To the Finland Station

EDMUND WILSON was born on May 8, 1895, in Red Bank, New Jersey, and was educated at Princeton. He is the author of a novel, *I Thought of Daisy* (1929), short stories, *Memoirs of Hecate County* (1946), a volume of poetry, *Poets, Farewell* (1929), and several plays. He is primarily known, however, for his works of criticism, among them *Axel's Castle* (1931), *The Triple Thinkers* (1938), *The Wound and the Bow* (1941), *Classics and Commercials* (1950), and the recent *The Shores of Light*.

To THE FINLAND STATION, Wilson's one historical study, was first published in 1940.

DOUBLEDAY ANCHOR BOOKS

TO

THE FINLAND

STATION

*A Study in the Writing and
Acting of History by*

EDMUND WILSON

Doubleday & Company, Inc., Garden City, N.Y.

The author has particularly to thank the following persons for criticism, information or the loan of materials: Max Eastman, Christian Gauss, Franz Höllering, Sidney Hook, Robert Jean Longuet, Mary McCarthy, Max Nomad, and Herbert Solow. He has leaned particularly hard in certain chapters on E. H. Carr's biography of Bakúnin, Arno Schirokauer's biography of Lassalle, and the first volume of Leon Trotsky's biography of Lenin; and he owes a special debt to Max Eastman's book, *Marx, Lenin, and the Science of Revolution*.

Acknowledgments are due *The New Republic* and the *Partisan Review*, in which certain sections first appeared.

The policy has been adopted, in the case of all Russian names, except those that have been Anglicized or are very familiar, of marking the accented syllables, in the hope of at least partially avoiding those prose-interrupting blurs which Russian names are likely to produce in an English text.

I:

II:

III:

I:

1 Michelet Discovers Vico

One day in the January of 1824, a young French professor named Jules Michelet, who was teaching philosophy and history, found the name of Giovanni Vico in a translator's note to a book he was reading. The reference to Vico interested him so much that he immediately set out to learn Italian.

Though Vico had lived and written a hundred years before, he had never been translated into French and was in fact little known outside Italy. He had been a poor scholar, born at Naples, the backward tail-end of Italy, at the time when the Italian Renaissance, obstructed by the Inquisition, had run pretty completely into the sands. Vico, by reason of his humble origin and his reputation of being a crank, had missed his academic career; but, finding his path of advancement blocked and driven back upon his own resources, he pushed further his unpopular ideas. He composed, and published in 1725, a work called *Principles of a New Science Dealing with the Nature of Nations, Through Which Are Shown Also New Principles of the Natural Law of Peoples*. Vico had read Francis Bacon, and had decided that it ought to be possible to apply to the study of human history methods similar to those proposed by Bacon for the study of the natural world. Later he had read Grotius, who had advocated an historical study of philosophy and theology in terms of the languages and actions of men, with a view to constructing a system of law which should embrace all the different moral systems and thus be universally acceptable.

The young Michelet had also been groping for the principles

of a new science of history. Among his projects had been a history of "the race considered as an individual," a series of "philosophical studies of the poets" and a work on "the character of peoples as revealed by their vocabularies." He had desired, he wrote, to "mingle history with philosophy" because they "completed each other." By July, he had gotten to Vico, and he read the first volume through without stopping. From the collision of Michelet's mind with Vico's, it is hardly too much to say that a whole new philosophical-artistic world was born: the world of re-created social history. Of this moment in Michelet's life he was afterwards to note: "1824. Vico. Effort, infernal shades, grandeur, the Golden Bough." "From 1824 on," he wrote, "I was seized by a frenzy caught from Vico, an incredible intoxication with his great historical principle."

And even reading Vico today, we can feel some of Michelet's excitement. It is strange and stirring to find in the *Scienza Nuova* the modern sociological and anthropological mind waking amid the dusts of a provincial school of jurisprudence of the end of the seventeenth century and speaking through the antiquated machinery of a half-scholastic treatise. Here, before the steady rays of Vico's insight—almost as if we were looking out on the landscape of the Mediterranean itself—we see the fogs that obscure the horizons of the remote reaches of time recede, the cloud-shapes of legend lift. In the shadows there are fewer monsters; the heroes and the gods float away. What we see now are men as we know them alone on the earth we know. The myths that have made us wonder are projections of a human imagination like our own and, if we look for the key inside ourselves and learn how to read them correctly, they will supply us with a record, inaccessible up to now, of the adventures of men like ourselves.

And a record of something more than mere adventures. Human history had hitherto always been written as a series of biographies of great men or as a chronicle of remarkable happenings or as a pageant directed by God. But now we can see that the developments of societies have been affected by their sources, their environments; and that like individual human beings they have passed through regular phases of growth. "The facts of known history," Vico writes, (I quote from the translation by Michelet, which sometimes departs from Vico's text) are to be "referred to their primitive origins, divorced from which they have seemed hitherto to possess neither a common basis, nor continuity nor coherence." And: "The nature of things is nothing other than that they come into being at certain times and in certain ways. Wherever the same circumstances are present, the same phenomena arise and no others." And: "In that dark night which shrouds from our eyes the most remote antiquity, a light appears which cannot lead us astray; I speak of this incontestable truth: *the social world is certainly the work of men;* and it follows that one can and should find its principles in the modifications of the human intelligence itself." And: "Governments must be conformable to the nature of the governed; governments are even a result of that nature."

All of these ideas which Michelet found in Vico were, though Vico had been their first exponent, not of course new to Michelet. The Enlightenment of the eighteenth century had occurred between Vico's time and his. Voltaire, before Michelet was born, had already cleared the gods and the heroes away; Montesquieu had shown how human institutions were related to racial habit and climate. And Michelet, furthermore, was soon afterwards to find in Herder an evolutionary theory of culture and in Hegel an exposition of the chemistry of social change. How was it then that the *Scienza Nuova* could come to a man of 1820 as an intoxicating revelation? Because Vico, by force of an imaginative genius of remarkable power and scope, had enabled him to grasp fully for the first time the *organic* character of human society and the importance of re-integrating through history the various forces and factors which actually compose human life. "I had no other master but Vico," he wrote. "His principle of living force, of humanity creating itself, made both my book and my teaching." Vico had described his achievement as an explanation of "the formation of human law" and an indication of "the specific phases and the regular process by which the customs which gave rise to law originally came into being: religions, languages, dominations, commerce, orders, empires, laws, arms, judgments, punish-

4

ments, wars, peace, alliances." Of all these social elements, he has shown, he says, "in terms of these phases and this process of growth, the eternal propriety by virtue of which the phase and the process must be thus and not otherwise." In August, we find Michelet preaching as follows on the occasion of the awarding of school prizes: "Woe be to him who tries to isolate one department of knowledge from the rest. . . . All science is one: language, literature and history, physics, mathematics and philosophy; subjects which seem the most remote from one another are in reality connected, or rather they all form a single system." And he was to begin in a few years his great application of the general principles of Vico to the actual presentation of history.

2 Michelet and the Middle Ages

There had become dominant with the eighteenth century Enlightenment and the French Revolution an idea which is not to be found in Vico, though it already existed in germ in his master Bacon: the idea of human progress, of the capacity of mankind for self-improvement. Vico, for all his originality, had never thoroughly emancipated himself from the theological point of view, which put the goal of improvement in Heaven, making salvation an individual matter dependent on the grace of God. He had been able to see that human societies pass through successive phases of development, but he seems to have imagined history as a series of repetitive cycles.

But Michelet, born in 1798, had the tradition of the Revolution. He had grown up under Napoleon and the Bourbon Restoration, and in his teens he had had himself baptized a Catholic; he had accepted the post of tutor to the young Princess de Parme at the Tuileries. But he had been poor: his family on both sides had belonged to the cultivated small bourgeoisie—one of his grandfathers had been organist in the Cathedral at Laon—and his father, a printer, had been ruined by Napoleon's suppression of the press. Two years before Jules was born, the printing shop had been raided for Jacobin literature: an incriminating manifesto, which would have cost Furcy Michelet his head, was lying in plain sight on the table and the inspector never thought to examine it; but Mme. Michelet, who was pregnant at the time, always believed that the stillbirth of her baby had been due to the shock of the raid. When

Jules Michelet was ten, his father was arrested for debt, and he went along with his mother while she accompanied her husband to jail. Later, Napoleon's police put the seals on the Michelets' press; and the incident caused Jules such anguish that he afterwards made a stipulation in his will that his wife should not be obliged to seal his coffin. The principles of the Revolution were never far below the surface in Michelet, even in those years of his early manhood when they appeared somewhat varnished over by what had come to be the conventional bourgeois opinions.

In the July of 1830, the reaction against Charles X resulted in an uprising of workers and students which held Paris for three days and drove the white flag back into exile. Michelet, still full of Vico, became possessed by a vision of his own, in which the reawakening idealism of the tradition of the great Revolution gave purpose to Vico's cycles. In a burst of emotion, he wrote at top speed an *Introduction to Universal History*. It had been dashed off, he said, "on the burning pavements" of Paris; and it opened with the following declaration: "With the world began a war which will end only with the world: the war of man against nature, of spirit against matter, of liberty against fatality. History is nothing other than the record of this interminable struggle." Christianity has given the world the moral gospel; now France must preach the social gospel. "The solutions to social and intellectual problems are always ineffective in Europe until they have been interpreted, translated, popularized, by France."

But the victory of the workers was premature; the provinces failed to support Paris; and the liberal bourgeoisie, instead of restoring the republic, sold out to the Orleanist party, who set up the constitutional monarch, Louis-Philippe. Michelet went back to the Tuileries, where he now had a new princess to tutor, Louis-Philippe's daughter. But he got also an appointment more important to him: he was made Conservateur des Archives, head of the Record Office. And with the charters, the statutes and the official correspondence of ancient France at his disposal, he embarked on his *History of the Middle Ages*.

When Michelet went into the Records, with Vico and the echoes of July in his head, a new past, for the first time the real past of France, seemed to revive for the imagination. The first volume or two of Michelet's history, dealing with the early races of Gaul, a period where documents are few and as to which, even in the light of later scholarship, we still remain considerably in the dark, were not particularly successful as "resurrection" of the past, the phrase Michelet applied to his method. It is only with the chapter called *Map of France* and devoted to the description of the country, that the characteristic Michelet appears. But as we get on into the ages where the materials are more plentiful, the miracle begins to take place.

Michelet's letters during this period supply a remarkable picture of his conception of his historian's task and the passion with which he attacked it.

"I believe I have found," he writes, "through concentration and reverberation, a flame sufficiently intense to melt down all the apparent diversities, to restore to them in history the unity they had in life. . . . I have not been able to interpret the least social fact without calling all the departments of human activity to my aid, and coming more and more to realize that our classifications do not hold. . . . To undertake to combine so many elements alien to one another is to harbor within oneself a great disturbing force. To reproduce so many passions is not to calm one's own. A lamp which is hot enough to fuse whole peoples is hot enough to consume its very hearth. . . . I have never yet [he is writing of the Renaissance now] lifted so great a mass, combined in a living unity so many apparently discordant elements. . . . I am trying to twist those threads which have never been woven together in science: law, art, etc., to show how a certain statue, a certain picture, is an event in the history of law, to follow the social movement from the stocky serf who upholds the niches of the feudal saints to the fantasy of the court (Goujon's Diana), even to Béranger. This double thread is twisted of industry and religion. It is easy for the imagination to catch a glimpse of this interaction, but to determine with any certitude the *manner,* the *quantity*, of the action, to found so new a theory scientifically, requires no small effort."

Behind the chronicles and legends of the Middle Ages, which that flame had rendered transparent, there now narrowed down into focus a new and distinct panorama. No one had really explored the French archives before; the histories had mostly been written from other histories. Michelet tells how in those "solitary galleries, where I wandered twenty years, in that deep silence, there had come to me the whispers of the souls who had suffered so long ago and who were smothered now in the past"—all the soldiers fallen in all the wars, reminding him of the hard reality and demanding of him bitterly whether he had come there to write romances in the manner of Walter Scott, prompting him to put into the record what had been left out by Monstrelet and Froissart, the "hired chroniclers" of the age of chivalry. One has heard Michelet called a romantic; and his history has plenty of movement and color and, in its early phases, passages of wordy rhetoric. But Michelet's fundamental attitude is certainly, as he insists, realistic and not romantic. He worked by himself, he says— the romantic movement "passed him by." "We are all more or less romantics," he had written in his journal at twenty-two. "It is a disease in the air we breathe. He is lucky who has equipped himself early with enough good sense and natural feeling to react against it."

The great mediaeval stories are in Michelet, and they are made vivid with a peculiar intensity; but the effect of the historian's treatment is to clear up the haze of myth about them. And they are presented in relation to a background of economic and social processes quite unknown to the school of romantic fiction of which Michelet disapproved. It was characteristic of the romantics to be interested in remarkable individuals for their own sake; Michelet was interested in remarkable individuals as representatives of movements and groups. The stately language of the old chronicles no longer gave its tapestry remoteness to the Crusades and the Hundred Years' War. Michelet made them take place on the same stage and pitched them at the same level of dignity as the wars of drilled regiments and artillery. What interests the historian more than the feats of individual prowess is the developing technique of warfare.

And we remember the terrible description of the peasants in the chapter on the peasant revolts when we have forgotten Philippe de Valois and Philippe le Bel: "Today," Michelet writes, "there are few châteaux left. The decrees of Richelieu and the Revolution have seen to that. Yet when we find ourselves even now in our travels under the walls of Taillebourg or Tancarville, when in the depths of the Ardennes forest, in the Montcornet gorge, we catch sight above our heads, of the squinting oblique eye watching us pass, our heart contracts and we feel something of the sufferings of those who for so many centuries wasted at the foot of those towers. To know it we do not even need to have read the old histories. The souls of our fathers still throb in us for pains that have been forgotten, almost as the man who has been wounded feels an ache in the hand he has lost."

Michelet has done a good deal, it is true, to make Jeanne d'Arc popular and famous; but it was as the spokesman for the national sense of the people, not as a mystic or a saint, that she interested him. "What legend is more beautiful," he writes, "than this incontestable story? But one must be careful not to make it into a legend. One must piously preserve all its circumstances, even the most human; one must respect its touching and terrible humanity. . . . However deeply the historian may have been moved in writing this gospel, he has kept a firm hold on the real and never yielded to the temptation of idealism." And he insisted that Jeanne d'Arc had established the modern type of hero of action, "contrary to passive Christianity." His approach was thus entirely rational, based squarely on the philosophy of the eighteenth century—anti-clerical, democratic. And for this reason, the History of the Middle Ages, important as it is, and for all its acute insight and its passages of marvelous eloquence, seems to me less satisfactory than the other parts of Michelet's history. What Michelet really admires are not the virtues which the chivalrous and Christian centuries cultivated, but the heroisms of the scientist and the artist, the Protestant in religion and politics, the efforts of man to understand his situation and rationally to control his development. Throughout the Middle Ages, Michelet is impatient for the Renaissance.

The reign of Louis XI, letting him down after Jeanne d'Arc, is too much for Michelet: though he is never precisely dull, he makes us feel during the periods which do not interest him his fatigue and his lack of sympathy. In the middle of Louis XI, he heaves a great sigh of oppression: "The history of the fifteenth century is a long history," he writes, "—long are its years and long its hours. They were so for those who lived them, and they are so for him who has to begin them again and relive them. I mean, for the historian, who, taking history as something more than a game, makes the effort in good faith to enter into the life of the past. . . . For where *is* the life here? Who can say here which are the living and which are the dead? In what party am I to take an interest? Is there one among these various figures who is not either dubious or false? Is there one on whom the eye may rest and find expressed in him clearly the ideas, the principles, on which the heart of man lives? We have descended low indeed into indifference and moral death. And we must descend lower still."

In the meantime, in Michelet's own century, the struggle between the reaction and the republic is pressing to an issue again. The clergy are denouncing Michelet's history; and the child of the Revolution is called again to vindicate its principles. The Princess Clémentine gets married, and Michelet resigns his post as tutor; and in his course at the Collège de France, where he is now a popular figure, he begins a series of lectures against the Jesuits. Among his colleagues were the militant Quinet and the exiled Polish patriot Mickiewicz. "Action, action!" Michelet wrote in July, 1842, "action alone can console us! We owe it not only to man, but to all that lower nature which struggles up toward man, which contains the potentiality of his thought—to carry on vigorously thought and action." From 1843 on, Michelet follows a definite and uncompromising line. He turns his back on the Middle Ages, having given them, as he believes, all the sympathetic attention they deserve. It has become dangerous now to idealize them; the cult of that past only leads to reaction; the old tyrannies come back with the romance. And Michelet, although he did not engage in political action, jumped his history forward from the fifteenth century to the French Revolution, whose purposes and achievements he felt had been obscured by the confusion of events which had followed it. He was now at the height of his power; and, under pressure of the mounting passion which was to burst forth in 1848, he threw himself into the epic of three centuries which was to occupy him all the rest of his life and to which the *History of the Middle Ages* was to serve as scarcely more than an introduction.

3 Michelet and the Revolution

The mature Michelet is a strange phenomenon. He is in many ways more comparable to a novelist like Balzac than to the ordinary historian. He had the novelist's social interest and grasp of character, the poet's imagination and passion. All this, by some unique combination of chances, instead of exercising itself freely on contemporary life, had been turned backward upon history and was united with a scientific appetite for facts which drove him into arduous researches.

He had grown up in isolation from his fellows and much thrown in on his own resources. Michelet's early life had been sad, poor and hard. Born in a dark and damp old church which had been deserted for many years and let in the wind and rain through broken windows, but which his father had got cheap for a printing office, he spent his youth and a good deal of his young manhood amidst surroundings peculiarly depressing. "I grew up," he wrote, "like a weed without sun between two paving stones of Paris." Up to the time that Jules Michelet was fifteen, the family had no meat and no wine; they lived on boiled vegetables and bread. And in the basement in which they were lodging during the years when Jules was going to school, they spent winter after winter without heat. Jules's hands got so badly chapped that he kept the scars all the rest of his life. Living at close quarters, the father and mother quarreled constantly, and the boy had to witness these quarrels. When he was seventeen, his mother died of cancer. At school, he was weakly, queer and shy, and a butt for the other boys. He could not make friends among them;

he came to them out of a different world. When the other boys left school, it was to go home to bourgeois comfort and leisure; when Jules went home, it was to work on the press. He had learned to set type at twelve.

But near the press in that bleak and unhealthy basement, he was building up for himself his own empire. In proportion as he was hungry and cold, so was he forced in for food and heat on his own mind and imagination. After all, he was an only child of whom his parents expected much and for whom they procured such advantages as they could. Later in life, he was to write to his son-in-law on the question of his grandson's schooling: "The most important matter is Etienne. I must *hand on to him what my parents did for me* in providing me by unexampled sacrifices with freedom, freedom to have time for my work. Let us not indulge in false democratic attitudes. The worker is a *slave* either of the will of others or of fate. I escaped that, thanks to my father and mother." And, after all, although, as we shall see, the damp and chill winters of Paris put their blight on all Michelet's youth, he was a Parisian, and that was to mean to him all his life to have been born to a great intellectual inheritance. He speaks in one of his letters of his eagerness to get back to "our Paris, that great keyboard with its hundred thousand keys that one can play on every day—I mean by that its innumerable intellectual resources."

And finally—what provided Michelet with a special kind of outlook and training—the Michelets were a family of printers, who had their printing press to give them a common interest and a sort of *esprit de corps*. The press was to become for Michelet the great symbol of the advance of modern thought, and printing a veritable religion. There was something in the Michelets still of the spirit of the great Renaissance printers such as the Etiennes and the Alduses, of whom Michelet gives so stirring an account—those extraordinary learned families who, transported by the discovery of antiquity and hardly stopping to sleep at night, managed not merely to set up the classics but to edit and elucidate them, too. So, up to the time of his death, Michelet's father worked with him over his history. And Michelet's interest in the freedom of the press and the progress of human science is that of a man to whom printing is still an adventure and a conquest. It is an essential part of Michelet's strength and charm that he should seem less like a nineteenth-century scholar than like the last great man of letters of the Renaissance. In his early years he mastered Latin and Greek with a thoroughness which was at that time already rare; and he later acquired English, Italian and German and devoured the literature and learning of those languages. With small means, he succeeded in traveling pretty much all over Western Europe, and those regions, such as the Slavic East, to which his actual travels did not penetrate, his insatiable mind invaded. The impression he makes on us is quite different from that of the ordinary modern scholar who has specialized in some narrowly delimited subject and gotten it up in a graduate school: we feel that Michelet has read all the books, been to look at all the monuments and pictures, interviewed personally all the authorities, and explored all the libraries and archives of Europe; and that he has it all under his hat. The Goncourts said that Michelet's attractiveness lay in the fact that his works "seem to be written by hand. They are free from the banality and impersonality which the printed thing has; they are like the autograph of a thought." But what Michelet really goes back to is an earlier stage of printing before either the journalistic or the academic formulas had come between first-hand knowledge and us. He is simply a man going to the sources and trying to get down on record what can be learned from them; and this role, which claims for itself, on the one hand, no academic sanctions, involves, on the other hand, a more direct responsibility to the reader.

Michelet thus learned from the beginning to fortify himself inside an intellectual citadel impregnable to hardship or disaster. The external circumstances of his life continued to be somber and distressing. After the death of Mme. Michelet, Jules's father was given an odd kind of employment presiding over an institution which was half boarding-house, half insane asylum. There Michelet spent some eight years of his youth in the company of cracked and impoverished persons left over from the old regime, and of the doctors and attendants who took care of them. Jules married the young companion of an old and feeble-minded marquise. She had little in common with Michelet and after fifteen years died of consumption, leaving him with two children. During these years, as a young professor, Michelet would get up at four in the morning and read, write and teach all day: he even took a book on his afternoon walk. He had made one close friend, a medical student, with whom he shared the intellectual passions which, as he said, "devoured" his youth; but this young man, to Michelet's anguish, had also come down with consumption, had sickened and wasted and died.

There is perhaps no more amazing example in literature of the expansion of a limited individual experience into a great work of the imagination. When the frail and solitary printer's son came to turn himself inside out in his books, he gave the world, not, as his romantic contemporaries did, personal exaltations and despairs swollen to heroic volume, but the agonizing drama of the emergence of the modern world out of feudalism. His history of France, immense though it is and with all its complexity, variation and detail, displays a bold emotional design which is easily referable to Michelet's own experience. The centuries which lead up to the Revolution are like a long and solitary youth waiting year after year for self-expression, release, the assertion of unacknowledged rights, the free association with others. The climax of the story is the moment of the founding of the Federations in the year after the taking of the Bastille, when communities all over France met together to swear fraternity and devotion to the Revolution. Michelet had been the first historian to investigate and emphasize this phenomenon. "At no other time, I believe," he wrote, "has the heart of man been wider and more spacious—at no other time have distinctions of class, of fortune and of party been more completely forgotten." But it was a moment only; after that, the back-flow of old instincts and interests among the purposes and hopes of the new was to bring years of confusion and disorder. The leaders were to find themselves undone by their own internal contradictions between the new and the old—as Michelet, before making his stand, had found himself between his royal patrons and his revolutionary tradition. Michelet was himself the child of that period of paradoxes;

and he was to become *par excellence* the historian of the perplexed personalities and political anomalies peculiar to an age
of social change. This idea of contradictions inside a social
system, which is to play, as we shall see, such a prominent role
in later social-economic thought, already pervades Michelet to
such an extent that we may trace to it the habit of verbal
paradox which grew on him in the later-written volumes of
his history, where he is dealing with the *impasses* of the old
regime. With Michelet, the typical internal antithesis—which
splits up and prevents from functioning the individual or the
political body—is between class solidarity on the one hand and
patriotic duty on the other; and beyond it, one is always aware
of the two opposite emotional poles which magnetize Michelet's world and give it its moral system: a cold and anti-social
egoism and the impulse toward human solidarity.

To return again to Michelet's own century, the Revolution
of 1848 had come and gone before Michelet had finished his
history of the Revolution of 1789. In 1848, on the eve of the
February revolution, Michelet's lectures had been considered
so inflammatory that his course had been suspended; but after
the revolution, he had been reinstated in his chair. When
Louis Bonaparte made himself Emperor in 1851, Michelet was
dismissed without a pension, and when he refused to take the
oath of allegiance, was deprived of his post at the Archives. He
was a poor man again now after a period of relative prosperity;
and from a position of direct public influence, he found himself alone with his history. "He who knows how to be poor
knows everything," he wrote. He had ended the *History of the
Revolution* with the fall of Robespierre, and now he set himself to fill up the gap between the death of Louis XI and the
taking of the Bastille. When he had done that, he picked up
the story again at the fall of Robespierre and brought it down
through Waterloo.

And as the years went on and volume after volume made
the long continuity of the *History of France*, Michelet, living
out three-quarters of the century, came to impress himself
upon it profoundly. He was the man who, above all others,
had supplied the French of his time with a past. He was read

with enthusiasm by writers as different as Lamartine, Montalembert, Victor Hugo, Heine, Herzen, Proudhon, Béranger, Renan, Taine, the Goncourts and Flaubert. He was an artist as well as a thinker, and so penetrated to parts of the intellectual world widely remote from one another and influenced a variety of writers in a curious variety of ways.

What Michelet regarded as his gospel we may leave for discussion later: his ideas were always expounded on a level more or less distinct from that on which his narrative was developed. Let us consider his history as a work of art and in its philosophical implications.

Two principal problems confronted Michelet in writing history in such a way as to render the organic character of society, of that "humanity creating itself" of which he had caught the conception from Vico. One of these was the nerve-trying task under which we have seen him gasping in his letters: that of fusing disparate materials, of indicating the interrelations between diverse forms of human activity. The other was to recapture, as it were, the peculiar shape and color of history as it must have seemed to the men who lived it—to return into the past as if it were present and see the world without definite foreknowledge of the as yet uncreated future. And in conceiving and carrying out these feats, Michelet seems to me to have proved himself a great intellect and a great artist.

One of the primary aspects of the fusing process was the relation of the individual to the mass; and Michelet's handling of this has probably never been surpassed, even in fiction. "Another thing," he wrote in the *History of the Revolution*, "which this History will clearly establish and which holds true in every connection, is that the people were usually more important than the leaders. The deeper I have excavated, the more surely I have satisfied myself that the best was underneath, in the obscure depths. And I have realized that it is quite wrong to take these brilliant and powerful talkers, who expressed the thought of the masses, for the sole actors in the drama. They were given the impulse by others much more than they gave it themselves. The principal actor is the people. To find the people again and put it back in its proper role, I have been obliged to reduce to their proportions the ambitious marionettes whose strings it manipulated and in whom hitherto we have looked for and thought to see the secret play of history." And in regard to remarkable persons in general, Michelet always shows them in their relation to the social group which has molded them and whose feelings they are finding expression for, whose needs they are attempting to satisfy. Yet even the personalities of the revolutionary leaders are made vivid and idiosyncratic; they are at intervals brought so close to us that we can note a change in their health or morale, their manner or their way of dressing; we follow their private relationships, enter into their love affairs. Michelet is equally successful in dealing with individuals and communities. The special personality of a city or a locality—Lyon, Avignon, the Vendée—is rendered with the same masterly sense of character; and the various social elements which compose it are shown in their interaction like the elements in a single human character. And then there are the persons of secondary importance, like Ravaillac, the assassin of Henri IV, or Madame Guyon, the eighteenth-century mystic, or the totally obscure persons like Grainville, the unfortunate schoolmaster of Amiens, who seemed to concentrate in his destiny all the disillusion and despair of the aftermath of the Revolution—those minor figures of whom Michelet will give us a portrait in a chapter, making us see clearly in the single cell some function or some malady of the body.

Michelet's skill at shifting back and forth between the close-up of the individual, the movement of the local group and the analytic survey of the whole, is one of the features of a technical virtuosity which becomes more and more amazing.

Michelet first begins really to master his method toward the middle of the *History of the Revolution,* where he has to range over an immense keyboard in relating the developments in the provinces to political events in Paris. I cannot allow Lytton Strachey's opinion that the centuries leading up to the Revolution are the most successful section of Michelet (the volumes on the sixteenth, seventeenth and eighteenth centuries were written after the volumes on the Revolution). The

Revolution is a much more disorderly and much more difficult subject; and the very crowdedness and jaggedness of Michelet's treatment of it are the signs of a determination to lay hold of a complex reality which had been simplified to make texts for many sermons, revolutionary and reactionary alike. It was with justice that Michelet claimed that, though there had been royalist and Robespierre histories of the Revolution—both "monarchist" versions, he insisted—he had written the first republican history. Yet in the volumes which deal with the centuries preceding, where Michelet has a clear stretch of slow developments, the great rhythmic recurrences of history are interwoven with a cumulative force and a symphonic effect which surely represent the extreme limit of the capacity of the artist to use historical fact as material. Michelet manipulates his themes, dropping them and picking them up at intervals, as if he were braiding a rope: the periodical assemblies of the States-General, gradually acquiring a new significance; the progressive sterilization and incompetence of the Court; the technical development of warfare; the books that mark the dawn of the Enlightenment; the episodes of the Protestant persecution; the series of witchcraft trials which show the decay of Catholicism in the convents. Yet the plaiting of a rope is too coarse an image. No image except that of life itself can convey the penetrating intelligence and the masterly skill of presentation with which, in the volumes on Louis XIV, for example, Michelet interrelates the intrigues of the Court, the subjects of Molière's comedies and the economic condition of France; or the completeness of the volume on the Regency—Michelet groans over his travail with this in his letters: "Nothing more difficult, more dispersed, more arduous to reconstruct!"—in which the good intentions of the liberal Regent are so subtly shown to prove ineffective by reason of his inextricable entanglement with the dying class to which he belongs—a story ending with one of those sharp incidents which Michelet is so good at finding to nail down a situation: the Duc d'Orléans, his reforms come to nothing and with only the solace of dissipation left, exclaiming bitterly, "Poor damned country, governed by a drunkard and a pimp!"

At intervals, Michelet halts his narrative to give a description of the general life of the time: the habits, the costumes, the moral atmosphere; and he here displays his peculiar genius for identifying himself with each period as he passes through it. This is one of the main differences between Michelet's method and the method of the ordinary historian. The ordinary historian knows what is going to happen in the course of his historical narrative, because he knows what has really happened; but Michelet is able to put us back at upper stages of the stream of time, so that we grope with the people of the past themselves, share their heroic faiths, are dismayed by their unexpected catastrophes, feel, for all our knowledge of after-the-event, that we do *not* know precisely what is coming. Michelet responds with the sensitivity of a poet to every change of tempo, movement or scope; and he develops an infinitely varied technique to register different phases. The genius which has been admired in his books on natural history and which enabled him to render the humming-bird's darting, the flap of the frigate bird, the lightness and song of the lark, the muffled swoop of the owl, with an accuracy almost Tennysonian, appears in his treatment of history in a much more extraordinary way. The processes which lead up to the Revolution are presented, as I have described, in a rotating series of episodes; we are made to see how things are going, without very much comment by Michelet, as we observe certain tendencies recurring and growing gradually more pronounced in the behavior of various individuals or groups. I do not know of anything in literature more remarkable in its way than the skill with which Michelet leads us, as we follow generation after generation of kings, to feel the old virtue passing out of them, the lapsing of their contact with the people. The great rooms of Fontainebleau and Versailles seem to get colder and larger and the figures smaller and more alone; they are not usually made odious so much as wretched—Michelet remembered the poor queer relics of the sanitarium in which he had lived; and we are finally startled but not surprised to find Louis the Sun King himself eclipsed in his windowless inside room, bored with the old and deaf Madame de Maintenon, nagged by the quarrels of the monks and losing his magnificent manners at last in his fury against the obstinate parliament. To give us a final symbol for the monarchy, Michelet has only to describe without comment the expense and the clumsy complication of the great waterworks at Marly which make the Versailles fountains play and which fill the air for miles around with their agonized creakings and groanings.

The chapters on the Federations are rhapsodic; the chapters on the last days of the Terror have an infernal, an almost intolerable intensity: with the overloaded cemeteries of Paris planted unbreathably in the background of our minds, Michelet confines us for chapter after chapter among the mutually repellent human units, in the constantly tightening atmosphere of panic of the committee rooms and assemblies of the capital. "I have already begun changing the rhythm of my history," he writes in one of his letters. "There are no more big chapters, but little sections, speeding by one after the other. The prodigious acceleration of pulse is the dominant phenomenon of the Terror." He takes history now day by day, instead of year by year or month by month—making even the weather play its part in the complex, when he can find out what it is: "October thirtieth dawned pale and rainy"—of the day when the Girondists were guillotined—"one of those livid days which have the weariness of winter but not its sinew, its salutary austerity. On those sad nerveless days the fiber weakens; many persons sink below themselves. And they took care to forbid that any stimulant be administered to the condemned." . . . Then the relief and awakening life of the Directory. The people coming out of the houses and going about the streets. And the great opening out of the scope and speeding up of the pace with Napoleon—till, lifted high above political bodies, we can look out on the breadth of Europe, taking it in from Ireland to Russia, and understand that we have to do with processes which involve the whole of the West.

One remarkable device of Michelet's has since been exploited and made famous by the novelist Marcel Proust. Proust, who invokes Michelet (though in a different connection) and who obviously owes a good deal in his volumes on Sodom and

Gomorrah to Michelet's picture of the processes of decadence, seems to have taken from him also the cue for his theory of the relativity of character. The more important actors in Michelet's history often produce sharply varying impressions as they are shown us at different ages and in different situations—that is, each is made to appear at any given moment in the particular role that he is playing at the moment, without reference to the roles he is later to play. Michelet explains what he is doing at the end of the fifth book of the *Revolution* —"History is time," he says; and this evidently contributed in Proust's case, along with other influences such as Tolstoy, to his deliberate adoption of that method of presenting his characters in a series of dramatically contrasting aspects by which he produces the effect of the long lines on economics charts fluctuating back through time. Michelet apparently, however, had arrived at his method naturally before he thought to take account of it and justify it, in the process of identifying himself so closely with the developing organism of society that he had come to see historical personalities as they appeared at the moment to their contemporaries, or, more accurately, to give them the value which they possessed at the moment for society. And he aims at making points by his contrasts quite different from the points of Proust. For he shows us, especially in dealing with the period of the Revolution, how the value of an individual may change, how his very personality may seem to vary, during the transition from one system to another. So Voltaire, between the refinement of the old regime and the pressing necessity for the new, is seen first as a clever young man like another playing the game of one of the cliques about the Court; then, after his beating by the Chevalier de Rohan and his flight to and return from England, as an intensely serious person, hiding himself away from society, shutting himself up to write; then, later, during his early years at Ferney, under the influence of his conventional niece, passing into intellectual eclipse as he allows her to establish about him on the precarious borders of France a miniature court of his own like the one he has left behind; then aroused to violent activity, as the new enlightened conscience of mankind, for the defense of Sirven and Calas; then, finally, after his death, when in

1791 the new generation have his body transferred to the Pantheon, rising gigantically out of his grave as the genius of the Revolution which he had only dimly apprehended. So the Abbé Sieyès appears formidable when he publishes under the old regime his pamphlet on the Third Estate; but later, in the Convention, feeble and timid. So even in the case of Napoleon, whom Michelet intensely dislikes and whose role he systemically belittles, we see him suddenly, under favorable conditions, expand to a moment of greatness at the time of his campaign in Egypt.

4 Michelet Tries to Live His History

Michelet's absorption in his history, his identification of himself with his subject, carried him to singular lengths. His emotions and the events of his own life are always breaking through into his narrative; and, conversely, the events of history seem to be happening to him. Proust has amusingly parodied this aspect of Michelet: "This was always my force, my weakness, also," he makes Michelet write, "this need of life. At the culminating point of the reign of Louis XV, when absolutism seemed to have killed all freedom in France, for two long years—more than a century (1680-1789)—strange headaches made me think every day that I should have to interrupt my history. It was only with the Oath of the Tennis Court (June 20, 1789) that I really recovered my force." But the examples that come to light in Michelet's letters are even more bizarre than Proust's parody: "I am accomplishing here the extremely tough task of reliving, reconstituting and suffering the Revolution. I have just gone through *September* and all the terrors of death; massacred at the Abbaye, I am on my way to the revolutionary tribunal, that is to say, to the guillotine"; and, "As for me, I have arrived at a thrice-solemn moment; I am about to enter the heart of the Convention, I stand at the gates of the Terror. At the same time, my wife is on the point of wresting forth a new *me* from her womb. . . . This moment of suspense, I assure you, is for me full of fear." We finally get to feel that Michelet is the human spirit itself fighting its way through the ages—enduring long degradations, triumphing in joyful rebirths, contending within itself in devastating and baffled conflicts. We are not surprised when, arriving at last at the year 1798, we find Michelet's own birth recorded as an event to which all that has gone before from the Merovingian and Carlovingian dynasties has in some sense been leading up. And the effect of this touch is not grotesque; it seems quite natural, of the essence of the subject. What he is really telling us is: "Under stress of this culminating experience, it became possible for the human consciousness to look back on human history with new insight and to understand all that I have shown you."

But one cannot enter into human history once it has taken place; nor can a man of the nineteenth century really recover the mentality of the sixteenth. One cannot reproduce the whole of history and yet keep to the forms and proportions of art. One cannot care so much about what has happened in the past and not care what is happening in one's own time. One cannot care about what is happening in one's own time without wanting to do something about it.

He was pulled in many directions. In the first place, his subject was so vast that it was always tending to burst out of the bounds which he had been forced by the limits of life and of human capacity to prescribe for it. The *History of France* proper overflowed into a whole series of smaller books which dealt more fully with special aspects of the subject. Michelet takes us through the ages, panting and talking at top speed: if he is sometimes elliptical and obscure, it is because he has so much to tell us. He explains in one of his prefaces, as it were apologetically, that if his narrative hasn't the ideal symmetry of art it is because the facts of history won't permit it; and he remarks in one of his letters, in connection with a one-volume history of France: "You would have difficulty in imagining how hard it is to reduce that long string of centuries to the unity of a work of art." At the same time, his scientific passion kept him feverishly grubbing in the archives. He was the first to write a history of the Revolution based on the actual records of the various revolutionary bodies; and as the Hôtel de Ville was soon afterwards burned, he was to remain the only historian who had made use of the records of the Commune. Gabriel Monod, his biographer and disciple, complains that he did not give his references in a genuinely scholarly fashion; but even the methodical Taine and the envious Sainte-Beuve were forced to confess that, though Michelet's way was as alien as possible from their ways, his work remained valid none the less.

Then, Michelet, reëntering the past, successful though he is at making us see things as they must have looked to the people of the past, has nevertheless, inescapably, the wisdom of the later time and cannot restrain himself from trying to intervene. He is always warning, advising, scolding his actors, whom, however, he cannot hope to influence. And in the meantime, contemporary events were continually soliciting his attention. He wrote pamphlets against the Jesuits; in vindication of the revolutionary tradition; in defense of France after 1870. According to the devoted but disquieted Monod, he turned his lectures into public speeches. He insisted that what he wanted was to get out of history "a principle of action," to produce "something more than intelligences—souls and wills." He was never, he complained, at one with himself; all his life, he was hurrying and straining to accomplish prodigious tasks which seemed to loom insurmountable before him. "Having strayed from the paths of harmony forever," he writes in one of his letters, "I have resumed the life I led so long: that of a cannon ball." Yet his history found its vein and its proportions; and he did not desert it for action. Even in 1848, when his excitement over public affairs was at its height and his friend and ally Quinet was running for political office, Michelet declined to take part in politics. His early years had conditioned him, as the behaviorists say, for self-dependence, literature, research—as his hair had turned white at twenty-five. He had made a second marriage late in life with a woman much younger than himself, who gave him sympathy and admiration; but the impression we get from his work is that of a man who has subsided into early-acquired habits of solitude. He worked at night, and made the centuries of the dead keep him company and lend him their strength and their faith that he might wake strength and faith in the living.

5 Michelet Between Nationalism and Socialism

What had he to tell them in his lectures and pamphlets? What were Michelet's conclusions from the crises which seemed continually, during his lifetime, to be reviving the revolutionary issues and in which the revolutionary tradition seemed always to be defeated? In what direction did he believe that human progress had manifested and was to manifest itself?

Not long before 1848, and just before beginning the *History of the Revolution*, Michelet wrote a little book called *The People*.

The first half, *Of Slavery and Hate*, contains an analysis of modern industrial society. Taking the classes up one by one, the author shows how all are tied into the social-economic web —each, exploiting or being exploited, and usually both extortionist and victim, generating by the very activities which are necessary to win its survival irreconcilable antagonisms with its neighbors, yet unable by climbing higher in the scale to escape the general degradation. The peasant, eternally in debt to the professional moneylender or the lawyer and in continual fear of being dispossessed, envies the industrial worker. The factory worker, virtually imprisoned and broken in will by submission to his machines, demoralizing himself still further by dissipation during the few moments of freedom he is allowed, envies the worker at a trade. But the apprentice to a trade belongs to his master, is servant as well as workman, and he is troubled by bourgeois aspirations. Among the bourgeoisie, on the other hand, the manufacturer, borrowing from the capitalist and always in danger of being wrecked on the shoal of overproduction, drives his employees as if the devil were driving him. He gets to hate them as the only uncertain element that impairs the perfect functioning of the mechanism; the workers take it out in hating the foreman. The merchant, under pressure of his customers, who are eager to get something for nothing, brings pressure on the manufacturer to supply him with shoddy goods; he leads perhaps the most miserable existence of all, compelled to be servile to his customers, hated by and hating his competitors, making nothing, organizing nothing. The civil servant, underpaid and struggling to keep up his respectability, always being shifted from place to place, has not merely to be polite like the tradesman, but to make sure that his political and religious views do not displease the administration. And, finally, the bourgeoisie of the leisure class have tied up their interests with the capitalists, the least public-spirited members of the nation; and they live in continual terror of communism. They have now wholly lost touch with the people. They have shut themselves up in their class; and inside their doors, locked so tightly, there is nothing but emptiness and chill.

What then? The second half of *The People* seems as ridiculous to us today as the first half seems acute. Michelet, like many nineteenth-century writers, is at his worst when he is preaching a gospel. We know them well in English, these nineteenth-century gospels: Ruskin's Beauty, Meredith's Nature, Matthew Arnold's Culture—large and abstract capitalized words, appearing in cloudy apocalypses, as remedies for practical evils. Once Michelet leaves history proper, once he gets outside his complex of events, he shows the liberal nineteenth century at its worst. Great displays of colored fire are set off, which daze the eye with crude lurid colors and hide everything they are supposed to illuminate. The bourgeois has lost touch with the people, Michelet tells us; he has betrayed his revolutionary tradition. All the classes hate one another. What is to be done about it, then? We must have love. We must become as little children; for truth, we must go to the simpleton, even to the patient animal. And Education!—the rich and the poor must go to school together: the poor must forget their envy; the rich must forget their pride. And there they must be taught Faith in the Fatherland. "Here," Michelet is forced to confess, "a serious objection arises: 'How shall I be able to give people faith when I have so little myself?' " "Look into yourself," he answers, "consider your children—there you will find France!"

With all this, he says some very searching things, of which he does not perceive the full implications. "Man has come to form his soul according to his material situation. What an amazing thing! Now there is a poor man's soul, a rich man's soul, a tradesman's soul. . . . Man seems to be only an accessory to his position." And his conception of the people, which at moments sounds mystical, comes down at the end to something that seems to be synonymous with humanity: "The people, in its highest idea, is difficult to find in the people. When I observe it here or there, it is not the people itself, but some class, some partial form of the people, ephemeral and deformed. In its authentic form, at its highest power, it is seen only in the man of genius; in him the great soul resides."

Socialism he rejects: property in France, he believes, has been too far subdivided, and the French have too strong a sense of property. And he is appalled by a nightmare of the national resources administered by French public officials. No: the bourgeoisie and the people must learn to know and love one another.

The Revolution of '48 followed. The Paris proletariat, led by Socialists and demanding the municipal workshops they had been promised, were shot down by the bourgeoisie. "Let the day be stricken out," he wrote in his journal; and "I should never write *The People* now," he said.

Yet he was to remain a man of his age, a man of a generation who had seen many political systems fail, who had been exposed to the Romantic idealism, and who had been played upon by a confusion of social forces. "Young and old, we are tired," he had written already in *The People*. "Why should we not confess it, almost at the end of that laborious day which now makes half a century? . . . Even with those who, like me, have passed through several classes and who have preserved through all sorts of trials the fecund instinct of the people, that has not saved them from losing on the way, in the conflicts they have waged within themselves, a considerable part of their forces." Michelet continued to elaborate a typical nineteenth-century moral gospel in a series of social studies which he alternated with the volumes of his history. *Love* and *Woman*, evidently inspired by his late second marriage after a series of unhappy or uncomfortable liaisons, were an attempt to hold the French family together by recalling the casual French to the sacredness of domestic relations; and Michelet was naïvely delighted when some mischievous person assured him that his book was driving the brothels out of business. *Our Sons* returned to education, the last hope of the liberal in all periods; and *The Bible of Humanity* was an effort —of a kind all too familiar in our own day—to provide a new substitute religion by combining all the best features of the old ones.

It was the positive pole of his nature keeping him steady against the pull of the negative, toward which his history in its later phases was gravitating; and we cannot grudge him a little well-meant nonsense in compensation for those terrible volumes written under the oppression of Napoleon III and dealing with the last days of the old regime. Here Michelet's chief literary vice, a kind of romantic verbiage, has entirely faded away; the influence of Tacitus, from his earliest reading one of Michelet's great admirations, seems to assert itself. Here he anatomizes politics and intrigue in a style which grows more and more incisive and terse and with a caustic coldness like Stendhal's; and, by an incomparable power of tragic horror, he weights this chronicle with the burden, ever more heavily dragging, of the lives of political prisoners and inconvenient nuns stifled in blind prisons and *in pace's,* the slaughter and eviction of whole Protestant communities by Louis XIV's *dragonnades,* the long tortures under the whips of the galleys of those whom thought or conscience had brought there— filling up the abysses of history with those millions of human beings who had been dropped out of life and forgotten, till we ourselves are almost ready to shut the book and hear no more about the past of humanity. Even Michelet's interest in natural history—inspired, also, by his new wife: it was one of her enthusiasms—which stimulated him during the same period to publish a succession of books, *The Insect, The Bird,* etc., that celebrate lyrically the marvels of nature, has a more sinister side in his history, where the doings of human beings begin to seem to have more and more in common with the doings of insects and birds. It was the moment of *The Origin of Species,* and Naturalism was already in the air.

The events of 1870–71 had a shattering effect on Michelet. He had been away from Paris at the time of the invasion; and at the news of the first French defeats, he returned in the belief that he was needed, that he could somehow be of use. In the course of the siege of Paris, the house in which he was living was burned; his apartment miraculously escaped, though the chair in which he had worked got scorched. Michelet was then in his seventies, and he retreated before the attack.

Before the declaration of war, he had signed, with Marx and Engels and others, an international pacifist manifesto; and he now brought out a pamphlet called *France Before Europe,* in which as "a worker to the workers of the world," he summoned them to create "an armed peace league." But his confusion between the cause of France and the cause of the workers of the world is very evident here. "The great labor party, the laboring, the industrious, the productive nations" are to arm against "the party of death," which is simply "Prusso-Russian militarism." He praises the moderation with which the revolution has thus far been carried on; only one man, he notes, has been killed. The Socialists have shown admirable restraint; and Socialism is largely a local matter: there are still only ten million industrial workers to twenty-six million peasants, and the peasants, who have made possible the Second Empire, are still strong on the side of property. All the classes are coöperating fraternally; France need not fear "the social question."

Not long afterwards, in his exile at Pisa, the news of the Paris Commune reached Michelet, following the news of the surrender of Paris; and he had an apoplectic stroke. It was the third workers' revolt during his lifetime; and this time a

Communist government was to hold Paris for two and a half months. The bourgeois government at Versailles shot its prisoners; the Commune slaughtered bourgeois hostages, including the Archbishop of Paris. The bourgeoisie bombarded the city; and the Commune burned public buildings. The population of Paris fought the Versailles troops for eight days and were finally defeated by the massacre of from twenty to thirty thousand men and women. When the reports of this civil war reached Michelet, he had a second and more serious stroke, which paralyzed his right arm and his organs of speech.

Yet he recovered to continue his task. He had brought his notes with him, and he returned with furious industry to his history, taking it up where he had dropped it, at the fall of Robespierre. The final volumes of Michelet are not merely somber, but bitter. Though his organic conception of history enabled him to see humanity as a whole, he was in the habit of thinking of it and dealing with it in terms of its components: nations. He had, however, a special version of nationalism which enabled him, in the case of France, to identify the *"patrie"* exclusively with the revolutionary tradition. In the name of the Revolution she had been chosen to lead and enlighten the world. But the old nationalism, the growing inspiration of common interest and purpose, of which Michelet had been following the development—the nationalism of which Jeanne d'Arc had been the prophet and the Federations of 1789 the explicit realization—was now turning into something which had nothing to do with the principles of '89: it was turning into modern imperialism. Napoleon, a foreigner among the French and a traitor to the Revolution—and how much more, Napoleon III—is for Michelet the mockery of the national ideal. Michelet's history, in its latest volumes, is bursting out of its old conception. "I was born," he writes in one of his prefaces, "in the midst of the great territorial revolution and I shall have lived to see the dawning of the great industrial revolution. Born under the terror of Babeuf, I have lived to see the terror of the International." The history of the nineteenth century may be summed up, he says, in three words: industrialism, militarism, socialism.

But he was too old to go far with that story: he breaks off with the banishment of Napoleon. The last words of his last volume are like an epitaph: "But by a singular blunder," he writes, "they situated him on St. Helena—so that of this high and conspicuous stage the scoundrel could make a Caucasus, exploiting the pity of the public and preparing, by force of his lies, a bloody second repetition of all the disasters of the Empire." They were to be Michelet's epitaph, too: not long after writing them, his heart failed, and he died (February 9, 1874); his last volumes came out after his death. He had intended to continue his history further; but, characteristically, he dropped it and died with it, at precisely the right moment, both of the story he was telling and of contemporary events. A new point of view, as we shall see, was needed to deal with what followed. Who can imagine Michelet confronted with the Third Republic?

But his work was complete in itself; and when we look back on it, we can see that the breaking-off leaves it as an artistic whole admirably proportioned and rounded. The early centuries of comparative barbarism succeed one another fast; they lead up to modern nationalism, Jeanne d'Arc; a brief lapse, then a great international movement of enlightenment and independence—the Renaissance, the Reformation—causes the story to overflow its frame (or, more accurately, Italy and Germany to overflow into the frame); then the Renaissance lapses, the pace slows up, the scale of presentation expands, we see the unification of France, the intensification of French nationalism, and, with them, the development of a new Renaissance, which has its climax in the Revolution; the scale becomes enormous, we trace the motives in every heart, a day may now sometimes last longer than a century of the Middle Ages; then, the great drama done, the pace accelerates and the scope opens out again; the interest of the revolutionary drama and of the national epic are both finished. I am not here interpreting history, nor even quite faithfully interpreting Michelet, if we follow all his statements and indications: I am describing the impression which he actually, by his proportioning and his emphasis, conveys. This was the story which he had to tell and which, through all the shifts of his contemporary world, the vicissitudes of his personal career, kept its consistency and reached its completion. We can study in it how far it is possible to reconcile the nationalistic ideal with a concern for the life of mankind.

The *History of France* stands unique, a great work of imagination and research of a kind perhaps never to occur again— the supreme effort in its time of a human being to enter into, to understand, to comprehend, the development of a modern nation. There is no book that makes us feel when we have finished it that we have lived through and known with such intimacy so many generations of men. And it makes us feel something more: that we ourselves are the last chapter of the story and that the next chapter is for us to create.

But what and how? Michelet cannot tell us. The fierce light of his intellect flickered out in a rhetoric smoky and acrid.

6 Decline of the Revolutionary Tradition: Renan

"You have that thing which is so rare," Michelet had once said to a younger writer, "that thing which they all [all the literary men] lack: the sense of the people and its sap. In my own case, I feel, as I reread what I have sent you [the first volume of the *History of the Revolution*], how much I still lack myself. . . . My poetry is sometimes obscure, inaccessible to the great number."

The French bourgeoisie, who in the great Revolution had seized power from the feudal aristocracy, had, through all the readjustments of the forms and accouterments of government and in the teeth both of monarchist reaction and of socialist working-class revolt, maintained its position as the dominant class; and, except when spasmodically reawakened by the Royalists, the Bonapartists or the clergy, its revolutionary tradition grew feeble. The word "revolution" was coming to connote working-class interference from below with bourgeois property arrangements. The nineteenth century in France was a great literary period, and a period perhaps comparable, for fiction and history, to the Elizabethan period for poetry or the Italian Renaissance for painting. But this literature, for all the immense range in it of the social imagination, was no longer a revolutionary literature. The enthusiasm for science of the Enlightenment persisted without the political enthusiasm of the Enlightenment; and since the Romantic movement, the conception of the literary art was becoming more elaborate and subtle than the mere eloquence, polish and skill which had distinguished the eighteenth century. And Michelet, for all his attempts to reaffirm, to keep always in the foreground of his activity, the original revolutionary principles, was turning out to be one of the chief ornaments of this highly developed literature. With his novelist's sympathetic insight into different kinds of human beings, his sense of social and moral complexity and his artistic virtuosity, he was to live to be read with delight by people who did not share his opinions.

Nevertheless, he was to pass out of fashion. The writer of an article called *Why Michelet Is No Longer Read* predicted in 1898, on the occasion of the Michelet centenary, that the celebration would not do Michelet justice. Michelet is no longer read, he says, because people no longer understand him. Though he was followed in his day by the whole generation of 1850, he commits for the skeptical young men of the end of the century the supreme sin of being an apostle, a man of passionate feeling and conviction. Michelet created the religion of the Revolution, and the Revolution is not popular today, when the Academicians put it in its place, when persons who would have been nothing without it veil their faces at the thought of the Jacobin terror, when even those who have nothing against it manage to patronize it. Besides, Michelet attacked the priesthood, and the Church is now treated with respect.

Let us take a last look at him, in Couture's drawing, before passing on to his successors: the Michelet of 1842, with his mask of determined will, which seems always to have been straining, never relaxed—the long plebeian jaw, the self-assertive chin, the set mouth, the fine trenchant nose with its distended and mettlesome nostrils, the eyes deep and sharp, sheltering a sensitiveness taxed by interior struggle, beneath eyebrows as heavy as wings, which make the creases of perpetual effort.

Now look at Renan and Taine. With Michelet, the man has created the mask. But here it is the profession that has made it: Renan, with his great belly, his pudgy hands, his round and puffy face, his heavily-drooping porcine eyelids—the most intelligent and honest of all the French abbés, but still fundamentally a French abbé; Taine (in Bonnat's portrait), with his spectacles and his myopic-looking eyes, his bald dome, his wilting imperial, his high conversational eyebrows— the most brilliant of all the French professors, but still from tip to toe a French professor. Michelet, the man of an un- settled and a passionate generation, has forged his own per- sonality, created his own trade and established his own place. Renan and Taine, on the other hand, are the members of learned castes. Both, like Michelet, set the search for truth above personal considerations: Renan, who had studied for the priesthood, left the seminary and stripped off his robe as soon as he knew that it was impossible for him to accept the Church's version of history, and the scandal of the *Life of Jesus* cost him his chair at the Collège de France; and the materialistic principles of Taine proved such a stumbling- block to his superiors throughout his academic career that he was finally obliged to give up the idea of teaching. But, though rejected by their professional colleagues, they came before long to be accepted as among the official wise men of their society, a society now temporarily stabilized. Both ended as members of the Academy ("When one is *someone*, why should one want to be *something*?" Gustave Flaubert wondered about Renan)—whereas it is only a few years ago that Michelet and Quinet were finally given burial in the Panthéon.

Both Renan and Taine, of the generation twenty or thirty years younger than Michelet, had felt his influence, and com- bining, as Michelet had done, immense learning with artistic gifts, were to continue his re-creation of the past. Renan tells us with what excitement he read Michelet's history at school: "The century reached me through the cracks in a broken ce- ment. . . . With amazement I discovered that there were lay- men who were serious and learned; I saw that there existed something outside of antiquity and the Church . . . the death of Louis XIV was no longer the end of the world for me. Ideas and feelings appeared that had never had any expression either in antiquity or in the seventeenth century."

Three years after Renan left the seminary, the Revolution of 1848 occurred, and "the problems of socialism," as he says, "seemed, as it were, to rise out of the earth and terrify the world." Renan attempted to deal with these problems in a book

called *The Future of Science,* in which he presented a vision
of progress recalling those of the eighteenth century, but conveyed in the sermonizing accents and bathed in the altar-light
which he had brought over from Saint-Sulpice. What humanity
needs, he says, is not a political formula or a change of bureaucrats in office, but "a morality and a faith." Augustin Thierry,
the historian, and others considered the book too "daring" for
the public: it would be better for him to "insinuate" his ideas
with an article here and there. "The French insistence upon
clearness and discretion, which sometimes, it must be confessed, restrains one from saying more than a part of what one
thinks, from doing justice to the depth of one's thought,
seemed to me," he wrote forty years later, when he finally
brought the book out, "a tyranny at that time. The French
language is adapted only to the expression of clear ideas; yet
those laws that are most important, those that govern the transformations of life, are not clear, they appear to us in a half-
light. Thus, though the French were the earliest to perceive
the principles of what is now known as Darwinism, they turned
out to be the last to accept it. They saw all that perfectly well;
but it lay outside the usual habits of their language and the
mold of the well-made phrase. The French have thus disregarded precious truths, not because they haven't been aware
of them, but because they have simply cast them aside, as useless or as impossible to express." But he took the advice of
his elders and refrained from bringing out his book. And the
general cooling-off of the French bourgeois in regard to politi-
cal-social issues may be seen very clearly in Renan. He continues to hope for progress; but it is a hope that still looks to
science without paying much attention to political science,
whose advances, indeed, he tends to disregard, as he says the
French naturalists had done with Darwinism. Where Michelet
had forfeited his posts rather than take the oath of allegiance
to Louis Bonaparte, Renan considered it a matter of no consequence: "My opinion is that only those should have refused
who had directly taken part in former governments . . . or
who at the time had the definite intention of entering into a
conspiracy against the new one. The refusal of others, though
admirable in itself if it is prompted by a delicacy of conscience,

is in my opinion regrettable. For besides depriving the public service of those who are best fitted to fill it, it implies that everything that is done and everything that happens ought to be taken seriously. . . . In my own case, nothing has yet been asked of me; I confess that I don't consider myself sufficiently important to make an exception among my colleagues, who are no more partisans of the present regime than I am. It is clear that for a very long time we must stand aside from politics. Let us not keep the burdens, if we do not want the advantages."

Yet there is here still an ideal of public service. Renan ran for the Chamber of Deputies in 1869 on a platform of, "No revolution; no war; a war will be as disastrous as a revolution." And even when the war was in progress and the Prussians were besieging Paris, he took an unpopular line in advocating peace negotiations.

The French bourgeois intellectual after 1870 found himself in the singular position of belonging at the same time to a dominant class and a defeated nation, of at the same time enjoying advantages and submitting to humiliation; and this paradox produced curious attitudes. Edmond de Goncourt, in his journal, gives an illuminating picture of Renan during the Franco-Prussian War and the Commune—we see him praising the Germans, to whom in his field he owed so much, in the face of the loud protests of his companions; waving his short arms and quoting Scripture against the prophets of French revenge; maintaining that for the "idealist," the emotion of patriotism had been rendered obsolete by Catholicism, that "the fatherland of the idealists is the country where they are allowed to think." One day when he had been standing at the window watching a regiment pass by amidst the shouts of the crowd, he contemptuously turned away: "There's not a man among them all," he cried, "who is capable of an act of virtue!"

But what did Renan mean by virtue? On what did he base his code? Renan's work, for all his smiling indulgence, has a certain austerity behind it. In what school had this virtue been

learned? It was the ecclesiastical discipline which had made
him: the sense of duty and the self-sufficiency which contributed to the very moral courage he was to display in opposition
to the Church had been derived from his training for the
priesthood, from that Catholicism which, as he said, had made
patriotism obsolete, but in which he had ceased to believe. It
is almost as if virtue were with Renan a mere habit which he
has been induced to acquire on false pretenses. Though his
devotion had been at first directed to the ends of the Enlightenment, to the scientific criticism of the Scriptures which supplemented the polemics of Voltaire, the Enlightenment itself,
as I have indicated, was in a sense on the wane with the
attainment by the French bourgeoisie of their social-economic
objects; and Renan's virtue came more and more to seem, not
like Michelet's, a social engine, but a luminary hung in the
void. In a hierarchy of moral merit drawn up in one of his
prefaces, he puts the saint at the top of the list and the man
of action at the bottom: moral excellence, he says, must always lose something as soon as it enters into practical activity
because it must lend itself to the imperfection of the world.
And this conception gave Michelet concern: he rebuked "the
disastrous doctrine, which our friend Renan has too much
commended, that passive internal freedom, preoccupied with
its own salvation, which delivers the world to evil." It is curious
to contrast the tone of Renan's speech at the inauguration of a
medallion of Michelet, Quinet and Mickiewicz at the Collège
de France in 1884 with that of his combative predecessors.
Renan's emphasis is all on the importance of the calm pursuit
of truth, though the turmoil may be raging around us of those
who are forced to make a practical issue of it. But he corrects
himself: "No, we are posted in sign of war; peace is not our
lot." Yet the relation between the rioter in the street and the
scholar in his study seems to have been completely dissolved.

In *The Origins of Christianity*, Renan's attitude toward his
own time appears very plainly through his story. In any sense
in which it is possible to describe human productions as impartial, this enchanting account of the decline of the ancient
world and the rise of the Christian religion may be said to be
impartial. The effort toward universal comprehension and jus-

tice is one of the most impressive things about Renan. But his very artistic form has its bias, the very fall of his sentences has its bias; and before he has finished his story, he *has* undeniably tipped the scales. In *The Origins of Christianity*, which begins with a volume on Jesus and ends with a volume on Marcus Aurelius, it must be confessed that somehow or other Marcus Aurelius gets the better of it. The *Life of Jesus*, which the Goncourts characterized as "Michelet Fénelonized," has always seemed to me the least successful section. Renan makes Jesus a "charming doctor," tends, in fact, to make him a sort of Renan, and minimizes the symbolic tragedy which was to fascinate and sustain the world. He does better perhaps with Paul, but makes us dislike him. The episode we remember best is Paul's arrival in Athens to preach the Christian gospel and his outcry against the Greek statues: "O chaste and lovely images," Renan cries out in his turn, "of the true gods and goddesses!—this ugly little Jew has stigmatized you with the name of idols!" And so when Renan comes to the Apocalypse, which he interprets as a radical tract directed against the Roman Empire, he does not fail to put the whole exploit in an ironical light from the beginning by commenting on the extreme inappropriateness of John's having selected the little island of Patmos, more suitable, as Renan remarks, for some delightful classical idyl of the type of *Daphnis and Chloë*, for the forging of his fulminations and the concoction of his esthetic monstrosities. The truth is that the moral earnestness of the Jews, to whose literature Renan has devoted his life, is coming to seem to him unsympathetic. And when we arrive at Marcus Aurelius, Renan's preference for the Graeco-Roman culture as contrasted with the agitation of the Christians unmistakably emerges and has the last word. We can note how, almost imperceptibly, his interest and emphasis have shifted since he published the *Life of Jesus* nearly twenty years before. "Marcus Aurelius and his noble masters," Renan had written then, "have had no enduring effect on the world. Marcus Aurelius leaves behind him delightful books, an execrable son, a dying world. Jesus remains for humanity an inexhaustible principle of moral regeneration. Philosophy, for the majority, is not enough; they must have sainthood." But

in the volume on Marcus Aurelius (published in 1881), Renan
manages to give us the impression that the Romans, through
their legal reforms, were tending by themselves and independently of the evangelism of the Christians, to put humanitarian
principles into practice. Was Christianity necessary, after all?
we are prompted to ask ourselves. Will not a society sufficiently
developed arrive at this point of view by itself? Marcus
Aurelius has all Jesus' love of virtue and is a Roman gentleman as well; and, ruminating sadly on human affairs as he
wages his uncongenial warfare against the forces battering in
the Empire, he is presented as the perfect exemplar for the
French intellectual world of the period after 1870—disillusioned with its political tradition, resigned to its national defeat, disgusted with contemporary tendencies, but persisting
in the individual pursuit of such ends, the private cultivation of
such qualities, as still seem to be valuable in themselves. "His
[Marcus Aurelius'] virtue was based, like ours, upon reason,
upon nature. Saint Louis was a very virtuous man and, according to the ideas of his time, a very great king, because he was
a Christian; Marcus Aurelius was the most pious of men, not
because he was a pagan, but because he was an emancipated
man. He was an honor to human nature, and not to a particular
religion. . . . He has achieved the perfect goodness, the absolute indulgence, the indifference tempered with pity and
scorn. 'To be resigned, as one passes one's life in the midst of
false and unjust men'—that was the sage's program. And he
was right. The most solid goodness is that which is based on
perfect ennui, on the clear realization that everything in this
world is frivolous and without real foundation. Never was
there a more legitimate cult, and it is still our cult today."
Such a morality is attractive to read about, but it will let down
rather than support its generation. What kind of champions
can be recruited by a preacher who is obliged to have recourse
for his sanctions to the stoicism of Marcus Aurelius?—by one
who begins by assuring us that we should value the saint above
all men, but ends by recommending as a model a sage who
plays the man of action with no conviction of the action's
value?

Renan himself was, however, sustained to accomplish his

historical work. And *The Origins of Christianity* is a master-piece—perhaps the greatest of all histories of ideas. What Renan can give us incomparably, what we get out of him so that we never forget it, is the sense of the way in which doctrines, conceptions, symbols, undergo continual transformations at the hands of different persons and races. With a sensitiveness of intelligence and a subtlety of presentation which have never been excelled, he follows the words and the story of Jesus as they pass into varied combinations and with every new combination become themselves something new: the Christianity of the Apostles is no longer the Christianity of Jesus; the Christianity of the Scriptures is modified as it is attracted toward the Greeks or the Jews; the Christianity of the Rome of Nero is something entirely different from the primitive Christianity of Judea. Our ideas are all spun from filaments, infinitely long and mingled, which have to be analyzed with an infinite delicacy.

But note that the emphasis with Renan is thus chiefly upon the relativity of religious and philosophical conceptions. There is a relativity, too, in Michelet—his actors play different roles in different historical situations, according to their personal capacities in relation to varying circumstances; but the dominating values are not in doubt. With Renan, of the later generation, the values themselves are beginning to waver; we find him talking about "the clear realization that everything in this world is frivolous and without real foundation." Note, furthermore, that whereas with Michelet we are in the midst of human happenings, among which the propagation of ideas figures merely as one of many kinds of activity, with Renan we are occupied primarily with ideas, behind which the rest of human history is merely filled in as a background—it is the frame on which the web has been woven, but what we are concerned with is tracing the web. Renan's function is to take us through the texts of the religion and wisdom of antiquity—even though by a spell of imagination he is creating about us as we read them the social atmosphere of the times in which they were written. Though *The Origins of Christianity* is still Michelet's organic history, it is the history no longer of the man as a whole but a man's formulated ideas.

7 Decline of the Revolutionary Tradition: Taine

Renan's style, so much admired in its day, shows certain definite signs of decadence. Renan was always insisting that French literature ought to return to the language of the seventeenth century, that the classical vocabulary was sufficient to deal with modern feelings and ideas; and his own style preserves in distinguished fashion the classical qualities of lucidity and sobriety. Yet this language of Renan's, which seems precise, has a way of leaving indistinct impressions. Compared to the language of Michelet, with its tightness, its vigor, its vibrations of excitement, Renan's prose is pale; it lacks relief. If we read him for long at a sitting, the sense blurs and he puts us to sleep.

With Taine, the effect is quite different. Taine is not trying to get back to the past; he has gone ahead with the present. But, in doing so, he has come to exhibit some of the most unattractive qualities of that present; and we may study in his form and his style the characteristics of the bourgeois nineteenth century, as they confront us as soon as we open him—before we pass on to his content.

Amiel complained of Taine: "This writer has a trying effect on me like a creaking of pulleys, a clicking of machines, a smell of the laboratory." And he was justified: Taine had perfected one of the great modern mechanical styles. His books have the indefatigable exactitude, the monotonous force, of machinery; and, for all his gifts of sympathetic intelligence and the doubts with which he was sometimes troubled on certain tendencies of his contemporary world, he is rarely shaken out of the cocksure and priggish tone, the comfortable conviction of solidity, of the bourgeois whom the machine is making rich. In this, he resembles Macaulay, whom he had at one time inordinately admired; but it is a Macaulay of the latter half of the century and a Macaulay of a more philosophical turn of mind, who is beginning to be sour instead of optimistic at the direction that the century is taking. It is curious to find Taine, in his chapter on Macaulay, condemning in his predecessor the very faults from which he suffers himself. For Taine himself, in spite of his repeated insistence on his attitude of naturalistic objectivity, was to become almost as emphatic as Macaulay with a sort of middle-class moral flatness. And the overdemonstration which he blames in Macaulay, the laboring of points already obvious, is certainly one of Taine's worst habits.

It is not precisely decadence that is seen here; Taine's immense sentences, vast paragraphs, solid sections, gigantic chapters, represent the never-slackening ever-multiplying production of a class that is still sure of itself. But there is a lack of human completeness somewhere, and this appears in Taine's real lack of taste. He manages to combine the rigor of the factory with the upholstery and the ornamentation of the nineteenth-century salon. A large area of the surface of Taine's writing is covered over with enormous similes, which have been laid on a coat of paint. These similes at their best are very good; but even when they are good, they are usually overelaborated; and all too often they are ludicrous or clumsy. "A creature of air and flame," he writes of Voltaire, "the most excitable who has ever lived, composed of atoms more ethereal and more vibrant than those of other men, there is none whose mental structure is finer nor whose balance is at the same time more unstable and more true. We may compare him to those precision scales which are susceptible of being disturbed by a breath, but beside which the other devices for measurement are inexact and coarse. Only very light weights should be placed in this scale, only samples as tiny as possible; but it will, on this condition, weigh any substance with strictness." This is splendid; it really states something which we had never quite realized about Voltaire. But a few pages before, we have had the following: "I compare the eighteenth century to a company of people at table: it is not enough that the food should be before them, that it should be prepared, presented, easy to get hold of and digest; it must also be a special course, or better a delicacy. The mind is a gourmet; let us furnish it with savory and delicate dishes, suited to its taste; it will eat all the more for sensuality's having whetted the appetite." Now why must we be told all this simply in order that we may learn that the writing of the eighteenth century was seasoned with "salt and spice"? The notion of wisdom seasoned with wit is surely a common enough one; the simple word was all that Taine needed. Yet, with the utmost complacency, he stages for us a banquet, and a banquet at which we are invited to entertain the forbidding hypothesis that unseasoned and un-appetizing food may be served, but at which we are finally re-lieved to see the diners, their appetite "whetted" by "sensuality," fall upon food that has been delicately prepared. Later in *The Origins of Contemporary France,* in the section on *The Revolutionary Government,* we find what is probably one of the worst figures in literature. Taine is trying to convey the situation of France at the time when, according to his picture, all the men of public spirit and brains had been exe-cuted or driven into exile or hiding, and only the ignorant and brutish held the power: "The overturn," he writes, "is complete: subjected to the revolutionary government, France resembles a human being who should be obliged to walk on his head and think with his feet." This is bad enough; but when we turn the page, we find the next chapter beginning as fol-lows: "Imagine a human being who has been obliged to walk with his feet up and his head down"—and he goes on to elabo-rate it for half a page. Compare Taine even at his best with the images in Michelet, which are struck off so much more spontaneously but which stick so much longer in the mind: the Renaissance sawed in two like the prophet Isaiah; the Revolution undermined by speculators like the termites in La Rochelle; the Tsar and the King of Sweden coming down like great polar bears from the north and prowling about the houses of Europe; the unspoken words, congealed by fear, unfreezing in the air of the Convention; the French language of the eighteenth century traveling around the world like light.

So much for the surface of Taine. It is significant of the difference between Michelet, on the one hand, and both Renan and Taine, on the other, that we should think of the latter as presenting surfaces. When we look back on Michelet, what we are aware of is not a surface, but the thing he is presenting, the living complex of the social being. Michelet's primary concern is to stick close to the men and events; he succeeds in dominating history, like Odysseus wrestling with Proteus, by seizing it and holding on to it through all its variety of metamorphoses; and in the course of this rough-and-tumble struggle, he works out an original kind of literary form. He has no preconceived ideas which hamper him; his ideas are in the nature of speculations, and they are merely set afloat in the upper air while his prime business is with what is actually happening. But both Renan and Taine practise systematizations which, in ordering the confusion of human life, seem always to keep it at a distance. Renan must never get so close to violent happenings or emotions that they can break up his sweet and even flow. Taine feeds history into a machine which automatically sorts out the phenomena, so that all the examples of one kind of thing turn up in one section or chapter and all the examples of another kind in another, and the things which do not easily lend themselves to Taine's large and simple generalizations do not turn up at all. The thesis is the prime consideration, and he will allow only a moderate variety in the phenomena that go to fill it in. Yet Taine, with his remarkable machine, did manufacture an article of value.

The generation of French artists and thinkers who came to manhood about 1850 had pretty well abandoned political interests. The *coup d'état* of Louis Bonaparte in 1851 depressed them and left them feeling helpless. Taine, like Renan, had declined to make an issue of the oath of allegiance to Napoleon III. He took the position that the voters, though imbeciles, had the right to confer power on whom they chose; that for a dissident like himself to refuse to submit to their choice would constitute an act of insurrection—the implication being that such an act would be wholly improper in itself, amounting to an attack on organized society. He refused, however, to sign a document presented to the university professors and eliciting an assurance of their "gratitude" and their "respectful devotion." "Political life," he wrote to a friend, "is forbidden us for perhaps ten years. The only path is pure literature or pure science."

Men like Taine were traveling away from romanticism, from the revolutionary enthusiasm and the emotional exuberance of the early part of the century, and setting themselves an ideal of objectivity, of exact scientific observation, which came to be known as Naturalism. Both Renan and Taine pretend to a detachment quite alien to the fierce partisanship of a Michelet; and both do a great deal more talking about science. The science of history is for Taine a pursuit very much less human than it had been for Michelet. He writes in 1852 of his ambition "to make of history a science by giving it like the organic world an anatomy and a physiology." And in the preface to his *Essay on Titus Livy,* he wrote in 1856 as follows: "Man, says Spinoza, is in nature, not as an empire in an empire, but as a part in a whole, and the movements of the spiritual automaton which is our being are governed by laws to the same extent as those of the material world in which it is contained." Note that it is no longer a question of humanity creating itself, of liberty warring against fatality; but of an automaton functioning in an automaton. In the famous introduction to the *History of English Literature,* published in 1863, Taine stated his full philosophy and program: in dealing with works of literature, "as in any other department, the only problem is a mechanical one: The total effect is a compound determined in its entirety by the magnitude and the direction of the forces which produce it." The only difference between moral problems and physical problems is that, in the case of the former, you haven't the same instruments of precision to measure the quantities involved. But "virtue and vice are products like vitriol and sugar"; and all works of literature may be analyzed in terms of the race, the milieu and the moment.

This theory in itself might have produced a criticism utterly arid; but Taine had a great appetite for literature and a gift for dramatizing literary events. In studying works of literature as the flowerings of periods and peoples, he developed superbly a special department of Michelet's "integral reconstitution of the past"; and literary criticism ever since has owed him an immense debt. From Taine's program, we might expect him to confine himself to an analysis of works of literature into their constituent chemical elements; but what he does rather is to exhibit them as specimens, and he delights in showing us how each of his specimens is perfectly developed in its kind. Nor is his interest in them, in spite of what he says, of a character purely zoological. Taine had strong moral prepossessions of a kind which made the literature of the English a peculiarly happy subject for him. Though he dismisses Dr. Johnson as "insupportable," he enjoys playing the Puritans off against the frivolities of the Restoration and gets one of his best effects by following a description of the Restoration dramatists with a peal of the voice of Milton growling at the "sons of Belial." One of his most eloquent chapters, however, one of the passages where he seems really great, is the contrast between Alfred de Musset and Tennyson, in which one kind of English morality gets the worst of it: "We think of that other poet away there in the Isle of Wight, who amuses himself by dressing up lost epics. How happy he is amongst his fine books, his friends, his honeysuckle and his roses! No matter. This other, even here amidst misery and filth, rose higher. From the heights of his doubt and despair, he saw the infinite as we see the sea from a storm-beaten promontory. Religions, their glory and their ruin, the human race, its pangs and its destiny, all that is sublime in the world appeared to him there in a flash. He felt, at least this once in his life, this inner tempest of deep sensations, gigantic dreams and intense delights, the desire for which enabled him to live, the lack of which forced him to die. He was not a mere dilettante; he was not content to taste and enjoy; he stamped his mark upon human thought; he told the world what man is, and love and truth and happiness. He suffered, but he imagined; he fainted, but he created. He tore forth with despair from his entrails the idea which he had conceived, and he held it up before the eyes of all, bloody and alive. That is harder and finer than to go fondling and gazing upon the ideas of others. There is in the world only one achievement worthy of a man: the bringing forth of a truth to which we give ourselves up and in which we believe. The people who have listened to Tennyson are better than our aristocracy of bourgeois and Bohemians; but I prefer Alfred de Musset to Tennyson."

This is not merely a vindication of Musset; it is a vindication of Taine. What sounds in this passage so stirringly is the tone of that real intellectual heroism which makes Taine himself command our respect. But it is significant that he should go back for his text to the generation of 1830. Outside the ideal of "pure science," to which he imagined he had devoted his life, there was little moral inspiration for Taine in the France of the Second Empire. He took courses in anatomy and psychology, frequented the alienists. Yet his determinism is not enough for him; and although he continues to affirm it, we find him smuggling himself out of his confinement within a mechanistic universe in various more or less illogical ways. When he comes to write his philosophy of art, he is obliged to introduce a moral value in the form of "the degree of beneficence of the character" of a given artist or painting. And in his last phase we are to see him responding to a sense of patriotic duty.

The French defeat and the Commune profoundly shocked and troubled Taine; and he sat down in the autumn of 1871 to an immense and uncongenial task which was to occupy him all the remaining twenty years of his life and to be left by him unfinished at his death. Taine set himself to master politics and economics, and to study the processes of government in France from the eve of the great Revolution down through Napoleon to contemporary society. It is in vain that he keeps insisting that his object is purely scientific, that he is as detached in his attitude toward France as he would be toward Florence or Athens: the *Origins of Contemporary France* has an obvious political purpose; and we may infer from it how far the enlightened bourgeois has traveled since the end of the preceding century in his relation to the revolution which made possible his present enlightenment and which established him in the present enjoyment of his property and his rights.

The first thing that strikes us, after Michelet and Renan, about the *Origins of Contemporary France* is that it is not a history at all, but simply an enormous essay. If Renan has become an historian of ideas, allowing other events to lapse into the background, Taine is an historian of literature and displays a truly startling ineptitude when he attempts to deal with parliaments and uprisings. Books and pictures may be pinned down and studied quietly in libraries and museums; and a social life sufficient to explain them may be reconstituted from conversation and travel; but though Taine can read all the documents on a great social struggle as he can read any other books, there is nothing in his own personality or experience which enables him to re-create in imagination the realities these documents represent. Note, in the specimens of his imagery which I have quoted, how awkward he is with a political generalization, but how brilliantly he comes to life when it is a question of a writer to be described. In the eternal generalizations and classifications which constitute the whole structure of his history, the movement of events is lost. In the first place, where Michelet, in attempting to tell everything, is always tending to expand beyond his frame, Taine has begun by laying out a plan which will exclude as many elements as possible. What he is undertaking, he tells us, is merely a "history of the public powers"; he leaves to others the history "of the diplomacy, the wars, the finances, the Church." Then he formulates a set of simplifications of general political and social tendencies, then marshals to the support of each of these a long array of documentary evidence. By Taine's time, the amassment of facts for their own sake was coming to be regarded as one of the proper functions of history; and Taine was always emphasizing the scientific value of the "little significant fact." Here, he says, he will merely present the evidence and allow us to make our own conclusions; but it never seems to occur to him that we may ask ourselves who it is that is selecting the evidence and why he is making this particular choice. It never seems to occur to him that we may accuse him of having conceived the simplification first and then having collected the evidence to fit it; or that we may have been made skeptical at the outset by the very assumption on his part that there is nothing he cannot catalogue with certainty under a definite number of heads with Roman numerals, in so complex, so confused, so disorderly and so rapid a human crisis as the great French Revolution.

As Renan, even after he has explained to us that in the decline of the ancient world it was saints rather than sages who were needed, makes us wonder whether the civilization represented by Marcus Aurelius might not after all have saved itself and done a much more agreeable job of it; so Taine, in the very act of demonstrating the inevitability of the breakdown of the old regime, assures us that its worst abuses were already being corrected by the governing class itself and keeps intimating that if only the people had been a little more reasonable and patient, the whole affair might have been quietly adjusted. Our conviction of the inevitability of religions and revolutions varies in proportion to our distance from them and our opportunity for untroubled reflection. Taine plays down the persecutions for religious belief and liberal thought under the regime of the monarchy and almost succeeds in keeping them out of his picture; and he tries somehow to convey the impression that there was nothing more to the capture of the Bastille than a barbarous and meaningless gesture, by telling us that it contained at the time, after all, only seven prisoners, and dwelling on the misdirected brutalities committed by the mob. Though in some admirable social-documentary chapters he has shown us the intolerable position of the peasants, his tone becomes curiously aggrieved as soon as they begin violating the old laws by seizing estates and stealing bread. Toward the Federations of 1789, which had so thrilling an effect on Michelet, he takes an ironic and patronizing tone. The spirit and achievements of the revolutionary army have been shut out from his scope in advance and are barely—though more respectfully—touched upon. And the revolutionary leaders are presented, with hardly a trace of sympathetic insight—from a strictly zoological point of view, he tells us—as a race of "crocodiles."

Where now is the Taine who, with Alfred de Musset, could

exult in the sense of humanity rising to greatness of vision through misery, conflict, dissipation? The human Proteus, in its convulsions and its disconcerting transformations, has thrown Taine and sent him away sulky, as soon as he has emerged from his library. Not only is he horrified by the Marats, but confronted by a Danton or a Madame Roland, he shrinks at once into professorial superiority. At the sight of men making fools and brutes of themselves, even though he himself owes to their struggles his culture and his privileged position, a remote disapproval chills his tone, all the bright colors of his fancy go dead. Where is the bold naturalist now who formerly made such obstinate headway against the squeamishness of academic circles? He is pressing upon us a social program which blends strangely the householder's timidity with the intellectual's independence. Don't let the State go too far, he pleads: we must, to be sure, maintain the army and the police to protect us against the foreigner and the ruffian; but the government must not be allowed to interfere with Honor and Conscience, Taine's pet pair of nineteenth-century abstractions, nor with the private operation of industry, which stimulates individual initiative and which alone can secure general prosperity.

The truth is that the mobs of the great Revolution and the revolutionary government of Paris have become identified now in Taine's mind with the socialist revolution of the Commune. Like Renan, he has been driven to imagining that his sole solidarity lies with a small number of superior persons who have been appointed as the salt of the earth; and he is even farther than Renan from Michelet's conception of the truly superior man as him who represents the people most completely. But, though not much liking his ordinary fellow bourgeois, he will rise to the defense of the bourgeois law and order as soon as there seems to be a danger of its being shaken by the wrong kind of superior people.

Yet something is wrong: his heart is not in this as it was in his early work. He does not like the old regime; he does not like the Revolution; he does not like the militaristic France which has been established by Napoleon and his nephew. And he never lived to write, as he had planned, the final glorification of the French family, which was to have given its moral basis to his system, nor the survey of contemporary France, in which he was apparently to have taken up the problem of the use and abuse of science: to have shown how, though beneficial when studied and applied by the elite, it became deadly in the hands of the vulgar.

8 Decline of the Revolutionary Tradition: Anatole France

Anatole France, of the generation twenty years younger than Renan and Taine, was twenty-seven at the time of the Commune. He had been declared unfit for service at the front and, as a member of the National Guard, had been reading Virgil on the fortifications. When the socialist government of Paris was set up and there seemed danger of his being pressed to its defense, he got away from Paris with a false name and a Belgian passport, and took refuge in Versailles, the head-quarters of the bourgeois government. From Versailles, he writes to his parents that he has had the satisfaction of seeing a group of Communard prisoners: "riffraff . . . they were hideous, as you may suppose." The explosion of a powder magazine in the Luxembourg was clearly heard in Versailles, and the people there were very much frightened. Young Anatole France watched the fire and worried about his family in Paris. Back at home, with the Commune suppressed and the Louvre and the National Library still intact, so that he was able to feel that "the intellectual life was not yet al-together lost in Paris," he writes a friend that "the government of Madness and Crime is rotting at last in the very hour when it was beginning to put its program into effect. Paris has run up the tricolor over the ruins."

He was the son of a Parisian bookseller, and the family shop on the Quai Voltaire was a clearing-house for that rich culture of Paris which became richer as the century wore on. The scholars, the novelists and the poets came there. The shop was within the shadow of the Academy, and when

Anatole France was fifteen, he drew one day at the end of one of his school themes, which had received honorable mention, a picture of the Thibault bookshop and the Cupola and drew a line connecting one with the other. Two years later, he wrote to his father, who had just attended a meeting of the Academy: "How shall I answer your letter now that you have actually sat within the holy precincts of the Institute, now that you have listened to the most eloquent voices and the most nobly inspired poems—I who know only the greenery of the fields, the blue of the sky, the thatched roofs of the farms?"

One of his great admirations was Renan. In *The Wedding at Corinth,* a play in verse, he dramatized *The Origins of Christianity;* and part of *The Crime of Sylvestre Bonnard,* the story of a kindly, innocent and subtle-minded old scholar, is said to have been based on Renan's adventures in Sicily. Out of the preface to a late book of Renan's, *Philosophical Dramas,* he got the phrase about approaching human life with an attitude of irony and pity which he was himself to exploit and make famous. The young Anatole France, in fact, achieved his first success by a sort of sweetened imitation of Renan in his old age. *The Crime of Sylvestre Bonnard,* which he afterwards grew to loathe, was aimed, he confessed, at the Academy. And the Academy duly crowned it. By fifty-two, Anatole France had taken his seat as an Academician. He was afterwards to say that he had done everything which would have pleased his mother on the Quai Voltaire.

Yet there was something else underneath the surface of the honey-voiced early France. Anatole France was a man of superior abilities who had taken some disagreeable snubs. At the ecclesiastical school to which he had been sent, the Collège Stanislas, the old scale of social values was still in force. In the whole course of his attendance there, France afterwards told his secretary, Jean-Jacques Brousson, he had never received a prize. The prizes all went to the pupils with aristocratic names—it was thus the masters advertised the school. "A few second-rate honors, to be sure, were thrown to the Third Estate, the sons of doctors or notaries or lawyers —prizes for recitation, drawing or religious instruction. But favoritism played its part even there in the distribution of the crumbs that fell from the high table." The masters told his parents he was dull and advised them to take him out: they were only wasting their money trying to educate him beyond his station. The elder France had been a shoemaker's son, who had begun his career as a farm boy and soldier, who had educated himself and worked up gradually to the book-shop on the Quai Voltaire; and Anatole was to cherish all his life the resentment of the petty bourgeois against the big bourgeoisie and the nobility. His unctuous manners are likely to break down when something happens to revive this resent-ment. He became furious with a vicomte of the Academy, who had promised to vote for him and then failed to do so: "You are mistaken, M. de——," he blasted him, when the Academi-cian tried to apologize. "You voted for me! You gave me your word. You're a gentleman: you don't break your word. You're mistaken, M. de——; you did vote for me!" And when one of the priests of the Collège Stanislas, who had told his parents to put him to work in the shop, tried to congratulate him after his election to the Academy, France repulsed him in a harsh burst of anger. France hated the priests all the more because he believed that the Catholic education was aimed at cramp-ing the natural instincts, that it was hostile to beauty and *volupté*.

All this side of Anatole France was to be brought out by the Dreyfus case. The condemnation of Dreyfus, which stirred up the French in 1895, when Anatole France was fifty, was not a genuine social crisis like the Commune, which called the whole structure of society in question. It was a conflict merely between, on the one hand, the liberal bour-geoisie, and, on the other, the army, the royalists, the Church. Anatole France, by himself rather timid and lazy, had at that time a Jewish friend, Mme. Caillavet, who made him work, gave him a salon in her house and generally promoted his advancement; and she probably had a good deal to do with his championship of Dreyfus, which contributed to bring about the retrial and pardon of 1899. Besides, the righting of injustice, the baiting of the forces of reaction, had by Rabelais and Voltaire been made a part of the French literary tradition, which France prided himself on representing. He made speeches, pamphleteered, turned for the moment into a satirist of the type of Bernard Shaw. The immensely amusing *Contemporary History,* with its smiling but deadly analysis of the upper strata of French society, is the product of the Dreyfus period. At the beginning of *The Elm Tree on the Mall,* as if as a keystone and justification of the work, France, evidently remembering his father, plants an intelligent cobbler's son. Piédagnel, the brilliant child of humble parents, has aroused the sympathetic interest of the Abbé at the head of the seminary where Piédagnel is studying for the priesthood. But the boy is weak in doctrine; he is found to have been copying down erotic poems by Verlaine and Leconte de Lisle. The Abbé begins to be afraid that he may be rearing another Renan, and, though reluctantly, he dismisses the boy just at the moment when the ritual of the Church is beginning esthetically to move him. Piédagnel, with no aptitude for a manual trade, is sent back to the cobbler's shop; the Church has abruptly closed to him the hopes which it had been encouraging, it is suppressing the same gifts which it has stimulated. But Piédagnel goes out with a passion in his heart which, France tells us, is to fill his whole life: the "hatred of the priest."

This incident told with the French brevity and coolness of which Anatole France was a master, with the art which does not allow us to feel the full force of what we have been reading till we have finished the last line, is one of the most effective things of the kind that Anatole France ever wrote. Yet we are somewhat surprised as we go on to discover that it is to have no sequel. From these first chapters we might have supposed that Piédagnel was to figure as a hero; but the cobbler's son never reappears. The character who turns into the hero is M. Bergeret, another Sylvestre Bonnard, less sentimentalized and more ironic. M. Bergeret is a humble professor of Latin, who has been compelled by the science department to hold his classes in a depressing basement (belles lettres by Anatole France's time are losing their faith in science and are no longer so eager for an alliance with it). Later, Bergeret takes a stand on Dreyfus, attracts a certain amount of public attention, goes to Paris and gets a better chair. What France has done is to telescope in Piédagnel his own situation with his father's—the shoemaker's grandson with the shoemaker's son; and then allow M. Bergeret, who corresponds to the mature France with the Collège Stanislas well behind him, to substitute himself for Piédagnel. A whole set of steps in the social ladder has been jumped between Bergeret in Paris and Piédagnel in his provincial town. And thereafter Anatole France himself is to be Bergeret successful.

The little bourgeois of the Quai Voltaire is by way of being a big bourgeois now. His books sell in never-ending editions; they are on sale at every railway station in France. He gets rich; he can buy all the pictures and books, all the fine furniture and bric-à-brac, he pleases. In the salon of Mme. Caillavet, he is the most sought-after literary figure in Paris. He loses his awkward manners and his stammer and becomes an entrancing salon talker. Then he takes a large house of his own, begins to detach himself from Mme. Caillavet, finally breaks with her altogether.

This lady, it is true, must have been trying; we cannot be surprised that France should, in the long run, have felt a desperate need to escape her. With her feverish merciless possessive affection, she had been attempting to control all his writing, to check up on all his movements. Yet during the period when her influence over him is dominant—say, from *The Red Lily* to *Crainquebille*—he appears as a more sympathetic and a much more clear-cut figure than either before or after. The challenge of political opposition arouses his more generous emotions and puts him on his mettle; his ideas seem to hang together better. And Mme. Caillavet was certainly right in trying to get him away from his eternal historical pastiches to write novels of contemporary life.

For France was much preoccupied with history; he wrote a whole series of novels and short stories—they make, indeed, the bulk of his writing—which attempt to catch the essence of various periods from Homer's Greece to Napoleon III's Paris. Even his studies of contemporary France he labels *Contemporary History*. But how far away now, in a few decades, Michelet's vision of history seems when we look back from Anatole France! It is characteristic of France that he should, as I have said, aim merely at catching the essence of a period. He has already become one of the great practitioners of a cult which is later to be carried further: the cultivation of intelligence for its own sake. Let us understand phenomena and appreciate them: it gives pleasure and it is a mark of superiority to be able to see how things work and how an infinite variety of things are good in an infinite variety of kinds. But there we may leave them; we need not attempt to systematize them or to draw conclusions on which we may act. France has not yet come quite so far as this. He does, as we shall see, sometimes try to build systems and he occasionally makes gestures of public action. But he no longer has anything like Michelet's exalted and unfading vision of the combat of liberty with fatality, man with nature, spirit with matter, which had been so plain in the dawn of the century. It becomes a favorite game of France's irony to show, with something not unlike complacency, how freedom, spirit and man are defeated. Homer's song of the evils that flowed from the wrath of Achilles is broken up by the quarreling of cowherds; Jeanne d'Arc, preaching war, finds a following and becomes a national heroine where a similarly hallucinated young woman who has been inspired to preach peace and Christian love, walking the walls at the siege of Paris, is promptly picked off by an arrow. Yet there is no general coherence to the picture. In *The Procurator of Judea,* France takes a cue from Renan. Renan, in telling about Paul before Gallio, had pointed out the irony of the incident: to Gallio, the man in authority, the cultivated Roman, Paul had been an unprepossessing nobody. Yet the civilization of Gallio was doomed; it was Paul who represented the future. In *The Procurator of Judea,* Pilate has forgotten Christ. But later France is to try it the other way: in *On the White Stone,* he demonstrates that in the long run the future was really to belong to Gallio, since it was to be the kind of civilization imagined by enlightened Romans that was ultimately to hold the field when Christianity had come and gone. Yet France wrote pretty travesties of saints' legends whose shades of ironic tenderness Voltaire would never have understood. And the affair of

Thaïs and Paphnuce is a drama where we sympathize equally with the courtesan and with the saint. Sometimes he amused himself with pure exercises of the historic imagination, such as the story of Caesar's conquests from the point of view of one of the Gallic chieftains whom the Romans are reducing to subjection. It is the miscellaneous learning of the bookstore, unorganized by any large purpose, the undisciplined undirected curiosity of the indolent lover of reading.

When we come to the period of the French Revolution, to which Anatole France devoted one of the most ambitious of his later books, we find him attacking the subject from an angle which the France of *Contemporary History* would never have led us to expect. *The Gods Are Thirsty* is a story of the Terror, and Anatole France opposes in it a harsh and puritanical petty Robespierre to a charming and epicurean formerly well-to-do Farmer-General—that is, the Revolution at its ugliest to the old regime at its most attractive. France had written in his youth of Louis XIV: "That grotesque and hateful being whom Michelet, with his eye of genius, has seen in all his baseness and all his misery, has no longer any right to foolish indulgence"; yet, though he thinks better of Louis XIV now, he would not even now choose an aristocrat for a hero. What he does do is take a cultivated bourgeois who has got rich under the old regime and enjoyed the best of the old society, and give him all the moral advantage. The Jacobin Gamelin becomes more and more fanatical and intolerant, and finally sends the gentle Brotteaux to the ax. Brotteaux is a later version of Bergeret; but a Bergeret—see the episode with the prostitute—toward whom France seems now to be relapsing into a mood of sentimentality reminiscent of Sylvestre Bonnard.

And who is Gamelin, after all, but our old friend Paphnuce of *Thaïs*, grown conspicuously less sympathetic? The comfortable bourgeois is getting the better of it. Brotteaux had been deprived of his fine house, his agreeable social life; but he had borne it with a classical fortitude and read Lucretius on the way to execution. Anatole France still has all his luxuries, and we feel it would be hard for him to part with them. Yet in the enjoyment of them he is not precisely happy. It has become the fashion to disparage France as a writer; but that is partly because people expect to find in him things that he cannot supply, even though he may sometimes attempt to do so—and not for the things that are actually there. For Anatole France does not represent merely a dimming of the eighteenth-century Enlightenment as Taine and Renan do; he shows that tradition in full disintegration; and what he is telling, with all his art and wit, is the story of an intellectual world where principles are going to pieces. The moralist in Anatole France, the Paphnuce, the Gamelin, is always in conflict with the sensualist, the great preacher of *volupté* as the sole solace for human futility; and the moralist becomes more and more odious as the sensualist becomes more and more sterile.

In his political role, France is a socialist; yet the whole purpose of two of his later books, *The Gods Are Thirsty* and *The Revolt of the Angels,* is to show that revolutions must eventually result in tyrannies at least as oppressive as those they were designed to displace. And when he undertakes, in *Penguin Island,* to write a sort of outline of history, he has modern industrial civilization blasted off the face of the earth by embittered proletarian anarchists. But no freer and more reasonable order succeeds: the rebels are wiped out with their masters, and such men as are left on earth return to their original condition as tillers of the soil. We are back with the cycles of Vico again and might as well not have got rid of God. *Penguin Island* is presented as a satire, to be sure; but we know from France's other work that this kind of idea haunted his mind. "Slowly, but surely," he had written at the head of his political papers, "humanity realizes the dreams of the wise"; but he had moments when this assurance was destroyed by the nightmares of science, which was no longer for France, as I have said, the school of discipline, the source of strength, that it had been for Taine or Renan or Zola. Taine is an avowed determinist, who derives from his mechanistic conceptions a solid method and a formal force of logic, but whose esthetic and moral values are really very little affected by his materialistic principles. Anatole France is a professed reformer and optimist, who is always relapsing into cynicism or gloom, and giving way to the worst suspicions of the mechanistic character of life and the total insignificance of humanity. He reads the astronomical articles in Larousse and makes great play with the vision of mankind alone in the awful empty universe, a mere disease on the face of the earth—a vision that has seemed terrible with Pascal, still tragic in Leopardi, still productive of nobly-ringing verses in the poetry of Alfred de Vigny, a little overdone and ridiculous in the novels of Thomas Hardy, and which has come down, in Anatole France, with his dressing-gown, his slippers and his Larousse, to the level of entertaining conversation.

Mr. Haakon M. Chevalier has shown in his admirable study of France how both his irony and his inveterate inability to construct a book on a large scale were due to the fluctuating character of his intellect: France's mockery works both ways because he is unable to reconcile in himself several quite different points of view and he can never hold to any system long enough to base a full-length piece of work upon it. More even than Voltaire, Anatole France comes finally to deserve the accusation of being a "chaos of clear ideas." The books of France's later years are more solid and more ambitious than anything he has done before; but they have the same lack of organic coherence. What do we find in them?—glowing hopes undermined by frightful sinkings, erotic imagination mixed with impulses of social protest, and—becoming more pronounced as he grows older—a nihilism black and hateful. He gets a certain intensity here, the intensity of a man actually tortured by his powerlessness to carry through any one of a number of contradictory impulses. For the first time his ridicule becomes truly ferocious. His sense of isolation deepens. He insists before Proust on that aloneness in love, that imprisoning impossibility of sharing one's emotions with another, which Proust is to take for his central theme and which he is to harp on and elaborate so inordinately. In both *The Red Lily* and *A Mummer's Tale* (*Histoire Comique*), with which the pathological early story *Jocaste* associates itself, the typical romantic situation of love rendered hopeless by barriers of marital duty, social convention or consanguinity has already turned into the situation of love rendered hopeless by neurotic obsession and inhibition. Michelet, too, had been an only child; Michelet, too, had suffered from social maladjustment; but he had derived from the Revolution just behind him a sense of solidarity with others engaged in a great human undertaking, and through his history he had succeeded in making himself a part of a human world of which he believed in the importance and the destiny. With France, the abysses of doubt and despair are always yawning under the tightropes and trapezes of the highly developed intelligence, and to perform on them becomes more and more ticklish.

In the meantime, during the period of the Dreyfus case, France sends back his Legion of Honor ribbon when the Legion strikes Zola off its rolls. He stays away from the séances of the Academy; but goes back to it, on entreaty, in old age. He makes speeches before working-class audiences at the time of the 1905 revolution in Russia. He supports the war of 1914, offers himself at seventy for military service; then, hearing of the rejection by the Allies of the peace proposals of the Central Powers, declines to lend his support to any more patriotic causes. "Yes," he told Marcel LeGoff, "I've written and talked like my concierge. I'm ashamed of it, but it had to be done." He would not protest, however, even in the War's later stages. He was frightened: his old friend Caillaux had been sent to jail by Clemenceau, his old ally of the Dreyfus case, and Clemenceau had threatened, it is said, to do the same thing to France if he opened his mouth to criticize the government. Surrounded by parasites and female admirers and a veritable museum of *objets d'art*, he would receive and talk with radicals, whom he called "Comrade." Brousson records that, on one occasion, when asked why he was "drawn toward socialism," France had answered: "Better be drawn than driven." To another caller, we are told by LeGoff, he said in answer to a question about the future: "The future? But, my poor friend, there is no future—there is nothing. Everything will begin the same again—people will build things and tear them down and so on forever. So long as men can't get outside themselves or free themselves from their passions, nothing will ever change. There will be some periods which will be more peaceful and others which will be more disturbed; men will go on killing each other and then go back to their affairs again." He sees too many people and is too polite and too malicious to all of them. Voltaire, we feel, was very fortunate in having an object that required all his malice. In Anatole France's day, after the flurry of the Dreyfus case, the Church no longer seems sufficiently formidable for the satirist to do very much more than tease it with ribald versions of sacred stories. He continues to preach the consolations of an easygoing epicureanism; but "if you could read in my soul," he once told Brousson, "you would be horrified." "He took my hands in his, feverish and trembling. He looked in my eyes, and I saw that his own were full of tears. His face was all ravaged. 'There is not,' he sighed, 'an unhappier creature in the whole universe than I! People think me happy. I have never been happy—not an hour—not a day!' "

And the nihilism, the bitter outbursts, begin to make the naïveté, which had once seemed so droll and delightful, sound off-key and insincere. Anatole France had an infantile side that we get to like less and less; and it is bound up with an attempt to get back to the more innocent ages of the language. The tendency toward archaizing which made him, in one of the Bergeret books, satirize contemporary politics in the language of Rabelais, and in the books about the Abbé Coignard, deliver criticisms of contemporary institutions in the accents of the eighteenth century, which caused him to lard even his own personal utterances with obsolete locutions and phrases, represented a genuine weakness. Now, in his old age, he takes refuge from his loneliness, from the War, from the death of his only daughter, who had been estranged from him by his divorce from his wife, in returning to a vein of childhood memories—the vein of *My Friend's Book* and *Pierre Nozière*—in which he had at one time been charming. But now, in spite of some fine passages such as the address to Racine, admirable exercises in that traditional French which he, like Renan, was to declare in these last years had only been debased since the eighteenth century, and to his labors over which the series of drafts of the book left unfinished at his death present such impressive testimony—in spite of this,

Little Peter and *Life in Bloom* seem self-conscious and coldly contrived. How much that is distressing he must be omitting—how much that is harsh, smoothing out! The smiling felicity of the art which has ripened in the sun of the nineteenth century can no longer, with the beginning of the twentieth, neutralize the taste of dust and ashes. And it is a long way from the France of Zorn's etching, leaning toward us over his table with his engaging ironic dark wide eyes and his moustache and pointed beard of the Second Empire, to the old man of Van Dongen's painting, which France himself detested and of which he correctly said that it made him look like a Camembert that was running.

At last, after the flattery and rewards of a lifetime, the younger generation is to reject him. His conception of "the succession of phenomena and the relativity of things"—to which France still assigned a certain reliability—was to be carried by the Symbolists and their successors to a point where it was to become, on the one hand, unintelligible to Anatole France and, where, on the other hand, France's interest in politics, the flickerings of his social conscience, were to cease to have meaning for them. With the Symbolists, the conviction of social isolation reached a point where they had not even the illusion of being disillusioned about society. When France died, his place at the Academy was filled by an eminent Symbolist, who used the occasion to disparage France; and that group of ultra-Symbolists, the Dadaists, together with some neo-romantic young writers, seized upon the day of his burial to bring out, under the title *A Corpse*, a fierce manifesto against him. "Without God, without touching love!" wrote Pierre Drieu de la Rochelle, "without insupportable despair, without magnificent anger, without definitive defeats, without conclusive triumphs!" And, "That skeptic, that amiable skeptic," protested Joseph Delteil, "leaves me cold. It is for passion that I become impassioned. It is optimism, faith, ardor and blood that arouse me!" They accuse him of compromise, of cowardice, of traditionalism, of patriotism, of realism, of betraying the Revolution.

Having reached the extreme stage of relativism, where it goes in for automatic writing and the documents produced by patients in insane asylums, making a duty of irresponsibility and a morality of moral anarchism, they completed the circuit of the varying relation of the individual, as writer, to society and came around to a point further back than that at which we first took up Michelet: they found that their necessary next progression took them out of the doctrine of relativity, which they had carried as far as was possible, and into beginning again with a creed and a code, fixed principles, a plan of action. Among the great Symbolist prototypes of the Dadaists, Rimbaud had fought for the Commune and Lautréamont was supposed to have participated in the agitation against the Second Empire and to have been murdered by Napoleon's police. In the *Second Surrealist Manifesto* of André Breton, the names of Rimbaud and Lautréamont turn up strangely beside those of Marx and Lenin. The next step from Dadaism was Communism; and one or two of the ex-Dadaists, at any rate, were serious enough to submit themselves to the discipline of the Communist Party.

But, having followed the tradition of the bourgeois revolution to its disintegration in Anatole France, we must go back and trace the inverse development of socialism.

II:

1 Origins of Socialism: Babeuf's Defense

The years of relaxation under the Directory which followed the fall of Robespierre were troubled by the activities of a man who called himself Gracchus Babeuf.

With the Directory the French Revolution had passed into the period of reaction which was to make possible the domination of Bonaparte. The great rising of the bourgeoisie, which, breaking out of the feudal forms of the monarchy, dispossessing the nobility and the clergy, had presented itself to society as a movement of liberation, had ended by depositing the wealth in the hands of a relatively small number of people and creating a new conflict of classes. With the reaction against the Terror, the ideals of the Revolution were allowed to go by the board. The five politicians of the Directory and the merchants and financiers allied with them were speculating in confiscated property, profiteering in army supplies, recklessly inflating the currency and gambling on the falling gold louis. And in the meantime, during the winter of 1795–96, the working people of Paris were dying of hunger and cold in the streets.

Babeuf was the son of a Protestant who had been sent abroad by the Calvinists to negotiate a union with the Lutherans and who had remained to serve as a major in the army of Maria Theresa and later to tutor her children. Returned to France, he had fallen into misery, and the son had had to learn his letters, he said, from papers picked up in the street. His father taught him Latin and mathematics. On his deathbed, the old man gave him a Plutarch and told him that he himself could have wished to play the role of Caius Gracchus. He made the boy swear on his sword that he would defend to the death the interests of the people.

This was in 1780. When the Revolution occurred, Babeuf was twenty-nine. He was present at the taking of the Bastille. He had been employed as a clerk to a registrar of seignorial rights in the little town of Roye in the Somme, and now he burned the seignorial archives. Thereafter, as journalist and official, he threw himself into the work of the Revolution with an earnestness that kept him in continual hot water. He incited the tavern-keepers of the Somme to rebel against paying the old wine tax, which the Constituent Assembly had abolished; he sold up the expropriated estates and divided the village common among the poor. Babeuf went too fast for his province. The landlords and the local authorities kept arresting him and clapping him in jail. At last in 1793 he was given a post in Paris in the Bureau of Subsistence of the Commune. The privation in Paris was terrible, and Babeuf found a leak in the bureau's accounts. He came to the conclusion that the authorities were deliberately producing a famine in order to exploit the demand for foodstuffs, and he had a commission of investigation appointed. The government suppressed the commission, and Babeuf soon found himself pursued for what were apparently framed charges of fraud in connection with his administration in the provinces.

After Thermidor, he rallied around him those elements of the Revolution who were trying to insist on its original aims. In his paper, *The Tribune of the People,* he denounced the new constitution of 1795, which had abolished universal suffrage and imposed a high property qualification. He demanded not merely political but also economic equality. He declared that he would prefer civil war itself to "this horrible concord which strangles the hungry." But the men who had expropriated the nobles and the Church remained loyal to the principle of property itself. *The Tribune of the People* was stopped, and Babeuf and his associates were sent to prison.

While Babeuf was in jail, his seven-year-old daughter died of hunger. He had managed to remain poor all his life. His popularity had been all with the poor. His official posts had earned him only trouble. Now, as soon as he was free again, he proceeded to found a political club, which opposed the policies of the Directory and which came to be known as the Society of the Equals. They demanded in a *Manifesto of the Equals* (not, however, at that time made public) that there should be "no more individual property in land; the land belonged to no one. . . . We declare that we can no longer endure, with the enormous majority of men, labor and sweat in the service and for the benefit of a small minority. It has now been long enough and too long that less than a million individuals have been disposing of that which belongs to more than twenty millions of their kind. . . . Never has a vaster design been conceived or put into execution. Certain men of genius, certain sages, have spoken of it from time to time in a low and trembling voice. Not one of them has had the courage to tell the whole truth. . . . People of France! open your eyes and your heart to the fullness of happiness. Recognize and proclaim with us the Republic of Equals!"

The Society of Equals was also suppressed; Bonaparte himself closed the club. But, driven underground, they now plotted an insurrection; they proposed to set up a new directory. And they drafted a constitution that provided for "a great national community of goods" and worked out with some precision the mechanics of a planned society. The cities were to be deflated and the population distributed in villages. The State was to "seize upon the new-born individual, watch over his early moments, guarantee the milk and care of his mother and bring him to the *maison nationale*, where he was to acquire the virtue and enlightenment of a true citizen." There was thus to be equal education for all. All able-bodied persons were to work, and the work that was unpleasant or arduous was to be accomplished by everybody's taking turns. The necessities of life were to be supplied by the government, and the people were to eat at communal tables. The government was to control all foreign trade and to pass on everything printed.

In the meantime, the value of the paper money had depreciated almost to zero. The Directory tried to save the situation by converting the currency into land warrants, which were at a discount of 82 per cent the day they were issued; and there was a general belief on the part of the public that the government had gone bankrupt. There were in Paris alone some five hundred thousand people in need of relief. The Babouvistes placarded the city with a manifesto of historical importance; they declared that Nature had given to every man an equal right to the enjoyment of every good, and it was the purpose of society to defend that right; that Nature had imposed on every man the obligation to work, and that no one could escape this obligation without committing a crime; that in "a true society" there would be neither rich nor poor; that the object of the Revolution had been to destroy every inequality and to establish the well-being of all; that the Revolution was therefore "not finished," and that those who had done away with the Constitution of 1793 were guilty of *lèse-majesté* against the people.

In the cafés, they were singing a song composed by a member of the society: "Dying of hunger, dying of cold, the people robbed of every right . . . newcomers gorged with gold, who have given neither work nor thought, are laying hold on the hive; while you, the toiling people, eat iron like an ostrich. . . . A brainless double council, five frightened directors; the soldier pampered and petted, the democrat crushed: *Voilà la République!*"

Babeuf's "insurrectionary committee" had agents in the army and the police, and they were doing such effective work that the government tried to send its troops out of Paris, and, when they refused to obey, disbanded them. During the early days of May, 1796, on the eve of the projected uprising, the Equals were betrayed by a stool pigeon and their leaders were arrested and put in jail. The followers of Babeuf made an attempt to rally a sympathetic police squadron, but were cut down by a new Battalion of the Guard which had been pressed into service for the occasion.

Babeuf was made a public example by being taken to Vendôme in a cage—an indignity which not long before had filled the Parisians with fury when the Austrians had inflicted it on a Frenchman.

His defense, which lasted for six sittings of the court and fills more than three hundred pages, is an impressive and moving document. Babeuf knew well that he was facing death and that the Revolution was doomed. The French had been finally exhausted by the birth-throes of the seven years that had passed since the taking of the Bastille. All the fervor of which they were still capable was siphoned off into the revolutionary army, which that spring was being led by Bonaparte to the victories of the Italian campaign. At home, since the Terror, they were shy of violence. Babeuf had united with the last of the Jacobins, and the people had had enough of *them*. Uncompromising principles and the guillotine were inextricably associated in their minds; they were glad to be free to live, and a period of frivolity had set in. And the bourgeois instinct for property was already becoming the overmastering motive, taking the place of other instincts and ideals: all those who had succeeded in getting anything clung to it with desperate tenacity; the idea of redistribution frightened them out of their wits. And the poor were no longer prepared to fight. Babeuf knew all this, and his defense has a realism and a sobriety which suggest much later phases of socialism. It is no longer the rhetoric of the Revolution, grandiose, passionate and confusing. At a time when people in general were able to think only of the present, Babeuf looked both backward and forward; at the moment when a society still talking the language of the ideals of the Revolution, libertarian, equalitarian and fraternal, had passed completely into the hands of a new owning class, with its new privileges, injustices and constraints, Babeuf, with great courage and insight, was able to analyze the ambiguous situation. His defense is like a summing-up of the unrealized ideas of the Enlightenment and a vindication of their ultimate necessity. And it has moments of grandeur which it is not absurd to compare to Socrates' *Apology*.

The real issue in this case, says Babeuf, is less the question of conspiracy against the government than the spreading of certain ideas subversive to the dominating class. He has seen under the Directory, he says, the sovereignty of the people disregarded, and the right to elect and be elected reserved to certain castes. He has seen privilege brought back again. He has seen the people deprived of freedom of the press and assembly, and the right to petition and the right to carry arms. He has seen even the right to ratify the laws taken away from the citizens and vested in a second chamber. He has seen an executive power set up which is out of the reach of the people and independent of popular control. He has seen relief and education forgotten. And finally he has seen the Constitution of 1793, which had been approved by nearly five million votes with genuine popular feeling behind them, replaced by an unpopular constitution, put over by scarcely a million dubious ones. So that if it were true that he had conspired (it *was* true, though at the trial he denied it), it would have been against an illegitimate authority. The cause of revolutions is the bending beyond what they can bear of the human springs of society. The people rebel against the pressure; and they are right, because the aim of society is the good of the greatest number. If the people still finds itself bent double, it doesn't matter what the rulers say: the revolution is not finished yet. Or if it is, the rulers have committed a crime.

Happiness, in Europe, is a new idea. But today we know that the unhappy are the really important powers of the earth; they have the right to speak as the real masters of the governments that neglect them. We know that every man has an equal right to the enjoyment of every benefit, and that the real purpose of society is to defend that right and to increase the common benefits. And work, like enjoyment, should be shared by all. Nature has decreed that we all must work: it is a crime to evade this duty. And it is a crime to take for oneself at the expense of other people the products of industry or the earth. In a society which was really sound, there would be neither poor nor rich. There would be no such system of property as ours. Our laws of heredity and inalienability are "humanicide" institutions. The monopoly of the land by individuals, their possession of its produce in excess of their wants, is nothing more nor less than theft; and all our civil institutions, our ordinary business transactions, are the deeds of a perpetual brigandage, authorized by barbarous laws.

But you say that it is my ideas, he goes on, which would

send society back to barbarism. The great philosophers of the century did not think so; and it is they whose disciple I am. You should be arraigning the monarchy for having shown itself so much less inquisitorial than the government of our present Republic; you should arraign it for not having prevented me from getting hold of the pernicious books of the Mablys, the Helvétius, the Diderots, the Jean-Jacques. Philanthropists of today! if it had not been for the poisons of these older philanthropists, I might share your moral principles and your virtues: I might have been moved by the tenderest solicitude for the minority of the mighty of this world; I might have been pitiless for the suffering mass. Didn't you know that you had included in your indictment a passage I had quoted from Rousseau, which was written in 1758? He had spoken of "men so odious as to dare to have more than enough while other men are dying of hunger." I do not hesitate to make this revelation because I am not afraid of compromising this new conspirator: he is beyond the jurisdiction of your tribunal. And Mably, the popular, the sensitive, the human, was not he an even deeper-dyed conspirator? "If you follow the chain of our vices," he said, "you will find that the first link is fastened to the inequality of wealth." The Manifesto of the Equals, which had never been brought out of the dust of the box where we had put it but about which so much fuss has been made, went no further than Mably and Rousseau. And Diderot, who said that from the scepter to the crozier, humanity was ruled by personal interest, and that personal interest arose from property, and that it was idle for philosophers to argue about the best possible form of government so long as the ax had not been laid to the roots of property itself— Diderot, who asked whether the instability, the periodic vicissitudes of empires, would be possible if all goods were held in common, and who asserted that every citizen should take from the community what he needed and give to the community what he could and that anyone who should try to restore the detestable principle of property should be locked up as an enemy of humanity and a dangerous lunatic!— Citizens, "dangerous lunatic" is precisely what you have called *me* for trying to introduce equality!

And Tallien and Armand de la Meuse, who are now sitting in the Directory and the legislature—why have they not been called to the bar? Tallien, only a few years ago when he was editing *The Sans-Culottes' Friend,* was telling us that "the anarchy would cease as soon as wealth was less unequal." And Armand de la Meuse was assuring the Convention that "every candid person must admit that political equality without real equality is only a tantalizing illusion," and that the "cruelest error of the revolutionary bodies has been their failure to mark the limits of property rights and their consequent abandonment of the people to the greedy speculations of the rich."

Christ has told us to love our neighbor and to do as we would be done by; but I admit that Christ's code of equality caused him to be prosecuted for conspiracy.

The way that things were going would have been brought home to me even if I had not been able to see them. When I was sent to jail for my writings, I left my wife and my three unfortunate children helpless during the horrible famine. My little girl of seven died when the allowance of bread was cut down to two ounces; and the others grew so thin that when I saw them again, I could hardly recognize them. And we were only one among thousands of families—the greater part of Paris, in fact—whose faces were blighted by the famine, who tottered when they walked.

And if I have desired for them a better system, it is not that I have expected to impose it by force. All I want is that the people should be enlightened and convinced of their own omnipotence, of the inviolability of their rights, and that the people should demand their rights. I want, if need be, that they should be shown the way to demand their rights; but I want nothing except subject to the people's consent.

But where Mably and Diderot and Rousseau and Helvétius have failed, how should I have hoped to succeed? I am a lesser disciple of theirs, and the Republic is less tolerant than the monarchy.

He reminded them of the fact that the royalists of the Vendémiaire conspiracy had all been pardoned and set free, and that the party of the Pretender had been openly saying that the new constitution would suit them very well if there were one director instead of five. The Society of Equals had reason to believe that a massacre was being plotted against them, like the massacres of republicans in the Midi, and Babeuf launched upon so provocative a picture of the hounding of the republicans by the forces of reaction that the judges made him stop his speech and would not let him go on till the next day.

Babeuf declared in conclusion that the death sentence would not surprise or frighten him. He had got used to prison and violent death in the course of his revolutionary mission. It was abundant consolation, he said, that his own wife and children and those of his followers had never been ashamed of what had happened to their husbands and fathers, but had come there to the courtroom to sustain them.

"But, oh, my children," he concluded, "I have from my place above these benches—the only place from which my voice can reach you, since they have even, contrary to law, made it impossible for me to see you—I have only one bitter regret to express to you: that, though I have wanted so much to leave you a heritage of that liberty which is the source of every good, I foresee for the future only slavery, and that I am leaving you a prey to every ill. I have nothing at all to give you! I would not leave you even my civic virtues, my profound hatred of tyranny, my ardent devotion to the cause of Liberty and Equality, my passionate love of the People. I should make you too disastrous a present. What would you do with it under the monarchic oppression which is infallibly going to descend on you? I am leaving you slaves, and it is this thought alone which will torture my soul in its final moments. I should equip you, in this situation, with advice as to how to bear your chains more patiently, but I do not feel that I am capable of it."

The vote, after much disagreement, went against Babeuf. One of his sons had smuggled in to him a tin dagger made out of a candlestick; and when he heard the verdict pronounced, he stabbed himself in the Roman fashion, but only wounded himself horribly and did not die. The next morning (May 27, 1797) he went to the guillotine. Of his followers thirty were executed and many sentenced to penal servitude or deportation.

Before he died, Babeuf had written to a friend, to whom he had confided his wife and children: "I believe that in some future day men will give thought again to the means of procuring for the human race the happiness which we have proposed for it."

His defense did not reach the world for almost a hundred years. The newspapers reported only part of it, and the full text was never published till 1884. His name remained a bugbear for decades.

2 Origins of Socialism: Saint-Simon's Hierarchy

Babeuf was like a last convulsive effort of the principles of the great French Revolution to work themselves out to their logical ends. The race of equalitarians and collectivists who came to prominence in the first years of the next century, though born at about the same time as Babeuf, belong to a different world.

The Comte de Saint-Simon is their prototype. He came of a younger branch of the family of the famous duke, the chronicler of the court of Louis XIV; and, although he had dropped his title and no longer believed, as his relative had, in the paramount importance of dukes, he was in his peculiar way equally convinced of the importance of the owning classes, and especially of the family of Saint-Simon. At seventeen, he had ordered his valet to wake him up every morning with the exhortation, "Get up, *monsieur le comte!* remember you have great things to do!"; and when he had been in prison during the Terror, he had imagined that his ancestor Charlemagne appeared to him and announced that it had been reserved for the Saint-Simon family alone to produce both a great hero and a great philosopher; he himself was to equal in the intellectual field the achievements of Charlemagne in the military.

Saint-Simon had stood aside from the Revolution. He believed that the old regime was doomed; but although he had gone earlier to America to fight on the side of the Colonies, he regarded the French Revolution, when it came, as a process, he said, mainly destructive, and could not bring himself to take an active part in it. He speculated in confiscated estates and made a certain amount of money; but was cheated out of a good deal of it by a partner. Then, instructed in his mission by Charlemagne, he set out with heroic naïveté systematically to make himself a great thinker.

First he took a house opposite the Polytechnic School and studied physics and mathematics; then he took a house near the Medical School and studied medicine. At one period, he led a life of dissipation, from motives, he said, of moral curiosity. He got married in order to have a salon. Then he divorced his wife and presented himself to Mme. de Staël, declaring that, since she was the most remarkable woman and he the most remarkable man of their time, it was plain that they ought to collaborate in producing a more than remarkable child. But Mme. de Staël only laughed. He traveled to both Germany and England in search of intellectual illumination, but came back disappointed from both.

When we read about Saint-Simon's life, we are likely to think him a little mad, till we observe that the other social idealists of this period were cranks of the same extravagant type. The first years of the nineteenth century were a highly confused epoch when it was still possible to have simple ideas. The rationalistic philosophy of the eighteenth century, upon which the French Revolution had been based, was still the background to most people's thinking (Saint-Simon's education had been supervised by d'Alembert); but this rationalistic philosophy, which had been expected to solve all the problems, had failed to rescue society from either despotism or poverty. Today the authority of the Church, the coherence of the old social system, were lost; and there was no longer any body of thought accepted as more or less authoritative, such as the work of the Encyclopaedists (one of Saint-Simon's projects was an encyclopedia for the nineteenth century). The mechanical inventions of which it had been expected that they would vastly improve the lot of humanity were obviously making many people miserable; but the encroachments of commerce and manufacture had not yet reached the overwhelming point where philanthropy and philosophy themselves were to come to seem out of date and merely the whims of ineffective persons. So that Frenchmen, deprived of the systems of the past and not yet foreseeing the society of the future, were free to propose any system, to hope for any future, they could conceive.

Some tried to return to the Catholic system in a more modified or more romantic form. But it is greatly to the credit of Saint-Simon that, descendant of Charlemagne though he was and admirer of the Middle Ages, he possessed the intellectual courage to take the post-revolutionary world as he found it and to plunge into its conflicting currents for principles which would render it intelligible and which would make possible a new systematization. Dilettante on an enormous scale, made restless by an all-trying curiosity, great noble of the old regime stranded in the new France and sworn to take a noble's responsibility for the whole of the new humanity, he was able to understand and to indicate—in a series of writings beginning in 1802 with the *Letters of an Inhabitant of Geneva*—certain fundamental elements of the present and certain trends toward the society of the future which were invisible to the professional thinkers.

The eighteenth century, said Saint-Simon, had committed a fundamental error: in assuming that human beings, on the one hand, were endowed with complete freedom of will while the processes of the physical world, on the other hand, were regulated by invariable laws, it had cut man off from Nature. For there were laws of society, too; there was a science of social development; and through the study of human history, we ought to be able to master it.

What Saint-Simon concluded from the examination of history was that society had alternate periods of equilibrium and breaking down. The Middle Ages, he thought, had been a period of equilibrium; the Reformation and the Revolution had been a period of breaking down. Now society was ripe for the consolidation of a new period of equilibrium. The whole world should now be organized scientifically; and this was obviously an industrial problem, not, as the eighteenth century had believed, a metaphysical one. The old politics of the Revolution had no relation to social realities; and the military dictatorship of Napoleon had as little relation to society's needs. Napoleon assumed that the objects of society were perpetual war and conquest, whereas its actual objects were production and consumption. The solution of social problems consisted in the adjustment of conflicting interests; and the real business of politics, then, was simply the control of work and of the conditions under which work was performed. The liberals were altogether wrong in their insistence on individual liberty; in society, the parts must be subordinated to the whole.

Get rid of the old liberals, then; get rid of the soldier in politics; and put the world into the hands of the scientists, the industrial captains and the artists. For the new society was to be organized, not, like Babeuf's, on the principle of equality, but according to a hierarchy of merit. Saint-Simon divided mankind into three classes: the *savants,* the propertied, and the unpropertied. The *savants* were to exercise the "spiritual power" and to supply the personnel of the supreme body, which was to be known as the Council of Newton—since it had been revealed to Saint-Simon in a vision that it was Newton and not the Pope whom God had elected to sit beside Him and to transmit to humanity His purposes. This council, according to one of Saint-Simon's prospectuses, was to be made up of three mathematicians, three physicians, three chemists, three physiologists, three *littérateurs,* three painters and three musicians; and it was to occupy itself with devising new inventions and works of art for the general improvement of humanity, and in especial with discovering a new law of gravitation applicable to the behavior of social bodies which would keep people in equilibrium with one another. (So the eighteenth-century communist philosopher Morellet, in a book called *The Code of Nature,* had asserted that the law of self-love was to play the same role in the moral sphere as the law of gravitation in the physical.) The salaries of the Council of Newton were to be paid by general subscription, because it was obviously to everybody's advantage that human destinies should be controlled by men of genius; the subscription would be international, because it would of course be to the advantage of all peoples to prevent international wars.

The actual governing, however, was to be done by those members of the community who possessed enough income to live on and could work for the State without pay. The unpropertied classes were to submit to this, because it was to their own best interests to do so. When they had tried to take things into their own hands at the time of the Revolution, they had made a most terrible mess of it and landed themselves in a famine. The propertied classes were to govern by reason of the fact that they possessed "more lights." But the purpose of all social institutions was to better, intellectually, morally and physically, the lot of "the poorest and most numerous class."

There were to be four great main divisions of government: French, English, German and Italian; and the inhabitants of the rest of the globe, whom Saint-Simon considered definitely inferior, were to be assigned to one or other jurisdiction and to subscribe to the maintenance of its council.

Saint-Simon, with his salon, his dissipations and his travels, had now managed to spend all his money and was able to investigate poverty at first hand. He had especially insisted on the importance of mixing with all classes of society, yet of looking at all classes from outside, of examining them in the spirit of science. And the *grand seigneur sansculotte,* as he was described by a contemporary who had admired him, with his gaiety, his cheerful open countenance and his long Don Quixote nose, who had lived in "cynical freedom" at the Palais-Royal, now became a copyist on Montmartre, working nine hours a day for small pay. A former valet in his service came to his rescue and gave him a place to live. No one except a very few disciples ever seemed to read the books he published; yet he kept on writing more of them, working on them now at night, the only time he had to himself.

And in his last book, *The New Christianity,* he restates his system from a new point of view. The beneficent power of genius alone no longer seems to Saint-Simon sufficient. He agrees with reactionaries like Joseph de Maistre that, in order to bring order out of the anarchy, a dominant religion is needed; but he rejects both the Catholic and the Protestant churches: it is time for a new kind of Christianity. The prime principle of Christ, *Love thy neighbor,* applied to modern society, compels us to recognize that the majority of our neighbors are destitute and wretched. The emphasis has now been shifted from the master mind at the top of the hierarchy to the "unpropertied" man at the bottom; but the hierarchy still stands as it was, as Saint-Simon's whole message is still his own peculiar version of the principle of *noblesse oblige.* The propertied classes must be made to understand that an improvement in the condition of the poor will mean an improvement in their condition, too; the *savants* must be shown that their interests are identical with those of the masses. Why not go straight to the people? he makes the interlocutor ask in his dialogue. Because we must try to prevent them from resorting to violence against their governments; we must try to persuade the other classes first.

And he ends—the last words he ever wrote—with an apostrophe to the Holy Alliance, the combination of Russia, Prussia and Austria which had been established upon the suppression of Napoleon. It was right, says Saint-Simon, to get rid of Napoleon; but what have they themselves but the sword? They have increased taxes, protected the rich; their church and their courts, their very attempts at progress, depend on nothing but force; they keep two million men under arms.

"Princes!" he concludes, "hear the voice of God, which speaks to you through my mouth: Become good Christians again; throw off the belief that the hired armies, the nobility, the heretical clergy, the corrupt judges, constitute your principal supporters; unite in the name of Christianity and learn to accomplish the duties which Christianity imposes on the powerful; remember that Christianity commands them to devote their energies to bettering as rapidly as possible the lot of the very poor!"

Saint-Simon himself was now worse off than ever. His valet-patron had died, and he was unable to get his books even printed. He was obliged to make copies of them himself. He continued to send them out in this form to the learned and distinguished persons whom he still hoped to interest in his views; but they ignored him as blankly as ever. "For fifteen days," he writes at this period, "I have been eating bread and drinking water. I work with no fire and I have even sold my clothes to make it possible to get my work copied. I have fallen into this distress through my passion for science and the public good, through my desire to find a way of bringing to an end without violence the terrible crisis in which today the whole of European society is involved. And I can therefore confess my misery without blushing, and ask for the necessary assistance to enable me to continue my work." He finally succeeded in getting his family to send him a small pension.

He tried to shoot himself in 1823, but survived and went on writing till 1825, an eventuality which caused him surprise: "Can you explain to me how a man with seven balls of buckshot in his head can go on living and thinking?" When he was dying in 1825, he declined to receive one of his relations for fear of breaking his train of thought.

"All my life," he is reported to have said by one of his disciples who was present at his deathbed, "all my life may be summed up in one idea: to guarantee to all men the free development of their faculties. Forty-eight hours after our second publication, the party of the workers will be organized: the future belongs to us!" . . . "He put his hand to his head and died."

3 Origins of Socialism: The Communities of Fourier
and Owen

The parties of the workers predicted by Saint-Simon were
actually to be organized very soon—though they were not to
proceed straight, as he had imagined, to the realization of the
new Christian society. But in the meantime, there appeared
other prophets, who were to try to create by themselves small
seminal new worlds inside the old.

Charles Fourier and Robert Owen, ten years younger than
Saint-Simon and Babeuf, are closely similar figures who follow
almost parallel careers, as they represent tendencies which
were specially characteristic of the first part of the nineteenth
century. Fourier was a draper's son from Besançon, who had
gone on the road as a traveling salesman; Owen was a Welsh
saddle-maker's son, who had worked as a draper's clerk. Both
had lost faith, as Saint-Simon had done, in the liberal politics
of the period and both stood outside its conventional culture.
Fourier was never tired of denouncing the tradition of European philosophy, in the light of whose guidance humanity
had "bathed itself in blood for twenty-three scientific centuries," and he believed that it was the purpose of God to
discredit the professional philosophers, to confute all "those
libraries of politics and morals," by selecting him, Charles
Fourier, "a shop clerk, almost an illiterate," as the expositor of
His secrets to mankind. The mistake of the statesmen for a
thousand years had been, according to Fourier, to occupy
themselves only with abuses of a religious and administrative
character. "The divine code should legislate first of all on

industry, the primordial function"; but it had been only very recently that the governments had begun to do this and then they had taken the wrong direction in favoring "industrial division and commercial fraud, dressed up as 'free competition.' " It is possible that Robert Owen had been influenced by William Godwin, the author of the *Enquiry Concerning Political Justice* (1793); but he seems never to have mentioned this or any other book of the kind and was never seen to read anything but statistics. His attempts to work through political machinery were unsuccessful and brief: he asserted that it was impossible to "expect anything resembling a rational 'something,' to relieve the widely extending distress of society" from "Radicals, Whigs or Tories—or from any particular religious sect."

Robert Owen has the look in his portraits of a great smooth meditative hare, with an assertive, independent English nose, but an elliptically oval face and deep innocent elliptical eyes that seem to stretch right around his cheeks; and Fourier's face, over its high white cravat, has something of the same odd simplification—though with the dignity of the strong old French rationalism, with its straight mouth and thin Roman nose and its lucid and religious eyes, a little too wide apart.

Both Owen and Fourier were persons of remarkable unworldliness and directness; both were capable of relentless persistency. Both combined in a peculiar fashion the deepest humanitarian sympathies with a passion for systematic exactitude. Both had had experience at first hand of the worst aspects of that industrial-commercial system which was coming at an accelerating pace to dominate Western society. Fourier had lost his patrimony and narrowly escaped the gullotine, at the time of the siege of Lyons by the revolutionary troops of the Convention; he had seen the population of Lyons reduced to the utmost degradation by the growth of the textile industry; and he had once watched a cargo of rice being thrown into the water at Marseilles after it had been purposely allowed to rot by his employers, who had succeeded in cornering the market and wanted to keep up the price during a famine. Fourier's abhorrence of cruelty, his almost insane capacity for pity, which had compelled him as a schoolboy to take frightful beatings in defense of his smaller companions and which at sixty sent him walking for hours in the rain in an effort to do something for a poor servant girl whom he had never even seen but of whom he had heard that her mistress ill-treated her—this stern overmastering impulse to render human life less painful inspired him with an optimistic certainty, and drove him to unrewarded labors, themselves almost insane. Not merely did he work out in his strange life of solitude all the complicated interrelations of the groups which were to compose his ideal communities and the precise proportions of the buildings that were to house them; but he believed himself able to calculate that the world would last precisely 80,000 years and that by the end of that time every soul would have traveled 810 times between the earth and certain other planets which he regarded as certainly inhabited; and would have experienced a succession of existences to the precise number of 1626.

Robert Owen, like Fourier, was peculiarly sensitive to suffering: he was to look back all his life on a dancing school to which he had been sent as a child and where he had seen the disappointment of little girls who had not been able to get partners, as a veritable place of torment. He had left home on his own at the age of ten and had made his way up so rapidly that at twenty he had found himself in sole charge of a cotton factory in Manchester, with five hundred workers under him. One of the earliest exploiters of the new cotton-spinning devices, he was soon struck by the terrible discrepancy between "the great attention given to the dead machinery, and the neglect and disregard of the living machinery"; and became aware that "bad and unwise as American slavery is and must continue to be, the white slavery in the manufactories of England was at this unrestricted period far worse than the house slaves whom I afterwards saw in the West Indies and in the United States, and in many respects, especially as regards health, food and clothing, the latter were much better provided for than were those oppressed and degraded children and work-people in the home manufactories of Great Britain"—let alone the tenants and servants on the great English country estates, as he had known them at the end of the eighteenth century. Nor was it the work-people merely who suffered: their employers themselves were debased. "I was completely tired of partners who were merely trained to buy cheap and sell dear. This occupation deteriorates and often destroys the finest and best faculties of our nature. From an experience of a long life, in which I passed through all the gradations of trade, manufactures and commerce, I am thoroughly convinced that there can be no superior character formed under this thoroughly selfish system. Truth, honesty, virtue, will be mere names, as they are now, and as they have ever been. Under this system, there can be no true civilization; for by it all are trained civilly to oppose and often to destroy one another by their created opposition of interests. It is a low, vulgar, ignorant and inferior mode of conducting the affairs of society; and no permanent, general and substantial improvement can arise until it shall be superseded by a superior mode of forming character and creating wealth."

But though Fourier believed that he had repudiated the philosophy of the Revolution and Owen claimed to have reached his conclusions from observation alone, both based their proposals on a doctrine of Rousseau which so permeated the air of the time that one did not need to imbibe it by reading: the doctrine that mankind is naturally good and that it is only institutions which have perverted it. Fourier asserted that human nature could be unpacked like the contents of a tool-chest into a limited number of human "passions"—that is, of instincts and interests—which had been given us by God for different ends. All were necessary, and the trouble with modern society was simply that these "passions" were misused. If only the proper passions could be directed to the proper uses, the reign of "Harmony" would prevail. And the whole career of Robert Owen was one long reiteration of the principle that men had been made what they were by education and early influences over which they had no control and that if only the right things instead of the wrong could be taught them during their formative years, they could be rendered, as he put it, with "mathematical precision"—universally happy and good.

In order to demonstrate that the interest of each was compatible with the interest of all, both Fourier and Owen proposed that limited self-contained societies should be organized inside the larger society.

The communities demanded by Fourier were to be dependent on private capital, and they were not to aim at complete equality. There was to be universal suffrage, and the children of the rich and the poor were to be given the same education; and Fourier saw the undesirability of including in the same community people of too widely differing incomes. Yet there were to be differences of income and a hierarchy—though a hierarchy of an unconventional kind: the capitalists were not to stand at the top. In the distribution of income by dividend (after a minimum subsistence had been guaranteed), capital was to get only four-twelfths while five-twelfths was to go to labor and three-twelfths to talent. Disagreeable work was to be paid for at a higher rate than work not unpleasant; and necessary work was to rank higher than work that was merely useful, as useful work was to take precedence over work that produced merely luxuries.

It was to Fourier simply a question of organizing the people in relation to the work in such a way that all the human "passions" should be made to serve beneficent ends. There was something that everybody liked to do, so there was no reason why everything should not get done. There was a good use for every human impulse, so there was no reason why they should not all be satisfied. And there was therefore no reason why anybody's work should not be attractive to him. It was not even necessary that people should bore or fatigue themselves by working continually at one task: everyone had his own set of tastes, his own combination of passions, but it would be possible for him to gratify them all by engaging in various activities. Industrial efficiency was to be stimulated by the rivalry of different groups. Fourier had worked out a scheme which, besides making everyone happy, was to result in increased producion. Two problems which had troubled him— why boys love dirt and how the refuse of the community was to be got rid of—were found to solve one another reciprocally: the boys were to dispose of the refuse.

Robert Owen's communities, on the other hand, were to realize absolute equality. Their only hierarchy was based on age: the mature who should not yet have become aged were to constitute the governing council. The children were to be taken from their parents at three and brought up by special educators and nurses. The unit of the medium of exchange was to be an hour's worth of labor.

Fourier had announced to the public that he would be at home at noon every day, ready to discuss his projects with any rich persons who might be interested in financing them. But though he was there every day on the dot for ten years, no patron ever appeared. Fourier died in 1837, still firm in his faith, but deeply disappointed.

Owen did, however, succeed in creating his ideal community. He asserted that Fourier, who had at one time looked to him for help, had learned from him his basic idea of practising communism in limited groups; and, in any case, it is Robert Owen who is the principal figure here—and one of the most amazing figures of his time.

Robert Owen's actual exploits sound today as fantastic as the romances of his period: the *Caleb Williamses* and the *Frankensteins.* A social idealist as disinterested as Fourier, he had a career which recalls that of Henry Ford. When Owen first took possession of the cotton mills at New Lanark, Scotland, they were operated by a crew of dirty and drunken and extremely unreliable men and women—at that time it implied a lack of self-respect to work in a mill at all—and by children between five and ten shipped in from the orphan asylums. Out of the material of this wretched population, to which he had come with the special disadvantage of being a Welshman among the Scotch, he was able to create in a quarter of a century a community with a high standard of living and a considerable degree of education, and a community by whom Owen himself was adored. He paid them higher wages and had them work shorter hours than any of his competitors did, and he carried them through periods of slump. He limited to a fixed amount the returns to be paid to his partners and he put the rest back into the community in improvements. Was it not obvious, he kept asking the world, that this was how the whole of society should be run? If only all the children were educated as he educated his workers' children, taking them from their parents early and training them without punishment or harshness, should we not have a new human race?

It did not occur to Owen at first to ask where the human materials were to be found or where the conditions for molding them were to be possible. He did not see that human beings were so universally imperfect that the prime questions were where to begin and who was to be trusted to do the beginning. He himself had begun at New Lanark on the most unpromising human beings conceivable. And it had never occurred to him that he himself was a man of exceptionally high character and that it was he and not the natural goodness of the children of those ill-conditioned parents who had made New Lanark a model community. He did not understand that New Lanark was a machine which he himself had built and which he had to control and keep going.

For Robert Owen in his factory played the role of a benevolent but omnipotent God. When he discovered that his urgings were not enough to make his employees industrious and honest, he worked out ways to check up on them and restrain them. He had hung up over his workers at their work little four-sided pieces of wood, which had a different color on each side and a different grade of conduct assigned to each color. He could then see on any day when he walked through, from the color turned out by the foreman, how each employee had behaved the day before. Whenever he encountered one of the colors which signified "bad or inferior conduct," he would simply fix his eyes on the delinquent worker as he passed. Under this system, he was gratified to observe that the colors changed gradually from black to blue, from blue to yellow, and finally to white. These gradings were all entered in a register so that he could always find out after an absence how the workers had been behaving while he was away. And he devised an infallible method for detecting and locating thefts. Yet Owen, who had never realized that he had created this moral universe himself, was always surprised that his schoolmasters went elsewhere and could not get the same results as at New Lanark, and that his communities failed to prosper when left to the direction of others. (William Lovett, one of the leaders of the Chartists, who worked with him afterwards in the coöperative movement, says that Owen was essentially despotic and quite impossible to collaborate with on any democratic basis.)

Gradually, however, as Owen discovered that his partners were sure to rebel against his methods, that he was always being obliged to look for new partners, and that it was becoming harder and harder to find them, he was forced to face the fact that the capitalists were a greedy and unenlightened lot. And his faith was further shaken when a bill against child labor (the first to be introduced in England), which he had tried to lobby through Parliament, was not only fiercely opposed by the cotton-spinners but ultimately emasculated at their insistence by politicians like Peel whom he had trusted. Looking for light to the political economists in London, he was amazed to find them men of no practical experience, who were engaged, as he contended, simply in constructing systems to rationalize the bad practices of the manufacturers. When he was invited to attend a conference on the desperate economic conditions which had followed the Napoleonic wars, a conference composed of people who had formerly impressed him by reputation, prominent economists, philanthropists, statesmen and business men, and presided over by the Archbishop of Canterbury, he discovered that he, an uneducated man, was the only person present who understood that the current unemployment had been caused by the release of men from the services and by the sudden collapse of the market which had been created by the needs of the war; and that he was able to astound the assembly by explaining to them that millions of people had been thrown out of work by machinery. When in his youth he had been manager of the cotton factory, the owner, who lived quite near, had never come to visit it but once—in order to show it to a visitor from abroad; but Robert Owen had never drawn the moral. Now he began to be afraid that it would take longer than he had thought to make people understand the truth.

Yet, at that time, they gave him their attention, the prime

ministers, the archbishops, the princes: they had begun to be gravely alarmed by the unrest of the lower orders, and here was a man who had given proof that he knew how to keep the lower orders happy. Owen was still able to believe in their disinterestedness: it had never occurred to him that for persons like them, in positions of high responsibility, it would be possible to desire anything other than the general amelioration of humanity. Then a critical incident occurred which caused him to change his mind.

He attended in 1817 a Congress of Sovereigns at Aix-la-Chapelle, and he met there a veteran diplomat, the secretary of the Congress. Owen explained to this personage that it was now possible, through the extraordinary progress of science—if only mankind could be persuaded to coöperate in its own best interests—for the whole of the human race, and no longer merely the privileged few, to be well-educated, well-nourished and well-bred. He had been telling all sorts of people this; but now he was to be startled by the secretary's reply. Yes, the veteran diplomat said, they all knew that very well—the governing powers of Europe which he himself represented—and that was just what they didn't want. If the masses became well-off and independent, how were the governing classes to control them? "After this confession by the secretary, the discussion lost much of its interest in my mind, for I had discovered that I had a long and arduous task before me, to convince governments and governed of the gross ignorance under which they were contending against each other, in direct opposition to the real interests and true happiness of both. I now foresaw that the prejudices which I had to overcome in all classes in all countries were of the most formidable character, and that, in addition to illimitable patience and perseverance, it would require the wisdom said to be possessed by the serpent, with the harmlessness of the dove, and the courage of the lion." However, he had "passed the Rubicon, and was strongly impressed to proceed onward in a straight course."

But the authorities had already begun to realize that in Owen they had to do with a subversive idealist force. He had declared on a public platform that the chief enemy of truth was religion; and he had attacked not merely religion, but property and the family as well (thus going much farther than Fourier, who had attempted, in his projected community, to keep modified forms of all three). Now the churches began to oppose him, and his friends became afraid to be seen with him.

He decided that Europe was diseased, that he must resort to a fresh part of the world, if he was to get the new society started. He came to the United States and took over from a German religious sect, the Rappites, the town of New Harmony, Indiana, with thirty thousand acres. He promulgated on July 4, 1826, a *Declaration of Mental Independence* from the three great oppressors of humanity: "Private Property, Irrational Religion and Marriage," and he invited to join his community "the industrious and well disposed of all nations." Then he went back to Europe and left it. But the Americans were no better than the English—indeed, at New Harmony they proved worse. The Westerners were not so docile as the Scotch proletariat of New Lanark; and the unrestricted invitation had brought all sorts of drifters and rascals. Owen had taken into partnership an unscrupulous character named Taylor, whom, when he returned, he thought it desirable to get rid of. Taylor made Owen buy him out with a tract of land, on which he (Taylor) said he wanted to found a community of his own. The night before the deal was settled, Taylor smuggled a lot of farm implements and cattle onto the property, so that they were included in the transfer the next day. Then he flouted Owen's preachments of temperance by setting up a whisky distillery on the place; and opened a tan-yard which competed with Owen's. New Harmony hardly lasted three years. Owen finally sold the property to individuals.

He made other such attempts in England and Ireland and sank a good deal of money in these communities. He seems to have had singularly little head for money. In the early days in New Lanark, when the cotton trade had been booming, when he had had only his original community and had been able to supervise it himself, this weakness had not been apparent; but now he would squander great sums on equipment and plant for other people, with no notion as to how they were to be maintained.

He was finally reduced to such straits that his sons were obliged to support him.

And now, no longer a rich manufacturer, and out of favor with the governing classes, he began to play an entirely new role. The Reform Act of 1832 had won the vote for the middle class only, and left the working class disillusioned and rebellious. Owen, disillusioned, too, allied himself with the working class. He was not even any longer an employer; he had given up even New Lanark. And he now allowed himself to be associated with an Owenite Coöperative Movement, and with the Grand National Consolidated Trades Union.

But he was still too impatient of political methods, too convinced, in spite of all his experience, of the obviousness and necessity of his system, to be able to serve with much effect in the long grinding battle of labor. The trade-union movement went to pieces within a year after he had organized it. He had very little interest in or sympathy with the Chartist Movement and the Corn Law Agitation: it was still impossible for him not to believe that it would be much easier to establish equality at a stroke and once and for all. And, finding mankind still so backward, he had recourse to superterrestrial forces. He came in his last days to believe that all the magnanimous souls he had known, Shelley, Thomas Jefferson, Channing, the Duke of Kent (though he forgot that the latter had failed to pay back the considerable sums of money he had borrowed from him)—all those who when living had listened to him with sympathy, of whom he had felt that they had really shared his vision, and who were lost to him now through death—he came to believe that they were returning from the other world, to make appointments with him and keep them, to talk to him and reassure him.

He needed them to confirm those intuitions which had come to him many years before and of which the time was not giving proof—intimations that "some change of high import, scarcely yet perhaps to be scanned by the present ill-taught race of men," was "evidently in progress"; that "fortunately for mankind, the system of individual opposing interests" had "now reached the extreme point of error and inconsistency," since "in the midst of the most ample means to create wealth, all are in poverty, or in imminent danger from the effects of poverty upon others"; that the "principle of union" was very soon to take the place of the "principle of disunion," and that then all men should understand that "the happiness of self" could "only be attained by conduct that must promote the happiness of the community."

Robert Owen, his money made and spent, went back in 1858 to die in a house next to his father's saddle-shop in the little town in Wales where he had been born, and from which he had set out at ten on that fabulous rise in the world which had landed him on the ground floor of the cotton trade.

4 Origins of Socialism: Enfantin and the American Socialists

The peculiar combination of qualities that we find in Saint-Simon, Fourier and Owen is something characteristic of the time. Their counterpart in literature proper is Owen's friend, Shelley. All were distinguished by lives of a pure and philosophical eccentricity; by a rarefied rhetoric which today seems inspired; and by fundamental social insights which were to remain of the highest value.

We have seen in such later French historians as Michelet, Renan and Taine, how this rhetoric was to grow more gaudy and to solidify in hypostasized abstractions. The industrial-commercial system whose tendencies had seemed to the earlier prophets so obviously inhuman and unpractical that it would be quite easy to check and divert them, was coming to take up the whole space, and absorbing and demoralizing critics. The future was no longer a free expanse which men like Fourier and Owen could assume as a field for innovation. The bourgeoisie were there to stay, and the typical social critic was the much-respected professor to whom the insights of Saint-Simon, Fourier and Owen were as alien as their fantastic behavior. If he was a brilliant professor, he was able to edify his audience by flourishing capitalized ideals such as Taine's Conscience and Honor. Insisting more and more on individual liberty, these thinkers became less and less bold. It is curious to compare, for example, the personal recklessness of Saint-Simon, who believed that the rights of the individual should be limited in the interests of the community, with the personal timidity of Taine, who insisted that individual Conscience and

the private operation of industry should be free from interference by the State.

The failure of the doctrines of Saint-Simon in the hands of
his disciples after his death is interesting in this connection.
Saint-Simon had, as I have said, come to believe that the
new society could never be brought into being without the
help of a new religion; and he had asserted that he spoke "in
the name of God." One of his disciples, Olinde Rodriques, a
young Jew who had been present at Saint-Simon's deathbed
and who had received his last words on religion, assumed the
role of consecrated apostle, and there grew up a Saint-Simonist
cult.

It was not, however, Rodriques, but a French engineer,
Prosper Enfantin, who eventually became the leader of this
cult. The Saint-Simonists in 1825, the year of Saint-Simon's
death, began by publishing a paper which aimed to recruit
the working class to a program of collectivism, internationalism
and the abolition of private property and tariffs; the idea of
the enslavement and exploitation of the working class by the
owning class appears already fully developed in their writings.
But gradually Enfantin became persuaded to consider himself
a Messiah, and he and another of the disciples became the
"Fathers" of the Saint-Simonist "Family." One morning at half
past six, before Enfantin was out of bed, he was visited by a
man named d'Eichthal, a member of the brotherhood and also
a Jew. D'Eichthal was in a state of extreme exaltation; he had
been to communion at Notre Dame the night before, and there
it had been suddenly revealed to him that "Jesus lives in
Enfantin," and that Enfantin was one of a holy couple, the
Son and Daughter of God, who were to convey a new gospel
to humanity. Enfantin at first was cautious: until the appearance of the female Messiah, he told d'Eichthal, he could not
name himself nor could he be named, and in the meantime he
begged his apostle to let him go back to sleep. D'Eichthal
accordingly left him, but almost immediately returned, got
Enfantin up again, and insisted that the hour had struck, that
Enfantin must proclaim himself the Son of God. Enfantin now

arose, put on his stockings in silence and announced, *"Homo sum!"*

Thereafter Enfantin was known as "Christ" and "Pope." The Saint-Simonists adopted special costumes and elaborated religious rites. Enfantin grew a beard in evident imitation of Jesus and displayed the title *"Le Père"* embroidered on his shirt across his chest.

In Paris the Saint-Simonists were persecuted by the authorities, who closed their meeting hall. Enfantin took forty disciples and retreated to Ménilmontant, just outside the city, where he established a sort of monastery. They wore red, white and violet costumes and did all their own work. "When the proletariat presses our hands," they said, "they will feel that they are calloused like their own. We are inoculating ourselves with the proletarian nature."

But charges were now brought against them—it was the reign of Louis-Philippe—of preaching doctrines dangerous to public morality. Le Père Enfantin was made to serve a short sentence in jail, which broke his morale as a Messiah. He did not have the true fanatic's capacity, the capacity of Mrs. Eddy or Joseph Smith, for deceiving himself and others: he had kept waiting for the female Messiah, who should finally make the world believe in him and who should make him believe in himself. And now he returned to his trade, to the practical field of engineering. Saint-Simon had been strongly convinced of the future importance of engineering and had included the engineers among the groups who were to be entrusted with the supreme control of society. At the time of his visit to America, he had made an effort to interest the Mexican viceroy in the project of cutting a canal at Panama. And now Enfantin, during a trip to Egypt, did his best to promote what appeared to him the equally sound idea of cutting a canal at Suez—a service for which, when the canal was undertaken, he got scant recognition from de Lesseps. Finally he became a director of the Paris and Lyons railroad and played the leading role in its consolidation, in 1852, as the Paris-Lyon-Méditerranée.

In Prosper Enfantin, therefore, the gospel of Saint-Simon had produced one of the most bizarre, one of the most apparently incoherent, careers in history. Beginning as the Son of God, he had ended as a fairly able railroad director. Yet Enfantin's religion and his railroads were both justified by the teaching of Saint-Simon: for the new rapid transportation was a means of bringing people together, and a merger was a step toward unification. But the difficulty for Enfantin was that, on the one hand, he was much too hard-headed, too rational, too French, to dissociate himself from society and to identify himself with God, as the saint does; and that, on the other hand, as things were going, there seemed to be no way for the practical engineer, the manipulator of railroad combinations, to connect his activities with the religion of humanity.

None of these political idealists understood the real mechanics of social change nor could they foresee the inevitable development of the system which they so much detested. They could only devise imaginary systems as antithetical to the real one as possible and attempt to construct models of these, assuming that the example would be contagious. This was what the word *socialism* meant when it first began to be current in France and England about 1835.

But it was the United States, with its new social optimism and its enormous unoccupied spaces, which was to become the great nursery for these experiments. The split between the working and the owning classes, with the resultant organization of labor, was already quite marked in the American republic by 1825; the immigrants from feudalism and famine in Europe were finding in the crowded American cities new misery and new hard masters. And the socialist movement both relieved the congestion and revived the disillusioned political thinkers.

We have seen that Robert Owen came to America in 1824 and started an Owenite movement: there were at least a dozen Owenite communities; and Albert Brisbane, who had brought Fourierism back from Paris and had been given a rostrum by Horace Greeley in *The New York Tribune*, propagandized for it in the 1840's with such success that more than forty groups went out to build Fourierist phalansteries (which included Brook Farm in its second phase). This movement, which arose at the same time as the great tide of religious revivalism and which was entangled at various points with Transcendentalism, Swedenborgianism, Perfectionism and Spiritualism, persisted through the early fifties until the agitation for free farms in the West, culminating in the Homestead Act of 1863, diverted the attention of the dissatisfied from labor organization and socialism. It is hard to arrive at any precise estimate of the number of these communities, but there are records of at least a hundred and seventy-eight, including the religious communities practising communism, ranging in membership from fifteen to nine hundred; and Morris Hillquit, in his *History of American Socialism*, seems to believe there were many more, involving altogether "hundreds of thousands of members." The Owenite and Fourierist communities alone are supposed to have occupied some fifty thousand acres. There were communities entirely Yankee and communities, like the French Icarians and the German religious groups, made up entirely of immigrants. There were sectarian communities, communities merely Christian and communities full of Deists and unbelievers. There were communities that practised complete chastity and communities that practised "free love"; communities that went in for vegetarianism. Some aimed at pure communism of property and profit, and some—notably the Fourierist phalanxes—were organized as joint stock companies. Some, entirely discarding money, lived by barter with the outside world; some by building up industries and driving a good bargain. One follower of Owen, a Scotch woman, Frances Wright, founded a community on the Wolf River in Tennessee, which was intended to solve the Negro problem: it was partly made up of slaves whom she had begged or bought from their masters and whom the white members were to educate and set free.

One odd and very American development was actually an anti-communist community. A man named Josiah Warren, who had taken part in the Owenite community at New Harmony and who had come to the conclusion that its failure had been due to the idea of "combination" itself, evolved a doctrine of Individual Sovereignty and a program for Equitable Commerce. He first wandered about Ohio and Indiana, open-

ing up a succession of "Time Stores," in which the customer
paid in cash the wholesale cost of his purchase, plus a small
percentage for the upkeep of the store, but paid with a "Labor
note" for the amount of time consumed by Mr. Warren in the
transaction. He handed this idea on to Robert Owen, who tried
a large-scale labor exchange in London. Later on, Warren
founded on Long Island the village of Modern Times, which
was to give scope to Individual Sovereignty in property, occupation and taste. There were to be, as Warren announced,
"no organization, no delegated power, no constitutions, no
laws or by-laws," no "rules or regulations but such as each
individual makes for himself and his own business; no officers,
no prophets nor priests." If they had meetings, it was not for
the purpose of agreeing on common plans, but merely "for
friendly conversation," for music, for dancing or for "some
other pleasant pastime." "Not even a single lecture upon the
principles upon which we were acting" had ever "been given
on the premises. It was not necessary; for, as a lady remarked,
'the subject once stated and understood, there is nothing left
to talk about: all is action after that.'" The village of Modern
Times in turn proliferated Henry Edger, who became one of
the ten apostles appointed by Auguste Comte, a disciple of
Saint-Simon, to preach the scientific religion which he called
Positivism and who later attempted a Comtist community; a
man named Stephen Pearl Andrews, who developed a system
of "Universology" and an intellectual and spiritual hierarchy
called the "Pantarchy"; and a Dr. Thomas L. Nichols, who
published an "Esoteric Anthropology," inaugurated the Free
Love movement by bringing out a list of the names of persons,
scattered all over the United States, who were looking for and
wished to become "affinities," and ended up as a Roman
Catholic.

"Seating myself in the venerable orchard," said a visitor to
the Trumbull Phalanx in Trumbull County, Ohio, in the August
of 1844, "with the temporary dwellings on the opposite side,
the joiners at their benches in their open shops under the
green boughs, and hearing on every side the sound of industry,
the roll of wheels in the mills, and many voices, I could not
help exclaiming mentally: Indeed my eyes see men making

haste to free the slave of all names, nations and tongues, and my ears hear them driving, thick and fast, nails into the coffin of despotism. I can but look on the establishment of this Phalanx as a step of as much importance as any which secured our political independence; and much greater than that which gained the Magna Charta, the foundation of English liberty."

With their saw mills and grist mills and flour mills and their expanses of untried acres, with their communal dormitories and dining halls, they achieved some genuinely stimulating, harmonious and productive years, but more quarreling and impoverished failures. A very few of these communities lasted longer than a decade, but a great many never completed two years. They had against them sources of dissension within and pressure of public opinion from without, incapacity of lower-class groups to live up to socialist ideals and incapacity of upper-class groups to adapt themselves to manual labor. And all kinds of calamities befell them: fires and typhoid epidemics. A creek would overflow on swampy ground and they would all come down with fever and ague. They would be baffled by land which they had had the bad judgment to buy while it was under snow. They would start off with inadequate equipment or insufficient supplies and never be able to make them go round; or with debts that would get heavier and heavier and finally drag them down. They would get into legal difficulties about their land titles; they would be unbusinesslike and make messes of their accounts. They would be disrupted by the bigotries of the religious and by jealousies among the women. They would suffer, as was said by a member of the Marlboro Association in Ohio, from "lack of faith in those who had the funds and lack of funds in those who had the faith"; and from "accepting the needy, the disabled and the sick." They would end up in acrimonious lawsuits brought by members against the association; or in the event of their actually having been able to increase the value of their property, there would be members unable to resist the temptation to speculate and sell the community out.

The story of the Icarians is a longer one. Etienne Cabet was a cooper's son, to whom the French Revolution had opened the career of a lawyer and political figure. His loyalty to the revolutionary principles made him conspicuous and extremely uncomfortable to the Bourbon Restoration and to Louis-Philippe alike; and as he found himself consigned to remote posts, persecuted for his opposition in the Chamber and finally given his choice between imprisonment and exile, he was driven farther and farther toward the extreme Left, which was still represented by the old Buonarotti, the great-nephew of Michael Angelo who had been a companion-in-arms of Babeuf. During his exile in England, Cabet composed a novel called *Voyage en Icarie,* which described a utopia on a communist island, where the inhabitants enjoyed a progressive income tax, abolition of the right of inheritance, state regulation of wages, national workshops, public education, the eugenic control of marriage and a single newspaper controlled by the government.

The effect of this romance on the French working class during the reign of Louis-Philippe was so immense that by 1847 Cabet had acquired a following variously estimated at from two to four hundred thousand. These disciples were eager to put Icarianism into practice; and Cabet published a manifesto: *"Allons en Icarie!"* Icaria was to be in America: Cabet had become convinced that Europe was now past mending even by a general revolution. He had consulted Robert Owen, who had recommended the state of Texas, then just admitted to the Union and in need of population; and Cabet signed a contract with an American company for, as he supposed, a million acres. When the first band of sixty-nine Icarians signed on the pier at Havre, just before sailing, "social contracts," which pledged them to communism, Cabet announced that "in view of men like those in the advance guard," he could not "doubt the regeneration of the human race." But when the Icarians got to New Orleans, in March, 1848, they discovered that they had been swindled by the Americans: that their domain, instead of touching the Red River, was located two hundred and fifty miles inland in the midst of an untraveled wilderness, and that they were able to claim only ten thousand acres, and those scattered instead of all in one piece. They got there, however, by ox-teams. Everybody came down with malaria, and the doctor went insane.

Cabet and other immigrants later joined them, and, after terrible sufferings and labors, they established themselves successfully at Nauvoo, Illinois, which had recently been abandoned by the Mormons (themselves in their Utah phase, up to the death of Brigham Young, an example of a successful coöperative community).

But though the Icarians did not dissolve until almost the end of the century, their moments of prosperity were modest and few. With all their efforts they seemed never to get ahead; they were dependent on money sent them from France, and after the 1848 Revolution, with its promise of national workshops, the enthusiasm for Icarianism declined—so that they were always dragging heavy debts. They cultivated the land in a small way, tried to produce everything they needed. It seems to have taken them decades to learn English. They were always holding political meetings at which they would deliver interminable French speeches. And they were repeatedly torn and split by dissensions. What was primarily at issue in these dissensions was the conflict between the instincts of the American pioneer and the principles of the French doctrinaire. Cabet, with his typically eighteenth-century mind, had worked out what he considered a perfect system which would be sure to recommend itself to people because it would be sure to make them happy. The utopia contemplated in his novel had had a president and a parliamentary system that derived from the French Revolutionary Convention and the American Constitution; but, once established in the actual community, he felt compelled to impose himself as a dictator. And he seems to have had none of the real spiritual superiority of a Robert Owen or a Noyes. He was the most bourgeois of the communist leaders. He had no real imagination for the possibilities of either agriculture or industry; and, always trimming the community down to the most cautious scale of small French economy, he forbade them tobacco and whisky, supervised their private affairs, and sapped the morale of the members by setting them to spy on one another. He finally became such a tyrant that they sang the *Marseillaise* outside his windows, and defied him in open meeting: "Have we traveled three thousand miles not to be free?" In 1856, a majority overruled him and drove him out, and the old man died immediately afterwards in St. Louis.

A second Icarian revolution cut the other way. The younger members, excited by the Workers' International and the Paris Commune of 1871, rebelled against the older elements, who had subsided into practical American farmers. They demanded equal political rights for women and the communization of the little private gardens which had become one of the principal pleasures of the old people's meager lives. Another secession took place, which ended in California and petered out. The old Icarians—there were only a handful left—liquidated themselves in 1895. They were just like everybody else now, they said.

But by far the most successful of these experiments was the Oneida Community in New York State, which lasted for thirty-two years, from 1847 to 1879, on its original collectivist basis; and its leader, John Humphrey Noyes, was by far the most remarkable figure produced by the movement in America.

He came from Brattleboro, Vermont (he was born in 1811), from a family of some political distinction, and studied for the ministry at Yale, but began early to profess a heresy known as Perfectionism. According to the doctrine of the Perfectionists, it was not necessary to die to be saved: one could rid oneself of sin in this world. But a visit to New York City, where he had never before been, threw the young Noyes into a state of panic: he felt that the temptations of the flesh were dragging him down to the threshold of Hell, and, unable to sleep at night, he would walk the streets and go into the brothels and preach present salvation to the inmates. Unlike the other socialists of his epoch (Joseph Smith is his religious counterpart), he was profoundly concerned with sex, and in the community which he afterwards founded developed a technique of love-making which, in eliminating the danger of children, put love on a new communal basis. In some cases irregular children came also to be permitted. Beginning with the members of his own family, Noyes exerted so powerful an influence over his followers and exercised so strict a discipline over himself that he was able to control these difficult situations and actually succeeded to his own satisfaction and to that of those respectable Vermonters in dissociating the idea of sexual enjoyment from the idea of Hell and sin, and so accommodating it among the elements of the state of salvation on earth.

Noyes, who was a man of real intellectual ability, carefully studied the other communities with the purpose of profiting by their experience, and wrote a valuable book about them, *A History of American Socialisms*. He came to the conclusion that their failures and their various degrees of success were traceable to definite factors. He perfectly saw the absurdity of a system like that of Fourier, which adopted certain abstract principles and then deduced from them an ideal community which could be put together in a vacuum and which would then begin to work automatically. In the first place, it was important to start out with members who knew and trusted one another. Then it was important not to go too far away from the big centers and not to depend too much on land, which was much harder to get an income out of than industry. Then it was very important for the master mind to live in and lead the community himself: it was Noyes's opinion that "a prohibitory duty" should be put on "the importation of socialistic theories, that have not been worked out, as well as written out, by the inventors themselves. It is certainly cruel to set vast numbers of simple people agog with utopian projects that will cost them their all, while the inventors and promulgators do nothing but write and talk." But, most fundamental of all, neither socialism nor religion by itself was enough to make a successful community: you had to have both together; and you had to have an inspiration—what Noyes called an "afflatus"—strong enough to decompose the old family unit and to reassemble the members in the new organism, the new home, of the community. He believed that the most important practical example had been set by the religious communities of the Shakers, who had first settled at Watervliet, New York, in 1776, who had lasted and prospered through the whole nineteenth century, while, as Horace

Greeley pointed out, "hundreds of banks and factories, and thousands of mercantile concerns, managed by shrewd, strong men, have gone into bankruptcy and perished," and who, as I learn from a newspaper as I write, can still muster, out of their maximum of nearly five thousand, six old men and one old woman. Noyes considered that the validity of the Shaker movement had been due to the fact that, like Mormonism and Christianity, it had been able to produce a second great leader to rescue it from the period of confusion after the death of its first leader, Mother Ann.

And he endeavored to realize these conditions in the case of the Oneida Community by taking full responsibility for everything himself, by developing a highly profitable steel-trap factory and other successful industries (one of which, Community Plate, still survives), and by keeping up the afflatus of the religious end. He was actually able in a late phase of the community (between 1869 and 1879) to put into practice a breeding system which he called "stirpiculture" and which involved the picking of mates and the prohibition of unions by a board of supervisors, in the interests of the production of better children; and Noyes himself, though already in his sixties, became the father of nine. But he failed in the last of his conditions for success: he was not able to find a Brigham Young. As he grew old, the Oneida Community, with its dangerous stresses and strains, began to get out of hand; the parsons raised an outcry against it; and it was obliged to give up Complex Marriage. Eventually, after Noyes had had to leave it as a result of the dissensions that had arisen, it relapsed into individual ownership.

It is significant that Noyes, who had thought more deeply and who had achieved a more remarkable success than any other of the early socialist leaders, should have been unable to find any hope for the future save in the very unrealistic notion that the requisite combination of socialism and religion might be made universally to prevail by the conversion of the "local churches" to communism.

Only a few weeks before I write, I read in my local paper of the destruction of a part of the "phalanstery" put up near

Red Bank, New Jersey, by the longest-lived of the Fourierist communities, the North American Phalanx, which adhered to its Fourierist form from 1843 to 1855. Here descendants of the original members still live on alone in the ragged New Jersey woodland in the same old long-galleried building, unpainted and gray now for decades but constructed with a certain grandeur according to Fourier's specifications and so quaintly unassignable to the categories of either mansion, barracks or hotel; here they still put up tomatoes in the old factory, which, according to Fourier's provision, is removed at some distance from the phalanstery and concealed by an avenue of trees. Here, in the middle years of the last century, came Greeley, Dana, Channing and Margaret Fuller. Here the faithful from Brook Farm ultimately migrated; and here found refuge the political exiles from France. Here died George Arnold, the poet, who, brought up in the Fourierist community and having watched it go to pieces in his teens, would return to the old refuge at intervals to write, among the honeysuckle or the crickets, his poems of epicurean loafing or elegiac resignation; and here was born Alexander Woollcott, who learned here whatever it is in him that compels him to throw up his radio engagement rather than refrain from criticism of the Nazis.

Here in the great wing, which had been growing unsafe and which has just been pulled down, was the communal hall where they ate, where they listened to lectures and concerts, and where they held banquets and balls; where the women both waited on table and danced, and where they were proud to appear in skirts that reached only to the knees and with trousers like men's underneath. Here was the center of that pastoral little world through which, as one of the Fourierists said, they had been "desirous of escaping from the present hollow-hearted state of civilized society, in which fraud and heartless competition grind the more noble-minded of our citizens to the dust"; where they had hoped to lead the way for their age, through their resolute stand and pure example, toward an ideal of firm human fellowship, of planned production, happy labor, high culture—all those things from which the life of society seemed so strangely to be heading away.

5 Karl Marx: Prometheus and Lucifer

In the August of 1835, a young German-Jewish boy, a student at the Friedrich-Wilhelm Gymnasium at Trier on the Moselle, composed a theme for his final examination. It was called *Reflections of a Young Man on Choosing a Profession*, and it was radiant with those lofty ideals which are in order on such occasions and which in the present case have attracted attention only for the reason that the aspiring young man managed to live up to his aspirations. In choosing a profession, said Karl Marx at seventeen, one must be sure that one will not put oneself in the position of acting merely as a servile tool of others: in one's own sphere one must obtain independence; and one must make sure that one has a field to serve humanity—for though one may otherwise become famous as a scholar or a poet, one can never be a really great man. We shall never be able to fulfill ourselves truly unless we are working for the welfare of our fellows: then only shall our burdens not break us, then only shall our satisfactions not be confined to poor egoistic joys. And so we must be on guard against allowing ourselves to fall victims to that most dangerous of all temptations: the fascination of abstract thought.

One reflection—which the examiner has specially noted—comes to limit the flood of aspiration. "But we cannot always follow the profession to which we feel ourselves to have been called; our relationships in society have already to some extent been formed before we are in a position to determine them. Already our physical nature threateningly bars the way, and her claims may be mocked by none."

So for the mind of the young Marx the bondage of social relationships already appeared as an impediment to individual self-realization. Was it the conception, now so prevalent since Herder, of the molding of human cultures by physical and geographical conditions? Was it the consciousness of the disabilities which still obstructed the development of the Jews: the terrible special taxes, the special restrictions on movement, the prohibitions against holding public office, against engaging in agriculture or crafts?

Both, no doubt. There had been concentrated in Karl Marx the blood of several lines of Jewish rabbis. There had been rabbis in his mother's family for at least a century back; and the families of both his father's parents had produced unbroken successions of rabbis, some of them distinguished teachers of the fifteenth and eighteenth centuries. Karl Marx's paternal grandfather had been a rabbi in Trier; one of his uncles was a rabbi there. Hirschel Marx, Karl's father, was evidently the first man of brains in his family decisively to abandon the rabbinate and to make himself a place in the larger community.

The German Jews of the eighteenth century were breaking away from the world of the Ghetto, with its social isolation and its closed system of religious culture. It was an incident of the liquidation of medieval institutions and ideas. Moses Mendelssohn, the Jewish philosopher, through his translation of the Bible into German, had brought his people into contact with the culture of the outside German world, and they were already by Karl Marx's generation beginning to play a role of importance in the literature and thought of the day. But Mendelssohn, who had been the original of Lessing's Nathan the Wise, produced a result far beyond what he had intended: instead of guiding the Jews as he had hoped to a revivified and purified Judaism, he opened to them the doors of the Enlightenment. For the young Jews, the traditional body of their culture seemed at once to collapse in dust like a corpse in an unsealed tomb. Mendelssohn's daughters already belonged to a group of sophisticated Jewish women with salons and "philosopher" lovers, who were having themselves baptized Protestants and Catholics. Hirschel Marx was a Kantian free-thinker, who had left Judaism and Jewry behind. Living in Trier, on the border between Germany and France, he had been nourished on Rousseau and Voltaire as well as on the philosophy of the Germans. Under the influence of the French Revolution, some of the restrictions on the Jews had been relaxed, and it had been possible for him to study law and to make himself a successful career. When the Prussians expelled Napoleon and it became illegal again for Jews to hold office, he changed his name to Heinrich, had his whole family baptized Christians and rose to be Justizrat and head of the Trier bar.

Next door to the Marxes in Trier lived a family named van Westphalen. Baron von Westphalen, though a Prussian official, was also a product of eighteenth-century civilization: his father had been confidential secretary to the liberal Duke Ferdinand of Brunswick, the friend of Winckelmann and Voltaire, and had been ennobled by him. Ludwig von Westphalen read seven languages, loved Shakespeare and knew Homer by heart. He used to take young Karl Marx for walks among the vineyard-covered hills of the Moselle and tell him about the Frenchman, Saint-Simon, who wanted society organized scientifically in the interests of Christian charity: Saint-Simon had made an impression on Herr von Westphalen. The Marxes had their international background of Holland, Poland and Italy and so back through the nations and the ages; Ludwig von Westphalen was half-German, half-Scotch; his mother was of the family of the Dukes of Argyle; he spoke German and English equally well. Both the Westphalens and the Marxes belonged to a small community of Protestant officials—numbering only a scant three hundred among a population of eleven thousand Catholics, and most of them transferred to Trier from other provinces—in that old city, once a stronghold of the Romans, then a bishopric of the Middle Ages, which during the lifetimes of the Westphalens and Marxes had been ruled alternately by the Germans and the French. Their children played together in the Westphalens' large garden. Karl's sister and Jenny von Westphalen became one another's favorite friends. Then Karl fell in love with Jenny.

In the summer of Karl's eighteenth year, when he was home on his vacation from college, Jenny von Westphalen promised to marry him. She was four years older than Karl and was considered one of the belles of Trier, was much courted by the sons of officials and landlords and army officers; but she waited for Karl seven years. She was intelligent, had character, talked well; had been trained by a remarkable father. Karl Marx had conceived for her a devotion which lasted through his whole life. He wrote her bad romantic poetry from college.

This early student poetry of Marx, which he himself denounced as rhetorical almost as soon as he had written it, is nevertheless not without its power, and it is of interest in presenting the whole repertoire of his characteristic impulses and emotions before they are harnessed to the pistons of his system. The style, already harsh and tight-knotted, which suits his satirical subjects, is usually quite inappropriate to his more numerous romantic ones; but even the lyrics have something of the hard and dark crystallization which is afterwards to distinguish Marx's writing, and they leave in the mind of the reader certain recurrent symbols.

In these poems, we find a woful old man, all bones, lying at the bottom of the water, but the waves make him dance when the moon is out, for they are cold in heart and mind and feel nothing. There is a man in a yellow house, a little man with a lean horror of a wife; the poet must pull down the shade so that they may not scare off his fancies. There are doctors, damned Philistines, who think the world is a bag of bones, whose psychology is confined to the notion that our dreams are due to noodles and dumplings, whose metaphysics consists of the belief that if it were possible to locate the soul, a pill would quite easily expel it. There are also sentimental souls who weep at the idea of a calf's being slaughtered: yet, after all, are there not asses, like Balaam's, that are human enough to talk?

In one of Karl Marx's ballads, a mariner is roused from his bed by the storm: he will go forth, he will leave behind him the warm and quiet towns; will put to sea, and let his ship's sail swell, keep his course by the changeless stars, contend with the waves and the wind, feel the joy of all his forces at full strain, blood pounding in his breast at the danger—he will defy and he will conquer the sea, which is picking the bones of his brother. In another ballad, a second skipper, assaulted by the songs of the sirens—very different from the sailors of Heine, whose bones have whitened the rocks—declares to their faces that their charms are specious, that for them in their cold abysses there burns no eternal God; but that in *his* breast the gods preside in their might, all the gods, and under their governance no deviation is possible. The sirens, discouraged, sink. In another, a Promethean hero curses a god who has stripped him of his all; but he swears that he will have his revenge, though his strength be but a patchwork of weaknesses: out of his pain and horror he will fashion a fortress, iron and cold, which will strike the beholder livid and against which the thunderbolts will rebound. Prometheus is to be Marx's favorite myth: he is to prefix to his doctor's dissertation the speech of Aeschylus' Prometheus to Zeus, "Know well I would never be willing to exchange my misfortune for that bondage of yours. For better do I deem it to be bound to this rock than to spend my life as Father Zeus's faithful messenger"; and a contemporary cartoon on the suppression of the paper he is later to edit is to show him chained to his press with the Prussian eagle preying on his vitals.

In yet another of Karl Marx's poems, he proclaims that the grandeurs and splendors of the pygmy-giants of earth are doomed to fall to ruins. They do not count beside the soul's aspiration; even vanquished, shall the soul remain defiant, shall still build itself a throne of giant scorn: "Jenny! if we can but weld our souls together, then with contempt shall I fling my glove in the world's face, then shall I stride through the wreckage a creator!"

Old Heinrich, who said that his parents had given him nothing but his existence and his mother's love, hoped that Karl, with more advantages than he had had himself, would take his place at the Trier bar. He recognized that Karl's abilities were exceptional, but he disapproved of what seemed to him his uncanalized energies, his all-embracing intellectual ambitions. Though he, too, talks of Karl's working for the "welfare of humanity," he is exceedingly anxious for his son to establish good connections, gives him letters to influential persons who may be of use to him in making his career. His letters to his son are a mixture of excited admiration and apprehension lest Karl's genius miscarry; and they have the insistence of jealous affection. Old Heinrich reproaches the boy with egoism, with lack of consideration for his parents—Karl rarely seems to have answered his family's letters; he cries out continually over Karl's frequent demands for money: does the young gentleman think his father is made of gold? etc. His mother writes him that he must not neglect to keep his rooms clean, that he must scrub himself every week with sponge and soap, that his Muse must be made to understand that the higher and better things will be promoted through attention to the more humble.

In the meantime, at the University of Bonn, to which he had gone in the fall of 1835, Karl had joined a convivial tavern club, contracted considerable debts, got into trouble with the university authorities for "nocturnal drunkenness and riot," become a member of a Poets' Club suspected of subversive ideas and under the surveillance of the political police, taken part in a row which had arisen between the plebeian tavern clubs and the aristocratic Korps associations, and finally—in the summer of 1836—fought a duel and got a wound over the eye. In a lithograph of the members of his tavern club, made this same year, when Karl Marx was eighteen, he is shown in the background, but with his head held high under its heavy black helmet of hair and thrown back with a look of brooding fierceness from thick and strong black brows and black eyes.—It was decided, with his father's emphatic approval, that he should be transferred to the University of Berlin, which has been described by a contemporary as a "workhouse" in contrast to the "Bacchanalian" character of the other German universities.

At Berlin, where he remained till March 30, 1841, he

studied law in compliance with his father's wishes, but neglected it in favor of philosophy, which was at that time in the German universities the great subject of intellectual interest and of which Karl was a born addict and master. Now he shuts himself up to think and study, "repulses friendships," as he says, "neglects nature, art and society, sits up through many nights, fights through many battles, undergoes many agitations both from outward and inward causes," reads gigantically, plans immense labors, writes poetry, philosophy, makes translations.

His father's letters grow continually more troubled. Has Karl more brains and brilliance than heart? Is it a divine or a Faustian daemon that possesses him? Will he ever be capable of domestic happiness, of making those around him happy? Old Marx is impressive in his letters. His son, Karl's daughter tells us, enormously admired his father and was never tired of talking about him; he carried a picture of him about all his life, and Engels put it in his coffin when he was dead. But much as he got from his father that was valuable, it was vital for the son to reject much. Heinrich's correspondence with Karl has a certain dramatic interest. It reaches a climax in a letter of huge length and tragic emotional force, written (December 9, 1837) five months before the old man's death—a last desperate effort to save his son from turning into something which the father dreads. He hopes, he tells Karl, that the denying genius may develop into a solid thinker, that he will realize that art is to be acquired only through intercourse with well-bred people; Karl must learn to present himself to the world in an agreeable and advantageous light, he must win consideration and affection. Above all, he must be careful of Jenny, who is bringing to him all her devotion and sacrificing her social position: in return, he must provide her with a place in actual human society, not merely in some smoked-up room beside a bad-smelling oil-lamp, shut in with a crazy scholar.

The old man, who was fond of Jenny and who had done what he could to promote the match, already foresaw the future and felt himself helpless against it. For Karl seems already to have shaken from him the barbarian social world of the beer-swilling and saber-brandishing German students and to have returned to the rabbinical world. He had made his social isolation complete—he was never again to encourage any friends save those who fed his intellectual interests; and he had worked himself into a decline. Sent away to the country to recover, he had read through the whole of Hegel and gone on to the works of Hegel's disciples. He was already on his way to becoming the great secular rabbi of his century. Salomon Maimon, in the century before, had tried to reconcile rabbinical philosophy with Kant. Karl Marx, also a teacher in the Jewish tradition but now quite free of the Judaic system and with all the thought of Western Europe at his disposal, was to play an unprecedented role as a leader in the modern world.

We shall revert to this aspect of Marx later on: but it may be said here that Karl Marx was too profoundly and completely a Jew to worry much about the Jewish problem in the terms in which it was discussed during his lifetime. The only opinion he would express on this issue was that the usurious activities of the Jews, which had made them unpopular with their neighbors and which to him were more objectionable still, were simply a special malignant symptom of capitalism, which would disappear with the capitalist system. In his own case, the pride and independence, the conviction of moral superiority, which give his life its heroic dignity, seem to go back to the great days of Israel and to be unconscious of the miseries between.

Yet are they? Two of Marx's poems he rewrote and finally published in 1841. In one of them a wild violinist appears, in a white gown and with a saber at his side. Why does he fiddle so madly? asks the speaker. Why does he cause the blood to leap? Why does he lash his bow to shreds?—Why do the waves roar? the spirit demands in answer. That, thundering, they may crash on the cliff—that the soul may crash on the floor of Hell.—But, musician, with mockery thou tearest thy heart! That art which a bright god has lent thee thou shouldst send to swell the music of the spheres. Nay, the apparition replies, with this blood-black saber I pierce the soul. God knows not, nor honors, Art: it rises from the vapors of Hell—it maddens the brain and it alters the heart. 'Tis the Devil who beats me the time and the Dead March the tune I must play.—Lucifer was to hover behind Prometheus through the whole of Karl Marx's life: he was the malevolent obverse side of the rebel benefactor of man. In a satirical poem by Engels and Edgar Bauer, written at about this time, Marx is described as the "black fellow from Trier," a savage and sinewy monster, who creeps not, but leaps, upon his prey, who stretches his arms toward the heavens as if he would tear down their canopy, who clenches his fist and raves as if a thousand devils had him by the hair; and through the years of his later life he was to be familiarly known as "Old Nick." His little son used to call him "Devil." True: the devil as well as the rebel was one of the conventional masks of the romantic; but there is something other than romantic perversity in this assumption of a diabolic role.

The second poem is a dialogue between sweethearts. Beloved, says the lover, thy grief stings thee—thou tremblest beneath my breath. Thou hast drunken of the soul: shine, my jewel—shine, shine, O blood of youth!—Darling, replies the maiden, thou lookest so pale, speakest so strangely seldom. See with what celestial music the worlds pass across the heavens!—My dear, says the lover, they pass and they shine— let us, too, flee away, let us merge our souls in one.—Then, whispering, with terrified glance: My dear, thou hast drunk of poison; thou must needs depart with me now. Night has fallen; I can no longer see the light.—With violence he clasps her to his heart, death in his breast and breath. She is pierced by a deeper pain; never more will she open her eyes.

Heinrich Marx had died in the May of 1838; Karl Marx was married to Jenny von Westphalen in the June of 1843, two years after he had graduated at Berlin.

6 Karl Marx Decides to Change the World

The great task of Karl Marx's first period was to engage German philosophical thought in the actualities of contemporary Germany.

The world of German philosophy seems queer to us when we come to it from the French Revolution. The abstractions of the French—whether Liberty, Fraternity and Equality or the Harmonies and Passionate Attractions of Fourier—are social principles which are intended to evoke visions of social and political improvement; but the abstractions of the Germans, by comparison, are like foggy and amorphous myths, which hang in the gray heavens above the flat land of Königsberg and Berlin, only descending into reality in the role of intervening gods. Marx and Engels were to come to the conclusion that the failure of the German philosophers to supply principles for man as a social being had been due to their actual helplessness under an obsolete feudal regime: as, for example, the "self-determination" of Kant had been the intellectual reflection of the effect of the French Revolution on the minds of the German bourgeoisie, which had the impulse but not yet the power to free itself from the old institutions—so that this "will" remained a "will-in-and-for-itself . . . a purely ideological determination and moral postulate," with no influence on actual society.

Hegel had held that society, "the State," was the realization of absolute reason, to which the individual must subordinate himself. He afterwards said that what he had meant was the *perfect* state; but his politics and position in his later years gave ground for the assumption that he regarded this perfection as already having been achieved by the contemporary Prussian state of Friedrich Wilhelm III. Society had ceased to develop, was consummated and petrified in a mold. Yet at the same time this consummated state was itself merely a mystical entity in the shadowland of German idealism, for it was conceived as merely a product and aspect of a primordial divine "Idea," which realized itself through reason. The king, who had thus been supplied with a Divine Right and had the permanence of his office guaranteed in terms of the most advanced thinking, patronized and promoted the Hegelians: they had become pillars of the administration.

Yet there was a revolutionary principle in Hegel, who had been swept up in his early years, before he had stiffened into a Prussian professor, by the surge of the French Revolution. He had reviewed the whole of history as he knew it and he had shown the organic processes, recurrent and ineluctable, by which old societies turn into new. Why, then, should these processes be suddenly arrested? The Revolution of 1830 in France had awakened agitation in Germany. This had been put down and had been followed by a reaction, of which one of the features had been an attempt to revive orthodox religion. A new school of Hegelians appeared, who used Hegelianism to liquidate Christianity. In 1835, David Friedrich Strauss published his *Life of Jesus*. It had been one of the achievements of Hegel to direct the attention of the Germans to the development of human institutions as special expressions of the genius of various peoples. D. F. Strauss, even in asserting like Hegel that Christianity represented ideal truth, shocked Germany with the contention that the Gospels were not historical documents at all but only myths, that, though they could be traced back to an authentic germ of fact, they had largely been created unconsciously by a communal imagination which had flowed through the minds of the early Christians. Bruno Bauer, in criticisms of the Gospels published in 1840 and 1841, tried to clear away this mythopoeic possession, itself something in the nature of a myth, by examining the New Testament documents as the products of specific human hands and concluding that the whole thing was a for-

gery, known and intended as a fraud by its first perpetrator:
Jesus had never existed. Bauer had thus got rid of Christianity
but, Hegelian as he still remained, later elaborated a doctrine
of "self-consciousness," which, denying the existence of matter as a reality distinct from spirit, left humanity still disem-
bodied, still suspended in the philosophic void.

Karl Marx, a young student at Berlin, had been admitted
in 1837 to a Doktorklub of which Bauer was a member and in
which a "Young Hegelian" movement arose. Marx had succumbed to the Hegelian philosophy, which was still the most
powerful system of thought in Germany, but almost immediately commenced to resist it. The deicide principle in Marx
rebelled against the Absolute Idea. "Philosophy makes no
secret of the fact," he wrote in a doctor's thesis which is nevertheless full of Hegelian method: "Her creed is the creed of
Prometheus—'In a word, I detest all the gods.' This is her
device against all deities of heaven or earth who do not
recognize as the highest divinity the human self-consciousness
itself." Nor, as we shall see, was this human self-consciousness
to remain merely a universal abstraction like the self-
consciousness defined by Bruno Bauer.

Bauer himself was by this time a professor at Bonn, and he
had promised Marx to get him a post there. Marx had counted
on joining him; they had collaborated on a satire against pious
Hegelians, talked about publishing an Atheist Review. But in
the meanwhile, by the time Marx had graduated, Bruno
Bauer was already getting into trouble for his anti-religious
and pro-constitutional activities; and he was dismissed from
his chair the next spring. The possibility that the ablest
philosopher of the new German generation—of whom it had
already been predicted by a contemporary that, as soon as he
should make his appearance in a lecture room, he would draw
upon him the eyes of all Germany—the possibility that the
young Dr. Marx might follow the example of his great predecessors, Kant and Fichte and Hegel, and expound his system
from an academic pulpit, was thereby destroyed forever.

The accession in 1840 of Friedrich Wilhelm IV, of whom
liberal reforms had been expected, had brought only a new

feudal reaction. From that point on, the necessity for political action became continually more urgent for Germans. In the fourth decade of the nineteenth century, they had no parliament, no trial by jury, no rights of free speech or assembly; and the new king, with his royal romanticism that idealized the Middle Ages, made it quite plain that he would give them none of these things. In the meantime the doctrines of the utopian socialists had come to trouble German philosophy and politics. They leaked over first from their sources in France into the Rhineland, already partly Gallicized, where they found for other reasons, also, a particularly favorable field. The wine-growing peasants of the Moselle were being impoverished, since Prussia's customs union with Hessia, by the competition of the wine industry outside; and they had still some remnants from the Middle Ages of the communal ownership of land. Saint-Simonism spread so rapidly along the Moselle that the archbishop had to denounce it as a heresy; and in 1835 a German named Ludwig Gall published in Trier a socialist pamphlet in which he declared that the propertied class and the laboring class had directly conflicting interests. Heinrich Marx had in 1834 taken a leading part in political banquets at which the demand for a real parliament had been pressed and at which the *Marseillaise* had been sung, but of which the Trier papers had been forbidden to publish any report and which had been rebuked by the Crown Prince himself—with the result that the club in which they had been held had been put under the supervision of the police.

Karl Marx in the first months of 1842 wrote an article on the new Prussian censorship, in which we see him for the first time at his best: here the implacable logic and crushing wit are trained full on Marx's lifelong enemies: the deniers to human beings of human rights. The censor himself, it is true, blocked the publication of the article in Germany, and it was only printed a year later in Switzerland. But the new note has already been sounded which, though it is long to be muffled or ignored, will yet gradually pierce with its tough metallic timbre through all the tissues of ideas of the West.

Marx now begins to write for the *Rheinische Zeitung*, a liberal newspaper published in Cologne, the center of the in-

dustrialized Rhineland, and supported by the wealthy manufacturers and merchants who had found their ideas and their
railroads obstructed by the old Catholic society. It was written
by the young intelligentsia; and Karl Marx became editor-in-
chief in October, 1842.

Marx's work for the *Rheinische Zeitung* brought him up for
the first time against problems for which, as he said, no solution had been provided for him by Hegel. In commenting on
the proceedings of the Rhenish Diet which Friedrich Wilhelm
IV had convened, he had had to deal with the debate on a
bill for punishing the picking-up of wood in forests, and it had
been plain to him that the new government was attempting
to deprive the peasants of even those communal privileges
which had remained with them from the Middle Ages. By a
first stroke of that irony of "fetishes" which was afterwards to
play so important a part in his work, he pointed out that the
trees had been given rights to which the rights of the people
were being sacrificed; and through arguments of a semi-
scholastic subtlety he proved that an administration that made
no distinction between wood-gathering and common theft as
offenses against private property were inviting the persons
they prosecuted so unfairly to disregard the distinction between the offense against property involved in common theft
and the offense against property involved in owning a great
deal of property and preventing other people from having
any. The subject leads for Marx at twenty-four to a passage
of exhilarating eloquence, in which he declares that the code
of the feudal world has no relation to general human justice
but has perpetuated itself from a time when men were essentially animals, and simply guarantees their right to eat one
another up—with the exception that among the bees, at least
it was the workers that killed the drones and not the drones
that killed the workers. Later, people began writing to the
paper about the misery of the wine-growers on the Moselle.
Marx investigated, found out that conditions were really extremely bad, and got into a controversy with the governor of
the Rhine Province. In the meantime the *Rheinische Zeitung*
had become involved in polemics with a conservative paper
rival, which had accused it of communist tendencies. Karl

Marx knew very little about communism; but he decided to study the subject forthwith.

The *Rheinische Zeitung,* under Marx's direction, lasted five months. It was suppressed, at the instance of the Ambassador to Russia, for criticizing the government of the Tsar.

It seems always to have been with something of relief that Karl Marx turned away from politics and devoted himself to research and the following-out of large unifying ideas. The atmosphere, he said, had got too stifling. "It is bad to work for freedom in servitude and to fight with pins instead of clubs. I am sick of the hypocrisy, the stupidity, the brutal authority, and of our cringing and complying and quibbling and tergiversation. And now the government has given me back my freedom." In the same letter to a friend, he goes on to say that he has now fallen out with his family: he has no claims on his father's estate while his mother is still alive; but he is engaged to Jenny von Westphalen and neither can nor will go without her. "There is in Germany no possible further career for me. One debases one's value here."

Before he leaves the Fatherland, however, he sets himself to grapple with Hegel, whose idealism has dominated his mind hitherto. It will be better to leave the discussion of Marx's political thought as it splits off from Hegel's philosophy of Law, till after the beginning of his collaboration with Engels; but we may anticipate a few years in order to indicate how he eventually threw out a bridge—reversing the procedure in *The Rhinegold,* where the gods cross the rainbow to Valhalla, leaving behind them the harsh scene of human greed—from the self of German idealistic philosophy, which could never really know the outside world, to the landowners of the Rhenish Diet tightening their halters around the necks of the peasants, and Marx himself excluded from the lecture-room, forbidden to express himself in print.

There had been, besides Strauss and Bauer, a third critic of religion named Ludwig Feuerbach, who had made a great impression on Marx's generation in 1841 by a book called *The Essence of Christianity.* Hegel's Absolute Idea, said Feuerbach, which was supposed to have incorporated itself in matter for the purpose of realizing reason, had been a gratuitous presupposition which Hegel was unable to prove. What the Absolute Idea really was, was a substitute for the Word become Flesh; and Hegel was actually merely the last of the great apologists for Christianity. Let us forget about the Absolute Idea; let us start an investigation with man and the world as we find them. When we do so, it becomes perfectly obvious that the legends and the rituals of religion are merely the expressions of human minds.

Feuerbach succeeded in dragging religion down out of the communal imagination of Strauss, in rescuing the ethical instinct from the pure self-consciousness into which it had rebounded with Bruno Bauer after he had rejected its Scriptural sanctions, and in tying both religion and morality inescapably to the habits of men. But he still believes in the permanent necessity for religion. He tries himself to produce a substitute religion, a cult of love based on sex and friendship. And he imagines an abstract humanity endowed with a common reason.

It now presented itself to Marx as his further task to get rid of religion altogether and to put the emotions, the moralities, of man into relation with the vicissitudes of society. It was also his task to convert the "Will" of German philosophy, which had been "a purely ideological postulate" and which even Fichte, though he had contemplated it in action, had not assumed to be necessarily successful but had regarded as an end in itself—Marx's problem was to convert this abstraction into a force in the practical world.

In a remarkable set of notes on Feuerbach which he wrote down in 1845, he asserted that the defect of all previous materialisms had been their representing external objects only as acting upon the mind, which remained passive, while the defect of idealism had been that what it perceived could not act upon the world. The truth was that the reality or unreality of thought except as thought enters into action was a purely academic question: all that we can know we know is our own action in relation to the external world. On this external world we seek to act: when we find that we succeed in transforming it, we know that our conceptions are correct.

Utopians like Robert Owen had believed that a different education would produce a different kind of human beings. But this utopian was in reality a materialist; and, as a materialist, he was unable to explain how he himself, who was presumably the product of antecedent conditions, had come to be differentiated in such a way as to be in a position to educate others. Were there, then, two kinds of human beings? No: there was a dynamic principle at work in the whole of human activity. How else could one explain the coincidence between the changes in things which we perceive and our purposive human effort?

Feuerbach had imagined an abstract man with abstract religious feelings; but in reality man was always social, and his religious feelings, like all his other feelings, were related to his environment and time. The problems which had given rise to the supernatural conceptions of religion were actually practical problems, which could only be solved by man's action in transforming the practical world.

As for traditional materialism, its conceptions were equally non-social: it contemplated human beings only as separate individuals who went to make up a "civic" association. The new materialism proposed by Marx was to look at mankind from the more organic point of view of "human society or of socialized humanity."

I have here given my own paraphrase of this document, which has inspired so much controversy and commentary; I have not analyzed it or criticized its assumptions. Marx never really developed this philosophy. It was the eve of 1848, and he was impatient to put behind him the old kind of philosophical discussion and to be about his revolutionary business: he gave the matter only just enough thought to sketch a position that would bring him into action. He compresses the whole situation into the two lines of the last of his notes: "The philosophers hitherto have only interpreted the world in various ways: the thing is, however, to change it."

7 Friedrich Engels: The Young Man from Manchester

In the fall of 1842, when Marx was editing the *Rheinische Zeitung,* a highly intelligent young man who had been contributing to the paper came to see him. The son of a Rhineland manufacturer, he had just been converted to communism. He was passing through Cologne on his way to England, whither he was going with the double object of learning his father's business in Manchester and of studying the Chartist movement.

Karl Marx, who was only beginning to read the communists and who as yet knew little or nothing about Manchester, received him with the utmost coldness. He was then in the midst of one of those feuds with former associates which were to be a recurrent feature of his life. The result of the all-powerful reaction had been to cause the young Hegelians in Berlin to recoil into a theoretical intransigence; and since their position of pure atheism and pure communism, which made no contact with actual society, excluded all possibility of affecting the course of events by ordinary agitation, they had resorted to a policy of clowning not unlike that by which the Dadaists of our own post-war period attempted, in a similar fashion, to shock a world of which they totally despaired and which they could only desire to insult. Karl Marx hated the clowning and considered the intransigence futile: he was trying to make his paper a practical political force. He had been cutting and refusing to publish the contributions of his friends in Berlin; and it was to be increasingly characteristic of Marx that he passed readily from a critical mistrust, based on sound intellectual grounds, to an unhealthy and hateful suspicion. In this case, he assumed that the young traveler was an emissary from his enemies in Berlin, and he sent Friedrich Engels away without ever finding out what there was in him or understanding what he was up to.

Engels was two and a half years younger than Marx, but he had already some reputation as a writer. He had been born (November 28, 1820) in the industrial town of Barmen, where good stone houses lined a well-paved street. Between the houses one sometimes got a glimpse of a clear little river called the Wupper, which flowed away into the Rhine between softly rolling banks, with green bleacheries, red-roofed houses, gardens, meadows and woods. So he described it in a pseudonymous letter—written when Engels was eighteen, and written remarkably well—for a paper which Gutzkow was editing. But on the opposite bank of the Wupper, he wrote, one found the narrow and characterless streets of Elberfeld, where the first spinning machine in Germany had been set up; and the river, as it ran through the double town, was flanked by the textile factories and muddied with purple dye. Friedrich Engels was already aware that "the fresh and vigorous popular life, which existed almost all over Germany," had disappeared in his native town. One never heard the old folk-songs in Barmen-Elberfeld: the songs that the mill-workers sang were invariably smutty and low—and they sang them howling drunk in the streets. Drinking beer and Rhine wine, he reflected, had once been a jolly affair; but now that cheap spirits were being sent in from Prussia, the tavern life was becoming more and more brutal. The workers got drunk every night; they were always fighting and sometimes killed one another. When they were turned out of their grog-shops at closing time, they would go to sleep in the haylofts or stables or fall down on people's dungheaps or front steps.

The reasons for this, Engels wrote, were quite plain. All day they had been working in low-ceilinged rooms, where they had been breathing more dust and coal smoke than oxygen; they had been crouching above their looms and scorching their backs against the stove. From the time that they had been six years old, everything possible had been done to deprive them of strength and the enjoyment of life. There was nothing left for them but evangelism and brandy.

Young Friedrich Engels' father was in the textile business himself, and he was strong for the evangelism, if not for the brandy. He had factories both in Manchester and in Barmen. His grandfather had founded the business in the last half of the eighteenth century, and was said to have been the first manufacturer to build up a permanent industrial community by giving homes to those of the workers, a floating population at that date, who had commended themselves through industry and conduct, and subtracting the cost from their wages. Friedrich's father was progressive in the sense that he was the first manufacturer of the Rhineland to install English machines in his mills; but he was a pillar of the most rigorous party of the Calvinism that dominated the locality, and a bigot of the most crushing kind.

Friedrich Engels, with his natural gaiety and his enthusiasm for literature and music, grew up in a cage of theology, from which it took him a long time to escape. For the "Pietism" which his father professed, righteousness meant unremitting work; and work meant his own kind of business. He would not allow novels in the house; and young Friedrich hoped to be a poet. Old Caspar, who felt that the boy needed steadying, sent him to Bremen to live with a pastor and to work in an export office. There Strauss's *Life of Jesus* set in motion for Friedrich the machinery of rationalist criticism. Yet for months he still declared himself a "supernaturalist"; and the truth was that his religious instincts were not to be extinguished but rather fed by the new doctrine with which he now became preoccupied. He was to find his lost God again in the Absolute Idea of Hegel.

He wrote notices of theater and opera, travel sketches, mythological stories; poems on oriental subjects in the manner of Freiligrath: the old rebuke from the brave faraway to the dismal and pedestrian present. He adored and translated Shelley; and he wrote revolutionary rhapsodies of his own to the freedom which was surely coming and which was apparently to make all Germany as good-natured and laughter-loving and frank as an ideal unindustrialized Rhineland: the new sun, the new wine, the new song!

The young Engels is an attractive figure. He was tall and slender, with brown hair and bright and piercing blue eyes. Unlike the obdurately brooding Marx, he was flexible, lively and active. In Bremen he loved to fence, loved to ride; swam the Weser once four times at a stretch. He was observant and filled his letters with drawings of the people he saw: broad brokers who always began everything they said with "According to my way of thinking—"; young men with dashing mustaches, heavy fringes of beard, and foils; a queer old party who got drunk every morning and came out in front of his house and slapped himself on the chest and declared to the world: "I am a burgher!"; wagoners riding without saddles and bargemen loading coffee at the docks; seedy-looking *Weltschmerz* poets, one of whom Engels insists is writing a book on *Weltschmerz* as the only sure way of getting thin. He himself seems to have written verse almost as easily as prose; and he picked up languages with marvelous facility: one of the things that seems chiefly to have pleased him at the young business men's club that he frequented was the variety of foreign papers. He loved good wine and did an immense amount of drinking: one of the most amusing of his incidental drawings depicts a disgusted elderly connoisseur who has just tasted some sour wine, contrasted with the urbane and cheerful countenance of the traveling salesman who has just induced him to buy it. He liked music, joined a singing society and composed some choral pieces for it. He writes his sister that Liszt has just given a concert in Bremen, and that Liszt is a wonderful man: the ladies have been swooning all over him and keeping the dregs from his tea in cologne bottles, but the master had left them cold and gone out to drink with some students, and he had run up a bill in the public house of no less than three thousand thaler—let alone what he'd put away in other places!

What is to be noted in Engels from the beginning is his sympathetic interest in life. Marx's thinking, though realistic in a moral sense and though sometimes enriched by a peculiar kind of imagery, always tends to state social processes in terms of abstract logical developments or to project mythological personifications; he almost never perceives ordinary human beings. Engels' sense of the world is quite different: he sees naturally and with a certain simplicity of heart into the lives of other people. Where Karl Marx during his years at the university seems to have written to his family rarely and then only to tell them of his ambitions, Engels continues through imagination and feeling to participate in the life of his, even after he has gone to Bremen. Whenever he writes to his sister, he is able to see his own experience through her eyes—from the day in 1838 when he describes to her in such accurate detail a hen with her seven little chickens, one of which is black and will eat bugs off your hand, to the day in 1842 when he tells her about his new spaniel, which has "displayed a great talent for tavern life" and goes the rounds of the tables to be fed, and which he has taught to growl in the most savage manner when he says, "There's an aristocrat!" And he can see them all there at home; he sends his sister a little scene in dramatic form depicting current goings-on in the household—a large well-to-do middle-class family; evidently, in spite of old Caspar's relentless Bible-reading, pretty cultivated, good-humored and lively. He follows Marie in imagination to her boarding-school, returns with her to Barmen when she leaves and sees her entering on her new young lady's life of freedom. He writes her a mocking and charming set of verses about a lame student she has met at Bonn, whom she is supposed to have found more attractive than more aristocratic and prepossessing beaux.

One day he went down to the docks to visit a ship that was sailing for America. The first cabin was "elegant and comfortably furnished, like an aristocratic salon, in mahogany ornamented with gold"; but when he descended to the steerage, he found the people "packed in like the paving-stones in the streets," men, women and children, sick and well, dumped together among their baggage, and he pictured them to himself in a storm, which would churn them all around in a heap and compel them to close up the porthole through which they had had their only ventilation. He saw that they were good strong honest Germans, "certainly by no means the worst that the Fatherland produces," who had been bedeviled by the feudal estates between serfdom and independence till they had decided to abandon their Fatherland.

From Bremen he removed to Berlin in the autumn of 1841 to put in his year of military service. He had chosen Berlin on account of the university: he had had no academic training, and he wanted to study Philosophy. There he fell in with the same set of young Hegelians who had had so stimulating an effect on Marx. It was the year of the publication of Feuerbach's *Essence of Christianity*, which for Engels performed the service of setting him free from theology and standing him firmly in the world of human action; and it was also the year of *The European Triarchy*, a book by a man named Moses Hess, the son of a Jewish manufacturer, who had traveled in England and France and who had come to the conclusion that it was impossible to eliminate the hatreds between nations without getting rid of commercial competition. Hess seems to have been the first German writer to canalize the current of Saint-Simonism into the main stream of German thought, and when the young Engels met him later at Cologne, Hess quickly converted him to communism.

The next November Friedrich Engels went to England and remained there for twenty-two months. It was a period of economic depression of unprecedented severity for the English. The cotton mills of Manchester were standing idle; and the streets were full of unemployed workmen, who begged from the passers-by with the threatening demeanor of rebels. The Chartist movement for universal suffrage and representation of the working class in Parliament had come to a climax the summer before in a general strike of the whole North of England, which had only been broken when the constabulary had fired on one of these formidable crowds. The next May there was a strike of the brickmakers, which resulted in a bloody riot. In Wales the impoverished peasants were destroying the tollkeepers' houses.

Friedrich Engels brought to the city of Manchester the comprehensive and anatomizing eye of a highly intelligent foreigner. He explored it till, so he said, he had come to know it as well as his own town. Barmen-Elberfeld had given him the clue to it. He studied the layout of the city and saw its commercial center surrounded by a girdle of working-class sections, and, outside the working-class girdle, the villas and gardens of the owners merging pleasantly with the country around; and he saw how the owners had arranged it so that it was possible for them to travel back and forth between the Exchange and their homes without ever being obliged to take cognizance of the condition of the working-class quarters, because the streets by which they passed through these sections were solidly lined with shops that hid the misery and dirt behind them. Yet it was impossible to walk through Manchester without encountering people strangely crippled, people with knock-knees and crooked spines: reminders of that suppressed and stunted race whose energies kept Manchester going.

This race Engels carefully observed. He was having a love affair with an Irish girl named Mary Burns, who worked in the factory of Ermen & Engels and had been promoted to run a new machine called a "self-actor." She seems to have been a woman of some independence of character, as she is said to have refused his offer to relieve her of the necessity of working. She had, however, allowed him to set up her and her sister in a little house in the suburb of Salford, where the coal-barges and chimneys of Manchester gave way to the woods and the fields. There he had already begun that strange double life which was to be kept up through the whole of his business career. While maintaining a lodging in town and going to his office during the day, he spent his evenings in the society of the Burns sisters, working on the materials for a book which should show the dark side of industrial life. Mary Burns was a fierce Irish patriot and she fed Engels' revolutionary enthusiasm at the same time that she served him as guide to the infernal abysses of the city.

He saw the working people living like rats in the wretched little dens of their dwellings, whole families, sometimes more than one family, swarming in a single room, well and diseased, adults and children, close relations sleeping together, sometimes even without beds to sleep on when all the furniture had been sold for firewood, sometimes in damp, underground cellars which had to be bailed out when the weather was wet, sometimes living in the same room with the pigs; ill nourished on flour mixed with gypsum and cocoa mixed with dirt, poisoned by ptomaine from tainted meat, doping themselves and their wailing children with laudanum; spending their lives, without a sewage system, among the piles of their excrement and garbage; spreading epidemics of typhus and cholera which even made inroads into the well-to-do sections.

The increasing demand for women and children at the factories was throwing the fathers of families permanently out of work, arresting the physical development of the girls, letting the women in for illegitimate motherhood and yet compelling them to come to work when they were pregnant or before they had recovered from having their babies, and ultimately turning a good many of them into prostitutes; while the children, fed into the factories at the age of five or six, receiving little care from mothers who were themselves at the factory all day and no education at all from a community which wanted them only to perform mechanical operations, would drop exhausted when they were let out of their prisons, too tired to wash or eat, let alone study or play, sometimes too tired to get home at all. In the iron and coal mines, also, women and children as well as men spent the better part of their lives crawling underground in narrow tunnels, and, emerging, found themselves caught in the meshes of the company cottage and the company store and of the two-week postponement of wages. They were being killed off at the rate of fourteen hundred a year through the breaking of rotten ropes, the caving-in of workings due to overexcavated seams and the explosions due to bad ventilation and to the negligence of tired children; if they escaped catastrophic accidents, the lung diseases eventually got them. The agricultural population, for its part, deprived by the industrial development of their old status of handicraftsmen and yeomen who either owned their own land and homes or were taken care of with more or less certainty by a landlord on whose estate they were tenants, had been transformed into wandering day laborers, for whom nobody took responsibility and who were punished by jail or transportation if they ventured in times of need to steal and eat the landlord's game.

It seemed to Engels that the medieval serf, who had at least been attached to the land and had a definite position in society, had had an advantage over the factory worker. At that period when legislation for the protection of labor had hardly seriously gotten under way, the old peasantry and hand-workers of England, and even the old petty middle class, were being shoveled into the mines and the mills like so much raw material for the prices their finished products would bring, with no attempt even to dispose of the waste. In years of depression the surplus people, so useful in years of good business, were turned out upon the town to become peddlers, crossing-sweepers, scavengers or simply beggars—sometimes whole families were seen begging in the streets—and, almost as frequently, whores and thieves. Thomas Malthus, said Engels, had asserted that the increase of population was always pressing on the means of subsistence so that it was necessary for considerable numbers to be exterminated by hardship and vice; and the new Poor Law had put this doctrine into practice by turning the poorhouses into prisons so inhuman that the poor preferred to starve outside.

All this brought a revelation to Engels. He saw the pressure of labor conditions in Parliament, where debate on the Poor Relief Bill and the Factory Act had recently crowded into the background the middle-class movement against the Corn Laws, and he came to the conclusion that "class antagonisms" were "completely changing the aspect of political life." He now clearly understood for the first time the importance of economic interests, which had hitherto been assigned by the historians either a trifling role or no role at all. Engels concluded that, under modern conditions at any rate, these were undoubtedly a decisive factor.

In London he found a city of more people than he had ever seen together before, but they seemed to him a population of atoms. Were they not, "the hundreds of thousands of all classes and ranks crowding past one another," all nevertheless "human beings with the same facilities and powers, and with the same interest in being happy? And have they not in the end to seek happiness in the same way, by the same means? And still they crowd by one another as though they had nothing in common, nothing to do with one another, and as if their only agreement were the tacit one that each shall keep to his own side of the pavement, in order not to delay the opposing streams of the crowd, while it never occurs to anyone to honor his fellow with so much as a glance. The brutal indifference, the unfeeling isolation of each in his private interest becomes the more repellent and offensive, the more these individuals are herded together within a limited space."

This conception of the individual in modern society as helpless, sterile and selfish was one of the main themes of nineteenth-century thought, and in our own time it has been felt, if possible, even more intensely. We have seen how the historian Michelet, writing at the same moment as Engels, was tending increasingly to interpret the world in terms of an antisocial egoism opposed to an ideal of solidarity, how he succeeded by a return to the past in escaping from that sinister solitude by identifying himself with the French nation, and how he later tried to find reassurance against the antagonisms that he felt in society through a mystical belief in "the People." We have seen how one of the first ideas of the young Marx was that there was a danger in egoistic interests if preferred to the service of humanity. With Saint-Simon, the disintegration of Catholicism and the feudal system with which his heredity connected him, had caused him, in the years of disorder that followed the Revolution, to elaborate a new system of hierarchies which should win unity and order for the future. The utopian socialists like Fourier, who found competitive society intolerable, were protecting themselves in a similar fashion against the feeling of isolation from their fellows by imagining a new kind of coöperation.

The further advance of industrial civilization created more murderous conflicts; and an intimate contact with it sharpened the conviction of the need for a new reconciliation. To Engels, in his early twenties, it seemed that a society so divided must be headed straight for civil war and for the consequent abolition of the system of competition and exploitation. The middle class in England was swiftly being absorbed from both sides, and there would soon be nothing left of English society but a desperate proletariat confronting an overrich owning class. From this owning class it appeared to him impossible to expect even a working arrangement: they seemed to him determined to ignore the situation. On one occasion when he had come into Manchester in the company of an English bourgeois, he had spoken of the terrible misery and said he had "never seen so ill-built a city"; the gentleman had quietly listened and then remarked at the corner when they were parting: "And yet there is a great deal of money made here; good morning, sir."

It seemed to Engels that the "educated classes," whose sole education consisted in having been annoyed with Latin and Greek in their school days, read nothing but Biblical commentaries and long novels. Only Carlyle in his just-published *Past and Present* had shown anything approaching a consciousness of the seriousness of English conditions; and Carlyle was unfortunately full of the wrong kind of German philosophy: the intoxication with ideas about God which prevented people from believing in mankind. What the English badly needed, he declared, was the new kind of German philosophy, which showed how man could at last become his own master.

But in the meantime the English workers would certainly demand their rights in a revolt that would make the French Revolution look gentle; and when the workers had come to power, they would certainly establish the only kind of regime that could give society a real coherence. Engels imagined a consummation in communism not very much different from that which Saint-Simon had proclaimed before his death; but for the first time he conceived this consummation as the consequence of something other than a vague spontaneous movement: it was to be the upshot of definite events. Engels was sure that he saw it already in the slogan evolved by the Chartists: "Political power our means, social happiness our end."

8 The Partnership of Marx and Engels

In the meantime, Marx had gotten married and had taken Jenny to Paris in October, 1843. He had been reading up with his usual thoroughness on French communism and studying the French Revolution, about which he was planning to write a book.

But early in 1844 there came under his eye an essay which Engels had written from England for the *Deutsch-Französische Jahrbücher,* to which Karl Marx was also contributing. It was an original and brilliant discussion of the "political economy" of the British, which Engels on his side had been reading up. Engels held that the theories of Adam Smith and Ricardo, of MacCulloch and James Mill, were fundamentally hypocritical rationalizations of the greedy motives behind the system of private property which was destroying the British peoples: the Wealth of Nations made most people poor; Free Trade and Competition left the people still enslaved, and consolidated the monopoly of the bourgeoisie on everything that was worth having—all the philosophies of trade themselves only sanctified the huckster's fraud; the discussions of abstract value were kept abstract on purpose to avoid taking cognizance of the actual conditions under which all commercial transactions took place: the exploitation and destruction of the working class, the alternation of prosperity with crisis. Marx at once began to correspond with Engels, and he set himself to master as much of the British economists as he could find translated into French.

Engels arrived back from Lancashire about the end of

August and stopped in Paris on his way home to Barmen. He immediately looked up Marx, and they found that they had so much to say to one another that they spent ten days together. Their literary as well as their intellectual collaboration began from that first moment of their meeting. They had been working toward similar conclusions, and now they were able to supplement one another. Like the copper and zinc electrodes of the voltaic cell of which they used to debate the mystery—the conductor liquid would be Hegel diluted in the political atmosphere of the eve of 1848—the two young Germans between them were able to generate a current that was to give energy to new social motors. The setting-up of this Marxist current is the central event of our chronicle and one of the great intellectual events of the century; and even this electrical image is inadequate to render the organic vitality with which the Marx-Engels system in its growth was able to absorb such a variety of elements—the philosophies of three great countries, the ideas of both the working class and the cultured, the fruits of many departments of thought. Marx and Engels performed the feat of all great thinkers in summing up immense accumulations of knowledge, in combining many streams of speculation, and in endowing a new point of view with more vivid and compelling life.

It would not be worth while here to attempt to trace in detail the influence of all the thinkers that Marx and Engels laid under contribution. In a sense, such attempts are futile. The spotlighting method that I have used in this book must not be allowed to mislead the reader into assuming that great ideas are the creations of a special race of great men. I have discussed some of the conspicuous figures who gave currency to socialist ideas; and Professor Sidney Hook in his admirable *From Hegel to Marx* has indicated with exactitude the relation of Marx to his background of German philosophy. But behind these conspicuous figures were certainly sources less well-known or quite obscure: all the agitators, the politicians, the newspaper writers; the pamphlets, the conversations, the intimations; the implications of conduct deriving from inarticulate or half-unconscious thoughts, the implications of unthinking instincts.

It is appropriate, nevertheless, to point this out at this particular moment, because it was precisely the conception of intellectual movements as representative of social situations which Marx and Engels were to do so much to implant; and it may be interesting to fill in a little more completely the background of early nineteenth-century thought out of which Marx and Engels grew as well as to understand the relation of these two thinkers to one another.

The great thing that Marx and Engels and their contemporaries had gotten out of the philosophy of Hegel was the conception of historical change. Hegel had delivered his lectures on the *Philosophy of History* at Berlin University during the winter of 1822–23 (Michelet, it may be remembered, had first come in contact with Vico the next year); and, for all his abstract and mystical way of talking, he had shown a very firm grasp on the idea that the great revolutionary figures of history were not simply remarkable individuals, who moved mountains by their single wills, but the agents through which the forces of the societies behind them accomplished their unconscious purposes. Julius Caesar, says Hegel, for example, did of course fight and conquer his rivals, and destroy the constitution of Rome in order to win his own position of supremacy, but what gave him his importance for the world was the fact that he was performing the necessary feat—only possible through autocratic control—of unifying the Roman Empire.

"It was not then merely his private gain but an unconscious impulse," writes Hegel, "that occasioned the accomplishment of that for which the time was ripe. Such are all great historical men—whose own particular aims involve those large issues which are the will of the World-Spirit. They may be called Heroes, inasmuch as they have derived their purposes and their vocation, not from the calm, regular course of things, sanctioned by the existing order; but from a concealed fount —one which has not attained to phenomenal, present existence —from that inner Spirit, still hidden beneath the surface, which, impinging on the outer world as on a shell, bursts it in pieces, because it is another kernel than that which belonged to the shell in question. They present themselves, therefore, as men who appear to draw the impulse of their life from themselves; and whose deeds have produced a condition of things and a complex of historical relations which appear to be only *their* interest, and *their* work.

"Such individuals have had no consciousness of the general Idea they were unfolding, while prosecuting those aims of theirs; on the contrary, they were practical, political men. But at the same time they were thinking men, who had an insight into the requirements of the time—*what was ripe for development*. This was the very Truth for their age, for their world; the species next in order, so to speak, and which was already formed in the womb of time. It was theirs to know this nascent principle; the necessary, directly sequent step in progress, which their world was to take; to make this their aim, and to expend their energy in promoting it. World-historical men—the Heroes of an epoch—must, therefore, be recognized as its clear-sighted ones; *their* deeds, *their* words are the best of that time. Great men have formed their purposes to satisfy themselves, not others. Whatever prudent designs and counsels they might have learned from others, would be the more limited and inconsistent features in their career; for it was they who best understood affairs; it was they from whom *others* learned and approved—or at least acquiesced in—their policy. For that Spirit which had taken this fresh step in history is the inmost soul of all individuals; but abides in a state of unconsciousness from which the great men in question aroused it. Their fellows, therefore, follow these soul-leaders; for they feel the irresistible power of their own inner spirit thus embodied."

We shall examine a little later the peculiar dynamics of Hegel's conception of historical change. It is enough to note further for the moment that he regarded each of the epochs of human society as constituting an indivisible whole. "We shall have to show," he announces, "that the constitution adopted by a people makes one substance, one spirit, with its religion, its art and philosophy, or, at least, with its conceptions and thoughts: its culture generally; not to expatiate upon the additional influences, *ab extra*, of climate, of neighbors, of its place in the world. A State is an individual totality, of which you cannot select any particular aspect, not even such a supremely important one as its political constitution, and deliberate and decide respecting it in that isolated form."

But where Hegel had tended to assume that the development of history through revolution, the progressive realization of the "Idea," had culminated in the contemporary Prussian state, Marx and Engels, accepting the revolutionary progress but repudiating the divine Idea, looked for a consummation of change to the future, when the realization of the communist idea should have resulted from the next revolution.

They had by this time their own new notions about communism. They had taken stock of their predecessors and, with their own sharp and realistic minds, they had lopped off the sentimentality and fantasy which had surrounded the practical perceptions of the utopians. From Saint-Simon they accepted as valid his discovery that modern politics was simply the science of regulating production; from Fourier, his arraignment of the bourgeois, his consciousness of the ironic contrast between "the frenzy of speculation, the spirit of all-devouring commercialism," which were rampant under the reign of the bourgeoisie and "the brilliant promises of the Enlightenment" which had preceded them; from Owen, the realization that the factory system must be the root of the social revolution. But they saw that the mistake of the utopian socialists had been to imagine that socialism was to be imposed upon society from above by disinterested members of the upper classes. The bourgeoisie as a whole, they believed, could not be induced to go against its own interests. The educator, as Marx was to write in his *Theses on Feuerbach*, must, after all, first have been educated: he is not really confronting disciples with a doctrine that has been supplied him by God; he is merely directing a movement of which he is himself a member and which energizes him and gives him his purpose. Marx and Engels combined the aims of the utopians with Hegel's process of organic development. By the mid-century they were thus able to see quite clearly, as even John Humphrey Noyes did not do, that it was impossible for small communist units by themselves to effect the salvation of society or even to survive in the teeth of the commercial system; that it was not merely unfortunate accidents and disagreeable personal relations which had rendered the American communist movement futile but its ignorance of the mechanics of the class struggle.

Of this class struggle Marx had learned first from his reading of the French historians after he had come to Paris. Augustin Thierry in his *History of the Conquest of England,* published in 1825, had presented the Norman Conquest in terms of a class struggle between the conquerors and the Saxons. Guizot, in his *History of the English Revolution,* had shown, from the bourgeois point of view, the struggle between the middle class and the monarchy.

But it remained to root the class struggle in economics. We have seen how Friedrich Engels had come to appreciate the importance of economics as the result of his experience in Manchester. Karl Marx owed more to his reading. The idea of the fundamental importance of economic interests was not new in the eighteen-forties. A French lawyer named Antoine Barnave, who had been president of the revolutionary Assembly of 1790, had asserted that the difference between classes was the result of economic inequalities, that the class which was in power at any epoch not only made laws for the whole of society in order to guarantee its own hold on its property but also "directed its habits and created its prejudices," that society was constantly changing under the pressure of economic necessities, and that the rising and triumphant bourgeoisie which had displaced the feudal nobility would in turn produce a new aristocracy. Barnave, who was a moderate in politics and compromised himself with the royal family, was guillotined in 1793. A collected edition of his writings was published in 1843; but Marx never seems to have mentioned him, and it is not known whether he had ever read him. In any case, the thought of the period was converging during the first years of the forties toward the Marxist point of view. Friedrich List, the patriotic German economist, had published in 1841 his work on *The National System of Political Economy,* in which he had described the development of society in terms of its industrial phases; and in 1842 a French communist named Dézamy, a former associate of

Cabet, published his *Code de la Communauté*. Karl Marx had read Dézamy at Cologne. This writer had criticized Cabet for believing that anything could be done for labor by invoking the aid of the bourgeoisie, and, accepting the brute fact of the class struggle, had projected a somewhat new kind of community, based on materialism, atheism and science. Though Dézamy had not as yet arrived at any ideas about proletarian tactics, he was sure that the proletariat, among whom he included the peasants, must unite and liberate itself. And it may be noted that the importance of the bottom class had already been emphasized by Babeuf when he had declared in the course of his defense that "the mass of the expropriated, of the proletarians" was generally "agreed to be frightful," that it constituted now "the majority of a nation totally rotten."

In the December of 1843, Marx had written for the *Deutsch-Französische Jahrbücher* a *Critique of the Hegelian Philosophy of Law,* in which he had postulated the proletariat as the class which was to play the new Hegelian role in effecting the emancipation of Germany: "A class in *radical chains,* one of the classes of bourgeois society which does not belong to bourgeois society, an order which brings the break-up of all orders, a sphere which has a universal character by virtue of its universal suffering and lays claim to no *particular right,* because no *particular wrong,* but complete wrong, is being perpetrated against it, which can no longer invoke an *historical* title but only a *human* title, which stands not in a one-sided antagonism to the consequences of the German state but in an absolute antagonism to its assumptions, a sphere, finally, which cannot emancipate itself without freeing itself from all the other spheres of society and thereby freeing all these other spheres themselves, which in a word, as it represents the *complete forfeiting* of humanity itself, can only redeem itself through the *redemption of the whole of humanity.* The *proletariat* represents the dissolution of society as a special order."

Yet even though Marx has got so far, the proletariat remains for him still something in the nature of a philosophical abstraction. The primary emotional motivation in the role which he assigns to the proletariat seems to have been borrowed from his own position as a Jew. "The social emancipation of the Jew is the emancipation of society from Judaism"; "a sphere, finally, which cannot emancipate itself without emancipating all the other spheres of society"—these are the conclusions in almost identical words of two essays written one after the other and published, as it were, side by side. Marx, on the one hand, knew nothing of the industrial proletariat and, on the other hand, refused to take Judaism seriously or to participate in current discussions of the Jewish problem from the point of view of the special case of Jewish culture, holding that the special position of the Jew was vitally involved with his money-lending and banking, and that it would be impossible for him to dissociate himself from these until the system of which they were part should be abolished. The result was that the animus and rebellion which were due to the social disabilities of the Jew as well as the moral insight and the world vision which were derived from his religious tradition were transferred in all their formidable power to an imaginary proletariat.

Perhaps the most important service that Engels performed for Marx at this period was to fill in the blank face and figure of Marx's abstract proletarian and to place him in a real house and real factory. Engels had brought back from England the materials for his book on *The Condition of the Working Class in England in 1844*, and he now sat down at once to get it written. Here was the social background which would make Marx's vision authentic; and here were cycles of industrial prosperity which always collapsed into industrial depressions —due, as Engels could see, to the blind appetites of the competing manufacturers—and which could only result in a general crash: that millennial catastrophe that for Marx was ultimately to dethrone the gods and set the wise spirit of man in their place.

And for Engels, on his side, here in Marx was the backing of moral conviction and of intellectual strength which was to enable him to keep his compass straight in his relation to that contemporary society whose crimes he understood so well, but out of which he himself had grown, and to which he was still organically bound as Marx was not. Besides, Marx had more weight and more will. Engels wrote with lucidity and ease; he had sensibility and measure and humor. He is so much more like a French writer of the Enlightenment—something between a Condorcet and a Diderot—than a philosopher of the German school that one is inclined to accept the tradition that his family had French Protestant blood. This young man without academic training was an immensely accomplished fellow: he had already learned to write English so well that he was able to contribute to Robert Owen's paper; and his French was as good as his English. He had a facility in acquiring information and a journalist's sense of how things were going; his collaborator Marx used to say that Engels was always ahead of him. But Engels had not Marx's drive; it is what we miss in his writing. From the beginning Marx is able to find such quarrel in matters like the wood-theft debates that he can shake us with indignation against all violators of human relations; while Engels, with his larger experience of the cruelties and degradations of industrial life, does not—even in *The Condition of the Working Class in England*—rouse us to protest or to fight but tends rather to resolve the conflict in an optimistic feeling about the outcome. "Marx was a genius," wrote Engels later. "The rest of us were talented at best."

It is perhaps not indulging too far the current tendency toward this kind of speculation to suggest that Marx took over for Engels something of the prestige of paternal authority which the younger man had rejected in his own father. There was always something boyish about Engels: he writes Marx in the September of 1847, when he is twenty-seven, that he does not want to accept the vice-presidency of one of their communist committees, because he looks "so frightfully youthful." Young Friedrich had been rebelling since his teens against old Caspar Engels' combination of the serious crassness of business with the intolerance of religion; but old Engels' decisions for his son had hitherto determined his practical career. And, in spite of Friedrich's final enfranchisement from theology, some of the fervor of his father's faith had nevertheless been communicated to him. He had grown up in Barmen-Elberfeld under the pulpit of the great Calvinist preacher, Friedrich

Wilhelm Krummacher, who with an eloquence that Engels had found impressive had used to alternate the legends of the Bible and a majestic oratory drawn from its language with illustrations from ordinary life and who had harrowed and subdued his congregations with the terrible Calvinist logic, which led them either to damnation or grace. Karl Marx was a great moralist, too, and, on occasion, a formidable preacher. He seems to have provided the young apostate from Pietism with a new spiritual center of gravity.

When Engels went back to Barmen, at any rate, to live with his family and work in the family business, he continued to correspond with Marx; and he grew more and more dissatisfied and uncomfortable in an impatience which this correspondence must have fed.

He had evidently contracted some sort of engagement with a young lady of his own class and locality before he had left Barmen for Manchester; and now this seems to involve in his mind—his letters to Marx leave it all rather dark—the obligation to go to work for the firm. "I have let myself in through the persuasions of my brother-in-law and the melancholy faces of my parents for at least an attempt at this filthy trade, and for fourteen days now I've been working in the office—the outlook in connection with my love affair has also brought me to it; but I was depressed before I started in: money-grubbing is too frightful; Barmen is too frightful, the waste of time is too frightful, and above all it is too frightful to continue to be, not merely a bourgeois, but actually a manufacturer, a bourgeois working against the proletariat. A few days in my old man's factory have compelled me to recognize the horror of it, which I'd rather overlooked before. . . . If it weren't for the fact that I apply myself every day to getting down on paper in my book the most dreadful accounts of English conditions, I believe I should have gone to seed already, but this has at least kept the rage in my bones. One can very well be a communist and yet keep up a bourgeois position, if only one *doesn't write;* but to work at serious communist propaganda and at industry and trade at the same time—that's really absolutely impossible."

He was holding working-class meetings with Moses Hess, who had become his ally in the Wuppertal; and they were getting out a communist paper in Elberfeld. As the weeks go on, his letters to Marx become irradiated by his characteristic hopefulness. One found communists everywhere now, he wrote.

But now old Engels became indignant, tragic. He could not stand Friedrich's associating with Hess, he could not stand his preaching communism in Barmen. "If it were not for the sake of my mother, who has a sweet and human nature and is only powerless against my father, and whom I really love, it would never occur to me for a moment to make even the pettiest concession to my fanatical and despotic old man. But my mother is gradually grieving herself sick and gets a headache that lasts for eight days every time she is specially worried about me—so I can't endure it any longer, I must get away, and I hardly know how I'm going to be able to get through the few weeks that I'll still have to stay."

Finally, he learned that the police were lying in wait for him, and he left Barmen in the spring of '45. There is a passage in one of his letters from which it is possible to form the conjecture that he had been rather hoping to get into trouble in order to be forced to part with, as well as perhaps to be compromised in the eyes of, the young lady to whom he was somehow committed.

He joined Karl Marx in Brussels. The latter had himself had to leave Paris as a result of expulsion from France at the insistence of the German government, which was worried by the activities in Paris of revolutionary German refugees, and on an order from that Guizot, now Prime Minister, who had helped teach Marx the mechanics of the class struggle.

Then Engels went straight back to Manchester to find his friend Mary Burns again and to bring her over to France. He took Karl Marx along on the trip—exhibited to him the activities of Manchester and introduced him to the work of the English political economists. He reminded him a quarter of a century later of how they had used to look out through the colored panes of the bay-window of the Manchester library on weather that was always fine. It had been the light of that human intellect which they felt was now coming to maturity and which would vindicate the dignity of man, in the midst of that inhuman horror of filthiness and deformity and disease that hemmed the city in.

9 Marx and Engels: Grinding the Lens

The role which Marx performed for Engels—that of compass that kept him from sailing off his course—he performed also for the Left as a whole.

We have seen how the tradition of the French Revolution passed first into democratic rhetoric, then into skeptical humanism and anti-democratic science, and finally into anti-social nihilism, in proportion as the French historians came more and more to identify their interests with those of the French bourgeoisie and as the ideals of the bourgeoisie became more overwhelming and more vulgar. As a Jew, Marx stood somewhat outside society; as a man of genius, above it. With none of the handicaps of the proletarian from the point of view of intellectual training or of general knowledge of the world, he was yet not a middle-class man—not even a member of that middle-class "élite" in whom men like Renan and Flaubert believed; and he had a character that could not be sidetracked by the threats or baits of bourgeois society. Certainly his character was domineering; certainly his personality was arrogant, and abnormally mistrustful and jealous; certainly he was capable of vindictiveness and of what seems to us gratuitous malignity. But if we are repelled by these traits in Marx, we must remember that a normally polite and friendly person could hardly have accomplished the task which it was the destiny of Marx to carry through—a task that required the fortitude to resist or to break off all those ties which—as they involve us in the general life of society—limit our views and cause our purposes to shift. We must remember that such a man as, say, Renan, who advises us "to accept every human being as good and to treat him with amiability till we have actual proof that he is not" and who confesses that he has sometimes lied in his relations with contemporary writers "not out of interest but out of kindness"— we must remember that the moral force of Renan becomes ultimately dissolved and enfeebled in proportion as it is diffused by his urbanity.

Marx and Engels in their books of this period between their meeting and the Revolution of 1848—*The Holy Family, The German Ideology, The Poverty of Philosophy*—were attempting to arrive at a definite formulation of their own revolutionary point of view, and this involved a good deal of destructive work, especially on their German contemporaries, as they extricated the insights that seemed to them valid from the cobwebs of metaphysics and from the divagations by which the bourgeois thinkers, as a result of their stake in the *status quo,* were escaping the logical conclusions from their premises.

The early Marx and Engels are quite exhilarating and very funny when they are knocking the philosophers' heads together with the brutal but not ungenial German humor and performing variations on the theme which they quote from their friend and disciple Heine: "The land belongs to the Russians and French, The sea belongs to the British; But we possess in the cloudland of dreams The uncontested dominion." One must imagine a more profound Mencken and Nathan engaged on a greater task. Marx and Engels did find themselves with a marvelous field for the exercise of satirical criticism: their butt, as in the case of Mencken and Nathan, was the whole intellectual life of a nation. And so many of their old allies, as time went on, took to professing compromise forms of Christianity, editing conservative papers or whooping it up for Prussian imperialism. Even Moses Hess, from whom Engels had learned so much, was associated with that school of "True Socialists," who seemed to the inventors of Marxism to have arrived at the principles of socialism only to transport them back again into the pure empyrean of abstraction and who seemed also to be playing into the hands of the reaction by opposing the agitation for a constitution on the part of the big bourgeoisie, under the impression that they were being uncompromising but actually—so Marx and Engels believed— in order to defend their own petty-bourgeois interests.

Marx by himself is not so genial. His own opinions seem always to have been arrived at through a close criticism of the opinions of others, as if the sharpness and force of his mind could only really exert themselves in attacks on the minds of others, as if he could only find out what he thought by making distinctions that excluded the thoughts of others. In following this method, he is sometimes merely peevish, sometimes unbearably boring; it is true, as Franz Mehring has said, that in his polemical writings of this period he is as likely to make a merely pedantic or a far-fetched and silly point as a piercing and decisive one. When Marx, in *The Holy Family*, attacked Bruno Bauer and his brothers, even Engels protested that the inordinate length of Marx's analysis was out of all proportion to the contempt he expressed for his subjects.

Engels himself is usually flowing and limpid; but it is characteristic of Marx that he should alternate between a blind derisive nagging with which he persists in worrying his opponent through endless unnecessary pages, reluctant to let him drop, an arid exercise of the Hegelian dialectic which simply hypnotizes the reader with its paradoxes and eventually puts him to sleep—and the lightning of a divine insight. In spite of all Marx's enthusiasm for the "human," he is either inhumanly dark and dead or almost superhumanly brilliant. He always is either contracted inside his own ego till he is actually unable to summon enough fellow-feeling to get on with other human beings at all or he has expanded to a comprehensive world-view which, skipping over individuals altogether, as his former attitude was unable to reach them, takes in continents, classes, long ages.

We may note the episode of his polemics with Proudhon as the type of his relationships of this period, which remained the type, even intensified with time, of his relationships through the whole of his life. It has also a special importance in the development by Marx of his system.

Marx had made the acquaintance of Proudhon in the summer of 1844. P.-J. Proudhon was a barrelmaker's son, who had risen to be a printer and who had educated himself in a remarkable way, teaching himself to read Greek, Latin and Hebrew. In 1840, he had published a book of which the title had asked the question, "What Is Property?" and in which he had given an answer: "Property is theft," that had made its impression on the age. Marx had felt considerable respect for Proudhon and during long nocturnal sessions in Paris, had expounded to him the doctrine of Hegel.

Two years later Marx wrote Proudhon from Brussels inviting him to contribute to an organized correspondence, designed to keep the Communists in different countries in touch with one another, which he and Engels were getting up. He took the occasion to warn Proudhon in a postscript against a journalist named Karl Grün, one of the "True Socialists," against whom he makes charges rather indefinite but stinging in tone and sinister in implication.

Proudhon replies that he will be glad to participate, but that other business "combined with natural laziness" will prevent his really doing much about it; and he goes on to "take the liberty of making certain reservations, which are suggested by various passages of your letter." "Let us by all means collaborate," says Proudhon, "in trying to discover the laws of society, the way in which these laws work out, the best method to go about investigating them; but for God's sake, after we have demolished all the dogmatisms *a priori*, let us not of all things attempt in our turn to instil another kind of doctrine into the people; let us not fall into the contradiction of your compatriot Martin Luther, who, after overthrowing the Catholic theology, immediately addressed himself to the task, with a great armory of excommunications and anathemas, of establishing a Protestant theology. Germany for three centuries now has been obliged to occupy herself exclusively with the problem of getting rid of M. Luther's job of reconstruction; let us not, by contriving any more such restorations, leave any more such tasks for the human race. I applaud with all my heart your idea of bringing to light all the varieties of opinion; let us have good and sincere polemics; let us show the world an example of a learned and far-sighted tolerance; but simply because we are at the head of a movement, let us not set ourselves up as the leaders of a new intolerance, let us not pose as the apostles of a new religion—even though this religion be the religion of logic, the religion of reason itself. Let us welcome, let us encourage all the protests; let us condemn all the exclusions, all the mysticisms; let us never regard a question as closed, and even after we have exhausted our last argument, let us begin again, if necessary, with eloquence and irony. On that condition, I shall be delighted to take part in your association—but otherwise, no!"

Proudhon added that M. Grün was in exile with no financial resources and with a wife and children to support, and that, though he, Proudhon, understood Marx's "philosophic wrath," he could not regard it as unnatural that M. Grün should, as Marx had accused him of doing, "exploit modern ideas in order to live." As a matter of fact, M. Grün was about to undertake a translation of Proudhon's own work, and Proudhon hoped that M. Marx, correcting an unfavorable opinion produced by a moment of irritation, would do what he could to help M. Grün out of his straits by promoting the sale of the product.

The result of this incident was that Marx was to set upon Proudhon's new book with a ferocity entirely inconsonant with the opinion of the value of Proudhon's earlier work which he had expressed and which he was to reiterate later. But in the course of vivisecting Proudhon and exposing his basic assumptions, Marx was led to lay down for the first time in a book that reached the public his own set of counter-assumptions. Karl Marx had originally praised Proudhon for his achievement in "subjecting private property, which is the basis of political economy, to . . . the first examination of a decisive, relentless and at the same time scientific character." Now Marx saw that the axiom "Property is theft," in referring to a violation of property, itself presupposed real rights in property.

It was the old Abstract Man again, who in this case had an inalienable right to own things and who actually concealed the petty bourgeois. Proudhon declared strikes to be crimes against a fundamental "economic system," against "the necessities of the established order"; and out of the Hegelian theory of development, which Marx had been attempting to explain to him, he had produced a new kind of utopian socialism, which did not require for its realization a genuine Hegelian emergence of the working class as the new force that was to overthrow the old, but which was an affair merely of succoring the poor under the existing system of property relations.

Marx himself now went back to Hegel to get away from the Abstract Man, whom Feuerbach had assumed as well as Proudhon, and to restore the Historical Man, whose principles together with his subsistence were always bound up with the special conditions of the period in which he lived. New conditions could not be inculcated; they had to be developed out of the old conditions through the conflict of class with class.

And here we encounter what Karl Marx himself claimed to be one of his only original contributions to the system that afterwards came to be known as Marxism. Engels says that when he, Engels, arrived in Brussels in the spring of 1845, Marx put before him the fully developed theory that all history was a succession of struggles between an exploiting and an exploited class. These struggles were thus the results of the methods of production which prevailed during the various periods—that is, of the methods by which people succeeded in providing themselves with food and clothing and the other requirements of life. Such apparently inspired and independent phenomena as politics, philosophy and religion arose in reality from the social phenomena. The current struggle between the exploiters and the exploited had reached a point at which the exploited, the proletariat, had been robbed of all its human rights and had so come to stand for the primary rights of humanity, and at which the class that owned and controlled the industrial machine was becoming increasingly unable to distribute its products—so that the victory of the workers over the owners, the taking-over by the former of the machine, would mean the end of class society altogether and the liberation of the spirit of man.

Marx and Engels—who had assimilated with remarkable rapidity the social and historical thinking of their time—thus emerged with a complete and coherent theory, which cleared up more mysteries of the past, simplified more complications of the present and opened up into the future a more practicable-appearing path, than any such theory which had been hitherto proposed. And they had done more: they had introduced a "dynamic principle" (a phrase of Marx's in his doctor's dissertation)—we shall have more to say of it later—which got the whole system going, motivated convincingly a progression in history, as none of the other historical generalizations had done, and which not only compelled one's interest in a great drama but forced one to recognize that one was part of it and aroused one to play a noble role.

Of this theory they had given the first full account in the opening section of *The German Ideology*, begun that autumn in Brussels; but, as this book was never published, it was not till the *Communist Manifesto*, written for the international Communist League at the turn of the year, 1847–48, that their ideas really reached the world.

Here their glass has been turned quite away from the large and vague abstract shapes that have inhabited the German heavens—they are not concerned any longer even to mock at them—and directed upon the anatomy of actual society. The *Communist Manifesto* combines the terseness and trenchancy of Marx, his logic which anchors the present in the past, with the candor and humanity of Engels, his sense of the trend of the age. But nowhere can we see demonstrated more strikingly what Engels owed to Marx than at this point where we can compare the first draught by Engels with the material after it had been worked over by Marx. The *Principles of Communism* by Engels—written, it is true, in haste—is a lucid and authoritative account of the contemporary industrial situation, which generates little emotion and leads up to no compelling climax. The *Communist Manifesto* is dense with the packed power of high explosives. It compresses with terrific vigor into forty or fifty pages a general theory of history, an analysis of European society and a program for revolutionary action.

This program was "the forcible overthrow of the whole extant social order," and the putting in force of the following measures: "1. Expropriation of landed property, and the use of land rents to defray state expenditures; 2. A vigorously graded income tax; 3. Abolition of the right of inheritance; 4. Confiscation of the property of all émigrés and rebels; 5. Centralization of credit in the hands of the State, by means of a national bank with state capital and an exclusive monopoly; 6. Centralization of the means of transport in the hands of the State; 7. Increase of national factories and means of production, cultivation of uncultivated land, and improvement of cultivated land in accordance with a general plan; 8. Universal and equal obligation to work; organization of industrial armies, especially for agriculture; 9. Agriculture and urban industry to work hand-in-hand, in such a way as, by degrees, to obliterate the distinction between town and country; 10. Public and free education of all children. Abolition of factory work for children in its present form. Education and material production to be combined."

But to present the *Communist Manifesto* from the point of view of its evolution is to deprive it of its impact on the emotions and of its effect of a searching shaft of light. The case against the Marxist attitude has been put at its most eloquent by Proudhon in the letter we have quoted above. It is true that Marx and Engels were dogmatic; it is true that they were unjust to individuals—for Engels had now become almost as intolerant as Marx, almost as intolerant as old Caspar, his father. But such boldness and such ruthlessness were required to blow down the delusions of that age. We have indicated how both the historians and the socialists had been addicted to dealing with troublesome problems by opposing to them the capitalized ideals—a special export, precisely, from Germany —of abstract virtues, ideas, institutions. These words had been performing the same function as "that blessed word Mesopotamia," from which the pious old woman in the story explained that she had absorbed so much comfort in the exercise of reading her Bible; and they were never really the same again after the *Communist Manifesto*.

To those people who talked about Justice, Marx and Engels replied, "Justice for whom? Under capitalism it is the proletariat who get caught most often and punished most severely, and who also, since they must starve when they are jobless, are driven to commit most of the crimes." To people who talked about Liberty, they answered, "Liberty for whom?— You will never be able to liberate the worker without restricting the liberty of the owner." To people who talked about Family Life and Love—which communism was supposed to be destroying—they answered that these things, as society stood, were the exclusive possession of the bourgeoisie, since the families of the proletariat had been dismembered by the employment of women and children in the factories and its young women reduced to love-making in mills and mines or to selling themselves when mills and mines were shut down. To people who talked about the Good and the True, Marx and Engels replied that we should never know what these meant till we had moralists and philosophers who were no longer involved in societies based on exploitation and so could have no possible stake in oppression.

With all this, the *Communist Manifesto* gave expression to the bitterest protest that had perhaps yet been put into print against the versions of all these fine ideals which had come to prevail during the bourgeois era: "Wherever the bourgeoisie has risen to power, it has destroyed all feudal, patriarchal and idyllic relationships. It has ruthlessly torn asunder the motley feudal ties that bound men to their 'natural superiors'; it has left no other bond between man and man but crude self-interest and callous 'cash-payment.' It has drowned pious zeal, chivalrous enthusiasm and popular sentimentalism in the chill waters of selfish calculation. It has degraded personal dignity to the level of exchange value; and in place of countless dearly bought chartered freedoms, it has set up one solitary unscrupulous freedom—that is, freedom of trade. In a word, it has replaced exploitation veiled in religious and political illusions by exploitation that is open, unashamed, direct and brutal."

The last words of the *Communist Manifesto*, with their declaration of war against the bourgeoisie, mark a turning-point in socialist thought. The slogan of the League of the Just had been: "All men are brothers." But to this Marx and Engels would not subscribe: Marx declared that there were whole categories of men whom he did not care to recognize as brothers; and they provided the new slogan which was to stand at the end: "Let the ruling classes tremble at the prospect of a communist revolution. Proletarians have nothing to lose but their chains. They have a world to win. PROLETARIANS OF ALL LANDS, UNITE!" The idea of righteous war, and with it the idea of righteous hatred, has been substituted for the socialism of Saint-Simon, which had presented itself as a new kind of Christianity. All men are no longer brothers; there is no longer any merely *human* solidarity. The "truly human" is that which is to be realized when we shall have arrived at the society without classes. In the meantime, those elements of society which alone can bring about such a future —the disfranchised proletariat and the revolutionary bourgeois thinkers—in proportion as they feel group solidarity among themselves, must cease to feel human solidarity with their antagonists. Their antagonists—who have "left between man and man no bond except self-interest and callous 'cash-payment' "—have irreparably destroyed that solidarity.

We have hitherto described Marx and Engels in terms of their national and personal origins. The *Communist Manifesto* may be taken to mark the point at which they attain their full moral stature, at which they assume, with full consciousness of what they are doing, the responsibilities of a new and heroic role. They were the first great social thinkers of their century to try to make themselves, by deliberate discipline, both classless and international. They were able to look out on Western Europe and to penetrate, through patriotic sentiments, political catchwords, philosophical theorizings and the practical demands of labor, to the general social processes which were everywhere at work in the background; and it seemed clear to them that all the movements of opposition were converging toward the same great end.

The *Communist Manifesto* was little read when it was first printed—in London—in February, 1848. Copies were sent to the few hundred members of the Communist League; but it was never at that time put on sale. It probably had no serious influence on the events of 1848; and afterwards it passed into eclipse with the defeat of the workers' movement in Paris. Yet it gradually permeated the Western world. The authors wrote in 1872 that two translations had been made into French and that twelve editions had appeared in Germany. There had been early translations into Polish and Danish; and in 1850, it had appeared in English. There had been no mention in the *Communist Manifesto* of either Russia or the United States: both at that time seemed to Marx and Engels the "pillars of the European social order"—Russia as a "bulwark of reaction," a source of raw materials for Western Europe and a market for manufactured goods, the United States as a market and source of supply and as an outlet for European emigration. But it had been found worth while by the early sixties to translate the Manifesto into Russian; and in the year 1871 three translations appeared in the United States. So it did actually reach that audience of the "workers of all lands" to whom it had been addressed: it made its way to all continents, both hemispheres, rivaling the Christian Bible. As I write, it has just been translated into Afrikaans, a Dutch dialect spoken in South Africa.

Marx and Engels, still in their youth and still with the hope of '48 ahead of them, had in a moment of clairvoyance and confidence such as they were never quite to know again, spoken, and spoken to be heard, to all who had been crushed by the industrial system and who could think and were ready to fight.

10 Marx and Engels Take a Hand at Making History

We were concerned in the first sections of this study with writers who were attempting retrospectively to dominate the confusion of history by imposing on it the harmony of art, who participated in the affairs of the present only at most through polemical lectures like Michelet (whose suspension from the Collège de France elicited from Engels only the comment that it would combine with his bourgeois ideas to promote the popularity of his history); or, like Renan, in running once for office and failing to get elected. With Marx and Engels we come to men of equal genius who are trying to make the historical imagination intervene in human affairs as a direct constructive force.

There are several reasons why Marx and Engels have been inadequately appreciated as writers. Certainly one is that their conclusions ran counter to the interests of the classes who read most and who create the reputations of writers. The tendency to boycott Marx and Engels on the part of literary historians as well as on the part of economists has given a striking corroboration of their theory of the influence of class upon culture. But there is also another reason. Marx and Engels were no longer aiming at philosophical or literary glory. They believed that they had discovered the levers by which to regulate the processes of human society, to release and canalize its forces; and, though neither had any gifts as a speaker or much talent for handling men in a political way, they attempted to make their intellectual abilities count as directly as possible for the accomplishment of revolutionary ends. They were trying to make their writing what has in architecture come to be called "functional" as even the journalism of Marat or the oratory of Danton had not been. Because their aims were international, they did not care even to make their mark in German thought. Thus Marx cast his reply to Proudhon in French; and the writings of Marx and Engels during this period show a mixture of French, German and English—a body of work in newspaper articles, polemics and manifestoes, which has only recently been got together by the Russians and published in a complete form.

Marx and Engels had, to be sure, had their difficulties in getting their full-length philosophical writings published—difficulties due to the same kind of causes which have since prevented their being circulated and read. *The German Ideology*, for example, which had cost them a good deal of labor, was never printed except in fragments during their lifetimes. But though it contained the first complete formulation of their general point of view, they reconciled themselves to its suppression with the thought that this formulation was important primarily to themselves: "We had no wish," says Engels, "to propound these new scientific conclusions in ponderous tomes for professional wiseacres. On the contrary. We had both of us entered bag and baggage into the political movement; we had certain connections with the educated world . . . and close ties with the organized proletariat. We were in duty bound to base our point of view upon a firm scientific foundation; but it was no less incumbent upon us to convince the European proletariat in general and the German proletariat in particular. No sooner had we made the matter clear to ourselves than we set to work to do so."

We must realize how radical and how difficult a step for German intellectuals of the forties was this getting into relations with the working class. Herzen says of Heine and his circle that they never "knew the people . . . to understand the moan of humanity lost in the bogs of today, they had to translate it into Latin and to arrive at their ideas through the Gracchi and the proletariat of Rome"; that on the occasions when they emerged from their "sublimated world," like Faust in Auerbach's cellar, they were hindered like him by "a spirit of scholastic scepticism from simply looking and seeing" and "would immediately hasten back from living sources to the sources of history: there they felt more at home."

Heine tells us himself of his embarrassment on meeting the Communist tailor Weitling: "What particularly offended my pride was the fellow's utter lack of respect while he conversed with me. He did not remove his cap and, while I was standing before him, he remained sitting, with his right knee raised by the aid of his right hand to his very chin and steadily rubbing the raised leg with his left hand just above the ankle. At first, I assumed that this disrespectful attitude was the result of a habit he had acquired while working at the tailoring trade, but I was soon convinced of my error. When I asked him why he was always rubbing his leg in this way, Weitling replied in a nonchalant manner, as if it were the most ordinary occurrence, that he had been compelled to wear chains in the various German prisons in which he had been confined and that as the iron ring which held his knee had frequently been too small, he had developed a chronic irritation of the skin, which was the cause of his perpetual scratching of his leg. I confess that I recoiled when the tailor Weitling told me about these chains. I, who had once in Münster kissed with burning lips the relics of the tailor John of Leyden—the chains he had worn, the pincers with which he had been tortured and which are preserved in the Münster City Hall—I who had made an exalted cult of the dead tailor, now felt an insurmountable aversion for this living tailor, William Weitling, though both were apostles and martyrs in the same cause."

Karl Marx's relations with Weitling were strikingly different.

Wilhelm Weitling was the illegitimate son of a German laundress and one of Napoleon's officers, who had abandoned the mother and the child and whose name the son did not even know. He had been apprenticed as a boy to a tailor, but he hated the army so much that when his time came to do military service, he ran away and took to the road. He had educated himself, learned the ancient languages, had a project for a universal language; at twenty-seven he had written a book called *Humanity as It Is and as It Ought to Be*. At that time—in the thirties—the tradition of Babeuf had revived in the working-class quarters of Paris; and a society called the League of the Just had been founded in association with the Babouvist movement by a group of refugee German tailors. Weitling became a member and presently emerged into prominence as the most important German leader of the working class. In 1842, at that moment when the air was becoming saturated with the ideas which were so soon to condense into Marxism, Weitling had published a communist book called *Guarantees of Harmony and Freedom*, which Marx had hailed as the "tremendous and brilliant debut of the German working class." In the meantime, Weitling had been expelled from Paris as the result of taking part in Blanqui's insurrection of May 12, 1838; and, seeking asylum in Switzerland, had there been convicted of blasphemy and sentenced to six months in jail, in consequence of publishing a book in which he had described Jesus Christ as both a communist and an illegitimate child. Thereafter he was hounded from pillar to post, becoming in the process, not unnaturally, a crank with something like delusions of persecutions as well as a communist saint. He lived a life of ascetic simplicity, and owned no property save the tools of his trade.

At last, he turned up in Brussels, and Marx and Engels had to decide how to deal with him. Engels says that he was received by the Marxes "with well-nigh superhuman forbearance"; but Marx was never the man to forbear very long with a rival. Nor was he ever able to refrain very long from reminding self-educated thinkers who had lifted themselves out of the lower classes, as Proudhon and Weitling had done, that they were not doctors of philosophy like himself. (Wilhelm Liebknecht, who was a licensed philologist, tells how Marx used to delight to try to embarrass him by showing him passages in Aristotle and Aeschylus which he felt sure he would be unable to translate.)

Weitling was invited to a meeting (March 30, 1846) held by the Brussels communists "for the purpose of agreeing, if possible, on a common tactic for the working-class movement." The occasion has been reported by a Russian, a young intellectual named Annenkov, who was traveling and had a letter to Marx.

Annenkov has left a vivid description. Marx presented, he says, "a type of man all compact of energy, force of character and unshakable conviction—a type who was highly remarkable in his outward appearance as well. With a thick black mane of hair, his hands all covered with hair and his coat buttoned up askew, he gave one the impression of a man who had the right and the power to command respect, even though his aspect and his behavior might seem to be rather odd. His movements were awkward, but bold and self-assured; his manners violated all the social conventions. But they were proud and slightly contemptuous, and the metallic timbre of his voice was remarkably well adapted to the radical verdicts which he delivered on men and things. He never spoke at all except in judgments that brooked no denial and that were rendered even sharper, and rather disagreeable, by the harsh tone of everything he said. This note expressed his firm conviction of his mission to impress himself on men's minds, to dominate their wills, and to compel them to follow in his train. . . .

"The tailor-agitator Weitling was a good-looking blond young man in rather a foppishly cut frock-coat and with a beard rather foppishly trimmed, and resembled a commercial traveler rather than the stern and embittered worker whom I had imagined.

"After we had been casually introduced to one another—which was accompanied on Weitling's part by a certain affected politeness—we sat down at a little green table, at the head of which Marx took his place, pencil in hand and with his leonine head bent over a sheet of paper, while his inseparable friend and companion in propaganda, the tall erect Engels, with his English distinction and gravity, opened the meeting with a speech. He talked about the necessity for labor reformers' arriving at some sort of clarity out of the confusion of their opposing views and formulating some common doctrine which should serve as a banner to rally around for all those followers who had neither the time nor the ability to occupy themselves with questions of theory. But before

Engels had finished his speech, Marx suddenly raised his head and hurled at Weitling the following question:

" 'Tell us, Weitling, you who have made so much stir in Germany with your communist propaganda and have won over so many workers so that they have thereby lost their work and their bread, with what arguments do you defend your social-revolutionary activity and on what basis do you propose to ground them?' . . .

"A painful discussion began, which, however, as I shall show, did not last very long.

"Weitling seemed to want to keep the discussion on the plane of the commonplaces of liberal rhetoric. With a serious and troubled face, he began to explain that it was not his task to develop new economic theories, but to make use of those which, as was to be seen in France, were best adapted to open the eyes of the workers to their terrible situation, to all the wrongs committed against them." . . .

"He spoke at length, but, to my surprise and in contrast to the speech of Engels, unclearly and even with confused delivery, frequently repeating and correcting himself; and he had difficulty in reaching the conclusions that sometimes followed, sometimes preceded, his premises." He was confronted at this meeting, says Annenkov, with an audience of quite a different kind from that which had come to his workshop or read his writings.

"He would no doubt have spoken even longer, had not Marx broken in upon him with angrily glowering brows." Marx sarcastically declared "that it was simple fraud to arouse the people without any sound and considered basis for their activity. The awakening of fantastic hopes . . . would never lead to the salvation of those who suffered, but on the contrary to their undoing. 'To go to the workers in Germany without strictly scientific ideas and concrete doctrine would mean an empty and unscrupulous playing with propaganda, which would inevitably involve, on the one hand, the setting-up of an inspired apostle and, on the other hand, simply asses who would listen to him with open mouth.' " Weitling's role, he added, with a gesture toward Annenkov, might be all very well in Russia; but in a civilized country like Germany, one could do nothing without solid doctrine.

"The pale cheeks of Weitling colored, and his speech became animated and direct. In a voice that quivered with excitement, he began to insist that an individual who had brought together hundreds of men in the name of the ideas of Justice, Solidarity and Brotherly Love, could hardly be characterized as a lazy and empty fellow; that he, Weitling, was able to console himself against the present attack by recalling the hundreds of grateful letters, declarations and demonstrations, that had come to him from all the ends of the fatherland; and that it might be that his modest efforts for the common good were more important than closet analysis and criticism carried out far from the suffering world and the oppression of the people.

"These last words made Marx lose his temper: enraged, he struck his fist on the table with such violence that he shook the lamp, and, leaping up, he shouted: 'Ignorance has never helped anybody yet!'

"We followed his example and stood up, too. The conference was at an end."

Annenkov, "extremely astonished," quickly said good-by to Marx, who was still transported with rage. When Annenkov left, he was striding up and down the room.

It was the first Marxist party purge (the next victim was an unfortunate German named Kriege who had gone to the United States and who was bringing out a communist paper consecrated to the spirit of Love); and it will be seen that Karl Marx did not hesitate, in his search for the springs of power in the working class, to break with or even to break the working-class leaders themselves. He could not persuade or win; except in the case of a very few devoted disciples, he had no ability to evoke personal loyalty; he was unable to induce people to work for him who challenged him or with whom he disagreed; and, in relation to the working class particularly, although he was not like Heine afraid of them, his connections with them remained rather remote. Yet he was right in his criticism of Weitling: it was a matter of primary importance to disillusion the labor movement with the old-fashioned utopian socialism. It was his task to make the working class understand that they must study the processes of history, must watch for tides and judge situations; to convince them, in a word, once for all that what they needed was not mere preaching, but statesmanship. Karl Schurz, who saw Marx at Cologne during the Revolution of 1848, declared that Marx's manner was habitually so "provoking and intolerable" that his proposals were invariably voted down, "because everyone whose feelings had been hurt by his conduct was inclined to support everything that Marx did not favor." Yet his arrogance and coldness were negative distortions which were compensated for by the positive strength of his capacity to look at politics objectively and of his patience in the interests of the long view. The labor movement did have to learn from Marx.

Certainly he played during the events of 1848–49 a stout and energetic part.

He had joined the League of the Just—which was renamed the Communist League—in the spring of 1847. In the meantime, the rapid building of the European railroads that had taken place during 1846 and 1847 had been followed by a severe depression, in which something like fifty thousand men were thrown out of work. The revolution broke out in France in February, 1848, after the unprovoked firing by soldiers on a peaceful democratic demonstration, with the immediate fall of Louis-Philippe and the proclamation of the French Republic. Karl Marx, still in Brussels, helped to draft an address to be sent to the French Provisional Government. A Belgian police report says that he contributed to buy arms for the Belgian workers five thousand of the six thousand francs which he had induced his mother to give him in settlement of his claims against his father's estate. He was expelled by the Belgian authorities; went to Paris, and there established a new headquarters for the Communist League. He opposed a revolutionary expedition undertaken by a group of exiles, courageous but vague about their objectives, who marched into Germany and were put to rout as soon as they had crossed the Rhine.

Marx and Engels themselves returned to Germany, arrived on April 10 in Cologne, where a branch of the Communist League had set in motion throughout the Rhineland a movement of petitions for reform and where a repercussion to February 23 had just occurred when soldiers had shot into a demonstration led by the Communist League. The head of the League was a man named Gottschalk, the son of a Jewish butcher, who had studied medicine and practised among the poor in the working-class quarters of Cologne. He was a passionate partisan of these people and had organized a Workers' Union. When the Prussians, under pressure of agitation, granted a national assembly, Gottschalk advocated a boycott by the workers. Karl Marx was opposed to this: he believed that it was useless for the working class to strike for their own demands until the bourgeois revolution had been won. He got control of a newspaper, the *Neue Rheinische Zeitung;* put into it all that was left of his patrimony as well as such money as Jenny possessed; liquidated the Communist League, in the teeth of the protests of its other leaders, on the ground that, since he now had an organ through which to exercise his guidance, the organization was no longer necessary; and carried on a campaign for "democracy," in which working-class interests as well as communism were carefully kept out of sight. He also got control of the Workers' Union, while Gottschalk was in prison.

These months of the *Neue Rheinische Zeitung* were certainly Marx's most formidable period as a publicist. Engels, who handled the foreign policy, declared afterwards that every one of their articles had struck like a shell and burst; and Lenin said in 1914 that the paper was still the "unsurpassed" model of what an "organ of the revolutionary proletariat" ought to be. Day after day and month after month, Marx's goad dug the shanks of the Assembly, inciting it to bolder action; the breath of his freezing criticism blasted the backs of their necks. But the deputies, unused to political power, debated philosophical principles and could not agree as to what kind of central executive to set up at a time when authority was vital. The result was that the Prussian Friedrich Wilhelm concluded a truce in the war with Denmark without consulting the National Assembly, refused to become a constitutional monarch when it elected him, sent troops to put down insurrections on behalf of the constitution it had prepared, and finally—in June, 1849—sent the deputies about their business. Gottschalk before this had been released from jail and had led an attack on Marx which recalls the reproaches of Weitling: "They are not in earnest about the salvation of the oppressed. The distress of the workers, the hunger of the poor, have only a scientific doctrinaire interest for them." And, "Why should we, men of the proletariat, spill our blood for this? Must we really plunge deliberately into the purgatory of a decrepit capitalist domination in order to avoid a medieval hell, as you, Mister Preacher, proclaim to us, in order to attain from there the nebulous heaven of your Communist creed?" Engels, questioned later in life about Gottschalk, asserted that he had been "a total hollow-head," "a perfect demagogue for the conditions of that time," "a true prophet, above every scruple, and so, capable of any low act." Between them, they split the Workers' Union, and the Reaction did the rest. Gottschalk went back to his practice, worked in the slums during the cholera epidemic, caught the disease and died that autumn.

Marx put up a tough fight to the end. Cologne was full of soldiers that spring; and the authorities did their best to intimidate him. Berlin sent agents to watch him and to try to get something on him; but the Cologne government would not let them operate. Two non-commissioned officers appeared to beard him in his house one day, declaring he had insulted their rank; but he held them at bay in his dressing-gown by the threat of an unloaded revolver. Summoned to court for inciting the people to refuse to pay the taxes, he proved by one of his subtle disquisitions that all law was merely the reflection of social relations, that when the social relations were changed, the laws became invalid, and that, in consequence, it was not he who had broken laws that the Revolution had made obsolete but the government which had violated the rights that were to be guaranteed, according to its promise, by the imminent constitution: the effect on the jury was so great that Marx was thanked on their behalf by the foreman for his "extremely informative speech." The circulation of the *Neue Rheinische Zeitung* rose to six thousand, but this increased the immediate printing expenses. The well-to-do bourgeoisie had been scared by it and could not be induced to give it any more support, so Marx went out on a money-raising tour. He got only one contribution—from an *agent provocateur,* who traveled back with him to Cologne. There he found an order for his expulsion. It was just after the putting-down of the May uprisings in Dresden and Baden. The authorities, lacking any better pretext, had banished him as an undesirable alien, alleging that by living abroad he had forfeited his Prussian nationality. He brought out the last number of his paper printed entirely in red. Twenty thousand copies were disposed of; some of them brought a thaler, and the possessors had them framed. The editors announced that their last word would "always and everywhere be: 'The emancipation of the working class!'"

In the meantime, during 1848, Engels had exposed himself to prosecution by speaking at public meetings and inciting the Frankfort Assembly to resist the attempts to disarm it; and in September, when martial law had been declared, he had been charged with high treason. He took refuge in Barmen while his parents were away; but when they came back, they made him such scenes that he left Germany altogether for Brussels. The Belgian police shoved him on to France.

But in Paris, which he had always loved as "the head and the heart of the world," he found that he "couldn't stand this dead city," which, dead, "was no longer Paris." "On the boulevards, only bourgeois and police spies; the balls and the theater desolate; the gamins in Mobile Guard jackets vanished, bought by the honest Republic for thirty sous a day." He decided to go to Switzerland, and, having no money, walked; but he refrained from taking the shortest way, because "nobody is glad to leave France." He compares the other countries to France: Spain with its stony wastes; Italy left a backwater by world trade; England with its coal smoke and its leaden sky; Germany with its "flat sandy plain in the north, cut off from the European South by the granite wall of the Alps—Germany poor in wine, land of beer and schnaps and rye-bread, of rivers and revolutions that both run into the sands." But France, with its five great rivers, with its frontage on three seas—with its wheat, its corn and rice, its olives and flax and silk, and everywhere almost, the wine. "And what wine!" He enumerates his favorite brands, from Bordeaux to Ai Mousseux; "and when one considers that each one of these wines produces a different intoxication, from the mad desire of the Cancan to the fever of the *Marseillaise!*" It is a mood of exhilaration which any ex-soldier will recognize who has ever escaped on furlough to wander for a breathing-space through France. Engels, too, was leaving behind him a war, as he walked among the hills, heavy with vineyards and just bronzing in the first suns of autumn, which, as he says, in spite of contours less imposing than the towering rocky ramparts of Switzerland or the Rhine, have some harmony and richness of "ensemble" which gives the beholder an incomparable satisfaction.

In these pages, from the literary point of view among the most brilliant Engels wrote, we are pulled up by a sharp realization of the species of Jekyll-and-Hyde personality which Engels is developing in his relationship with Marx. In Engels' letters to Marx during the years before the Revolution, he has been doing his best to imitate the contemptuous estimates of his friend, Marx's cynical interpretations of motives: everybody else in the revolutionary movement, close associates as well as opponents, is either a *"Hund,"* a *"Wanz,"* a *"Tölpel,"* a *"Rüpel,"* a *"Hanswurst,"* a *"Schafskopf,"* a *"Schlingel"* or a *"Vieh,"* and as the years go on, the word *Esel* seems almost to become synonymous with *human being.* Even in connection with an old ally like Moses Hess, who had been one of the first to appreciate Marx's greatness and who had originally converted Engels to communism and had worked with him in his agitation in the Rhineland, Engels' tone becomes brutal and scathing—"Shall we never escape from that imbecile?" he is later to write Marx; nor are the rank and file of the workers forgiven their stupidity or their ignorance. But now, as he sets out along the valley of the Loire, it is as if his natural exuberance and amiability had suddenly been released. In the farms and the tiny villages, he repays the hospitality of the inhabitants by drawing his inevitable little pictures for the children—caricatures of Louis Napoleon and General Cavaignac, which he assures them are wonderful likenesses.

At Dampierre, he finds three or four hundred Parisian workers, "the remains of the former national workshops," whom the government had sent to build a dam. They showed, he says, "no trace whatever of a concern for their class interests or for the political questions of the day that touch them so nearly." Their relatively comfortable life as well as their separation from Paris had "markedly contracted their outlook." They were in process, he thought, of turning into peasants. Engels analyzes with his usual acumen the political point of view of the French peasant, whose father has won his property from the old nobility and clergy and who has been able to see no reason for disturbing himself in behalf of a revolution in Paris which has appeared to be directed against property; who is unable to understand as yet that the new bankers with their mortgages are dispossessing him just as surely as the old privileged classes did. Yet in Burgundy he finds these people "so naïve, so good-natured, so confiding," so full of "mother-wit within their accustomed world," that one cannot but "forgive them at once their utter political nullity and their enthusiasm for Louis Napoleon." In Burgundy, the streets were running blood, but not from the guillotine; it was the overwhelming vintage of '48; the red republic of the town of Auxerre would have turned the Paris deputies pale; the people were pouring out last year's wine in order to make room for this year's. And the women of those little Burgundian towns, who had acquired through the traffic of the wine trade some of the high civilization of France—the girls, so clean and so slim: his countrymen might never forgive him for preferring them to the German cow-girls, with their dragoon stride and their long flat backs that gave them the aspect of calico-covered boards, but he squandered so many hours eating grapes and drinking among them, lying in the grass and chattering and laughing, that he might easily have ascended the Jungfrau in the time he took to climb the hill.

In Switzerland, hearing nothing from Marx, on whom he had counted to send him money, he seems to have been as-

sailed by a fear lest his terrible ally might have dropped him
as readily and unregretfully as he had seen him do with others.
But it turned out that Marx had attended to his affair: "That
I could leave you in the lurch for an instant," Marx reassures
him in a letter, "is sheer imagination. You remain always my
intimate friend, as I hope that I do yours."

By the beginning of 1849, Engels was able to go back to
Cologne. While Marx was away raising money, he stayed by
the paper and wrote the leaders. He had great hopes of the
Hungarian revolution, thought the French would be aroused
again by the campaign of the Austrians in northern Italy.
When the Prussians called out the militia against the defenders
of the constitution and thereby precipitated civil war, it was
in Elberfeld that the violence began. The town was full of
unemployed mill workers. Barricades had been built in the
streets in May; the prison had been broken into; a Committee
of Public Safety had taken over the administration of the town.
This was followed by the insurrections in Dresden and Baden.
The Hungarians were about to invade Austria. Engels went
back to Elberfeld, was assigned by the Committee of Public
Safety to a commission of town defense. But he terrified the
bourgeoisie by attempting to arm the workers. On the morning
of his first Sunday in Elberfeld, with a red sash and in the highest spirits, he was in the act of directing the gunners on the
bridge between Elberfeld and Barmen, when old Caspar, apparently on his way to church, came by and ran into his son.
A distressing scene ensued, which made the final rupture between them. The report of the incident was spread and threw
the burghers into fierce indignation: old Engels was one of
their worthiest citizens. The town was soon placarded with
posters requesting Friedrich Engels to leave.

When the *Neue Rheinische Zeitung* was suspended, he went
with Marx, first to Frankfort, in an unsuccessful effort to spur
the parliament into fighting for their constitution; then to
Baden and the Palatinate, where he and Marx had at last to
realize that the rebellion was not so serious as they had hoped.
On their way back, they were arrested, then set free. Marx left
the Rhineland for Paris; but Engels went back to the Palatinate. There was no political role possible for him now: he

would not accept the official posts that were offered him in the provisional government, which he could not regard as truly revolutionary; and the articles he tried to write for its paper were considered much too strong. He found the Palatinate all "a great pothouse," where people talked against the Prussians over their beer but nobody was really worried. It was characteristic of the German Revolution that Engels should have discovered only by accident in a back number of a paper from Cologne that the Prussians were already in the province. He broke the news to the natives and enlisted in the local army.

Engels took part in four engagements. "The whistle of bullets," he wrote to Jenny Marx, "is an altogether trifling affair; and throughout the whole campaign, in spite of a good deal of cowardice, I saw hardly a dozen men who were cowardly under fire. But all the more 'brave stupidity.' . . . After all, it's an excellent thing that one of the *Neue Rheinische Zeitung* staff should have been through it." His corps started out for Freiburg in an effort to prevent the government there from surrendering to the Prussians without a battle; but before they had reached the town, they learned that the government had fled. Engels and his commander, Willich, attempted to persuade their superiors to put up a last fight with such forces as were left; but they failed, and the army withdrew to Switzerland. It was one of the last corps to disband. Engels always looked back on their retreat through the Black Forest as a delightful holiday jaunt; it was July, and the mountains were spangled with the splendor of summer flowers. Willich, he wrote to Frau Marx, was a brave and resourceful soldier, but off the battlefield no better than a "True Socialist."

A charming holiday; the whistle of bullets; the colors of summer flowers.

But when we return to Marx, when we read his letters from Paris, we are back with all the weight of human woe, with the travail of the moral passion. Doomed to suffer and to make others suffer, he must forge on against the happiness of those he loves, against the course of natural human activity, against the ebb-tide of history itself, toward a victory which is to be also a tragedy.

Engels had fled that desolate Paris where the side he had been backing had lost. But all the darkness of the death of the ideal now oppresses the spirit of his leader. With the presidency of Louis Bonaparte, the reaction had shut down without hope. The city was full of cholera; the heat was heavy and sunless; the hearses, according to Herzen, would race with one another as they approached the cemeteries. The French Republican Army, which had been sent to defend Italy against Austria, had sold out republican Rome to the Pope. Karl Marx was completely penniless. When he had cleaned up the affairs of his paper, he had not kept a pfennig for himself, and Jenny Marx had had to sell her furniture to enable them to get out of Cologne. Now in Paris they pawned her family silver. Jenny had now three children and was afraid they would catch the cholera; and she was expecting a fourth baby that fall.

Stephan Born, then a young communist printer, later a working class leader of '48, knew the Marxes when they were living in Brussels "in a little house in a suburb, extremely modest, one might almost say poorly furnished," and speaks of their mutual devotion. Of Jenny, he declares that he has never known a woman "so harmoniously formed alike in outward appearance and heart and mind." She used to give recitations at the weekly meetings of a Workers' Educational Union which had been founded in connection with the League of the Just, after Karl had delivered his lectures. Born tells how, at one of their entertainments, Engels ventured to appear with Mary Burns. The Marxes held aloof from their friend; and, when Born came over to speak to them, Karl "gave me to understand by a glance and a significant smile, that his wife declined in the most rigorous manner to make the acquaintance of that . . . lady." (Born himself, it is illuminating to note, highly approves of Frau Marx's stand, as an example of her "intransigent" attitude "where the dignity and purity of conduct were concerned," and he considers it insolent of Engels to have reminded the workers present of "the reproach so often made against the rich sons of manufacturers that they are in a position to press the daughters of the people into the service of their pleasures.")

At the time of Marx's banishment from Belgium, Jenny Marx had herself been arrested on a charge of vagabondage as a result of her attempts to find out what they had done with him; at the police court, she had been shut up with some prostitutes and had had finally to share a bed with one. And now, in spite of the fact that Marx had taken an alias, a French police sergeant appeared to them one morning and told them that they would have to leave Paris within twenty-four hours. If they wanted to remain in France, they would have to consent to be exiled to the remote department of Morbihan. "The Pontine Marches of Brittany!" Marx exclaims in his letters; he believed that the authorities wanted to kill him.

He decided to take refuge in England and wrote Engels to join him there.

11   The Myth of the Dialectic

We must now give some more thoroughgoing description of the structure and mechanics of the system which the activities of Marx and Engels assumed.

They called their philosophy "Dialectical Materialism"—a name which has had the unfortunate effect of misleading the ordinary person in regard to the implications of Marxism, since in this label neither the word *dialectical* nor the word *materialism* is used in the ordinary sense.

The "Dialectic" of which Marx and Engels talked was not the argumentative method of Socrates, but a principle of change conceived by Hegel. The "dialectic" exploited by Plato was a technique of arriving at truth by reconciling two opposite statements; the "Dialectic" of Hegel was a law which also involved contradiction and reconciliation but which was imagined by Hegel as operating not only in the processes of logic but also in those of the natural world and in those of human history. The world is always changing, says Hegel; but its changes have this element of uniformity: that each of them must pass through a cycle of three phases.

The first of these, called by Hegel the *thesis,* is a process of affirmation and unification; the second, the *antithesis,* is a process of splitting off from the *thesis* and negating it; the third is a new unification, which reconciles the *antithesis* with the *thesis* and is known as the *synthesis.* These cycles are not simple recurrences, which leave the world the same as it was before: the *synthesis* is always an advance over the *thesis,* for it combines in a "higher" unification the best features of both the *thesis* and the *antithesis*. Thus, for Hegel, the unification represented by the early Roman Republic was a *thesis*. This prime unification had been accomplished by great patriots of the type of the Scipios; but as time goes on, the republican patriot is to take on a different character: this type turns into the "colossal individuality" of the age of Caesar and Pompey, an individuality which tends to disrupt the State in proportion as the republican order begins to decay under the influence of Roman prosperity—this is the *antithesis* which breaks off from the *thesis*. But at last Julius Caesar puts down his rivals, the other colossal individualities, and imposes upon Roman civilization a new order which is autocratic, a *synthesis*, which effects a larger unification: the Roman Empire.

Marx and Engels took this principle over, and they projected its action into the future as Hegel had not done. For them, the *thesis* was bourgeois society, which had originally been a unification out of the disintegrating feudal regime; the *antithesis* was the proletariat, who had originally been produced by the development of modern industry, but who had then been split off through specialization and debasement from the main body of modern society and who must eventually be turned against it; and the *synthesis* would be the communist society which would result from the conflict of the working class with the owning and employing classes and the taking-over of the industrial plant by the working class, and which would represent a higher unity because it would harmonize the interests of all mankind.

Let us pass now to the materialistic aspect of the Dialectical Materialism of Marxism. Hegel had been a philosophical idealist: he had regarded historical changes as the steps by which something called the Absolute Idea achieved progressive self-realization in the medium of the material world. Marx and Engels turned Hegel upside down, as they said, and so set him for the first time right side up. "For Hegel," writes Marx in *Das Kapital*, "the process of thought, which, under the name of the Idea, he even transforms into an independent subject, is the demiurge of the real world, while the real world is only its external appearance. With me, on the contrary, the ideal is nothing other than the material after it has been transposed and translated inside the human head." Marx and Engels had declared that all ideas were human and that every idea was bound up with some specific social situation, which had been produced in the first instance, in turn, by man's relation to specific material conditions.

But what did this mean precisely? To many simple-minded persons who have just heard about Marxism, it means something extremely simple: it means that people always act from motives of economic interest and that everything mankind has thought or done is susceptible of being explained in those terms. It appears to such persons that they have discovered in Marxism a key to all the complexities of human affairs and that they are in a position—what is even more gratifying—to belittle the achievement of others by pointing out the money motivation behind it. If such people were pressed to justify their assumptions and if they were capable of philosophical argument, they could only fall back on some variety of "mechanism," which would represent the phenomena of consciousness, with its accompaniment of the illusion of will, as something in the nature of a phosphorescence generated by mechanistic activity, or perhaps running parallel to it, but in either case incapable of affecting it. To lend itself to the misunderstanding of such people has been one of the main misfortunes of Marxism ever since the days when Engels had to tell Joseph Bloch in this connection that "many of the recent 'Marxists' [of 1890]" had certainly turned out "a rare kind of balderdash."

Marx and Engels had rejected what they called the "pure mechanism" of the French eighteenth-century philosophers. They saw, as Engels says, the impossibility of applying "the standards of mechanics to processes of a chemical and organic nature," in which, though the laws of mechanics had also a limited validity, they were certainly "pushed into the background by other and higher laws." And so in society, to quote another of Engels' letters, it was "not the case that the economic situation is the *sole active cause* and everything else only a passive effect."

What then? In what sense was it true that economics determined social relations and that ideas were derived from these?

If the ideas were not "passive effects," what was the nature and extent of their activity? How could they act upon economic conditions? How could the theories of Marx and Engels themselves help to produce a proletarian revolution?

Well, the truth is that Marx and Engels never worked out their own point of view in any very elaborate way. What is important and inspiring in it is the idea that the human spirit will be able to master its animal nature through reason; but they managed to make a great many people think they meant something the opposite of this: that mankind was hopelessly the victim of its appetites. For Marx had dropped philosophy proper with the fragments of the *Theses on Feuerbach;* he had intended to write a book on the Dialectic after he should have got done with *Das Kapital,* but he never lived to undertake it. Engels did attempt late in his life—first in *Anti-Dühring,* which had the approval of Marx, and then in his short work on Feuerbach and his long letters to various correspondents, written after Marx's death—to explain the general point of view. But Engels, who had confessed in his youth, at the time when he was studying philosophy most earnestly, that he had little natural aptitude for the subject, provided no more than a sketch for a system. And if you look up and piece together all that Marx and Engels wrote on the subject, you do not get a very satisfactory picture. Max Eastman, in his remarkable study, *Marx, Lenin, and the Science of Revolution,* has shown the discrepancies between the statements that Marx and Engels made at various times; Sidney Hook, in his extremely able but less acutely critical book, *Towards the Understanding of Karl Marx,* has tried to iron out the inconsistencies, to state with precision what has been left in the vague, and to formulate a presentable system. The main point about the philosophy of Marxism for us here is that its emphasis is considerably shifted between the first phase of its creators and their latest. If we read *The German Ideology* of 1845–46—into which an element of satire enters—we find that we are having it drummed into us that all the things that men think and imagine grow straight out of their vulgarest needs; if we read Engels' letters of the nineties, written at a time when people interested in Marxism were beginning to ask fundamental questions, we get an old man's soberest effort to state his notion of the nature of things, and it produces an entirely different impression. "Marx and I," he wrote, "are partly responsible for the fact that at times our disciples have laid more weight upon the economic factor than belongs to it. We were compelled to emphasize its central character in opposition to our opponents who denied it, and there wasn't always time, place and occasion to do justice to the other factors in the reciprocal interactions of the historical process."

Let us see now how Engels envisaged these "reciprocal interactions."

The first image which comes to our mind when we hear about the Marxist view of history—an image for which, as Engels says, he and Marx themselves are partly responsible—is a tree of which the roots are the methods of production, the trunk is the social relations, and the branches, or "superstructure," are law, politics, philosophy, religion and art—whose true relation to the trunk and the roots is concealed by "ideological" leaves. But this is not what Marx and Engels mean. The ideological activities of the superstructure are regarded by them neither merely as reflections of the economic base nor as simple ornamental fantasies which grow out of it. The conception is a great deal more complicated. Each of these higher departments of the superstructure—law, politics, philosophy, etc.—is always struggling to set itself free from its tether in economic interest and to evolve a professional group which shall be partly independent of class bias and the relation of whose work to the economic roots may be extremely indirect and obscure. These groups may act directly on one another and even back on the social-economic basis.

Engels, in one of these letters, tries to give some idea of what he means by examples from the department of law. The laws of inheritance, he says, have evidently an economic basis, because they must be supposed to correspond to various stages in the development of the family; but it would be very hard to prove that the freedom of testamentary disposition in England or the restricted right of disposition in France can wholly be traced to economic causes. Yet both these kinds of law have their effect on the economic system in that they influence the distribution of wealth. (It should be noted, by the way, that in *The Housing Question* [Section 3, II], published in 1872, he gives a rather more "materialistic" account of the development of legal systems.) Marx had once—in a first draught for an *Introduction to the Critique of Political Economy*—made some attempt to explore the difficulties of the connection between art and economic conditions. The periods of the highest development of art do not coincide, he says, with the highest developments of society. Great art—the Greek epic, for example— is not even necessarily the product of a high period of social development. In any given instance, it is possible to see why a particular kind of art should have flourished at a particular moment: the very naïveté of the Greeks, who had not yet invented the printing press, their closeness to primitive mythology at an epoch before the prevalence of lightning rods, when it was still possible for people to imagine that a thunderbolt meant the anger of Zeus, their childlike charm in the childhood of society—this rendered their art "in certain respects the standard and model beyond attainment." The difficulty lay only in discovering the *general laws* of the connection between artistic and social development. One would say that Marx had found a great deal of difficulty in explaining the above specific case and that his explanation was far from satisfactory. The trouble is that he has not gone into the question of what is meant when the epoch of the lightning rod is called a period of "higher" social development than the epoch of the Homeric epic. That he was working toward an inquiry into this matter is indicated by another passage from the same document: "The unequal relation, for example, between material and artistic production. *In general, the conception of progress is not to be taken in the sense of the usual abstraction* [italics mine]. In the case of art, etc., it is not so important and difficult to understand this disproportion as in that of practical social relations: for example, the relation between education in the United States and in Europe. The really difficult point, however, which has to be gone into here is that of the unequal development of relations of production as legal relations. As, for example, the connection between Roman civil law (this is

less true of criminal and public law) and modern production."
But this manuscript is remarkable chiefly—like the scraps of
the *Theses on Feuerbach*—for indicating that, though Marx
was aware of the importance of certain problems, he never
really got around to going into them. He dropped this discussion and never went on with it.

In regard to the role of science in their system, Marx and
Engels became quite confused, because their own work is
supposed to be scientific, and they must believe in its effect on
society at the same time that they are obliged to acknowledge
its kinship with the other ideologies of the superstructure. In
Marx's preface (a different work from the fragment mentioned
above) to his *Critique of Political Economy*, he says that, in
studying the transformations resulting from social revolutions,
"the distinction should always be made between the material
transformation of the economic conditions of production, which
can be determined with the precision of natural science, and
the legal, political, religious, aesthetic or philosophical—in
short, ideological forms, in which men become conscious of
this conflict and fight it out." Natural science then, is not to
be numbered among the ideological outgrowths of the superstructure, but has a precision of which they are incapable; and
this precision social science may share. Yet at the time when
he and Engels had been discrediting the "abstract man" of
Feuerbach, they pointed out in *The German Ideology* that
"even the 'pure' natural sciences begin by deriving their aims
as well as their materials from trade and industry, from the
sensible activity of men"; and he was later to declare in *Das
Kapital* that "in the domain of political economy, free scientific
research encounters not merely the same enemies that it encounters in the other domains," but others more formidable
still, because "the very nature of the subject with which it is
dealing brings into the field against it those passions which
are at once the most violent, the basest and the most abominable of which the human breast is capable: the furies of
personal interest." Engels in *Anti-Dühring* claims little for the
precision of science. In those sciences, he says, such as Mechanics and Physics, which are more or less susceptible of
mathematical treatment, one can speak of final and eternal

truths, though even in Mathematics itself there is plenty of room for uncertainty and error; in the sciences that deal with living organisms, the immutable truths consist solely of such platitudes as that all men are mortal and that all female mammals have lacteal glands; and in the sciences which he calls "historical," precision becomes still more difficult: "once we pass beyond the primitive stage of man, the so-called Stone Age, the repetition of conditions is the exception and not the rule, and when such repetitions occur, they never arise under exactly similar conditions," and when it does turn out, "by way of exception," that we come to be able to recognize "the inner connection between the social and political forms of an epoch, this only occurs, as a rule, when these forms are out of date and nearing extinction." And he adds that in the sciences that deal with the laws of human thought—Logic and Dialectics—the situation is not any better.

Conversely, in regard to politics, the interests of their doctrine demand that the value of institutions should be shown to be relative to class; but there are moments when they are forced to admit that in certain situations a political institution may have something like absolute value. It was one of the prime tenets of Marxism that the State had no meaning or existence save as an instrument of class domination. Yet not only does Marx demonstrate in *The Eighteenth Brumaire* that the government of Louis Bonaparte did for a time represent an equilibrium between the various classes of French society; but Engels in *The Origin of the Family* asserts that "by way of exception . . . there are periods when the warring classes so nearly attain equilibrium that the State power, ostensibly appearing as a mediator, assumes for the moment a certain independence in relation to both. Such were the absolute monarchies of the seventeenth and eighteenth centuries, which balanced the nobles and burghers against each other; the Bonapartism of the First and, more especially, of the Second Empire in France, which played off the proletariat against the bourgeoisie and the bourgeoisie against the proletariat."

And yet Marx and Engels were never skeptical about their own theory of the social revolution; they never doubted that the purpose they derived from this theory would eventually be accomplished. Nor did they trouble themselves much to explain how their own brand of "ideology," avowedly itself a class ideology designed to promote the interests of the proletariat, could have some different kind of validity from that of others.

Where do these validities begin and end? the reader may ask today of Marx and Engels. How shall we determine to what extent a law or a work of art, for example, is the product of class delusion and to what extent it has some more general application? To what extent and under what conditions do the ideas of human beings react upon their economic bases? The last word that Engels leaves us on the subject (in his letter to Joseph Bloch, September 21, 1890) is his assertion that, though the economic factor is not "the *sole* determining factor," yet "the production and reproduction of real life constitutes in the *last instance* the determining factor in history" [italics in both cases Engels']. But what about the carry-over value of a system of law or a literary culture? No doubt the Roman Empire, "in the last instance," ran itself into an economic *impasse*. But did the Roman jurists and Virgil really perish with the passing of Rome? What does "the last instance" mean? No doubt there would be no Aeneid without Augustus; but then it is equally true that there would be no Aeneid, as we know it, without Virgil's Alexandrian predecessor, Apollonius Rhodius; and to what degree does Virgil, in turn, enter as a principle of cultural life into the new forms of society which are to follow him? Is the "last instance" last in time or is it ultimate in the quite different sense of being the fundamental motive of human behavior?

We may perhaps clear up the difficulty for ourselves by putting it that races or classes who are starving will be incapable of producing culture at all, but that as soon as they prosper, they reach out to one another across the countries and classes, and collaborate in a common work; that the economic ruin of a society unquestionably destroys the persons who compose it, but that the results of their common work may survive to be taken up and continued by other societies that have risen to the level from which the preceding one had declined. But Marx and Engels do not clear up this problem. Marx, who had studied Roman law, was evidently about to address himself to the subject in the notes I have quoted above. Why did he never do so? Why, in a word, were he and Engels content to leave the discussion of the relation between man's conscious creative will and the relatively blind battle for survival at such meager generalizations as the statements that "men make their own history, but not just as they please. They do not choose the circumstances for themselves, but have to work upon circumstances as they find them, have to fashion the material handed down by the past" (Marx: *The Eighteenth Brumaire of Louis Bonaparte*, 1852); or that "men make their own history, but not until now with a collective will according to a collective plan" (Engels' letter to Hans Starkenburg, 1894)?

Engels' fullest attempt to state the point of view is in his essay, written in 1886, on *Ludwig Feuerbach and the Outcome of German Classical Philosophy*. "Men make their own history," he writes, "whatever its outcome may be, in that each person follows his own consciously desired end; and it is precisely the resultant of these many wills operating in different directions and of their manifold effects upon the outer world that constitutes history. Thus it is also a question of what the many individuals desire. The will is determined by passion or deliberation. But the levers which immediately determine passion or deliberation are of very different kinds. Partly they may be external objects, partly ideal motives, ambition, 'enthusiasm for truth and justice,' personal hatred or even purely individual whims of all sorts. But, on the one hand, we have seen that, for the most part, the many individual wills active in history produce quite different results from those they intended—results often, in fact, quite the opposite; so that in relation to the total result, their motives are also of only secondary significance. On the other hand, the further question arises: what driving forces, in turn, stand behind these motives? What are the historical causes which, in the brains of the actors, transform themselves into these motives? The old materialism never put itself this question."

Engels answers with "class struggle for economic emancipation." But *he* never puts to himself the question of precisely how the "ideal motives" can in turn affect the progress of the class struggle.

The point is that Marx and Engels from the beginning had had something that had prevented their putting these questions in the terms in which we have been discussing them above: they had the Hegelian Dialectic. From the moment that they had admitted the Dialectic into their semi-materialistic system, they had admitted an element of mysticism.

Marx and Engels had both begun as idealists. They imagined they had brought Hegel down to earth; and certainly nobody had ever labored more deliberately and energetically than they had to discredit men's futile illusions, to rub men's noses in their human miseries, to hold men's minds to their practical problems. And yet the very fact of their insistent effort—which an Englishman or a Frenchman would never have found necessary—betrays their contrary predisposition. They had actually carried along with them a good deal of the German idealism that they thought they were warring against. The young Marx who had lampooned the doctors for imagining the soul could be purged with a pill was still present in the dialectical materialist.

The abstractions of German philosophy, which may seem to us unmeaning or clumsy if we encounter them in English or French, convey in German, through their capitalized solidity, almost the impression of primitive gods. They are substantial, and yet they are a kind of pure beings; they are abstract, and yet they nourish. They have the power to hallow, to console, to intoxicate, to render warlike, as perhaps only the songs and the old epics of other peoples do. It is as if the old tribal deities of the North had first been converted to Christianity, while still maintaining their self-assertive pagan nature; and as if then, as the Christian theology became displaced by French eighteenth-century rationalism, they had put on the mask of pure reason. But for becoming less anthropomorphic, they were not the less mythopoeic creations. The Germans, who have done so little in the field of social observation, who have produced so few great social novels or dramas, have retained and developed to an amazing degree the genius for creating myths. The *Ewig-Weibliche* of Goethe, the *kategorische Imperativ* of Kant, the *Weltgeist* with its *Idee* of Hegel—these have dominated the minds of the Germans and haunted European thought in general like great hovering legendary divinities. Karl Marx, in the passage I have quoted above, described the Idea of Hegel as a "demiurge": this demiurge continued to walk by his side even after he imagined he had dismissed it. He still believed in the triad of Hegel: the *These*, and *Antithese* and the *Synthese;* and this triad was simply the old Trinity, taken over from the Christian theology, as the Christians had taken it over from Plato. It was the mythical and magical triangle which from the time of Pythagoras and before had stood as a symbol for certainty and power and which probably derived its significance from its correspondence to the male sexual organs. "Philosophy," Marx once wrote, "stands in the same relation to the study of the actual world as onanism to sexual love"; but into his study of the actual world he insisted on bringing the Dialectic. Certainly the one-in-three, three-in-one of the *Thesis,* the *Antithesis* and the *Synthesis* has had upon Marxists a compelling effect which it would be impossible to justify through reason. (It is almost a wonder that Richard Wagner never composed a music-drama on the Dialectic: indeed, there does seem to be something of the kind implied in the Nibelungen cycle by the relations between Wotan, Brunhilde and Siegfried.)

The Dialectic lies deep in all Marx's work; it remained with him all his life. It formed his technique of thought and with it his literary style. His method of stating ideas was a dialectical sequence of paradoxes, of concepts turning into their opposites; and it contains a large element of pure incantation. It is most obvious in his earlier writings, where it is sometimes extremely effective, sometimes artificial and tiresome: "Luther vanquished servility based upon devotion, because he replaced it by servility based upon conviction. He shattered faith in authority, because he restored the authority of faith. He transformed parsons into laymen, because he transformed laymen into parsons. He liberated men from outward religiosity, because he made religiosity an inward affair of the heart. He emancipated

the body from chains, because he laid chains upon the heart."
But it continued to figure in his writing up to the time when
he brought *Das Kapital* to its climax with his phrase about
expropriating the expropriators.

In later life, he devoted much time to the study of Higher
Mathematics, in which, as he told Lafargue, he "found the
dialectical movement again in its most logical as well as its
simplest form." And Engels worked at Mathematics and Physics, Chemistry and Zoölogy, in an effort to prove that the
dialectical process governed the natural world. The Russians
since the Revolution have carried on these researches and
speculations; and with the spread of political Marxism, they
have been cropping up in other countries. Recent examples are
the distinguished British scientists, J. D. Bernal and J. B. S.
Haldane, who have been trying to show the workings of the
Dialectic in Physics and Chemistry and in Biology, respectively. One's attitude toward this sort of thinking is naturally
determined by one's appetite for pure metaphysics. To anyone
who has always found it difficult to feel the inevitability of any
metaphysical system and who tends to regard metaphysics in
general as the poetry of imaginative people who think in abstractions instead of in images, the conceptions of the dialectical materialists recommend themselves only moderately.
They do provide a dramatic formula for the dynamics of certain social changes; but they are obviously impossible to apply
to others.

It has not been difficult for the critics of Engels—who took
certain of his examples straight from Hegel's *Logic*—to show
that he was straining a point when he asserted that the "negation of the negation" (that is, the action of the *antithesis*
against the *thesis*) was demonstrated in mathematics by the
fact that the negation of the negation of a was $+ a^2$, "the original positive magnitude, but at a higher level." The negation of
$-a$ is obviously not a^2, but a; and if you want to get a^2, you do
not have to negate at all: you can simply multiply a *plus* by a
plus. Engels did, to be sure, admit that one has so to construct
the first negation that the second "remains or becomes possible." But since in that case the dialectical materialist has
always to provide his own conditions in order to arrive at dia-

lectical results, what becomes of his claim that the Dialectic is inherent in all the processes of nature? And so with the "transition of quantity into quality," an Hegelian principle of which Marx believed he could see the operation both in the growth by a gradual process of the medieval guildmaster into a capitalist and in the transformations, through the addition of molecules, of the compounds of the carbon series. Professor Hook, in his paper on *Dialectic and Nature* in the second number of the *Marxist Quarterly*, has pointed out that, in the case of such an example of Engels' as the sudden transformation at certain temperatures of water into steam or ice, the transformation for a different observer would take place at a different moment and would be a different transformation: for a person from whose point of view the water was concealed in a radiator, the sudden transition of which he would be aware would be that—perhaps marked by a sneeze—of the dropping of the temperature of the room from a comfortable warmth to distinct chilliness. And who knows but that the application to water of a microscope which would disclose its component electrons would banish the illusion that, at the point of boiling, it begins to change from a liquid to a vapor?

And so with the examples given by Bernal and Haldane. After all, the various discoveries invoked by Bernal were arrived at quite without the intervention of dialectical thinking —just as Mendeleyev's Periodic Table, which so much impressed Engels as an instance of quality determined by quantity, owed nothing to the *antithesis* and the *synthesis*; and it is difficult to see how they are improved by being fitted into the Dialectic. In the case of one of them, the Relativity Theory of Einstein, the discoverer has himself gone on record as of the opinion that the writings of Engels did not have "any special interest either from the point of view of present-day Physics or from that of the history of Physics." In the case of another of Bernal's examples, the Freudian theory of repressed desires, the dialectical cycle is certainly far from inevitable. The instinct is the *thesis*; the repression is the *antithesis*; the sublimation is the *synthesis*: good! But suppose the patient goes insane instead of being able to sublimate; suppose he kills himself: where is the reconciliation of opposites in the *synthesis?* Where is the progression from the lower to the higher? Certainly it is true in various fields that changes occur through accumulation which look to us like changes in kind. It may be true, as J. B. S. Haldane says, that the transformation of ice into water is still a mysterious phenomenon. But in what way does this prove the dialectical Trinity? In what way is that Trinity proved when Professor Haldane maps out the processes of mutation and selection as triads any more than it was proved by Hegel when he arranged all his arguments in three parts—or, for that matter, for Vico, when he persisted in seeing everything in threes: three kinds of languages, three systems of law, three kinds of government, etc., or by Dante, when he divided his poem into three sections with thirty-three cantos each?

In an interesting recent controversy in the Marxist quarterly, *Science and Society,* Professor A. P. Lerner of the London School of Economics has brought against Professor Haldane what would seem to be the all too obvious charge that he is trying to pin the Dialectic on Biology, which has hitherto derived nothing from it, in a purely gratuitous effort to bring his science into the Marxist Church. Professor Haldane replies, however, that since he was "compelled" by one of the State publishing houses in Moscow to formulate the Mendelian theory of evolution in terms of the Dialectic, he has found the dialectical way of thinking a great help to him in his laboratory work. He does not go so far as to claim, he admits, that the result of his researches "could not have been attained without a study of Engels"; he merely states "that they were not reached without such a study." So far from "suffering," as Professor Lerner has suggested, "from an overpowering emotional urge to embrace the Dialectic," Professor Haldane, who has been active in the defense of Madrid and who takes care to let the reader know it in the course of his first paper, explains that the process of embracing the Dialectic has taken him "some six years, so it was hardly love at first sight." "And I hope," he goes on, "that no student of biology will become a user of the Dialectic unless he or she is persuaded that it is (as I believe and Dr. Lerner does not) an aid both to the understanding of known biological facts and to the discovery of new ones." He "must thank" Professor Lerner "for his stimulating criticism . . . But the most valuable criticism would be from workers who were engaged in the same branch of science as myself and had accepted Marxist principles."

"I hope no —— will become a —— until he or she is persuaded that it is (as I believe and Dr. Lerner does not) an aid to the understanding, etc. . . . But the most valuable criticism would be from workers who had accepted —— principles." Where have we heard these accents before? Was it not from the lips of the convert to Buchmanism or Roman Catholicism?

The Dialectic then is a religious myth, disencumbered of divine personality and tied up with the history of mankind. "I hate all the gods," Marx had said in his youth; but he had also projected himself into the character of the resolute seaman who carried the authority of the gods in his breast, and in one of his early *Rheinische Zeitung* articles on the freedom of the press, he declares that the writer must "in his way adopt the principles of the preacher of religion, adopt the principle, 'Obey God rather than man,' in relation to those human beings among whom he himself is confined by his human desires and needs." And as for Engels, his boyhood had been spent under the pulpit of the great Calvinist evangelist Friedrich Wilhelm Krummacher, who preached every Sunday in Elberfeld and reduced his congregation to weeping and stupefaction. Engels tells in one of his *Letters from the Wupperthal* how Krummacher would subdue his auditors by the logic of his terrible argument. Given the preacher's primary assumption—the total "incapacity of man by dint of his own effort to will the good, let alone to accomplish it"—it followed that God must give man this capability; and since the will of God himself was free, the allotment of this capability must be arbitrary; it followed that "the few who were chosen would *nolentes volentes* be blessed, while the others would be damned forever. 'Forever?' Krummacher would query; and answer, 'Yes, forever!'" This seems to have made an immense impression on the young Engels.

Karl Marx had identified his own will with the *antithesis* of the dialectical process. "The philosophers have only interpreted the world," he had written in his *Theses on Feuerbach*. "Our business is to change it." The will had always tended in German philosophy to play the role of a superhuman force; and this will had been salvaged by Marx and incorporated in Dialectical Materialism, where it communicated to his revolutionary ideas their drive and their compelling power.

For an active and purposeful man like Lenin it may be an added source of strength to have the conviction that history is with him, that he is certain of achieving his goal. The Dialectic so simplifies the whole picture: it seems to concentrate the complexities of society into an obvious protagonist and antagonist; it gives the confidence not only that the upshot of the struggle will certainly be successful, but that it will resolve all such struggles forever. The triad of the Dialectic has thus had its real validity as a symbol for the recurring insurgence of the young and growing forces of life against the old and the sterile, for the coöperative instincts of society against the barbarous and the anarchic. It is an improvement over the earlier point of view it superseded: "Down with the tyrant! Let us have freedom!"—in that it conceives revolutionary progress as an organic development out of the past, for which the reactionary forces have themselves in their way been preparing and which combines the different resources of both sides instead of merely substituting one thing for another.

But conversion to the belief in a divine power does not have always an energizing effect. It was in vain that Marx tried to bar out Providence: "*History does nothing*," he had insisted in *The Holy Family*; "it 'possesses *no* colossal riches'; it 'fights no fight.' It is rather *man*—real, living man—who acts, possesses and fights in everything. It is by no means 'History' which uses man as a means to carry out *its* ends, as if it were a person apart; rather History is *nothing* but the activity of man in pursuit of his ends." But as long as he keeps talking as if the proletariat were the chosen instrument of a Dialectic, as if its victory were predetermined, he does assume an extra-human power. In the Middle Ages in Germany, he was to tell the English Chartists in a speech of 1856, there had existed a secret tribunal called the Vehmgericht "to take vengeance for the misdeeds of the ruling class. If a red cross was seen marked on a house, people knew that its owner was doomed by the Vehm. All the houses of Europe are now marked by the mysterious red cross. History is the judge; its executioner, the proletarian." There is then a higher tribunal for which the working class is only the hangman. There is a non-personal entity called "History" which accomplishes things on its own hook and which will make the human story come out right, no matter what you or your opponent may do. The doctrine of salvation by works, as the history of Christianity shows, is liable to pass all too readily into the doctrine of salvation by grace. All too naturally, by identifying himself with the *antithesis* of the Dialectic, that is, by professing a religious faith, the Marxist puts himself into the state of mind of a man going upstairs on an escalator. The Marxist Will, which once resolved to change the world, has been transformed into the invisible power which supplies the motive force to run the escalator; and if you simply take your stand on the bottom step, the escalator will get you to the top, that is, to the blessed condition of the *synthesis*. The only other situation conceivable is that of a man who tries to walk down the same escalator and who either is able to make no progress or goes backwards. Though there is in Marxism a strong element of morality that makes the escalator too mechanical a simile—since the man who is on the way up knows with certainty that he is a noble fellow, though he may not exert himself to move a step, while the man who has had the misfortune to move against the upcoming stairway, though he may be full of the most admirable intentions, is doomed, like the damned of Pastor Krummacher, to be carried, not merely rear-end foremost toward the *synthesis*, but into inevitable ignominy and torment. So the German Social-Democrats of the Second International, assuming that the advent of socialism was sure, were found supporting an imperialist war which was to deprive the working class of all its liberties; so the Communists of the Third International, leaving history to the dialectical demiurge, have acquiesced in the despotism of Stalin while he was uprooting Russian Marxism itself.

Karl Marx, with his rigorous morality and his international

point of view, had tried to harness the primitive German Will to a movement which should lead all humanity to prosperity, happiness and freedom. But insofar as this movement involves, under the disguise of the Dialectic, a semi-divine principle of History, to which it is possible to shift the human responsibility for thinking, for deciding, for acting—and we are living at the present time in a period of the decadence of Marxism—it lends itself to the repressions of the tyrant. The parent stream of the old German Will, which stayed at home and remained patriotic, became canalized as the philosophy of German imperialism and ultimately of the Nazi movement. Both the Russian and the German branches threw out all that had been good in Christianity along with all that had been bad. The demiurge of German idealism was never a God of love, nor did it recognize human imperfection: it did not recommend humility for oneself or charity toward one's fellows. Karl Marx, with his Old Testament sternness, did nothing to humanize its workings. He desired that humanity should be united and happy; but he put that off till the achievement of the *synthesis,* and for the present he did not believe in human brotherhood. He was closer than he could ever have imagined to that imperialistic Germany he detested. After all, the German Nazis, too—also, the agents of an historical mission—believe that humanity will be happy and united when it is all Aryan and all submissive to Hitler.

What Marx and Engels were getting at, however, was something which, though it may sometimes be played off the stage by the myth of the Dialectic and though an insistence on the problems it raises may seem to reduce it to disintegration, came nevertheless in its day as a point of view of revolutionary importance and which may still be accepted as partly valid in our own. Let us dissociate it from the Dialectic and try to state it in the most general form:

"The inhabitants of civilized countries, insofar as they have been able to function as creative and rational beings, have been striving after disciplines and designs which would bring order, beauty and health into their lives; but so long as they continue to be divided into groups which have an interest in injuring one another, they will still be hampered by inescapable limitations. Only from that moment when they have become conscious of these conflicts and have set their hands to the task of getting rid of them will they find themselves on the road to arriving at a really human code of ethics or political system or school of art as distinguished from these lame and cramped ones we know. But the current of human endeavor is always running in this direction. Each of the great political movements that surges up across social barriers brings about a new and broader merging of the rising aggressive element with the element it assaults and absorbs. The human spirit is always expanding against predatory animal pressure, to make larger and larger units of human beings, until we shall finally have realized once for all that the human race itself is one and that it must not injure itself. Then it will base on this realization a morality, a society and an art more profound and more comprehensive than man can at present imagine.

"And though it is true that we can no longer depend on God to give us laws that transcend human limitations, though it is true that we cannot even pretend that any of the intellectual constructions of man has a reality independent of the special set of earthly conditions which has stimulated certain men to build it, yet we may claim for our new science of social change, rudimentary though this still is, that it may more truly be described as universal and objective than any previous theory of history. For Marxist science has been developed in reaction to a situation in which it has finally become apparent that if society is to survive at all, it must be reorganized on new principles of equality; so that *we* have been forced to make a criticism of history from the point of view of the imminent necessity of a world set free from nationalisms and classes. If we have committed ourselves to fight for the interests of the proletariat, it is because we are really trying to work for the interests of humanity as a whole. In this future the human spirit as represented by the proletariat will expand to make the larger unity of which its mind is already compassing the vision."

12 Marx and Engels Go Back to Writing History

In any case, the discovery of economic motivation had equipped Marx and Engels with an instrument which was to enable them to write a new kind of history as with a biting pyrographic needle.

They were entering upon a phase of their lives in which they were to suffer a relative political eclipse; and now, in their journalism, their pamphlets, their books, and in that extraordinary correspondence which plays for the nineteenth century a role somewhat similar to that of those of Voltaire and the Encyclopaedists for the eighteenth, they were to apply their new method of analysis to the events of the past and the present. Karl Marx inaugurated this work with a product of his mature genius at its most brilliant, the study called *The Class Struggles in France* (1848–50), written in London during the first year of his exile and printed in a magazine called *Revue der Neuen Rheinischen Zeitung*, which he and Engels published and wrote. It was followed in 1852 by *The Eighteenth Brumaire of Louis Bonaparte*, dealing with the *coup d'état* of December 1851; and later, in 1871, by *The Civil War in France*, which analyzed the episode of the Commune.

This whole series, which aims at a profounder interpretation and is sustained on a higher level of expression than the run of Marx's newspaper commentary, is in fact one of the great cardinal productions of the modern art-science of history.

Let us look back again at the French historians who have

been serving as our point of reference in situating the positions of Marxism. It is obvious that these men were perplexed by the confused and complex series of changes which had been taking place in France during their time and in the course of which republic, monarchy, proletarian uprising and empire had been alternating, existing simultaneously, exchanging one another's masks. Now Marx knocks away the masks, and he provides a chart of the currents that have been running below the surface of French politics—a chart which has thrown overboard completely the traditional revolutionary language made up of general slogans and abstract concepts and which has been worked out exclusively in terms of the propulsions deriving from such interests as the bread and wine wrung by the peasants out of their tight little plots of land, and as the Parisian security and luxury obtainable through speculation in office. In Michelet's work of this period, it is, to be sure, becoming possible for him to see that what, for example, had been at the bottom of the imbroglio in the industrial city of Lyons in 1793, when the Convention had played the game of the rich against Joseph Chalier, the revolutionary leader, had been the struggle between the exploited and the exploiters; but this, as he says, he has learned from the socialists, and he fails to follow the clue.

But now Marx, in *The Eighteenth Brumaire,* never relinquishing this economic thread, is able to penetrate all the pageantry of Legitimists and Orleanists and Bonapartists and Republicans and Party of Order, and to show what had really happened in France after the abdication of Louis-Philippe: The great industrials, the great landlords and the financiers had combined against the small bourgeoisie and the workers; all the political parties had found themselves frustrated in their efforts to achieve their ends through the medium of parliamentary government; and it had then been possible for Louis Bonaparte to take over, not through sheer force of Napoleonic magic, but through the support of a class of farm-holding peasants, who had not been able to organize politically but who wanted a father-protector to stand between them and the bourgeoisie—together with the interested backing of a group of professional bureaucrats, created by the centralization of the government. For a moment, says Marx, Louis Bonaparte will be able to hold all groups in equilibrium; but as it will be impossible for him to do anything for one group without discriminating somehow against the others, he will in time arouse them all against him. And in the meantime, the so-called democrats, who had been trying to unite in a Social Democratic Party the socialist working class with the republican petty bourgeoisie, had, although they had "arrogated to themselves a position of superiority to class conflicts," been defeated between bourgeoisie and workers, as a result of their inability to rise above the intellectual limitations of the petty bourgeoisie and to do as Marx himself is doing here: grasp the class interests actually involved. Never, after we have read *The Eighteenth Brumaire*, can the language, the conventions, the combinations, the pretensions, of parliamentary bodies, if we have had any illusions about them, seem the same to us again. They lose their consistency and color—evaporate before our eyes. The old sport of competition for office, the old game of political debate, look foolish and obsolete; for now we can see for the first time through the shadow-play to the conflict of appetites and needs which, partly unknown to the actors themselves, throw these thin silhouettes on the screen.

These writings of Marx are electrical. Nowhere perhaps in the history of thought is the reader so made to feel the excitement of a new intellectual discovery. Marx is here at his most vivid and his most vigorous—in the closeness and the exactitude of political observation; in the energy of the faculty that combines, articulating at the same time that it compresses; in the wit and the metaphorical phantasmagoria that transfigures the prosaic phenomena of politics, and in the pulse of the tragic invective—we have heard its echo in Bernard Shaw —which can turn the collapse of an incompetent parliament, divided between contradictory tendencies, into the downfall of a damned soul of Shakespeare.

At the same time—the summer of 1850—Engels was turning back the high-powered torch on the events of a remoter past. A man named Wilhelm Zimmerman had published in 1841 a history of the German Peasant War of 1525. Zimmerman, who was to figure later on in the extreme Left of the Frankfort Assembly, had written from a point of view sympathetic to the rebellious peasants; but he was an idealist and had conceived the whole story as a struggle between Good and Evil—whereas Engels could see through his picture into the anatomy of a relationship between classes of which Zimmerman had hardly been aware. He was struck by an analogy with the recent revolution of 1848–49.

In a short work called *The Peasant War in Germany,* he analyzed the complicated society of the end of the sixteenth century, when the hierarchy of feudalism was falling apart and the new city republics were rising, and tried to trace the social-economic motives behind the heresies of the Middle Ages and Reformation. He showed how the revolt of Luther had been converted into a middle-class movement for breaking down the political authority and taking away the wealth of the clergy; and yet how Luther's defiance of the Catholic Church had provided an impetus which carried further the more seriously discontented elements: the peasants, crushed under the bankruptcy of feudalism, the impoverished plebeians of the towns. The peasants, organizing in widespread conspiracies, had finally drawn up a set of demands, which included the abolition of serfdom, the reduction of their crushing taxes, the guarantee of a few rudimentary legal rights, the democratic control of the clergy, and the cutting-down of their salaries and titles. Their leader was a Protestant preacher named Thomas Münzer, who advocated the immediate establishment of the Kingdom of God on earth. This was in reality a sort of primitive Christian communism; and Münzer's professing it had caused a break with Luther. When the general peasant insurrection blazed out in April, 1525, Luther turned against this more drastic anticlericalism, denounced Münzer as a tool of Satan, and urged the princes to strangle their peasants like mad dogs. His own movement was taken under the protection of these princes, who had acquired the estates of the Church. Thomas Münzer was captured and beheaded, and the uncoördinated movement destroyed.

Engels regards Münzer as a genius, whose perception of the necessity of communism reached too far beyond the conditions of his time. What in Münzer's time was directly ahead was a society the antithesis of communistic. Woe to him who, like Münzer at Mülhausen in 1525, like so many whom Engels had known in Frankfort in 1848, finds himself, in the heat of his struggle for a society which will abolish social classes, compromised in a governing body which, in the slow evolution of things, can do nothing but further the interests of the, to him alien, propertied classes, while he must feed the dispossessed with empty promises!

In the midst of this literary activity, so congenial to him and Marx, Engels exclaims at the foolishness or hypocrisy of any real revolutionary of the Left who can still desire at that date to hold office.

For the fires of '48 had now faded.

That movement which had had its first stimulus in Switzerland from the defeat of the Catholic cantons by the Radicals and which had resulted in insurrections in France, Italy, Germany, Austria and Hungary, had ended with the suppression of the Hungarian revolt by the Austrian and Russian emperors. All the efforts of the proletariat had served only, as Engels said, to pull the bourgeoisie's chestnuts out of the fire. He and Marx were still continuing to count, for a year after they got to England, on a new crisis that would start trouble again. Marx believed that a new rebellion on the part of the petty bourgeoisie would upset the big bourgeoisie in France; and they hoped that their *Revue der Neuen Rheinischen Zeitung* would be able to preserve the bulb of the old paper for a new sprouting of revolution in Germany. But as they studied the depression of the forties which had precipitated the events of '48, they had come to see that political developments were connected in a way they had not realized with the fluctuations of world trade. They saw by the fall of 1850 that a new period of bourgeois prosperity had commenced; and they announced in the last number of the *Revue* that "a revolution can hope for success only when the modern factors of production and the bourgeois technique of production are at variance. A new revolution is possible only after a new crisis."

The brave boasts of 1848 had now definitely to be dropped behind with the rest of romantic literature; and out of the old confused and candid talk about fatherland, brotherhood and freedom emerged cold problems of long-distance strategy. The Communist League had been revived after the failure of the German Revolution; but now it was split between August Willich, Engels' former commander in the Baden campaign, who continued to demand immediate action and whom Engels, now completely at the orders of his intellectual commander, vied with the master in deriding; and Marx, who insisted that the workers had before them "fifteen, twenty or fifty years of civil war and national wars, not merely in order to change your conditions, but in order to change yourselves and become qualified for political power." Willich's faction, says Marx, "treats *pure will* as the motive power of revolution instead of actual conditions." It is the moment when the dynamic self-assertion of the philosophy of pre-'48 abates and relinquishes its purpose to what inevitably come to be conceived as the more automatic forces of history. At a meeting on September 15, 1850, it turned out that Marx had a majority of the members of the Executive Committee; but he knew that the rank and file were for Willich, so he transferred the headquarters to Cologne. At this time there was an attempt on the life of Friedrich Wilhelm IV; and eleven of the Communists in Cologne were arrested and indicted by means of documents clumsily forged by the police. Marx and Engels exposed this evidence so effectively that it was abandoned by the prosecution; but in cases where political prejudice is involved, it is not enough, as we know, to prove the falsity of evidence; and the jury sentenced seven of the accused men to from three to six years in jail. This was the end of the Communist League, which was dissolved in November, 1852. Nor did the Chartist movement, on which Engels had counted, long outlast 1848. In the spring of 1848, the Chartists had been quite active in the North and had gotten up a demonstration in London which had so seriously disquieted the authorities that they had called out the Duke of Wellington and put the Bank of England in a state of defense. But, after that, with the new boom, the movement lapsed. Marx helped them with one of their papers, but it died.

Later on—June, 1855—a Sunday Trading Bill was passed

which, in the interests of keeping the lower classes sober, deprived them of their Sunday beer; and the common people of London congregated every Sunday in Hyde Park to the number of from a quarter to half a million and insubordinately howled "Go to church!" at the holiday-making toffs. Marx was ready to believe that it was "the beginning of the English revolution" and took himself so active a part in the demonstration that on one occasion he was nearly arrested and only escaped by entangling the policeman in one of his irresistible disputations. But the government gave the people back their beer, and nothing came of the agitation.

Marx and Engels in February, 1851, are congratulating one another on the isolation in which they find themselves. "It corresponds to our position and our principles," says Marx. "The system of reciprocal concessions, of half-measures tolerated for appearances, and the obligation to share in public with all these asses in the general absurdity of the party—we're done with all that now." "From now on," Engels answers, "we are responsible for ourselves alone; and when the moment arrives when these gentlemen find they need us, we shall be in a position to dictate our own terms." He tells Marx that they must write "substantial books," in which they will not even "need to mention these spiders." What will all the malignant gossip of all the revolutionary rabble count for when Marx answers them with his Political Economy?

The next June Marx obtained admission to the British Museum reading room, and there he sat from ten to seven every day. He got hold of and read very carefully some blue books of factory reports which had been sold by members of Parliament to a dealer in old books whom he frequented. Those who did not sell them, it seems, were in the habit of using them as targets, measuring the force of their fire-arms by the number of pages they pierced.

Intellectually, again, they were free; but there is no real way for the revolutionary leader to beat the game of the society he is opposing. Marx was to have no peace, and Engels was to have no leisure.

The failure of their review had left them penniless. They

had depended for circulation on the German émigrés in London; but as they made a habit of insulting in their commentary all the more influential of these latter, their paper had been coldly received. They had managed to get out four numbers, then later a double number; then they had been obliged to stop. Marx had put into it the last penny of some money that he had raised by selling the last remnants of his father's estate. His mother refused to give him any more, though he threatened to draw a note on her and, if she protested it, go back to Germany and let himself be put in jail. For a time he was expecting to make something out of the publication of his collected writings. One of the communists in Cologne had bought a printing business and had undertaken to bring them out in two volumes; but this man was arrested in the police raids of May, 1851, when only the first volume had been published (it seems, however, to have had a pretty good sale). *The Eighteenth Brumaire of Louis Bonaparte* might never have appeared at all if an immigrant German tailor in New York had not put up his whole savings, forty dollars, to have it published there. A thousand copies were printed, and a third of them were sent to Europe; but all these latter had eventually to be distributed among sympathizers and friends: not a bookseller could be persuaded to touch it.

Marx, when he first came to England, had taken furnished lodgings for his family in the fashionable suburb of Camberwell; but they were evicted in the spring of 1850 for inability to pay the rent, and had resorted to a poor street in Soho. There the whole family lived in two small dark unventilated rooms: there were six of them now, with the children, and with the maid, Helene Demuth, called Lenchen, whom Jenny's mother had given her as a wedding present and who, though they rarely had the money to pay her, was to stay with them to the end of their lives. The boy that Jenny had borne a few days after coming to England died in this place that November. They had been turned out while she was still nursing the baby; and she has left a vivid record of the incident in a letter to the wife of a comrade.

"I shall describe to you a day of this life just as it is, and you will see that perhaps few other refugees have gone through anything like it. Since wet-nurses are here much too expensive for us, I decided, in spite of continual and terrible pains in my breasts and back, to nurse the child myself. But the poor little angel drank in from me so much secret sorrow and grief with the milk that he was constantly unwell, lay in violent pain night and day. He has not slept a single night since he came into the world—two or three hours at most. Now lately he has been having violent cramps, so that the poor child is always hovering between life and death. In this pain he used to suck so hard that my nipple got sore and bled; often the blood would stream into his little quivering mouth. As I was sitting like this one day, our landlady suddenly appeared. We have paid her in the course of the winter over two hundred and fifty thalers, and we had made an arrangement with her that in future we were not to pay her but the landlord, who had put in an execution. Now she denied this agreement and demanded five pounds, which we still owed her; and as we were unable to produce this sum at once, two bailiffs entered the house, took possession of all my little belongings: beds, linen, clothes, everything, even my poor baby's cradle, and the best of the toys that belonged to the little girls, who were standing by in bitter tears. They threatened to take everything away in two hours' time—in which case I should have had to lie flat on the floor with my freezing children and my sore breast. Our friend Schramm hurried to town to get help. He got into a cab, and the horses bolted. He jumped out and was brought bleeding into the house, where I was in misery with my poor shivering children.

"The next day we had to leave the house. It was cold and rainy and dreary. My husband tried to find a place for us to live, but no one was willing to have us when we mentioned the four children. At last a friend came to our rescue, we paid, and I quickly sold all my beds, in order to settle with the chemist, the baker, the butcher and the milkman, who had been alarmed by the scandal of the bailiffs' arrival and who had come wildly to present their bills. The beds which I had sold were taken out of doors and loaded on to a cart—and do you know what happened then? It was long after sunset by this time, and it is illegal in England to move furniture so late.

The landlord produced the police and said that there might be some of his things among them, we might be escaping to a foreign country. In less than five minutes, there were two or three hundred people standing in front of our door, the whole Chelsea mob. The beds came back again—they could not be delivered to the purchasers till after sunrise the next day . . ."

She apologizes for talking so much about her troubles, but says that she feels the need of pouring out her heart for once to a friend. "Don't imagine that these petty sufferings have bent me. I know only too well that our struggle is no isolated one, and that I in particular belong to the specially fortunate and favored, for my dear husband, the mainstay of my life, is still by my side. The only thing that really crushes me and makes my heart bleed is that he is obliged to endure so much pettiness, that there should be so few to come to his aid, and that he who has so willingly and gladly come to the aid of so many, should find himself so helpless here."

They were to remain in Dean Street, Soho, six years. As Jenny said, few would help her husband; and it turned out, as time went on, that he would not do much to help himself. And now we must confront a curious fact. Karl Marx was neurotic about money. It was one of the most striking "contradictions" of Marx's whole career that the man who had done more than any other to call attention to economic motivation should have been incapable of doing anything for gain. For difficult though it may have been for an émigré to find regular work, it can hardly have been impossible. Liebknecht, Willich and Kossuth managed to support themselves in London. Yet on only one recorded occasion during the whole of Marx's thirty years' stay did he attempt to find regular employment.

This resistance to the idea of earning a livelihood may, at least partly, have been due to an impulse to lean over backwards in order to forestall the imputation of commercialism which was always being brought against the Jews. Certainly the animus of those of his writings which are sometimes characterized as anti-Semitic is mainly directed against the Jew as moneychanger or as truckler to bourgeois society. Take the passage in *Herr Vogt*, for example, in which he so remorselessly rubs it in that a certain newspaper editor in London has taken to spelling his name "Levy" instead of "Levi" and made a practice of publishing attacks on Disraeli, in order to be accepted as an Englishman, and elaborates with more stridency than taste on the salience of Levy's nose and its uses in sniffing the sewers of gossip. The point is that this man—who has libeled Marx—is a toady and a purveyor of scandal. And Marx's charge against another Jew, who has been profiteering out of the Second Empire, is that he has "augmented the nine Greek muses with a tenth Hebraic muse, the 'Muse of the Age,' which is what he calls the Stock Exchange." If Marx is contemptuous of his race, it is primarily perhaps with the anger of Moses at finding the Children of Israel dancing before the Golden Calf.

In any case, there is no question at all that Marx's antipathy to writing for money was bound up with an almost maniacal idealism. "The writer," he had insisted in his youth in the article already quoted, "must earn money in order to be able to live and write, but he must by no means live and write for the purpose of making money. . . . The writer in no wise considers his works a means. They are *ends in themselves;* so little are they a means either for himself or for others that, if necessary, he sacrifices *his own* existence to *their* existence and, in his own way, like the preacher of religion, takes for his principle, 'Obey God rather than man,' in relation to those human beings among whom he himself is confined by his human desires and needs." This was written, of course, before Marx had developed his Dialectical Materialism; but he was to act on this principle all his life. "I must follow my goal through thick and thin," he writes in a letter of 1859, "and I shall not allow bourgeois society to turn me into a money-making machine." Note Marx's curious language: the writer is "confined" ("*eingeschlossen*") among men. Instinctively Marx thinks of himself as a being set above their world.

Yet he *is* confined in this world by his "human needs and desires"; and if he will not allow himself to be turned into a money-making machine, somebody else will have to turn himself into one in order to make money for him.

Engels had written in *The Peasant War in Germany* of the

ascetism indispensable to proletarian movements both in the Middle Ages and modern times: "This ascetic austerity of behavior, this insistence on the renunciation of all the amenities and pleasures of life, on the one hand sets up in contrast to the ruling classes the principle of Spartan equality, and on the other hand constitutes a necessary transitional stage, without which the lowest stratum of society would never be able to launch a movement. In order to develop their revolutionary energy, in order to feel clearly their hostile position in relation to all the other elements of society, in order to concentrate themselves as a class, they must begin by stripping themselves of everything that could reconcile them to the existing social order, must deny themselves even the smallest enjoyment which could make their oppressed position tolerable for a moment and of which even the severest pressure cannot deprive them." Karl Marx, as the proletariat's Münzer, exemplified something of the sort; and Engels had made a resolute effort to dissociate himself from his bourgeois origins. But the miseries of the Marxes in London weighed upon Engels' mind. From almost the beginning of the Marx-Engels correspondence, when Engels writes to his friend about hunting for a lodging for him in Ostend, with details about the *déjeuners* and cigars, and gives him specific instructions about trains in a tone which suggests that Marx could not be depended upon to catch them, there is apparent a sort of loving solicitude in which the protector is combined with the disciple; and now, by the autumn of 1850, that terrible year for the Marxes, Engels has decided that there is nothing for it but to return to the "filthy trade" against which he had so rebelled in Barmen. After all, the revolution had been adjourned; and Marx had to have the leisure to accomplish his own work.

Engels went back to Ermen & Engels in Manchester and began sending over to his father highly competent reports on the business. The old man came on the next spring. Engels wrote Marx that he had blasted old Caspar with "a few words and an angry look" when, trusting in his son's sense of decency in the presence of one of the Ermens, he had ventured to "give voice to a dithyramb" on the subject of Prussian institutions; and that this had made them as frigid as before. Friedrich evaded a plan on his father's part to put him at the head of the Manchester counting-house; but he made an arrangement with him to stay there three years without binding himself in any way which would interfere with his political writing or with his leaving if the events demanded. He went to work in the "gloomy room of a warehouse looking out on the yard of a public-house." He had always detested Manchester, and he complained of being lonely and dull there, in spite of the fact that he had gone back to his former arrangement of living with Mary Burns: he had always to keep up his bachelor establishment, too. He still attempted to make a life apart from that society which was based on the cotton trade. When his father gave him a horse one Christmas, he wrote Marx that it made him uncomfortable "that I should be keeping a horse here while you and your family are in straits in London." "If I'd known about you, I'd have waited a couple of months and saved the cost of upkeep. But never mind: I don't have to pay right away." He loved riding: it was, he once wrote Marx, after spending seven hours in the saddle, "the greatest physical pleasure I know." He was soon fox-hunting with the gentry whom he disdained, and telling Marx that it was "the real school for the cavalry" and hence valuable as military training for the European Armageddon which—as he was coming to believe in the later fifties—would soon be upon them now.

Thus he was able to send his friend regular remittances; and in the August of 1851 a new source of income opened for Marx. He was invited by Charles A. Dana to write regularly for *The New York Tribune*. Horace Greeley, the editor of *The Tribune*, had at that time declared himself a socialist and had been giving Fourierism a great deal of publicity; and Dana, his managing editor, had been himself one of the trustees of Brook Farm. He had met Marx and been deeply impressed by him in Cologne in 1848; and now he asked him to contribute a bi-weekly article on European affairs.

Marx accepted, but, pleading the badness of his English and his having his "hands full" with his economic studies, requested Engels to write the articles. Engels complied, with some inconvenience to himself, as he had now only his evenings free, and for a year turned out a series called *Germany: Revolution and Counter-Revolution,* that did for recent events in that country, though with something less of brilliance and passion, what Marx was doing for France. They appeared over Marx's name, and even when Kautsky brought them out in a volume after Engels' death, were still credited by the editor to Marx. By the beginning of 1853, however, Marx was writing most of the articles himself. Through 1853–56 he was largely concerned with the Crimean War; Engels, who had applied himself seriously to the study of military strategy in the belief that revolutionists would need to master it, contributed opinions on the military situation. In the fall of 1854, they reported on the Spanish Revolution; and during 1861–62, on the American Civil War. Marx also supplied a commentary on British politics both for *The Tribune* and for the Chartist *People's Paper.*

This journalism, though not as a rule so remarkable as such an analysis as *The Class Struggles in France,* which Marx had written for his own review and into which he had been able to put all his thought, may nevertheless still be read with profit and with that intellectual satisfaction which is to be derived from all Marx's work. Marx differed from the ordinary political correspondent in that he had no contact with politicians: he was assisted by no inside gossip, by no official informants. But what he did have were all the relevant documents available in the British Museum; and as he was incapable of making a perfunctory job of anything, he put as much reading into these dispatches—both of the histories of such large subjects as Spain and India and of all sorts of diplomatic correspondence and parliamentary reports—as has often sufficed respectable writers for whole books. He was quite justified in complaining to Engels that he had been giving those fellows too much for their money.

One of the most striking features of all this commentary of Marx and Engels, if we return to it after the journalism and the political "theses" of the later phases of Marxism, is precisely its flexibility, its readiness to take account of new facts. Though the mainspring of the Dialectic was conceived as a very simple mechanism, the day-by-day phenomena of society were regarded by Marx and Engels as infinitely varied and complex. If they were mystical about the goal, they were realistic about the means of getting there. Certain assumptions—we shall examine them later—they had carried over from the more idealistic era of the *Communist Manifesto;* but these never blocked their realization that their hypothesis must fit actual facts. There are many respects in which Marx and Engels may be contrasted with the crude pedants and fanatics who have pretended to speak for the movement which Marx and Engels started; but none is more obvious than the honesty of these innovators in recognizing and respecting events and their willingness to learn from experience.

With this went an omnivorous interest in all kinds of intellectual activity and an appreciation of the work of others. This last may not seem easily reconcilable with the tendency we have noticed in Marx to split off from and to shut out other thinkers or with his habitual tone of scornful superiority and the earnest imitation of it by Engels. There are many passages in the Marx-Engels correspondence in which these two masters, who, like Dante (much quoted for such utterances by Marx), have decided to make a party by themselves, seem perversely, even insanely, determined to grant no merit to the ideas of anyone else. Yet it is as if this relentless exclusion of others were an indispensable condition for preserving their own sharply-angled point of view. It is as if they had developed their special cutting comic tone, their detached and implacable attitude, their personal polyglot language ("Apropos! Einige Portwein und Claret wird mir sehr wohl tun under present circumstances"; "Die verfluchte vestry hat mich bon gré mal gré zum 'constable of the vestry of St. Pancras' erwählt") in proportion as they have come to realize that they can take in more and more of the world, that they can comprehend it better and better, while other men, vulgarly addicted to the conviviality of political rhetoric, have never caught the sense of history at all, have no idea what is happening about them. Inside that reciprocal relationship, limited to the interchange of two men, all is clarity, coolness, intellectual exhilaration, self-confidence. The secret conspiracy and the practical joke conceal a watch-tower and a laboratory.

And here, in the general field of thought, if not always in that of practical politics, Marx and Engels are candidly alert for anything in science or literature that can help them to understand man and society. The timid man who seizes a formula because he wants above everything certainty, the snob who accepts a doctrine because it will make him feel superior to his fellows, the second-rate man who is looking for an excuse that will allow him to disparage the first-rate—all these have an interest in ruling out, in discrediting, in ridiculing, in slandering; and the truculence of Marx and Engels, which has come down as a part of the tradition, is the only part of their equipment they can imitate. But to the real pioneers of the frontiers of thought, to those who have accepted the responsibility for directing the ideas of mankind, to supply the right answer to every problem is far from appearing so easy. Such pioneers are painfully aware how little men already know, how few human beings can be counted on even to try to find out anything new, to construct a fresh picture of experience. Though Marx and Engels trusted the Dialectic, they did not believe it would do everything for them without initiative or research on their part nor did they imagine that it relieved them of the necessity of acquainting themselves with the ideas of other men. Hypercritical and harsh though Marx is in his strictures on such competitors as Proudhon, his sense of intellectual reality did compel him to do them justice—though it must be admitted that he was likely, as in the cases of Lassalle and Ernest Jones, to wait until after they were dead; and he was punctilious to the point of pedantry in making acknowledgments not merely to such predecessors as Ricardo and Adam Smith, but even to the author of an anonymous pamphlet published in 1740, in which he had found the first suggestion of the Labor Theory of Value.

Also, the Marxism of the founders themselves never developed into that further phase, where it was to be felt by the noblest of those working-class leaders who had accepted Dialectical Materialism, that all their thought should be strictly functional—that is, agitational and strategic; that they must turn their backs on non-political interests, not because these

were lacking in value but because they were irrelevant to
what had to be done. The tradition of the Renaissance still
hung about Marx and Engels: they had only partly emerged
from its matrix. They wanted to act on the course of history,
but they also loved learning for its own sake—or perhaps it
would be more correct to say that they believed that learning
gave power; and for all the intensity of Marx's desire to defeat
the antagonist in the class struggle, he declared that his favorite maxim was *"Nihil humanum alienum puto"*; and he and
Engels approached the past with a respect that had nothing
in common with the impulse which, justified on Marxist
grounds, figured in one phase of the Russian Revolution and
which was imitated by Marxists in other countries: the impulse to make a clean slate of culture.

Engels' championship of the Humanities in *Anti-Dühring*
might indeed be cordially approved by any defender of the
"Liberal Arts" education. "The people's school of the future"
projected by Herr Dühring, says Engels, is to be "merely a
somewhat 'ennobled' Prussian grammar school in which Greek
and Latin are replaced by a little more pure and applied
Mathematics and in particular by the elements of the philosophy of reality, and the teaching of German brought back
to Becker, that is, to about a Third Form level." Dühring
"wants to do away with the two levers that in the world as it
is today give at least the opportunity of rising above the narrow national standpoint: knowledge of the ancient languages,
which opens a wider common horizon at least to those who
have had a classical education; and knowledge of modern
languages, through the medium of which alone the people
of different nations can make themselves understood by one
another and acquaint themselves with what is happening beyond their own frontiers." "As for the aesthetic side of education, Herr Dühring will have to fashion it all anew. The poetry
of the past is worthless. Where all religion is prohibited, it
goes without saying that the 'mythological or other religious
trimmings' characteristic of poets in the past cannot be tolerated in this school. 'Poetic mysticism,' too, 'such as, for example, Goethe practised so extensively' is to be condemned.
Well, Herr Dühring will have to make up his mind to produce

for us those poetic masterpieces which 'are in accord with the higher claims of an imagination reconciled to reason,' and which represent the pure ideal that 'denotes the perfection of the world.' Let him lose no time about it! The conquest of the world will be achieved by the economic commune [proposed by Herr Dühring] only on that day when the latter, reconciled with reason, comes in at double time in Alexandrines."

And Marx and Engels had always before them—something which the later Marxists have sometimes quite lost sight of—the ideal man of the Renaissance of the type of Leonardo or Machiavelli, who had a head for both the sciences and the arts, who was both thinker and man of action. It was, in fact, one of their chief objections to the stratified industrial society that it specialized people in occupations in such a way as to make it impossible for them to develop more than a single aptitude; and it was one of their great arguments for communism that it would produce "complete" men again. They themselves had shied desperately away from the pundits of idealist Germany, whom they regarded as just as fatally deformed through a specialization in intellectual activity as the proletarian who worked in the factory through his concentration on mechanical operations; and they desired themselves, insofar as it was possible, to lead the lives of "complete" men. Something of the kind Engels certainly achieved, with his business, his conviviality, his sport, his languages, his natural sciences, his economics, his military studies, his article-writing, his books, his drawings and verses, and his politics; and what Marx lacked in practical ability and athletic skill he made up for by the immense range of his mind. It is true that the work of Marx himself, merging into and almost swamping that of Engels, had to become, under the pressure of the age, more exclusively economic; that the effects of the advance of machinery, which we have noted in the methods of Taine, are seen also in the later phases of Marxism, where it grows grimmer, more technical, more abstract. But there is still in Marx and Engels to the end that sense of a rich and various world, that comprehension of the many kinds of mastery possible for human beings, all interesting and all good in their kinds.

Engels' visits to London were always great events for the Marxes. Karl would become so much excited the day he was expecting his friend that he would be unable to do any work; and he and Engels would sit up all night, smoking and drinking and talking. But the life of the Marxes in England continued to be dismal and hard.

Marx had characteristically neglected to talk terms when he had been invited to write for *The Tribune*, and was taken aback when he learned that he was to get only five dollars an article. He supplied Dana with sixty articles during the first year that he was writing them himself. Dana liked them so well that he began running the best parts of them as leaders and leaving the remains to appear over Marx's name. Marx protested, but the best he could do was to get Dana to run the whole article anonymously in this way. Marx found himself reduced to two articles a week; and then—when the war was over and the boom of the early fifties collapsing, so that *The Tribune* began to retrench—to one; though Dana tried to make up for this by offering Marx supplementary work for *The American Encyclopaedia* and certain American magazines. In any case, Marx found that his income had now been cut down by two-thirds.

There is extant an apparently veracious account of the Marx household at the time when they were living in Soho, by a police agent who got to see them in 1853:

"[Marx] lives in one of the worst, therefore one of the cheapest neighborhoods in London. He occupies two rooms. The room looking out on the street is the parlor, and the bedroom is at the back. There is not one clean or decent piece of furniture in either room, but everything is broken, tattered and torn, with thick dust over everything and the greatest untidiness everywhere. In the middle of the parlor there is a large old-fashioned table covered with oilcloth. On it there are manuscripts, books and newspapers, as well as the children's toys, odds and ends from his wife's sewing-basket, cups with broken rims, dirty spoons, knives and forks, lamps, an ink-pot, tumblers, some Dutch clay-pipes, tobacco ashes—all in a pile on the same table.

"When you go into Marx's room, smoke and tobacco fumes make your eyes water to such an extent that for the first moment you seem to be groping about in a cavern, until you get used to it and manage to pick out certain objects in the haze. Everything is dirty and covered with dust, and sitting down is quite a dangerous business. Here is a chair with only three legs, then another, which happens to be whole, on which the children are playing at cooking. That is the one that is offered to the visitor, but the children's cooking is not removed, and if you sit down, you risk a pair of trousers. But all these things do not in the least embarrass Marx or his wife. You are received in the most friendly way and cordially offered pipes, tobacco and whatever else there may happen to be. Eventually a clever and interesting conversation arises which makes amends for all the domestic deficiencies, so that you find the discomfort bearable. You actually get used to the company, and find it interesting and original."

Sometimes they lived on bread and potatoes for days. Once when the baker had given them notice and asked for Marx when he brought the bread, the little boy, then seven and a half, had saved the situation by answering, "No, he ain't upstairs," and grabbing the bread and rushing off to deliver it to his father. They pawned everything at one time or another, including the children's shoes and Marx's coat—which prevented them from going out of doors. Jenny's family silver went to the pawnshop piece by piece. On one occasion, the pawnbroker, seeing the crest of the Duke of Argyll, sent for the police and had Marx locked up. It was Saturday night, and his respectable friends had all gone out of town for the week-end, so that he had to stay in jail till Monday morning. Sometimes Jenny would cry all night, and Karl would lose his temper: he was trying to write his book on economics.

The neighborhood was full of infections. They survived a cholera epidemic; but one winter they all had grippe at the same time. "My wife is sick. Jennychen is sick," Marx wrote Engels in the fall of '52. "Lenchen has a sort of nervous fever. I can't and haven't been able to call the doctor, because I

haven't any money for medicine." Marx was visited with piles
and boils, which made it impossible for him to sit down and
prevented his frequenting the library. In the March of 1851
another little girl was born, but she died of bronchitis a year
later. She had never had a cradle, and Jenny had to go to a
French refugee to borrow two pounds for a coffin: *"Quoique
de dure complexion,"* Marx wrote Engels on this occasion,
"griff mich diesmal die Scheisse bedeutend an." In January,
1855, another girl was born; but in April the surviving boy
died. Liebknecht says that he had "magnificent eyes and a
promising head, which was, however, much too heavy for his
body"; and he had shown signs of inheriting his father's brilliance: it was he who had outwitted the baker. But he was
delicate, and they had no way of taking care of him. Marx was
more affected by the death of this boy than by that of any of
his other children. "The house seems deserted and empty," he
writes Engels, "since the death of the child who was its living
soul. It is impossible to describe how much we constantly miss
him. I have suffered all sorts of bad luck, but now I know for
the first time what a genuine misfortune is. I feel myself
broken down [the last phrase is in English in the original].
. . . Among all the frightful miseries that I've been through
in these last days, the thought of you and your friendship
has always kept me up, and the hope that we still have something useful to accomplish in the world together." Two years
later Jenny gave birth to a still-born child under circumstances
so painful that Karl tells Engels he cannot bring himself to
write about them.

Jenny does not seem to have been a very good housekeeper;
the strong-minded Lenchen ran the household. But she had
much humor: her daughter Eleanor remembered her mother
and father as always laughing together; and she brought to
her unexpected role a dignity and loyalty that endured. To
the orphan Wilhelm Liebknecht, still in his twenties, another
socialist refugee from Germany, she appeared "now Iphigenia,
softening and educating the barbarian, now Eleonore, giving
peace to one who is slipping and doubts himself. She was
mother, friend, confidant, counselor. She was and she remains
for me still my ideal of what a woman should be. . . . If I

did not go under in London, body and soul, I owe it in a great measure to her, who, at the time when I thought I should be drowned in fighting the heavy sea of exile, appeared to me like Leucothea to the ship-wrecked Odysseus and gave me the courage to swim."

The police agent who has been quoted above said that Marx "as a husband and father, in spite of his wild and restless character, was the gentlest and mildest of men"; and everybody else bears him out. With his family Karl Marx was a patriarch, and where he dominated, he was able to love. He always turned off his cynical jokes and his bad language when there were women or children present; and if anybody said anything off-color, he would become nervous and even blush. He liked to play games with his children and is said to have written several of the biting pages of *The Eighteenth Brumaire of Louis Bonaparte* while they were sitting behind him playing horse, and whipping him to giddap. He used to tell them a long continued story about an imaginary character named Hans Röckle, who kept an enchanting toy-shop but who never had money in his pocket. He had men and women, dwarfs and giants, kings and queens, masters and journeymen, birds and four-footed beasts, as many as there were in Noah's Ark, tables and chairs, boxes and carriages, big and little, and all made out of wood. But in spite of the fact that he was a magician, he had debts to the butcher and the Devil, which he was never able to pay, and so he was forced to his great distress to sell all his beautiful things piece by piece to the Devil. And yet, after many adventures, some frightening and some funny, every one of them came back to him again.

Liebknecht, who called on the Marxes almost every day, gives a very genial picture of the family. They had Sunday outings on Hampstead Heath, with bread and cheese and beer and roast veal, which they carried along in a basket. The children were crazy for green things, and once they found some hyacinths in a corner of a field which had No Trespass signs but which they had had the temerity to invade. The walk home would be very gay: they would sing popular nigger songs and—"I assure you it's true," says Liebknecht—patriotic songs of the Fatherland, such as *"O Strassburg, O*

Strassburg, Du wunderschöne Stadt," which had been one of
the pieces that Karl had copied out in a collection of folk-
songs from different lands which he had made, when he was
a student, for Jenny; and Marx would recite *Faust* and *The
Divine Comedy,* and he and Jenny would take turns at
Shakespeare, which they had learned so to love from her
father. They made it a rule on these occasions that nobody
was to talk about politics or to complain about the miseries of
exile.

Sometimes little Jenny, who had the black eyes and big
forehead of her father, would burst out in what Liebknecht
describes as a "prophetic Pythian rapture." On one of these
walks one day she seemed to go into a trance and improvised
a kind of poem about another life on the stars. Her mother
became worried, and her father gave her a scolding and made
her stop.

The life of political exiles becomes infected with special
states of mind which are unimaginable for men who have a
country. Those precisely whose principles and interests have
raised them above the ordinary citizen, now, lacking the
citizen's base and his organic relation to society, find themselves contracted to something less. And, even aside from the
difficulties that the exile encounters in finding work and making friends in a foreign country, it is hard for him to take hold
in the new place, to build himself a real career there, because
he lives always in hope of going home when the regime by
which he has been banished shall have fallen.

For communists the situation is even harder. If they write
in their own language about what is happening at home, they
can print only on foreign presses works which have small
currency among the émigrés and which, sent back into the
fatherland, may compromise those who get them (see Engels'
letter to Marx on the subject of the latter's pamphlet exposing
the Communist trials in Cologne). And since the communist
has set himself against the whole complex of society, he must
try to live in it without being of it. He is thrown in upon his few
comrades and himself, and they develop bad nerves and bad
tempers; they are soon wasting their mental energies and their

emotions in sterile controversies and spiteful quarrels. Group enthusiasm turns to intrigue, and talent becomes diseased with vanity. The relationships of revolutionary brotherhood become degraded by jealousy and suspicion. Always braced against the pressure that bears down on them both as aliens and as enemies of society, the self-alienated man gives way to impulses to round upon his associates and accuse them of selling out the cause; always subject to secret espionage, always in danger of deportation or prison, he is obliged to suspect an informer in every person who seeks his acquaintance, becomes demoralized by shattering fears lest those closest to him be scheming to undo him by a betrayal for which his own poverty all too easily suggests a motive.

Of this danger Marx and Engels were well aware. "One comes to see more and more," Engels wrote Marx on February 12, 1851, "that the emigration is an institution which must turn everybody into a fool, an ass and a common knave, unless he manages to get completely away from it." But it was impossible for them really to get away: their letters continue to rasp with quarrels over revolutionary funds, sabotage of political meetings, ungenerous judgments, uneasy fears. Marx writes, in a letter to Weydemeyer of August 2 of the same year, that on top of all his other troubles he is obliged to support "the baseness of our enemies, who have never once attempted to attack me objectively, but who, revenging themselves for their own impotence, spread unspeakable slanders about me and try to blacken my reputation. . . . Several days ago, the 'famous' barrister Schramm meets an acquaintance on the street and immediately begins to whisper to him: 'However the revolution comes out, everybody agrees that Marx is done for. Rodbertus, who is the most likely to come to the top, will immediately order him shot.' And that's the way they all go on. So far as I myself am concerned, I laugh at all this idiocy, and it doesn't distract me from my work for a moment, but you can imagine that it does not produce any very salutary effect on my wife, who is ill and occupied from morning to night with problems of making both ends meet of the most depressing kind, and whose nervous system is run down, when every day foolish gossips bring her the stinking exhalations of the poisonous democratic sewer."

The crowning affront of this phase of Marx's life was an attack by a man named Karl Vogt, a German professor of Zoölogy, who had sat on the Left of the Frankfort Assembly and who had afterwards lived in exile in Switzerland. In the course of one of those wars of exiles, whose complications it would be unprofitable to trace, Vogt published in January, 1860, a brochure in which he accused Marx of blackmailing former revolutionists who were trying to go along with the regime in Germany, of fabricating counterfeit money in Switzerland, and of exploiting the workers for gain. This provoked Marx to write and publish in the November of the same year a long counter-attack on Vogt. His friends had done their best to dissuade him, telling him that he was wasting his time and his money (since he was printing the book at his own expense); but Marx insists that, filthy though the whole affair is, he owes it to his wife and children to make a defense of his character and career.

Herr Vogt did certainly vindicate Marx; and it made out a convincing case against Vogt on the basis of the charge which had been printed in a paper sponsored by Marx and which had started the polemics between him and Vogt: that the latter was a paid propagandist in the service of Napoleon III. Yet the reader is likely to agree with Marx's friends that Marx might better, as the Marxists say, have left his denouncer to History. For when the republican French government, after Sedan, published the archives of the Second Empire, it was found that Karl Vogt had indeed received forty thousand francs from the Emperor. And in the meantime Marx's book about him—in spite of a chapter of acute analysis of international events and a characteristically macabre caricature of one of those sordid police agents who were the plague of the exile's life—proved certainly one of the dreariest, most tedious and most exasperating productions of which a man of genius has ever been proud. Here Marx, by very force of his compulsion to go into every subject exhaustively, to fix each point with the last degree of exactitude, exposes a few ignoble lies and frauds with a machinery whose disproportion to its function only makes them appear more trivial. Marx's habitual sneer, which did duty for normal laughter and which sometimes seems almost passionate, can only here push mercilessly for pages jokes that are both forced and disgusting (Marx was almost as excremental as Swift).

And yet *Herr Vogt* itself is not without a moment of greatness which stands at the end like Marx's signature. When Vogt's charges had first been made, Marx had brought a libel suit in Germany against a paper which had given them currency. The Berlin court had refused his plea; he had appealed it and again been refused; he had taken it before the Supreme Court, and for the third time it had been rejected. Now, thwarted, he sets his brand of scorn with stinging and somber force on these judges of the petty courts of law who will not justify the higher judge. "It does not appear in the present case," the Royal Supreme Court had written, "that there has been any judicial error." So, says Marx, by a simple "not" (which has stood at the end of the sentence in German), a certain Herr von Schlickmann, in the name of the Royal Supreme Court, is empowered to reject his plea. It is a matter merely of writing that one word, without which the plea would have been granted. Herr von Schlickmann does not need to refute the arguments presented by Marx's counsel; he does not even need to discuss them; he does not need to mention them even. He has simply to tack a "not" on to a sentence.

"Wo also bleibt die *Begründung* der 'zurückweisenden' *Verfügung?* Wo die Antwort auf die sehr ausführliche Beschwerdeschrift meines Rechtsanwalts? Nämlich:

"SUB III: 'Ein solcher (Rechtsirrthum) *erhellt* jedoch im vorliegenden Falle nicht.'

"Streicht man aus diesem Satze SUB III das Wörtchen *nicht* weg, so lautet die Motivirung: 'Ein solcher (Rechtsirrthum) *erhellt* jedoch im vorliegenden Falle.' Damit wäre die Verfügung des Kammergerichts über den Hausen geworfen. Aufrecht erhalten wird sie also nur durch das am Ende aufpostirte Wörtchen '*Nicht*' womit Herr von *Schlickmann* im namen des Obertribunals die Beschwerdeschrift des Herr Justizrath Weber 'zurückweist.'

"Αὐτότατος ἔφη. *Nicht.* Herr von *Schlickmann* widerlegt die von meinem Rechtsanwalt entwickelten Rechtsbedenken *nicht,* er bespricht sie *nicht,* ja *erwähnt* sie *nicht.* Herr von *Schlickmann* hatte natürlich für seine 'Verfügung' hinreichende Gründe, aber er verschweigt sie. *Nicht!* Die Beweiskraft dieses Wörtleins liegt ausschliesslich in der Autorität, der hierarchischen Stellung der Person, die es in den Mund nimmt. An und für sich beweist Nicht Nichts. *Nicht!* Αὐτότατος ἔφη.

"So verbot mir auch das *Obertribunal* den 'Democrat' F. Zabel zu *verklagen.*

"So endete *mein Prozess mit den preussischen Gerichten.*"*

What is really behind the whole book, one realizes when one comes to this conclusion, is the helpless indignation of the man of integrity, whose principles have made him a rebel, in the face of a judicial system which, precisely because he is a rebel, will not recognize that integrity. One of the things that

---

* "Where then is the argument to be found on which this rejection is based? Where is the answer to the detailed petition drawn up by my attorney? Here it is:

"Under III: 'Now it does not appear in the present case that there has been such a judicial error.'

"If we strike out of this sentence under III the single little word 'not,' then the decision runs thus: 'Now it does appear in the present case that there has been such a judicial error.' In this way the order of the Court of Appeals is annulled and annihilated. It will only stand up through the interposition of that single little word 'not,' with which Herr von Schlickmann in the name of the Supreme Court rejects the petition of Herr Justizrath Weber.

"*He himself has spoken.* 'Not'! Herr von Schlickmann does 'not' refute the legal arguments adduced by my attorney; he does 'not' make any attempt to discuss them; he does 'not' mention them even. Herr von Schlickmann had of course his good and sufficient reasons for his order; but he prefers to keep silence about them. 'Not'! The power of demonstration possessed by this tiny word exclusively resides in the authority, in the hierarchical position, of the person who takes it in his mouth. In and by itself 'not' means 'nought.' 'Not'! *He himself has spoken.*

"So the Supreme Court has forbidden me to bring suit against the 'democrat' F. Zabel.

"So ended my case in the Prussian courts."

infuriated Marx most was a statement in the court's decision
that there had been nothing in the published slanders from
which Marx's reputation should suffer. And Marx's case is the
type of all such cases. The court says: You make war on
society; why should you expect vindication from its tribunals?
Had not the judges of Augsburg decided against Karl Vogt
in his suit against an Augsburg paper which had printed the
accusations against him, just as the judges of Berlin had decided against Karl Marx? Why not reduce the thing to absurdity by appealing to the bourgeois court to give you a good
character with your comrades as a sincere and self-denying
revolutionist?

For another kind of charge had been involved which was
serious enough and had enough truth in it to goad Marx—as
such charges always goaded him—more sharply perhaps than
all the foolish stories of counterfeit money and blackmail. Vogt
had included in his book a letter from a Prussian lieutenant
named Techow, written in 1850, at the time of the split in the
Communist League, of which Techow had been a member. "If
Marx," this former comrade had said, "had only as much heart
as intellect, if he had only as much love as hate, I would go
through fire for him, even though he has not only on several
occasions indicated his utter contempt for me, but has finally
expressed it quite frankly. He is the first and only one amongst
us whom I would trust for the capacity for leadership, the capacity for mastering a big situation without losing himself in
details." But Marx, said Techow, had come to be possessed by
the ambition for personal domination: he could now tolerate
only inferiors and despised his working-class supporters.

So Karl Marx must make his own court of justice, in which
he can vindicate his own moral superiority against the police
with their spies, the petty officials, the big officials, all the hol-
low simulacra of the Law, who are able, without effort, without suffering, without intellectual lights, to reject what ought
to be, what must certainly come, simply by writing that single
word "not."

Between *Herr Vogt* and *The Class Struggles in France* lies
a decade of the life of exile. The difference between them is
shocking. In Marx's writing of 1850, when he was a man in

his early thirties, for whom it was still a fine gesture to spend his patrimony on a revolutionary paper and pawn all his personal belongings, still flushed from his fight in Cologne, he had exulted in the consciousness of mastery of a vigorous and original mind with a new intellectual world before it; in *Herr Vogt* of 1860, half-atrophied in the monotony of London, with Jenny now in so bad a nervous condition that when she finally comes down with smallpox just as the book is being published, the doctor is to tell Karl that the infection has probably saved her from a mental collapse, he can only grind the wheels of his mind, spit out acid puns, rail reproachfully against that society which he has once so roundly defied.

And his protest itself will be stifled. He got rid of about eighty copies in England, but the book was never distributed in Germany, because of the failure of the German publisher who had brought it out in London. Marx's agreement with this young German had been that they should go halves on both profit and loss; but the young man had had a partner who did not hesitate to invoke the law and to claim the whole costs of printing, so that Marx not only lost what he had put up, but had to pay out almost as much again. He had never thought to get a written contract.

13   Historical Actors: Lassalle

There has never been any easy way of solving the problems that arise from the conflict of internationalism with nationalism. The wars of liberation of the French Revolution turned into the imperialism of Napoleon. The socialism of Marx and Engels called for the rising of an international proletariat, whose interests were everywhere the same, against the oppression of an international bourgeoisie; but since for this struggle to begin it was necessary that the industrial system should have run through the whole of its capitalist development, they came to regard the various countries as more or less "advanced" in proportion to the degree of this development; and this led, in actual struggles between nations, to backing the more "advanced" countries against the less—which in turn made it possible to disguise motives that were emotional and nationalistic in arguments that pretended to be based on a strategy demanded by socialist objectives.

This conflict has been productive of more paradoxes and absurdities perhaps than any other aspect of radical thought—Shaw's defense of the British policy in South Africa on the basis of the backwardness of the Boers; the position of those American socialists who approved the participation of the United States in the World War on the ground that in order to achieve socialism it was necessary to save capitalism first; and the contention of their former critics, the Communists of the Soviet Union, that the alliances desired by the Kremlin would somehow contribute to the proletarian revolution which the Kremlin was sabotaging in Spain. So that in contrast to much

hat has happened since, the handling by Marx and Engels of
hese problems—and especially in view of the fact that they
vere pioneers in international thinking—seems remarkably con-
cientious and sagacious. They did, however, land themselves
n some conspicuous contradictions. They denounced the imperialistic designs of Russia and the exploitation of Ireland
by England; yet their own attitude toward the Danes and the
Czechs was much like that of the English toward the Irish:
hey tended to regard them as troublesome little peoples
vhose pretensions to civilizations of their own were not to be
aken seriously. The unification of Germany at that time was
an essential part of their revolutionary program, and unifica-
ion led to making short shrift of the claims of non-German
neighbors in regions where Germans, too, were involved. The
only submerged neighbors of Germany to whose demands
hey paid attention were the Poles, because they were afraid
of the domination of Poland by Russia; and even here their
public championship of the Poles against the exploitation of
he Prussians in the days of the *Neue Rheinische Zeitung* did
not a little later prevent Engels from writing to Marx—on May
23, 1851—a letter proposing a hair-raising policy of German
Realpolitik in Poland, according to which, "under the pretext
of defending them," the Germans were to "occupy their for-
tresses, especially Posen" and "take away from the Poles of the
West everything that we can." "The more I reflect upon history, the more clearly I see that the Poles are completely
foutu as a nation and that they can only be useful as a means
to an end up to the time when Russia herself is drawn into the
agrarian revolution. From that moment Poland will no longer
have any *raison d'être* whatever. The Poles have never done
anything in history except commit courageous quarrelsome
stupidities. It would be impossible to cite a single occasion
when Poland, even as against Russia, has successfully represented progress or done anything whatever of historical significance. Russia, on the other hand, has shown herself
genuinely progressive against the East," etc. Engels also approved when the "energetic Yankees" took California away
from the "lazy Mexicans," because he believed that the former
were better fitted to work the country and open up the Pacific.

When the French were finally provoked to fight the Prussians by Bismarck's doctoring of the King's telegram, it put a tax on the philosophy of Marx and Engels to calculate the positions that would be correct at any given turn of affairs. They began by backing the Germans. "The French need a thrashing," Marx said. "If the Prussians win, then the centralization of the *state power* will help the centralization of the German working class. German preponderance, moreover, will shift the center of gravity of the working-class movement of Western Europe from France to Germany"—which would mean, he added, "the preponderance of *our* theory over those of Proudhon, etc." But when it became evident that the Prussians were not content simply to beat Louis Bonaparte, but were going on to grab Alsace and Lorraine, Marx and Engels began to protest, on the ground that this act of aggression would drive France into an alliance with the Tsar. In the meantime, they had been approving the resolutions drawn up by the French and German branches of the Workers' International, which condemned nationalistic wars in general—though the hostilities had at first been accepted by the German workers as a "defensive war" and an "unavoidable evil."

It was hard to deal realistically with the immediate situation and yet keep in mind the ultimate goal. After all, Bismarck stood, as the Republicans had, for German unification, and his war against France, which had the effect of compelling the South Germans to combine for defense with Prussia, was one of his means of accomplishing this. Marx and Engels were trying to keep clear the distinction between the national interests of Germany and the dynastic ambitions of Prussia. As Rhinelanders, they detested the Prussians; and perhaps the only serious case of a failure of realism in their political prognosis was their obstinate failure to recognize, even after it was well under way, the rise and domination of Prussia. It is curious to watch in their letters their reactions to what is happening in Germany. "It is nauseating," Marx writes Engels on the occasion of his visit to Berlin in the spring of 1851, "to see—especially in the theater—the predominance of uniforms." Engels is still able to hope in the May of 1866, just before the battle of Sadowa, which is to consolidate the power of Prussia, that if Bismarck makes war on Italy, "the Berliners will blow off the lid. If they would only proclaim the Republic, then Europe would be upside down in a few days." He was unable to bring himself to believe that Northern and Southern Germany were going to "come to blows simply because Bismarck wants them to do so"; predicted that, if this should occur, Prussia would be defeated; and then, even after the defeat by Prussia of Austria and of the North German states which had sided with her against Prussia, could still write: "The whole affair has this good feature: that it simplifies the situation and thereby makes a revolution easier, that it eliminates the riots of the petty capitals and in any case accelerates development. In the long run, a German parliament is something quite different from a Prussian chamber."

He relays to Marx the stories that are reaching him from friends in Germany, with a mixture of hatred of the Prussians and ridicule of the timidity and ineptitude of the people of such places as Frankfort and Nassau, which have just been annexed by the Prussians. "Wehner, who has just come back from Hanover, tells me that the Prussian officers have already made themselves thoroughly hated there, as well as the bureaucrats and the police." "The Sow-Prussians are certainly operating in the most admirable fashion. I should never have imagined that they could be so stupid; but actually it is impossible to imagine them stupid enough. All the better. The affair is under way, and we'll get the Revolution all the quicker." Yet he has just had a first-hand account of the tactics of the Nassau army. They had been confronted with the problem of bridging the Main and, after failing in their first attempt, as they declared, on account of a storm—"a storm on the Main!" exclaims Engels—they had discovered, when they returned to the task, that they had only enough pontoons to reach half-way across, and so they had written the people of Darmstadt to help them out with some more pontoons, "which they eventually received, and so the bridge over the terrible river was finished. Immediately after this, the Nassauese got the order to march south. They leave the bridge there completely unguarded, entrusting it to the sole care of an old boatman, who is to see that it's not swept off down the river. A few days afterwards the Prussians arrived, took possession of the convenient bridge, fortified it and marched across it!" It is the campaign in the Palatinate all over again; and yet Engels, who tells the story with a drollery that betrays affection, cannot believe in the triumph of Prussia.

These problems of the patriotic German socialist confronted with the constructive activities of Bismarck were involved in the relations of Marx and Engels with the great spokesman of the next phase of German socialism: Ferdinand Lassalle.

Lassalle was the only son of a well-to-do Jewish silk merchant of Breslau. He was born April 11, 1825, and so was seven years younger than Marx. His father had taken a name based on his own native town of Loslau, and the son afterwards gave it a French form. In his character and his relation to his family, he in some ways strikingly resembled Marx. He was an only son and, like Marx, he was gifted and adored by his father, whom he treated with passionate arrogance. Unlike Marx, he was emotional and tumultuous and vain of his person as well as of his attainments. He used to make terrible scenes with his sister, and he attempted to fight duels with his schoolmates, whom he would accuse of putting indignities upon him.

In Lassalle's case, the break with Judaism came not with the father as it had done in Marx's case, but with Ferdinand himself. He had been admitted at thirteen to the synagogue; and when he broke out into the freedom of secular thought, he became even more intoxicated than Marx, for whom old Heinrich had already set a tradition of rationalistic modern thought. Disdaining the family silk business, he demanded an academic training. The vision of Hegel had apparently taken hold of him, for when his father asked him what he wanted to study, he answered: "The greatest, the most comprehensive study in the universe, the study that is most closely associated with the most sacred interests of mankind: the study of History."

He had had a bad time at a commercial academy in Leipzig. His pride and his precocious brilliance as well as his uncontrolled temper made trouble for him with a prosaic headmaster, who told him that he had best become an actor because then he would be able to play Shylock. When at fifteen, full of Heine and Börne, he heard of the persecution of Jews in Damascus, he made a furious entry in his diary: "Even the Christians wonder at the sluggishness of our blood—wonder that we do not rise in revolt, in order that we may die on the battlefield rather than in the torture chamber." He once wrote Marx that he had been a revolutionist since that year, 1840— and a socialist since 1843. He applied at a Catholic *Gymnasium* to take university entrance examinations, believing that, in view of the alliance which the Catholics were making with the Jews against their common enemy Protestant Prussia, no discrimination against him would be shown; but he found that he was rejected on the pretext that he had not fulfilled all the formalities of application. He immediately appealed to the Minister for Public Worship and Education and actually persuaded him to arrange his admission. He did well in the examinations—in the oral examination came out first; but he was flunked by a Protestant professor of Theology who, in his capacity of government commissioner, was conducting the examination. The examiners protested to the commissioner; but the latter, pointing out that his own son had never been allowed to get beyond the Sixth Form, declared that Lassalle should never have been admitted to take the examinations in the first place, since he had improperly applied to the minister over the heads of the examining board. The boy now appealed to the minister again, but was told that he would have to resubmit himself. He was passed the next year and entered the University of Breslau.

But at Breslau he got into hot water, was punished by ten days' detention for demonstrating against a professor who had attacked Feuerbach and the Young Hegelians; and he went on to the University of Berlin. There he saturated himself with Hegel, got up at four in the morning to read him, became transported by the feeling that he was realizing himself as the Idea of the Hegelian World Spirit: "Through philosophy," he wrote his father, "I have become self-comprehending reason— that is to say, God aware of himself." He denounced the old man as a bourgeois and made frantic demands on him for money. If there was something of Marx about Lassalle, there was a good deal of Disraeli, too. On his way to Berlin from Breslau, he had passed through the Silesian villages where the weavers' strike was in progress and had listened to their songs of rebellion, and he already regarded himself as a champion of the proletariat. But he aimed also to succeed in society; he was a dandy and drove spirited horses, and he addressed himself to the conquest of women with the same compelling energy and eloquence that he was to display in his political speeches and legal arguments. Of his love letters he might have said as he did about one of his pamphlets, that he was "weaving out of logic and fire a web which will, I think, not fail of its effect." In his twenties, he was slender, with curly brown hair, a fine intellectual forehead and an incisive aquiline profile.

It was in a manner characteristically resourceful and characteristically unconventional that he found his first opportunity to make himself famous at the same time that he waged his first fight for the victims of an unjust society. There was a lady, the Countess Sophie von Hatzfeldt, a princess by birth and of one of the great German families, who had been married at seventeen to a man of a different branch of the same family for the purpose of settling a dispute about entail between this branch of the Hatzfeldts and her father's. Her husband conceived an implacable antagonism toward her; he took her share of the family money, was unfaithful; tried to deprive her of her children. He sent her daughters to a convent in Vienna; and finally, in 1846, threatened his fourteen-year-old son to disinherit him unless he consented to leave his mother. It was at this point that Lassalle stepped in. The Countess had been attempting to put through a divorce, but the tradition was all against it: German families were run by the males, and her brothers had sabotaged all her efforts. Now Lassalle, though he had been studying philosophy, not law, went to the Countess von Hatzfeldt and induced her to fight for her rights and to put the whole affair in his hands. She had turned out to be a woman of strong character; smoked cigars and is said to have produced a pistol and threatened to shoot an aide-de-camp of the King's who had been sent to get her son for the purpose of putting him away in a military academy. "Convinced," says Lassalle of the Countess, "that right was on her side, she had confidence in her own strength and in mine. She accepted my proposal with all her heart. Thereupon, I, a young Jew without influence, pitted myself against the most formidable forces—I alone against the world, against the power of rank and of the whole aristocracy, against the power of limitless wealth, against the government and against the whole hierarchy of officials, who are invariably the natural allies of rank and wealth, and against every possible prejudice. I had resolved to combat illusion with truth, rank with right, the power of money with the power of the spirit." For it was against the subjection of women itself that he was contending in the Countess's divorce suit: "You seem to overlook the fact," he once told her, "that your body has been borrowed by an idea of permanent historical importance."

He worked fast: he made his father give him money, and he bribed the Hatzfeldt peasants to testify against the Count and the press to arouse public opinion against him. The Count seemed about to capitulate and agree to a settlement on the Countess when Lassalle through a wilful gesture forfeited all he had won. Lassalle had sent to ask for a personal interview, and the Count had had the servant put out. The young man at once wrote an insolent letter, in which he threatened Hatzfeldt with violence unless he received an apology, and thereby so infuriated the Count that an arrangement became impossible. The contest went on for eight years. Lassalle worked unflaggingly, stopped at nothing. He engineered the theft from the Count's mistress of a casket which he believed to contain the bond of an annuity settled on the mistress against the interest of the Countess and her children. But the bond was not in the casket, and the friends of Lassalle who had taken it were found out and sent to jail. Lassalle only redoubled his attack: he launched a whole set of lawsuits against the Count, produced three hundred and fifty-eight witnesses, brought charges before thirty-six tribunals, and argued the case in court himself. He even led a demonstration of peasants against the Count on his own estate. Finally, Lassalle himself was arrested for his part in the casket theft and was put in jail in Cologne in February, 1848.

It was just a few days before the uprising in France. Lassalle pasted up on the wall of his cell a *Manifesto to the People* by Blanqui, which he had found in a Paris paper; and when he appeared in August for trial, he made a speech that lasted six hours, in which his defense in the matter of the casket was carried over into a general vindication of his "honest and indefatigable efforts to secure recognition for the violated rights of man." In the meantime, the Countess Hatzfeldt had been appearing at public meetings, denouncing the forces of reaction and declaring that she considered herself a proletarian. The jury did not fail to acquit Lassalle. He emerged a revolutionary hero. At Düsseldorf, the people unhitched the horses from the carriage in which he and the Countess were riding and drew them through the streets. His defense before the tribunals of revolutionary Cologne had made his reputation as an orator, and he now plunged furiously into political activity. He led a delegation from Düsseldorf to a mass meeting on the Rhine called by Engels for the purpose of declaring allegiance to the Frankfort Assembly against Prussia, which resounded through the whole of Germany; and he was arrested and put in jail in November for supporting the appeal signed by Marx which urged the people to refuse to pay taxes and to mobilize against the government. Marx and Engels did their best to get him out; but his case was not allowed to come to trial till May, 1849. In prison he had been harassing the authorities with a continual bombardment of petitions. He bullied the warden so unmercifully that the man finally complained to the governer; and when the governor visited his cell, Lassalle rebuked him for not saying "Good morning," refused to let him utter a word of protest and demanded facilities for filing a suit against the prison authorities. When he finally appeared in court, he had already had the speech he had written printed and sold in the town. This speech was an arraignment of the government for violating the reforms it had guaranteed and using the courts to persecute persons who were only trying to enforce those reforms, and of the Frankfort Assembly for not fighting. When he discovered that the public were to be excluded from the courtroom, he refused to deliver this speech, knowing well that the jury had read it, and simply demanded immediate acquittal. The jury brought in a verdict of not guilty; but the authorities, now convinced that he was dangerous, kept him in prison till 1851, and arrested the Countess Hatzfeldt.

The Countess' divorce, however, did go through in 1850; and by 1854 the Count had been so beaten down that he agreed to a settlement on terms very favorable to the Countess. Lassalle and she were now intimate allies. He seems to have had a low opinion of his mother, whom he once described as "the goose that had hatched out an eagle's egg"; and his relation to the Countess became filial—she was twenty years older than he. They lived together at Düsseldorf for years—since he was not allowed to return to Berlin. She had forfeited her social position; but Lassalle, on his side, through her tutelage, had grown steadier and more urbane. "I cannot associate with you any longer," he had said to one of the unfortunate Jewish friends whom he had involved in the casket scandal and who was just about to serve a term in jail for it. "You have become unpolished and rough." The same man, Arnold Mendelssohn, wrote him later: "It is inscribed in the book of Fate that you are to destroy yourself and your associates." Yet a letter from Mendelssohn to the Countess shows a loyalty to something noble which made itself felt through the arrogant exhibitionism.

The Countess herself he treated in the same driving and domineering way. When he finally maneuvered a return to Berlin in 1857, he gave her orders, against her vehement protest, not to come to join him in the capital, because the Queen so disapproved of her conduct that she would not have them both there at the same time, and he had been notified that if the Countess came, he would be obliged to leave. This was the period of his literary and social successes. He set himself up in a splendid establishment with, as he boasted, four great reception rooms and with an immense stock of books and wines. And here he entertained those members of the nobility and the fashionable and learned worlds who had the courage to come to see him. A young lady whom he wanted to marry, the daughter of a Russian official, has left an account of his house. The general effect, she says, was not attractive; it was cluttered with a great mixture of furnishings, obviously intended for effect: Turkish divans, wall brackets, bronzes, enormous mirrors, heavy satin hangings, great Japanese and Chinese jars; but his study was simple and serious and showed a more decent taste. He had just published a work on Heraclitus, on which he had been working for years and in which he tried to trace to the Greek philosopher the principles expounded by Hegel, but of which Marx and others have said that it had more bulk and show of learning than content; and he wrote also a blank-verse tragedy on a subject from the Peasant War, an Hegelian work on jurisprudence, and a pamphlet on foreign policy which, though intended to promote the interests of revolution, anticipated Bismarck's design of weakening the power of Austria. He speculated on the Stock Exchange, paid a visit to Garibaldi in Italy, thrashed with his cane a jealous official with whom he had come into conflict over the affections of a married lady, and courted the young Russian lady, whom he had met at Aix-la-Chapelle, writing her a forty-page letter and summoning the Countess to back him, at a time when he could hardly get around except in a wheel-chair. He had caught syphilis at twenty-two; it had got into the secondary stage and had never been satisfactorily cured, and now the bones in one of his legs were going. He had as yet no real political role and could only throw his energies away. This was already the end of 1860.

He had twice applied, after 1848, for membership in the Communist League; but the Communists had been suspicious of his ambitions and of his connection with the aristocratic Countess—so that, aside from raising funds and assisting escapes for the victims of the Cologne frame-up, he could play no part in the revolutionary movement. He had always admired Marx, and he was bound to respect Marx's position as the actual head of the movement. Lassalle had raised money for him at the time when Marx had first gone to England, had attempted at Marx's request to get him journalistic work on the Continent, had arranged for the publication of one of his books, and had worked to get him reinstated in Germany after Wilhelm, the new king, had declared, subject to many conditions, an amnesty of political exiles. Marx was irritated by

Lassalle's pretentiousness and resented his lordly tone; he probably envied his freedom of movement and his being on the spot in Germany. He obviously hated to owe anything to Lassalle's kindness, and he ridiculed him ferociously to Engels. Lassalle, in siding with Marx at the time of the Vogt affair, had ventured to take him to task for having believed the original charges against Vogt, and to lecture him on his suspicious disposition. Marx had also been suspecting Lassalle himself of holding up the publication of his, Marx's, book in order to make way for his own pamphlet, which was being printed by the same publisher in Germany; and this had come to Lassalle's knowledge. Marx, thereupon, to prove to Lassalle how extraordinarily free from suspicion he was, sent the latter a slanderous letter against him which he had received seven years before, referred to further accusations, which he said were in the archives of the League, and made a merit of having refrained from believing them. Lassalle overwhelmed him with irony: he stood up to Marx as he did to everyone. The result was that Marx soon suspected Lassalle of sabotaging the sale of his book. Yet Lassalle persuaded Marx to visit him in Berlin in the spring of 1861, had him photographed, fed him venison and mayonnaise; the Countess, "in order to insult the Royal Family," got him a seat for the ballet in a box that was right up against the royal one. And Lassalle set forth to Marx a project for bringing out a new radical daily paper, which the two of them were to publish together and for which the Countess was to put up the funds. With the advent of Wilhelm and the amnesty, the old revolutionists were returning; and Lassalle wanted to give them an organ.

But the authorities, in spite of Lassalle's efforts, would not have Marx back at any price; and his possible collaboration with Lassalle was wrecked on the very eve of a new workers' movement in Germany by personal considerations which miserably interfered with what Marx and Lassalle both regarded as their historic role. Lassalle returned Marx's visit by coming to London the next July. He was full of a new political agitation upon which he had just embarked in Germany. The uniforms which had angered Marx when he had sat next to the royal box the year before were beginning to meet opposition. A

liberal majority in the Prussian parliament had been obstructing the plans of the War Minister, who was demanding a
stronger army; and the result was that on March 11 King
Wilhelm dissolved this parliament. Four weeks later, Lassalle
had delivered before a factory workers' organization in Berlin
an address which he called a *Workers' Program*. The universal
manhood suffrage of 1848 had been transformed in 1849 into
a three-class system of suffrage graded according to direct
taxation, that is, according to income; and this practically excluded the working class and the petty bourgeoisie at a time
when they were being exploited indirectly through taxes on
food, stamps, etc., for the bulk of the expenditure of the
government. Lassalle presented himself as a leader in the
movement for universal suffrage; and in putting the case before his audience with characteristic clearness and force, he
also expounded to them the whole materialistic theory of
history: the class struggle, the development of industry, and
the role of the proletariat in the future, of which the fight for
universal suffrage merely counted as the momentary task:
"Insofar as the lower classes of society strive for the improvement of their situation *as a class*, the improvement of their
lot *as a class*, to precisely this extent will this *personal* interest
—instead of opposing the historical movement and finding itself
condemned to a completely immoral course—coincide in its
direction with the development of the entire *people*, with the
victory of the Idea, with the advances of civilization, with the
life principle of History itself, which is nothing other than
the development of *Freedom*. That is, as we have already seen
above, *your* cause is the cause of all *humanity*." He had also
begun talking to the liberals in terms of Marxist social dynamics: constitutional questions, he told them, were "not legal
questions but questions of power"; they could never get themselves a constitution by filling up a sheet of paper with words,
but only by changing the relationship of power. Lassalle was
aiming at coöperation between the workers and the bourgeois
liberals. The new elections in May had returned a liberal
majority even larger.

Marx was later in a letter to Engels to characterize the
Workers' Program as a "bad vulgarization of the *Manifesto*

and of other ideas which we have expounded so often that they have already become more or less commonplaces," and to ridicule in the same way for its obviousness Lassalle's speech on the constitution. But such criticisms, from the point of view of what Lassalle was trying to do—that is, making the Marxist principles effective in practical politics—were quite beside the point. And the question of the newspaper was still unsettled. Marx had written Engels that Lassalle could be useful only as one of the editorial staff and "under strict discipline." When he had suggested to Lassalle in Berlin that Engels should be asked to join them, Lassalle had answered that that would be all right, "if three wouldn't be too many," but that he could only allow Marx and Engels to have one vote between them, as otherwise he could always be outvoted. Now it happened that Marx found himself in the position of being obliged to repay the hospitality of Lassalle just at the moment when his own fortunes were at their lowest.

The Marxes had finally succeeded in getting away from Soho. Jenny Marx's mother had died in 1856 and left her £120, and in the October of that year they had purchased £40 worth of furniture and moved into a four-story house—a relatively magnificent residence, with ornamental window-frames of stone inlaid in the brick façade and half a bay with a pane of stained glass partitioned off from the house next door —in Grafton Terrace, Maitland Park, on Haverstock Hill. Marx wrote Engels that when he next came to London, he would find them in "ein vollständiges home." But hardly had they got themselves settled when *The Tribune* began to cut down on Marx's articles—so that, involved in heavier expenses— though "der show von respectability" had had the effect of doing something for his credit—he found his resources seriously reduced. Life in Maitland Park had turned out to be at least as difficult as life in Soho had been. He wanted to keep up appearances for his daughters: if it had been only a question of himself, he wrote Engels, or even if he had only had sons, he would willingly have gone to live in Whitechapel, "but for the girls at the time when they are growing up, such a meta-morphosis would hardly be suitable." The girls were extremely bright. Laura had won an accessit and Jenny a first prize for general scholarship when they were the youngest girls in the class at the private school to which Marx had sent them. He had also given them music lessons. But they were obliged to face the world and to make their way, with their poverty and the bitterness of their parents always dragging them back into the shadow. The year of Lassalle's visit, when the girls were seventeen and eighteen, young Jenny, the one who as a child had had the fantasy about life on the stars, showed signs of giving up the struggle. Her father wrote Engels in February that she had been two months under the care of the doctor: "The child has been visibly wasting away. Jenny is old enough now so that she feels the whole strain and mess of the conditions under which we live, and the ailment from which she is suffering is, I believe, chiefly due to this. . . . For she has gone to Mrs. Young, without telling us, to try, if you please, to get work in the theater."

"The poor children," he wrote in June, "are all the more a source of distress to me because all this [their straits had compelled them to pawn even the children's clothes and Lenchen's shoes] has happened during this Exhibition season when their friends are all enjoying themselves and they can only sit at home and be afraid someone will come to call on them and see the misery in which they live." And he says in the same letter that his wife wishes every day that she were in the grave with the children. Lassalle arrived in July. He had endeared himself already to the Marx ladies. The year before when Frau Marx had been recovering from an attack of smallpox and her face was pitted with scars, he had written her long and gallant letters and tried to make her feel more hopeful about her appearance. Her letters, he had told her, were so charming and kind that they made him want to kiss her hand at every word he read; and indeed Jenny's letters to Lassalle pour out a pathetic exuberance of gratitude. It was a long time since she had been the object of gallantry or even seen anything of men of the world. When Marx had sent her away to Ramsgate to recuperate from one of her breakdowns, she had made the acquaintance of what her husband described as "distinguished and, *horribile dictu,* intellectual English ladies"; and he wrote Engels that it seemed to have done her good, "after years of bad society or none," to "see something of people of her own kind." And Lassalle had sent the ladies all mantillas when Marx had come back from Berlin. She had put hers on and walked up and down the room, as little "Tussy," the youngest, had said in English: "Just like a peacock!" When finally he came to visit them in the height of the London season and at the time of the Exhibition, he brought with him the glamor of smart Berlin.

She made great efforts to entertain him; took to the pawnshop, as her husband wrote Engels, "everything not nailed and riveted down." But the wolves and the Furies outstripped her. The landlord, who had hitherto been quiet, demanded his £25, and threatened to send the bailiff in; the piano man, who was a brutal lout, threatened to haul Marx into court unless he paid up the £6 that was owing; the baker, the greengrocer and the tea grocer and all the rest of the Devil's crew had come down on him about their bills; and the tax-collector's notice about the taxes was there. At the same time the doctor had told them that young Jenny was in such serious condition that she would have to have two weeks at the seaside; and little Tussy was coming down with something that looked like jaundice. Lassalle talked about the five thousand thalers which he had just lost on a speculation; and he was spending, as Marx bitterly noted, at least £1 a day for cabs and cigars alone. Marx seems to have become daily more bitter. He tells Engels that the fellow assumes that because he, Marx, has no regular "business" but only "theoretical work," Lassalle is free to waste his time as he likes; and he furiously resents Lassalle's offering to help solve the problem of the Marx girls by installing one of them as companion to the Countess. He now finds Lassalle completely exasperating: "The everlasting chatter in the falsetto voice, the unlovely demonstrative gestures, the tone of setting you right about things." Marx thought Lassalle had changed since he had last seen him; he had become, he said, "quite insane": he was now "not only the greatest scholar, the deepest thinker, the most brilliant investigator, but also a Don Juan and a revolutionary Cardinal Richelieu." And it may be—later events seem to confirm it—that Marx's impression of a change in Lassalle was not due entirely to spleen: Lassalle showed doubtless at that time the doomed restlessness, the desperate superexcitation, of a man who felt the spirochaete of syphilis at work in his blood and his bones. Marx at any rate fixed upon him a terrible eye which shriveled him to the skeleton of a Marxist grotesque. He had already exhausted in his letters to Engels all the insulting nicknames he could think of based on the idea that Lassalle was a Jewish parvenu: "he must live like a Jewish baron or rather (through the Countess apparently) like a baronized Jew." But now, as he studies Lassalle's hair and the peculiar shape of his head, he decides that he must absolutely have Negro blood: "This combination of Jewry and Germanry with a fundamental Negro stock would give rise to a very singular product. The fellow's self-assertiveness is nigger, too."

One day Marx behaved so gloomily that Lassalle asked him about his finances. The tradesmen had now begun threatening to stop supplies and to sue him, and he put the situation before his friend, who offered at once to help. He would lend Marx £15 without conditions and as much more as he liked, on the security of Engels or someone else. Marx accepted the £15 and arranged to borrow £60 more. Lassalle left London; and in August Marx got a letter from him from Wildbad insisting on having a bond from Engels which should obligate Engels himself to pay the security eight days before the note fell due —"not, naturally, that I have any doubt that you are writing with his approval"; but he must be guaranteed against unforeseen circumstances or death. Marx took offense and wrote Lassalle sarcastically that his name on the note would never appear in any connection with the latter's "bourgeois existence" or compromise any "bourgeois drama." Lassalle, as usual, struck back. The affair got worse and worse. Six days before the note fell due, Lassalle wrote Marx an unpleasant letter, in which he demanded his money, and also asked him to send back an annotated book that he had lent him a year before; and he followed it with a curt note to Engels. The money was immediately paid; and Marx replied with something in the nature of an apology, which Lassalle might well have accepted: he confessed that he had been at fault in taking amiss

Lassalle's request for a bond from Engels, but that it had hardly been magnanimous of Lassalle to play the prosecuting attorney against him at a time when he had been in such a frightful state of mind that he would willingly have put a bullet through his head; he hoped that their friendship was strong enough to withstand such a (near-English) "chock"; he would send him back his book right away, but he had discovered that it would cost ten shillings. It was the end of their relationship.

Yet Lassalle had gone back to Germany to perform the great work of his life, for which he had only two years left. In August the Prussian Chamber refused to grant an appropriation for more than two years of army service. The war minister demanded three years: the first two years, it was said, to teach the soldier to shoot the foreign enemy; the third, to shoot his mother and father. The King was on the point of abdication, complaining with naïveté that he could not find a ministry which would permit him to rule without the approval of a parliamentary majority, when Bismarck came to the rescue by offering to form such a ministry and persuading the King to let him take over. Thinking only of the coming struggle with Austria, of the necessity of making Germany a great power, dominated and drilled by Prussia, he announced that the moment had come for a regime of "blood and iron." He proceeded to rule for four years without a parliamentary budget, putting through the army program and defying and insulting the parliament, on the pretext that the constitution failed to indicate what was to be done in the event of the King's and the parliament's being unable to agree on the budget. In the meantime, Lassalle's *Workers' Program* had been confiscated by the police as soon as it was published, and Lassalle was being prosecuted "for having publicly incited the non-possessing classes to hatred and contempt for the possessing classes." He now delivered another address in which he urged the Chamber to protest by suspending its sittings. But the German liberals of 1862 were as wordy and ineffective as those of 1848. They easily allowed their leadership to slip away in the practice of a parliamentary procedure which could no longer obtain recognition; and the leadership of the movement for reform now passed definitely to a different quarter.

At the beginning of December, a working-class delegate from Leipzig came to Lassalle and asked him to call a general congress of the German working class. He had already plunged with something even more than his usual feverish avidity into the study of economics; and he now launched upon an agitation unprecedented in mid-century Germany for its activity, its daring and its brilliance. In January of the following year, he stood trial for his *Workers' Program*. He spoke for four hours: assaulted the prosecutor, the son of Schelling, with quotations from the works of his father, overrode the lawyer's attempts to shut him up by insisting upon his right to be heard on the question of whether he ought to be silenced, and delivered a pro-proletarian speech which delighted the members of the Leipzig union who had come to Berlin to hear him. In March, he gives them a fighting manifesto: "A party of labor now exists. This party must be provided with a theoretical understanding and with a practical war-cry, even if it cost me my head three-and-thirty times." In May, he organizes this party as the General Union of German Workers.

He had already attracted the attention of Bismarck as a force that deserved serious consideration. The Minister-President had invited him to an interview, and they had discussed the situation of the working class. Lassalle was advocating at this time a program of State aid for productive associations of workers; the money was to be found by granting universal suffrage and having the workers themselves vote for loans. Lassalle differed most from Marx—though we have seen that Marx and Engels themselves were not always quite consistent in this respect—in conceiving the State, not merely as the instrument of a dominating class, undesirable in itself and at best a temporary necessity for that dictatorship of the proletariat which was to make possible the realization of communism, but as "a unity of individuals in a moral whole," which would be able to guarantee "a sum of education, power and freedom, that would be unattainable for them as a simple combination of individuals." He did not even object to the monarchy in itself, if it represented this "moral" state; Bismarck told the Reichstag after his death that Lassalle had "by no means" been a republican. At that time Lassalle and Bismarck had in common, though the levers with which they were working and their ultimate intentions were different, the desire to unseat the bourgeois liberals. (It ought also to be noted that Lassalle differed from Marx as well as from Bismarck in attempting to bring back into socialism the idea of brotherly love, which Marx had banished from it: "He who invokes the Idea of the workers' estate as the governing principle of society, . . . utters a cry that is not calculated to split and separate the social classes; he utters a cry of reconciliation, which embraces the whole of society, . . . a cry of *love*, which from the very first moment when it rises from the heart of the people, will *remain forever the true cry of the people* and continue by reason of its content to be essentially a *cry of love* even when it rings out as a battle-cry.")

Lassalle on his side treats Bismarck as if he were the head of one great power advising the head of another great power what to do for his own good. When the General Union was founded, he sent Bismarck a copy of its rules, with the message: "Herewith I send your Excellency the constitution of my realm, for which you will perhaps envy me." When Bismarck begins suppressing newspapers and prohibiting political discussion, Lassalle warns him that he is inviting revolution. He tours the Rhineland in triumph. At Solingen, a liberal burgomaster has the police break up one of his meetings, and Lassalle telegraphs to Bismarck, demanding "the promptest legal satisfaction." He runs into more serious trouble in Berlin; the liberals have won in the October elections, and his speeches give rise to riots. He is finally arrested for high treason at the behest of the Public Prosecutor, who, as Lassalle says, has never forgiven him for throwing in his teeth the ideas of his distinguished father; and he actually succeeds in inducing Bismarck to transfer Schelling to another town.

But by January, 1864, the war with Denmark was looming. Lassalle did his best to scare Bismarck into establishing universal suffrage before he committed Germany—declaring that a prolonged war would bring on riot and insurrection at home, with the result that the King would either dismiss him or that "History" would "take its fatal course" with "your government and with the monarchy." But Bismarck, by this time, as he afterwards said, felt that the power was all on his side. At the last interview he had with Lassalle, the junker, with the insolent cigar which he was so long to be puffing in the faces of diplomatic congresses and parliaments, advised him that if he wanted to make a career for himself, he should acquire "a landed estate and an ugly wife." By tricking the Danes into believing that England would come to their rescue—"The lie is a European power!" Lassalle had already said in one of his workers' manifestoes—Bismarck set off a war with Denmark which was so far from being prolonged that it was over in a month, and which brought Prussia Schleswig, Holstein and Lauenburg and the right to control the port of Kiel. He no longer now needed Lassalle to help him keep off the "progressives." He has an underling write him a note explaining that he is too busy to see him and that he is unable to make an appointment for the future. Lassalle tries a last move. He politely proposes a discussion of the issue between Prussia and Austria, which is involved in the Schleswig-Holstein question and which is to be Bismarck's great immediate preoccupation; but, after leaving the letter unmailed for three days, he cannot refrain from adding a postscript in which he expresses, not so politely, his surprise that his earlier letter should have been answered in this discourteous way, and tells Bismarck that any further advances must come from the Minister-President's side. It was the end of Lassalle's relations with Bismarck.

But he went on with his agitation. The authorities were now pursuing him more fiercely, and he was really going to pieces physically; but in his house, which the police were always searching, he continued to write pamphlet after pamphlet, to prepare speech after speech; when his voice suddenly left him, he had his throat painted with silver nitrate and so got a couple of hours more out of his vocal cords. He complained about the air in the meeting halls, said he detested the workers' delegations, and wished he could conduct the whole campaign from his study; but the workers no longer distrusted him as they had in the early days, because they knew he had the Devil's own courage. Again brought to court for high treason, he defends himself again, as he says, with "the fury of an Hyrcanian tiger," and causes the judges themselves to rise from their seats and howl with rage; and again gets himself acquitted. Then at last he is lassoed in Düsseldorf by a sentence of twelve months in prison. He appeals, but his extreme efforts can only reduce the sentence to six months.

He is not sure whether he can face it now. If in the autumn, when his sentence begins, he feels that his nerves will not hold up, he will simply have to escape abroad. But in the meantime he will go to a Swiss health resort and try to restore his forces. When he leaves Düsseldorf the last day of June, a gigantic demonstration of workers comes to see him off at the station.

At Rigi-Kaltbad, he ran into a young girl, whom he had formerly known in Berlin and with whom he had already had a flirtation, the daughter of an historian named von Dönniges. She had some Jewish blood and was thought physically to resemble Lassalle. She had beautiful red-gold hair and what is described as "a solid rebellious head." She must certainly have been both cleverer and more daring than most of the women of her milieu. She and Lassalle seem in imagination to have identified themselves with one another in the way which has sometimes so intoxicating an effect upon egoistic people but which has the danger of being liable to expose them to sudden and violent mutual repulsion. Helene calls him "eagle," "lord and master"; talks of his "daimonic presence"; says that she will run away with him to Egypt if she cannot get her parents' consent, but asks him to try to manage it respectably. He on his side has been preoccupied of late with the idea of a brilliant marriage. They go to Geneva to put it up to her family.

But the fatal pattern recurs. Old von Dönniges makes a terrible scene. Helene comes straight to Lassalle, where he has taken a room in a pension; collapses on the bed, tells him that she is his now forever, asks him to take her to France. But Lassalle will not accept her on these terms: her parents must recognize him; she must marry him in the ordinary way. He takes her home—and so loses her irrevocably. Her parents snatch her away from Geneva and make it impossible for him to see her again. He goes wild: mobilizes the Countess, who appeals to the Bishop of Mainz to act as an intermediary between Helene's father and Lassalle; summons to his side Colonel Rustow, a revolutionary military friend; makes an assault upon Richard Wagner—who finds him "extremely uncongenial" and declares that his "fundamental motives" are "only vanity and insincere pathos"—with the purpose of attempting to persuade him, since von Dönniges is a Bavarian official, to intervene with the King of Bavaria. At last he succeeds in inducing the Bavarian Minister of Foreign Affairs to bring pressure on Helene's father to let her see him. He has got up the legal aspect of the question and is able to prove by Munich law that her father has no right to coerce her. Von Dönniges consents to a meeting. Lassalle demands two hours; but Helene, who has been intimidated and has reacted against her transports, refuses to see him now. Ten minutes!—"when did Lassalle ever content himself with talking ten minutes?" She writes him that there can be no question of her marrying him, that she is going to marry a young man, a harmless young Rumanian nobleman, to whom she had formerly been engaged. Lassalle, in his role of reformer, had been opposed to the principle of the duel; but he now challenged both Helene's father and von Rakowitz, the young Rumanian. Von Rakowitz accepted the challenge for the morning of the twenty-eighth of August. Rustow advised his friend to get in some pistol practice beforehand; but Lassalle, in his self-confidence, refused. He was shot to death in the abdomen before he had managed to fire.

Marx and Engels were never more ghoulish than after the death of Lassalle. Engels tended to be jealous of other men who threatened to become collaborators of Marx's; and Marx seems to have played up to this tendency. The latter at any rate was infuriated by the working-class apotheosis of Lassalle which took place after his death, and wrote Engels with his characteristic sneer that they were trying to represent it as an evidence of Lassalle's superhuman powers that he should have continued to live for four days when he was suffering from peritonitis: people with peritonitis, said Marx, always lived two days at least; and Engels fed his friend's indignation by consulting a medical book and copying out for him passages which showed that peritonitis cases were likely to live any number of days—that a Paris worker who had been kicked by a horse had survived for sixty or seventy hours.

Yet Engels, though he said that Lassalle had been for them "at the present time a very uncertain friend and for the future a practically certain enemy" and demanded how it was possible for "a political man" like Lassalle to "fight a duel with a Rumanian adventurer?" (he and Marx had on an earlier occasion dissuaded Lassalle from a duel), yet admitted that their friend had been politically "the most important fellow in Germany," "the only man of whom the manufacturers and the swine of the Party of Progress are afraid." And Marx was quite plainly shocked: he almost expressed compunction. "*Dear Frederick:* [*] L's disaster has been damnably in my head all day. In spite of everything, he was still one of the *vieille souche* and the enemy of our enemies. Besides, the thing came so unexpectedly that *it's hard to believe that so bustling, stirring, pushing* an individual is now as dead as a mouse and must *entirely* hold his tongue. In regard to the cause of his death, you are quite right. It was one of the many tactless acts which he committed in the course of his life. *With all that* I'm sorry that our relationship should have been clouded in these last years, though to be sure through his own fault. On the other hand, I'm very glad that I resisted instigations from various directions and never attacked him during his 'Year of Jubilee.'" He had heard that the Countess Hatzfeldt was saying that he had let Lassalle down, and he wrote her: "Even aside from his abilities, I personally loved him. The unfortunate thing is that we concealed it from one another as if we were going to live forever."

There is perhaps some truth in Engels' idea, expressed in a letter to Marx, that Lassalle had fallen a victim to his own flighty and misdirected chivalry: "Der L ist offenbar daran

[*] From this point, the phrases in English as well as the phrases in French in the polyglot Marx-Engels correspondence will be italicized when the extracts are translated. Emphasized words will be indicated by spacing in the German fashion.

kaputt gegangen, dass er das Mensch nicht sofort in der Pension aufs Bett geworfen und gehörig hergenommen hat, sie wollte nicht seinen schönen Geist, sondern seinen jüdischen Riemen." But George Meredith, in *The Tragic Comedians*, which follows with close fidelity a memoir published by Helene von Dönniges, put his finger on the basic impulse that ruined the career of Lassalle. It was rather his pride than his chivalry that was excessive and a little insane. Though Meredith deals only with his love affair and does not carry the story back, it had been pride from the very beginning which had asserted itself as a stumbling-block to his projects at the same time that it had stimulated his heroism. He had overplayed his hand with Helene just as he had done with Count Hatzfeldt, whom he had irritated into fighting him for years when he might have obtained from him an immediate settlement; just as he had done with the authorities at Cologne, whom his demands and insulting behavior had evidently had the effect of arousing to keep him in prison for months after he had been acquitted; just as he had done with Marx, when the latter's neurotic cantankerousness had driven him (Lassalle) to mount his high horse with one of the few revolutionary comrades whose abilities were comparable to his own, and had made impossible collaboration between them; just as he had done with Bismarck, when he had made it as difficult as possible for the latter ever to see him again.

But it is not fair to assume, as Marx and Engels tended to do and as has sometimes been done since, that Lassalle would either have sold out to Bismarck or have gone the way that Bismarck was going. Lassalle, with a pride that like Swift's always took the form of insolence, was driven, for all his princely tastes, to fight for the dispossessed proletariat just as surely as Swift, for all his worldly ambitions, was driven to fight for the impoverished Irish. Such a man can never figure as a prince save in the realm of art, morals and thought; and he can never make deals and alliances—in this Lassalle is quite unlike Disraeli—with the princes of this world, let alone with their policemen and clerks. It may be possible to say theoretically that Lassalle would have enjoyed power for its own sake; but how, as a practical question, can it be possible for a man to achieve power who is always making issues over pretensions which the powerful by their position itself are unable to recognize? It is idle to speculate as to whether the State aid for workers' production of Lassalle could have turned into the State socialism of Bismarck: how can a man sell out to Bismarck who cannot refrain from insulting Bismarck? Lassalle, in his peculiar and tragic way, was one of the intransigents, too.

Those hard years of the early sixties, in which Marx decisively broke with Lassalle, threatened to put an end to the friendship even of Marx and Engels.

On the evening of January 7, 1863, Engels' mistress, Mary Burns, suddenly died of an apoplectic stroke. "I can't give you any idea how I feel," Engels wrote Marx in a note of a few lines. "The poor girl loved me with all her heart." In answering, Marx briefly remarked that the news had "surprised as much as shocked" him, that Mary had been "good-natured, witty and devoted"; and then went on to complain at length of the straits he himself was in and to explain the improbability of his being able to obtain a loan in London. "If only," he concludes, "instead of Mary, it had been my mother, who is full of physical infirmities, anyway, now and has had her fair span of life . . . ?" Yet, even here, a generalizing irony throws his cynicism into larger perspective: "You see what strange ideas can come into the heads of 'civilized people' under pressure of certain conditions."

In order to understand the effect that this letter of Marx's had on Engels, one must have followed the correspondence between the two men in the course of the eleven years since Engels had gone to Manchester. Year after year and week after week, Marx has been bewailing his miseries and importuning Engels for money. Engels had promised him some sort of allowance; but Marx was never able to keep inside it and was always forcing his friend to resort to financial juggleries that went against Engels' commercial conscience. But what was probably even more trying was Marx's practice of compelling Engels not only to support him out of his own earnings but also to write Marx's articles for him and let Marx collect the payment. Marx's continual nagging of Engels to get these articles done in time to catch the next boat during the years when his friend is working all day and sometimes also has business to transact at night—even allowing for the fact that Engels wrote fluently whereas for Marx composition was difficult—is the most unpleasant feature of their relationship. Engels' plight becomes comic and pathetic. On one occasion in 1852 when Engels has to stay at his office till eight o'clock every night, he writes Marx that he will have to spend the next evening writing an article which he has promised to the Chartists and cannot do the article for *The Tribune* till the next evening. "If your time is so taken up," replies Marx, "you would certainly do better to write for Dana than for Jones. The letter enclosed from Weydemeyer will make it even plainer how necessary it is that these articles should not be interrupted." Even after Engels has persuaded Marx to write the articles himself in German, he is still obliged to translate them; and even after Marx has learned to write passably in English, he still makes Engels supply a certain amount of copy on military and commercial affairs. Engels broke down in 1857, probably partly from overwork. He had undertaken to do a share of the pieces which Dana had arranged for Marx to write for the *American Encyclopaedia;* and it is touching to see him grinding away, before, during and after his illness and in spite of his protestations of ignorance, at articles on Army and Artillery and on generals beginning with A and B. When he writes Marx that he is well enough again to return to his favorite sport of riding, the latter answers: *"I congratulate you upon your equestrian performance.* Only don't take any too breakneck leaps: you'll soon have a more serious occasion for risking your neck. You seem *to ride somewhat hard this hobbyhorse."* "Don't you think you have enough material," he writes in 1858, after asking Engels to buy him a new book he needs, "to write something general on the *state of the British forces in India* and something conjectural for Friday? *It would be a great bonn* [*boon*] for me, for it will take me almost a week to read my own manuscript over." When Engels in 1859 has the ambition of writing a pamphlet for himself, Marx speaks to him as master to student: "Consider yourself entirely relieved from your *Tribune* collaboration (unless, what isn't very likely, some event of the war outdistances your pamphlet), till you've got the thing ready." "The £5 received. You must your *war-articles colour a little more,* since you're writing for *a general newspaper,* not for a scientific military journal. Something more descriptive and individual is easy to get out of the *Times* Correspondent and throw in. I can't stick it in myself, because there would be a discrepancy of style."

In the meantime, the contradiction involved for Engels between his communist opinions and aims and his situation as a practising business man continued to impose a strain, just as it had at Barmen, but now with no relief in sight. The falsity of his position is shown comically in a letter to Marx of November 15, 1857, which is full of excitement over the industrial depression: "The general aspect of the Stock Exchange here has been highly entertaining during the last weeks. The people are darkly annoyed over the particularly cheerful mood which has suddenly come upon me. *Indeed* the Stock Exchange is the only place where the *dulness* from which I have been suffering is transformed into elasticity and *bouncing.* And of course I always make gloomy prophecies—which irritates the asses all the more. On Thursday the situation was at its most deplorable; on Friday the gentlemen were brooding over the possible effect of the suspension of the Bank Act; and then as cotton goes up a penny, they say: We are over the worst. But yesterday the most gratifying *despondency* set in again; the whole power and the glory had departed, and hardly anybody was willing to buy, so that our market was as bad as before."

Yet Engels never shows impatience. Only for a moment when, just after the Marxes have moved into Grafton Terrace and their position has seemed to be sounder, he gets the news that Marx has been dropped from *The Tribune* and that his situation is now "more desperate than at any time during the last five years," does Engels betray that the prospect disconcerts him: "Your letter has landed on me like a thunderclap out of a clear sky. I thought that everything was at last in good order, that you were fixed up with a decent house and the *business* all settled; and now it seems that everything's uncertain. . . . Sometime in the first days of February, I'll send you £5 and you can count until further notice on getting the same sum every month. Even if I have to start the new fiscal year with a big load of debts, *c'est égal*." In 1862 he is writing him: "If I drew up for you a report of my expenses, it wasn't at all with the intention of discouraging you from what you call further 'squeezings.' On the contrary, I count on our continuing to help one another reciprocally whenever the occasion arises—it doesn't in the least matter which of us at any given moment is the 'squeezing' or the 'squeezed': the roles may always be reversed. The only motive for my going into all that was to show you the impossibility for the moment of my raising more than the £10."

This went on up to the death of Mary Burns. But there were, in Engels' reaction to Marx's letter, other factors involved as well. It must have cost a man as amiable as Engels a considerable conscious effort to keep up with Marx's relentless misanthropy. We feel it in reading their correspondence. Marx had the satanic genius of the satirist: his sneers are the true expression of his nature, and for this reason they are often effective: but Engels' sneers seem off-key. Though he can be humorous, he cannot be deadly: he simply commits faults of bad taste. Furthermore, the Marxes' treatment of Mary had evidently remained a sore subject. It will be noted that in speaking of her death in the letter quoted above, Marx includes no message from Jenny. Poor Engels, who had done what Marx had not: declared war on the bourgeois family— had sacrificed more by his bohemian life than it is easy today to understand. He had during these years become obsessed by a delusion that Mary Burns was the descendant of Robert Burns, apparently by way of Highland Mary; and he made trips to Scotland and Ireland with the object of verifying this theory, for which he never found a shred of evidence.

In any case, he did not answer till the thirteenth the note that Marx had written him the eighth, and then in the following terms:

"Dear Marx: You will understand that this misfortune of mine and your frigid attitude toward it have made it impossible for me to reply to you before.

"All my friends, including Philistine acquaintances, have shown me on this occasion, which was of course bound to touch me very closely, more sympathy and friendship than I could expect. You found it a suitable moment to demonstrate the superiority of your cold way of looking at things (*Denkungsart*)."

And he goes on to the money question: "You know how my finances stand; you know, too, that I do everything I can to help you out of the straits you are in. But the rather large sum you mention would be impossible for me to raise now, as you yourself must know." He lists three possible ways of procuring it and concludes: "Failing this, you must absolutely get it out of your Dutch uncle."

When Marx answers at the end of ten days, he apologizes and tells Engels that he had regretted the letter as soon as he had sent it off; but "under such *circumstances* I *generally* find that I can only fall back on cynicism." And he is still so deficient in tact and feeling that he then goes on to enlarge for pages on the miseries of his own situation and more or less to blame his letter on the pressure that his wife had brought to bear on him. But it is just as well, he says, that Engels should have written as he did, because now Jenny must see how impossible it is for them to keep up their present standard of living. Very good: he will declare himself bankrupt; he will have the girls go to work as governesses; he will let Lenchen find another place, and he and Jenny and little Tussy will go to live in a Model City Lodging House.

But his friend cannot of course allow this. He has recourse to a risky trick of kiting with a note which he knows he will be unable to pay on the date when it is to fall due, and sends Marx £100. Then he ceases to write to Marx at all for twenty-two days, leaving two letters unanswered. Poor Marx, in epistles that grow anxious in tone, continues to display his ineptitude: he tries to make it up to Engels by telling him how he has said to Jenny that none of their other troubles as the result of "these bourgeois annoyances" has been so serious as his having been reduced to bothering Engels about them; but this, he does not hesitate to go on, has only upset Jenny still more and made the domestic situation worse. He then requests from Engels an explanation of the machine called a "self-actor"—Mary Burns had operated one—and proceeds to regale him at inordinate length with an exceedingly subtle discussion of the difference between a "machine" and a "tool." There is in this letter a remarkable passage—it is impossible to tell whether or not Marx intended it as an apology or explanation for his tactlessness—which is profoundly significant in connection with Marx's whole life and thought. In writing to Engels of his own ignorance of machinery, he says that he is taking a course in practical mechanics, "purely experimental." "It is just the same with me," he says, "as in languages. I understand the mathematical laws, but the simplest technical reality, where intuition is needed, is harder for me than the knottiest problems." When Engels fails to answer this letter or the next, Marx fears he may again have offended him. "If I talked to you about machinery, it was only in order to distract you and to help you get your mind off your own sorrow." And it is perhaps true that he had intended to give his friend an opportunity to show his familiarity with factories at the expense, on Marx's own part—and he was probably capable of no severer sacrifice—of exposing his own limitations. But he had not been able to forbear from painting in his intervening letter a picture of his own desolation which could hardly have been expected to have the effect of cheering Engels up and which could have given him satisfaction only as testimony to the woes of atonement. It had been impossible for twelve days, says Marx, for him to read, to write or to smoke—"I have had a sort of eye infection, complicated by some kind of exceedingly disgusting affection of the nerves of the head . . . I used to give myself up to all sorts of psychological reveries about what it would be like to be blind or mad." And Marx vouchsafes one of his rare revelations of his involuntary personal feelings: "The place," he says to Engels about Manchester, "must have become damned lonely for you. I know from my own experience how much I still always get terrified by the neighborhood of Soho Square when I happen to be passing through it."

When Engels at last replies, he tells Marx he must excuse his long silence. He had tried to work himself out of his depression by studying the Slavic languages, "but the loneliness was intolerable to me." So, he implies, he had resorted to dissipation. "It helped: I'm myself again now." For a time he is a shade cavalier with Marx, seems to offend him by not coming to see him on the occasion of one of his visits to London. But soon enough they are back on the old basis, with only the difference perhaps that Engels' attitude now toward Marx has more in it of humorous benevolence. *"Voilà bien le père Marx!"* he wrote on a letter of 1867 which Marx had dated "1859"; and he had kidded him affectionately the previous fall for giving somebody a promissory note without noticing how much it was for.

A few months after Mary Burns's death, Engels began living with Mary's sister Lizzy, more pious than Mary but still comfortable enough. "She came of real Irish proletarian stock," he wrote about her once, "and the passionate feeling for her class, which was instinctive in her, was worth more to me than any of the blue-stockinged elegances of 'educated' and 'sensitive' bourgeois girls could have been." His life went on much as before.

These weeks of the January and February of 1863 must have been the darkest moment of the whole Marx-Engels exploit; and it is the triumph of Marx's greatness over the maddening defects of his character as well as of Engels' capacity for sympathy and understanding even where these were poorly repaid, that they got through it with so little damage.

14 Historical Actors: Bakúnin

And now a combination of circumstances for a time lifted
the life of Marx to a steadier and more dignified plane.
Wilhelm Wolff—one of the few German comrades whom Marx
and Engels trusted and with whom they remained friends:
Marx dedicated *Das Kapital* to his memory—died in the
spring of 1864 and left Marx £800; and in the fall of the same
year Engels became a partner in the Ermen & Engels firm,
and so was in a better position to send Marx money. Laura
Marx became engaged in the summer of 1866 to a young
doctor from Cuba named Paul Lafargue of mixed French,
Spanish, Negro and Indian blood; and they were married
two years later. Jenny married in the autumn of 1872 a
French socialist named Charles Longuet, who had had to
leave France after the Commune and who lectured at
University College in London. His daughters were thus provided for—though his sons-in-law from Marx's point of view
were not politically unexceptionable: "Longuet is the last
Proudhonist," he used to say, "and Lafargue the last Bakun-
inist—Devil take them!" In the spring of 1867 he completed
the first volume of *Das Kapital* and brought it out in the fall.
It was his first real expression of his general ideas in detailed
and developed form. The *Critique of Political Economy*,
which he had published in 1859, had baffled even Marx's
disciples by its relentless and opaque abstraction and had
made very little impression—though, significantly, it appeared
in the same year as Darwin's *Origin of Species* (a work which

Marx recognized as supplying a "basis in natural science" for the philosophy of Historical Materialism).

And today, after the reaction of a decade, the workers' rebellion was vigorously reviving, was achieving a new general solidarity. In England the Trade Union movement was taking the place of the Chartists. The growth of the industrial cities had caused a boom in the building and furnishing trades; and the workers in these trades had been left flat by the slump of the later fifties. Much the same thing had been happening in France, where Napoleon III had been rebuilding Paris, and where the followers of Proudhon and Blanqui were organizing the unemployed workers. We have seen how the movement of the Prussian workers had grown up under the leadership of Lassalle. Wilhelm Liebknecht, who had returned from exile in 1862, had converted to Marxist socialism a young turner named August Bebel and, after having been expelled from Prussia in 1865, had been organizing in South Germany a League of German Workers' Unions. The American Civil War of 1860–65, by shutting off the supply of cotton, had caused a crisis in the textile industry; and the American emancipation of the slaves of 1863, the abolition of serfdom in Russia in 1861, and the Polish uprising of 1863 had been giving a general impetus to liberal and revolutionary ideas. By the July of 1863 an international workers' movement was beginning to crystallize out. The English trade unions, whose action was being blocked by the importation of labor from Germany, France and Belgium, appealed to the workers of France for a common understanding against the employers; and the French, after delaying nearly a year, due to the uncertainty of the working-class leaders as to whether they should make the final break with the bourgeois political parties, accepted the proposal of the English. The International Working Men's Association was founded in St. Martin's Hall, London, on September 28, 1864. Thus, four weeks after the death of Lassalle, Marx was invited to attend the first meeting of the new working-class organization of which he was to become the directing mind, with his two sons-in-law among his lieutenants.

To read Marx's correspondence of this period is to be struck

—despite his ceaseless complaints of insomnia and physical ailments—by the effect on a personality even so self-dependent as Marx's, of relative financial security, of the sense of intellectual accomplishment, and of a decisive responsibility in a common undertaking with other men. One gets the impression that Marx is handling the affairs of the International with considerable sense and tact. He has to deal on the General Council with the men of various parties and doctrines of whose tendencies he disapproves: old Owenites and Chartists, followers of Blanqui and Proudhon, Polish and Italian patriots; and he manages for some time to work with them without allowing himself to become embroiled in any serious personal feuds. Perhaps the fact that he was intent on finishing his book may have induced him to avoid needless trouble. Certainly, the nightmare suspicions and the hysterically abusive bitterness of the days of the break-up of the Communist League are much less in evidence now. And he has now no Lassalle to compete with.

The Marx of this period—in spite of everything—has established himself as a power whom the bourgeois power through gendarme or sheriff can never expel or dispossess, and to whom men begin to come as if to learn permanent principles of truth in that age of political illusions, as if to secure for their new voyages a pilot who has never been stranded or swept away by the tides of revolution and reaction. Lafargue has left us a picture of Marx as he seemed to a young admirer in the sixties. His study on the first floor of the house gave on Maitland Park and let in a good light. It was furnished with a simple work-table, three feet long and two feet wide, a wooden arm chair, in which he sat to work, a leather-covered couch, and one or two other pieces of furniture. There was a fireplace opposite the window, with book-cases on either side. The book-shelves presented what seemed to Lafargue an inharmonious appearance because the books were arranged according to content, with quartoes and pamphlets side by side, and there were great packets of old newspapers and manuscript that piled the top shelves to the ceiling; and everything else in the room was littered with papers and books, mixed with cigars, matches, tobacco tins and ashes. But Marx knew where everything was: he had marked the books and turned down the pages regardless of handsome editions—and could show you at once passages or figures which he had cited in conversation. The books and papers obeyed him like his arms and legs: "They are my slaves," Marx used to say, "and they must serve me as I please." His mind, says Lafargue in a fine simile, was like a war-ship with her steam up, always ready at a moment's notice to start out in any direction on the sea of thought. The carpet had been worn down to the cord in a path between the door and the window which Marx had made by walking back and forth when he had been working and thinking alone. To this period of his later years belong the well-known photographs and portraits—distinctly different from the buttoned-up, constricted, self-conscious and hostile-eyed photograph which Lassalle had had taken in Berlin at the beginning of Marx's sixtieth year—in which something almost of benevolence, something certainly of imaginative amplitude and of the serenity of moral ascendancy, appears with the deep eyes and the broad brow, the handsome beard and mane, now whitening, that bend from the defiance of the rebel into the authority of the Biblical patriarch.

The inaugural address which Marx drafted for the International Working Men's Association had to steer, as I have already indicated, between shoals on every side: it had to satisfy English trade unionists, who were interested exclusively in winning strikes and cared nothing about their "historical role"; French Proudhonists, who were opposed to strikes and to the collectivization of the means of production, and who believed in coöperative societies and cheap credit; followers of the patriot Mazzini, who was chiefly interested in liberating Italy and who wanted to keep the class struggle out of it. Marx regretted, as he explained to Engels, that he had been obliged to put in some phrases about such abstractions as "duty" and "right" and a declaration that it was the aim of the International "to vindicate the simple laws of morality and justice, which ought to govern the relations of private individuals, as the rules paramount of the intercourse of nations." But he did get into it a blasting review of the results of industrial progress in England, which tied up with his own work on *Das Kapital*. He showed that while the imports and exports of England had trebled in twenty years, it nevertheless now appeared that, so far from pauperism's having been eliminated, as the middle-class apologists had said it would be, the industrial and agricultural populations were more debased and undernourished than ever. "In all countries of Europe it has now become a truth demonstrable to every unprejudiced mind, and only denied by those whose interest is to hedge other people in a fool's paradise, that no improvement of machinery, no appliance of science to production, no contrivances of communication, no new colonies, no emigration, no opening of markets, no free trade, nor all these things put together, will do away with the miseries of the industrious masses; but that, on the present false base, every fresh development of the productive powers of labor must tend to deepen social contrasts and point social antagonisms. Death of starvation rose [the English is Marx's own] almost to the rank of an institution, during this intoxicating epoch of economical progress, in the metropolis of the British empire. That epoch is marked in the annals of the world by the quickened return, the widening compass, and the deadlier effects of the social pest called a commercial and industrial crisis."

Marx continued to guide the International with surprising toleration and prudence through the Bâle Congress of 1869, at which the advocates of collectivization definitely defeated its opponents. He did not attend these annual congresses but controlled them through his lieutenants. He had been trying not to allow the International to take up too much of his time and on one occasion had let people believe that he had gone to the Continent on International business in order to be left in peace in London; but, as he wrote Engels: "Well, mon cher, que faire? Man muss B sagen, sobald man A gesagt." The organization grew every year more important. By the end of the sixties it is supposed to have had eight hundred thousand regular members; and its actual power was increased by alliances with other labor unions which had declared their solidarity with it. The press of the International boasted a strength of seven millions; and the estimates in the police reports put it as high as five millions. It organized strike relief and prevented the importation of strikebreakers. The very name of the International soon became such a bogey to the employers that it had sometimes only to threaten in order to bring them around. Marx and Engels had, as it were, unexpectedly, at a time when, having resigned themselves to reaction, they were preoccupied with literary work, found themselves actually in a position of leadership of an immense proletarian movement with revolutionary possibilities. *"Les choses marchent,"* Marx wrote Engels in September, 1867. "And by the time of the next revolution, which may perhaps be nearer than it seems, w e (that is, you and I) have this powerful *engine* i n o u r h a n d. *Compare with this the results of Mazzinis etc. operations since 30 years!* And without any financial resources! With the intrigues of the Proudhonists in Paris, of Mazzini in Italy, and of the jealous Odger, Cremer and Potter in London, with Schulze-Del [itzsch] and the Lassallians in Germany! We may consider ourselves very well satisfied!"

But again, and this time with more serious results, the authority of the sedentary Marx came into conflict with an active politician, and the Marxist point of view, so rationalistic and prudent, lost its grip on a labor movement which had now reached European proportions. It was at the Congress of Bâle that the Workers' International was first captivated by Michael Bakúnin.

He was a member of that unfortunate generation who had come to manhood in Russia during the reign of Nicholas I. Born on May 18, 1814, he had been eleven years old at the time of the Decembrist uprising—that upper-class conspiracy of officers and poets under the influence of Western ideas—in which the family of Bakúnin's mother had played an important part. The Russia of Pushkin and the Decembrists, of the dawn of the great culture of modern Russia, was extinguished by the thirty years of Nicholas, who aborted the intellectual movement by a terrible censorship of the press and did his best to make it difficult for Russians to circulate between Russia and Western Europe. Bakúnin was a product of this frustrated movement, like his friends Turgénev and

Herzen. Like them, he was driven by the oppression at home to look for freedom and light in the West, and then found himself doomed to live and work there with his mind always fretted by the problems of Russia. Herzen said that Bakúnin "had within him the latent power of a colossal activity for which there was no demand."

He came from the province of Tver, of a family of the landed gentry. He had spent his boyhood with his brothers and sisters on an estate of "five hundred souls" in a big eighteenth-century country house above a broad and slow Russian river; and in a sense this estate and this family, so beloved and so complete in themselves, remained the background of all his life. The childhood and youth of the Bakúnins were passed in an atmosphere of fantasy, of tender emotions and intellectual excitement, which sounds like Turgénev or Chékhov. Michael was the oldest boy of ten boys and girls, and so was in a position to dominate his sisters by his sex and his brothers by his age. His attitude toward both was protective, and he was their leader in conspiracies against their father, who had been forty when he married their mother and with whom his young wife always sided. Bakúnin, on his own confession, was in love with one of his sisters, and he seems to have been jealous of them all. When they began to have admirers and get married, Mikhaíl Alexándrovich would try to turn them against their suitors and husbands just as he incited his brothers to rebel against their father. Later on, he did the same thing with other women; but though he was able to get these ladies away from their husbands, he invariably let them down afterwards by failing to become their lover. He apparently remained impotent all his life, and was evidently a case of sexual inhibition based on the incest taboo. In Siberia, when he was forty-four, he married an eighteen-year-old girl, who eventually, while still living with Bakúnin, had two children by another man.

In Russia, the young Bakúnin became a member of a literary group so intoxicated with Hegelian idealism that even their love affairs were permeated by it, and who, volatilizing in the Russian way the portentous abstractions of the German, used to toast the Hegelian categories, proceeding through the metaphysical progression from Pure Existence to the divine Idea. At twenty-six—in 1840—Bakúnin decided to visit Berlin in order to drink Hegelianism at the fount and in order to rejoin a sister whom he had alienated from her husband and whom he had induced to take her child to Germany.

Bakúnin during his early years in Russia had remained a loyal subject of the Tsar—his only insubordination had been against his father. But in Berlin, under the influence of the Young Hegelians, he gravitated toward the Left. The critical turn of his conversion to the revolutionary interpretation of Hegel seems to have come at the moment when he definitely lost his hold over his maturing brothers and sisters. His married sister became reconciled with her husband and went back to Russia to live; a brother who had joined Michael in Germany, also returned and became an official; the sister whom he had loved most passionately and who was to have joined him in Germany, too, fell in love with his friend Turgénev and never left home at all. But Michael himself did not mature: he had no normal emotional development. Carried along by the current of the time, he now declared himself a political revolutionist—a revolutionist of the pure will and act, for whom upheaval was an historical necessity but who had no use for the strategy of Marx. For Bakúnin, the sincerity and the intensity of the gesture guaranteed its value, its effectiveness; and the gesture was primarily destructive. Discussing his character in his later years, he "attributed his passion for destruction to the influence of his mother, whose despotic character inspired him with an insensate hatred of every restriction on liberty." But it was evidently also an outlet for a frustrated sexual impulse. "The desire to destroy," he had already written in his early years in Germany, "is also a creative desire." He had visions of ecstatic conflagration: "the whole of Europe, with St. Petersburg, Paris and London, transformed into an enormous rubbish-heap." Herzen tells how, on one occasion, when Bakúnin was traveling from Paris to Prague, he had happened upon a revolt of German peasants, who were "making an uproar around the castle, not knowing what to do. Bakúnin got out of his conveyance, and, without wasting any time to find out what the dispute was about, formed the peasants into ranks and instructed them so skilfully [he had been an artillery officer in Russia] that by the time he resumed his seat to continue his journey, the castle was burning on all four sides." And he was always insisting on the importance, in time of revolution, of "unleashing the evil passions."

But he had also the magnanimity of a displaced and impersonal love: "The petty personal passions will not even have any place in the man possessed by passion; he is not even under the necessity of sacrificing them, because they do not exist in him any longer." He wanted—though in the name of destruction—to embrace the human race, and he was able to arouse in his followers a peculiar exhilaration of brotherly feeling.

With his colossal and commanding stature, his genius for popular oratory, Bakúnin should have figured like Garibaldi or Mazzini as the leader of a great national cause. But in Russia there was no cause for him to lead; and abroad he could never make an integral part of the national movements of other countries. He was condemned to play out his career in a series of unsuccessful attempts to intervene in foreign revolutions. When, for example, in 1848, the February days broke in France, Bakúnin sped to Paris at once and served in barracks with the Workers' National Guard—eliciting the famous verdict of the revolutionary Prefect of Police: "What a man! The first day of the revolution he is a perfect treasure; but on the next day he ought to be shot." And then, as soon as the German revolution had got under way in March, Bakúnin moved on to Germany, where he hoped to help the Poles to revolt. He had come to believe that the liberation of Russia could only be accomplished through a general pan-Slav revolution. But the Poles were suspicious of Bakúnin: the Russian Embassy in Paris had circulated the report that he was a spy; and he was obliged to go on to Prague, where he took part in an unsuccessful Czech insurrection. After months of wandering from place to place with false passports and always with the police at his heels, he happened to find himself in Dresden in May, 1849, when the revolutionary crisis there came. The King of Saxony was refusing to accept the constitution which had been framed by the Frankfort Assembly; and the pro-constitutional forces were taking to the barricades. Bakúnin had had no interest in the movement for the unification of Germany, and he did not believe that the revolution would succeed; but he could not stand by when there was trouble afoot. In the street he ran into Richard Wagner, then conductor of the Dresden opera, who was headed for the City Hall to see what was going on. Bakúnin went along. They found the Provisional Government just proclaimed. One speech was enough for Bakúnin: he presented himself to the leaders and advised them to fortify the city against the attack of the Prussian troops. The Prussians did arrive that night; the commander of the revolutionary forces, who may have been a traitor, obstructed the defense of the city; the revolutionary Polish officers, whom Bakúnin had been at pains to procure, gave the situation up and skipped out; two of the members of the provisional triumvirate also disappeared from the City Hall. The third member was left alone; and Bakúnin, with no stake in the conflict, stuck by this man to the end, making the rounds of the barricades to try to keep up the insurgents' morale. The Prussian and Saxon soldiers battled their way into the city, shot the rebels or threw them into the Elbe. Bakúnin tried to persuade his comrades to use all that was left of their powder to blow themselves up in the City Hall. But they withdrew to Freiburg, instead. Wagner urged them to move on to Chemnitz, declaring that the industrial population would certainly rally to their support. But when the Dresden insurgents got to Chemnitz, there were no signs of revolution whatever. They were arrested that night in their beds. Bakúnin was so dead with fatigue that he did not even try to make an escape, which he afterwards thought would have been easy. He was sent back to Dresden and put in jail with the rest.

He was to remain in prison eight years. Thirteen months in jail in Dresden and in the fortress of Königstein. Then a death sentence: they waked him one night and led him out as if he were to be beheaded. But the sentence had been commuted to life imprisonment, and he was merely being handed over to Austria, against which his incitement of the Czechs had been directed. Consigned to Prague as a military prisoner, he was shut up in a cell of the Hradčin citadel. Here he was denied legal representation, forbidden to answer or receive letters, and allowed only half an hour's exercise a day, when he was walked up and down a corridor under the guardianship of six armed men. When he had endured nine months of this, the authorities became alarmed by a rumor that his friends were planning a rescue, and removed him to the fortress of Olmütz, where he was fettered and chained to the wall. Two months later he was tried by a military court and condemned to be hanged for high treason. Yet his sentence was again commuted, and he was now handed over to Russia.

At the frontier, the Austrian guards took off his fetters, which they claimed as their national property, and the Russians put on worse ones of their own. The Tsar clapped him in the Peter-Paul Fortress and succeeded in extorting from him one of those "confessions" of wrongdoing and penitence which were inflicted by Nicholas I as a final humiliation and which have remained to this day a feature of the paternalistic Russian system. Bakúnin had scurvy, lost all his teeth, became stupefied and flabby with imprisonment. When the sister he had loved came to see him, he slipped out to her a despairing note: "You will never understand what it means to feel yourself buried alive, to say to yourself at every moment of the day and night: I am a slave, I am annihilated, reduced to lifelong impotence. To hear even in your cell the rumblings of the coming struggle, which will decide the most vital interests of humanity, and to be forced to remain idle and silent. To be rich in ideas, of which some at least might be beautiful, and not to realize one of them; to feel love in your heart, yes, love, despite this outward petrifaction, and not be able to expend it on anything or anyone. To feel yourself full of devotion and heroism to serve a sacred cause, and to see all your enthusiasm break against the four bare walls, my only witnesses and my only confidants." When Nicholas died in 1855 and the accession of Alexander seemed to promise a more liberal regime, Bakúnin's mother appealed to the Tsar. At first she had no success; and Bakúnin made his brother agree to bring him poison if she should definitely fail. But he was finally offered the alternative of exile for life in Siberia.

Once outside the prison walls, Bakúnin expanded and sped away like a genie let out of his bottle. He found in the governor of Eastern Siberia a relation on the Decembrist side of his family, who gave him a job in a trading company there. It was one of his duties to travel for the company, and at the end of four years of exile he succeeded in getting away. In the spring of 1861, he induced a Siberian merchant to pay the expenses of a journey to the mouth of the Amur River and got a letter to the commanders of ships on the Amur, instructing them to give him passage. Once there, he prevailed on the officials and captains to let him transfer from ship to ship till he finally steamed out of Yokohama on an American boat bound for San Francisco. Borrowing three hundred dollars from an English clergyman with whom he had made friends on board, he made his way from San Francisco to New York by way of Panama; got Herzen, then in London, to send him some more money, and reached London the last of November.

Herzen says that Bakúnin came back to Europe like the Decembrists returning from exile, who had seemed more youthful after their prisons than the crushed young people at home; that he was one of those extraordinary spirits who, instead of being ruined by punishment, seemed actually to have been preserved by it. For Bakúnin, the reaction of the fifties, which had discouraged the exiles in London, had never existed at all; he had, says Herzen, "read through" the events of those years as if they had been chapters in a book; and it was the February days in Paris, the uprisings in Dresden and Prague, which rang in his ears and swam before his vision. He had announced to Herzen from San Francisco that he was coming to devote himself again to "the utter destruction of the Austrian Empire" and the free federation of the Slav peoples. As soon as the Polish insurrection got under way in 1863, Bakúnin offered to organize a Russian legion; but the Poles were afraid that he would compromise them with his lurid record and his extravagant ideas, and tried to induce him to stay in London. This did not restrain him from taking flight to

Copenhagen in the hope of joining the rebellion or of embarrassing the Russian government by stirring up an insurrection in Finland. Eventually he embarked with a party of Poles, who had chartered a British vessel and were planning to land in Lithuania. The English captain seems to have liked his passengers—Bakúnin had talked of holding a revolver to his head—as little as the prospect of meeting Russian cruisers in the Baltic. He took the expedition back to Denmark.

Thereafter Bakúnin knocked around for some years between Sweden, Italy and Switzerland, subsisting on borrowed money and on the patronage of a Russian princess; associating himself with revolutionary movements and trying to cook up movements of his own. By 1866, he had definitely come to realize that the patriotic insurrections, such as those of the Italians, the Czechs and the Poles, on which he had counted so much, were not necessarily revolutionary save in relation to the national oppressors, but were likely—as had been the case with the Polish officers and landowners who had figured in the recent revolt—to be as deeply opposed to social innovation as their imperial masters themselves. Bakúnin now believed that the social revolution could only be international; and he succeeded in introducing into the program for a "United States of Europe" of the League for Peace and Freedom, an organization of bourgeois intellectuals in which he interested himself in '67, a paragraph about "the liberation of the working classes and the elimination of the proletariat."

In the summer of 1868, Bakúnin became a member of the Geneva section of the Workers' International and made an attempt to effect a merger between it and the pacifist League; but he ran up against the refusal of Marx, who called the League "the Geneva windbag," and the opposition of the League's own members. He then resigned from the League and set out to organize workers; but as it was impossible for him to content himself with merely building up the International and submitting to orders from Marx, he created a league of his own called the International Social-Democratic Alliance, whose activities were partly secret and whose relation to the International was ambiguous. Marx again refused, in the case of the Alliance, to allow it to merge with the original organization, and insisted that Bakúnin dissolve it and have the various sections join separately. Bakúnin complied publicly; but it can never have occurred to him for a moment to drop the web of the secret society. He thought of himself habitually as the head of a great underground organization. And he was becoming for the first time in his life a genuinely formidable power. He had, through his Italian connections, set up branches in Italy and Spain, where the International had never had any following; and he had succeeded in getting a very strong hold on certain working-class organizations in French Switzerland, where the International was to hold its next congress. He had gone among the watchmakers of the Jura, who were reduced to the bitterest misery by the competition of the new American watchmaking; had visited them in the little mountain towns and put on for them a wonderful show. And he had got from them the most useful of his lieutenants, a young schoolmaster named James Guillaume, who had the virtues of discipline and diligence that Bakúnin himself lacked. At the Bâle Congress of 1869 Bakúnin was in the position of controlling twelve of the seventy-five delegates.

The issue on which the battle was fought between the forces of Bakúnin and those of Marx was abolition of the right of inheritance. This was a measure which Bakúnin demanded passionately as "one of the indispensable conditions for the emancipation of labor"—perhaps because he had been trying unsuccessfully to induce his brothers in Russia to send him a share of the family estate. Marx contended with his usual logic that, since the inheritance of private property was merely a result of the property system, the primary thing was to attack the system rather than to bother with its incidental evils.

But Marx was away in London, and, though he had conveyed his desires to the Congress in a report from the General Council, his only spokesman was a German tailor, obedient and literal-minded, who had no powers to act for himself. Bakúnin, on the other hand, was there on the spot, an exhilarating, compelling personality. A spectator of one of his appearances at a meeting of the League of Peace and Freedom has described the immense impression that he was capable of making on an audience, "as he walked up the steps to the platform, with his heavy peasant gait . . . negligently dressed in his gray blouse, out of which there peeped not a shirt but a flannel vest . . . A great cry of 'Bakúnin!' went up. Garibaldi, who was in the chair, rose and went forward to embrace him. Many opponents of Bakúnin's were present, but the whole hall rose to its feet and it seemed as if the applause would never end." Of his oration at another meeting Baron Wrangel has written: "I no longer remember what Bakúnin said, and it would in any case scarcely be possible to reproduce it. His speech had neither logical sequence nor richness in ideas, but consisted of thrilling phrases and rousing appeals. It was something elemental and incandescent—a raging storm with lightning flashes and thunderclaps, and a roaring as of lions. The man was a born speaker, made for the revolution. The revolution was his natural being. His speech made a tremendous impression. If he had asked his hearers to cut each other's throats, they would have cheerfully obeyed him." For all the futility of his actual enterprises, he had acquired the power of a symbol. There is perhaps something in Bernard Shaw's idea that Wagner's Siegfried, conceived after his experience of the Dresden revolution, was based on the character of Bakúnin. In any case, despite the practical uselessness and the political inconsistency of Bakúnin's defiance of the Prussians, this defiance had come to signify the assertion of the disinterested bravery of the human spirit against human self-interest and timidity, just as his survival from the prisons of three despots and his escape which had encircled the world, had demonstrated the strength of that will to be free which Byron had said was "brightest in dungeons." Bakúnin appealed to the imagination as Marx had never been able to do: he had the superhuman simplification of a hero of romantic poetry, something very rare and strange in reality. And he poured forth at the Congress so eloquent an appeal in favor of the abolition of inheritance that for the first time in the history of the International a recommendation of the General Council was rejected. Bakúnin's resolution was voted down, with a number of delegates abstaining; but Marx's was voted down, too, and by a majority even larger. Eccarius, the unfortunate tailor—with whom Marx was later to quarrel—could only complain in distress: "Marx will be extremely displeased."

And now it became evident to Marx that Bakúnin was out to capture the International. Fate delivered Bakúnin into his hands.

The reign of Alexander II, the new reform tsar, in Russia had by the sixties reverted to reaction and given rise to a new revolutionary movement. But this was no longer a mere gentlemen's conspiracy like that of the Decembrists nor a ferment of intellectuals like the Petrashévtsy of the late forties: the agitators now were poor students for whom education was being made difficult by a government which had set out to advance it, but which had discovered that allowing people to learn anything meant encouraging contempt for the Tsar. One of these students was a young man named Necháev, the son of a former serf who had got himself sufficient schooling to enroll at the University of St. Petersburg. He had read about Babeuf and Blanqui, and his dreams were all of secret societies. In St. Petersburg he became the leader of the left wing of the students' movement and was obliged to flee to Moscow when the police set out to round this movement up. He decided to go to Geneva to see Bakúnin and the other Russian exiles, and he arrived there in the March of '69.

Bakúnin was fascinated by Necháev. Himself rather lazy and mild despite his impulses toward universal destruction, he seemed to find in this boy of twenty-one, energetic, determined and virulent, the type of the perfect conspirator, endowed with that *"diable au corps"* which he had described as indispensable to the revolutionary in one of the programs he had written for his Alliance. There was an element of Rimbaud-Verlaine about the relations between Necháev and Bakúnin. The older man saw in the younger some ideal of himself reborn—merciless, realistic, intent, speeding like a shot to his mark. He adored him, referred to him as "Boy," submitted to all his exactions.

Together—the original manuscript is supposed to have been in Bakúnin's handwriting—they concocted a hair-raising document called *The Catechism of a Revolutionist,* which, though it managed, as Marx and Engels said, to fuse into a single ideal the romantic attitudes of Rodolphe, Karl Moor, Monte Cristo and Macaire, must be noted for its importance as the first complete statement of a revolutionary point of view that was to continue to figure in Russian history. The revolutionist, says the *Catechism,* is a doomed man, with no personal interests or feelings, without even a name of his own. He has only one idea: the revolution; and he has broken with all the laws and codes of morals of the educated world. If he lives in it, pretending to be a part of it, it is only to destroy it the more surely; everything in it must be equally hateful to him. He must be cold: he must be ready to die, he must train himself to bear torture, and he must be ready to kill in himself any sentiment, including that of honor, the moment it interferes with his purpose. He may feel friendship only for those who serve his purpose; revolutionists of inferior caliber he must regard as capital to be spent. If a comrade gets into trouble, his fate is to be decided by his usefulness and by the expenditure of revolutionary force necessary to save him. As for established society, the revolutionist must classify its members, not in respect to their individual villainy, but in respect to their varying degrees of harmfulness to the cause of the revolutionist himself. The most dangerous must be immediately destroyed; but there are also other categories of persons who, if allowed temporarily at large, will promote the revolutionist's interests by perpetrating brutal acts and infuriating the population, or who may be exploited for the good of the cause by blackmail and intimidation. The category of liberals must be exploited by making them believe that one falls in with their programs and then compromising them by involving them with one's own. Other radicals must be pushed into doing things which in most cases will destroy them completely and, in a few, will make them real revolutionists. The sole aim of the revolutionist is the freedom and happiness of the manual workers, but, believing that this can only be accomplished by an all-destructive popular revolution, he must further with all his power the evils that will exhaust the people's patience. The Russian must repudiate squarely the classical model of revolution in vogue in the Western countries, which is always deferring to property and to the traditional social order of so-called civilization and morality, and which only replaces one State by another; the Russian revolutionist must eradicate the State, with all its traditions, institutions and classes. Thus the group that foments the revolution will not try to impose on the people any political organization from above: the organization of the future society will doubtless arise from the people themselves. Our business is simply destruction, terrible, complete, universal and ruthless; and for this purpose we must not only unite with the recalcitrant elements of the masses but also with the bold world of bandits, the only true revolutionists in Russia. It ought to be added that Bakúnin at this time was expressing admiration for the Jesuits and talking ominously about following their example.

Bakúnin and Necháev both had the mania of secret societies; but whereas Bakúnin seems merely to have deluded himself about the size and extent of his, Necháev was a systematic liar. He had already succeeded in creating a legend that he had escaped from the Peter-Paul Fortress, in which he had actually never been confined; and he had convinced Bakúnin that he was acting as the agent of a nationwide revolutionary committee. He now returned to Russia and passed himself off on the Moscow students as a member of a secret organization with iron discipline and terrible powers, which enjoined as one of the chief duties of its adherents the distribution of a certain poem on the death of the great revolutionist Necháev. One of the ablest and most disinterested of the student movement was a young man at the agricultural school named Ivánov, who was active in the coöperative enterprises of the students and devoted all his extra time to teaching the children of the peasants. He came soon to doubt the reality of Necháev's organization and, after challenging him to prove its existence, finally announced his intention of founding a serious organization of his own. Necháev then induced four of his companions to help him to murder Ivánov; and, this done, obtained a false passport and succeeded in getting away, leaving his comrades to take the rap. The police arrested three hundred young people; of the eighty-four brought to trial, almost all were imprisoned or exiled.

Nechâev had in the meantime returned to Geneva and got hold of some revolutionary friends and a Russian émigré paper; and he now began to treat Bakúnin as the *Revolutionary Catechism* said liberals ought to be treated after one had got out of them all that was possible. He would neither give Bakúnin any of the money nor allow him to collaborate on the paper; and he had in the meantime cut off for his old ally one of the latter's possible sources of income. Bakúnin had got a commission through a friend to translate *Das Kapital* into Russian and had received a considerable advance. But when he found the work difficult and slow and had already spent the advance, he allowed himself to be persuaded by Nechâev that such drudgery was a waste of time. Nechâev wrote a letter to the friend—apparently without the knowledge of Bakúnin—threatening him with a terrible punishment at the hands of the secret committee if he made any trouble about the money. And finally, he took the precaution of stealing a box of Bakúnin's correspondence in order always to be in a position to compromise him. Bakúnin now began writing letters to people all over Europe to warn them against Nechâev; and Nechâev resolved to plant a spy in Bakúnin's organization. He picked out for this purpose a Pole whom he believed to be a genuine revolutionary. But the Pole was a stoolpigeon for the Tsar and lost no time in turning Nechâev in.

But so far as the International was concerned, the damage was already done. At the trials of the Russian students in 1871, which brought the *Revolutionist's Catechism* to light, it came out that Nechâev had presented himself in Moscow as the authorized representative of the International. He had also in one of his publications referred the reader for the principles of his social theory to the *Communist Manifesto*. One can imagine the horror of Marx, who detested underground machinations and who had a morbid need to feel that everything was under his personal control, at discovering that a secret society, full of talk about invisible powers, initiates and inner circles, had been spreading its fibers inside the International and becoming identified with it.

It is no doubt true that Marx envied Bakúnin, just as he did Lassalle, for his ability to charm and command. Bakúnin had a peculiar combination of childlike candor with Russian slyness, which, together with his enthusiasm and his grandiose presence, enabled him to perform miracles of persuasion. There is a story that he once visited a bishop of the heretical Russian cult of Old Believers singing a religious song, and tried to convince him that their aims were identical; and it is certain that he quite innocently succeeded in turning into a tool of his own the Tsar's principal agent in Switzerland, who was masquerading as a retired Russian general: this man actually allowed Bakúnin to send him back to Russia as his own agent, to report on revolutionary activities there and to intercede with Bakúnin's family in the matter of the family estate; and he even became mesmerized to the point of helping Bakúnin out with a considerable sum of money, which the police agent obtained from the Tsar as expenditure in the line of duty. Bakúnin had also—what was perhaps even more remarkable— succeeded in charming Marx when, in the autumn of 1864, at the time of the founding of the International, they had seen one another in London. Bakúnin had asked warmly after Engels, regretted the death of Wolff, assured Marx that the Polish insurrection had failed because the landlords had not proclaimed "peasant socialism" and that he was resolved to devote himself henceforth to no cause but the socialist movement (later, he used to write Marx that he regarded himself as a disciple of his). Marx had written of Bakúnin to Engels in terms so favorable as to be almost unique in the Marx-Engels correspondence: Bakúnin was one of the few men, Marx had said, who had developed instead of retrograding during the previous sixteen years.

It is also true that in their writings against Bakúnin, Marx and Engels did not scruple to use against him certain of the misdeeds of Necháev for which Bakúnin was not directly responsible as well as entirely unfounded scandals about Bakúnin's career in Siberia. Yet it seems to me unfair, in this particular connection, to reproach them, as Mehring does, severely. Surely Bakúnin was a little cracked and politically quite irresponsible. All his life he was still playing at conspiracy as he had done with his brothers and sisters at home in his father's house, that isolated childhood domain where nothing could really happen to one, just as his eternal borrowing and then dismissing the debt from his mind was a survival of infantile dependence. He was able to catch people up by the spell of a personality part of whose power resided in the fact that it had the ingenuousness of a child's, and could launch them before they knew it on secret missions, reckless defiances, etc.; but his conspiracies were always partly imaginary, and he never himself seems quite to have known the difference between the actuality and the dream. His lack of the sense of reality was proved in the most disastrous way by his carelessness about compromising his agents and the comrades with whom he corresponded in Russia. Marx and Engels were rightly shocked by this. Bakúnin, though he reveled in secret codes, often failed to take ordinary precautions to keep his people out of the hands of the police. It is significant that, though up to his last days he was always able to recruit new disciples, he invariably eventually lost his old ones. Even the indispensable Guillaume in the long run found Bakúnin impossible.

Furthermore, he had since 1866 been promulgating a doctrine of "anarchism," of which the total abolition of the State demanded in the *Revolutionist's Catechism* was one of the fundamental tenets. He had been preaching this doctrine in a campaign against what he called Marx's German authoritarianism. What was sound in it was the notion that revolutionary organizations ought to come from the people themselves instead of being imposed from above, and that the units of a workers' association ought to be allowed to arrive at their decisions through a strictly democratic procedure. But Bakúnin was certainly no great theoretician, and his principles and his actual practice presented so many inconsistencies that it was quite easy for Marx and Engels to ridicule them with deadly effect when they had seriously set out to discredit him. They pointed out that, although he had boasted that the organization of the Alliance was to prefigure the future society in which the State should have been abolished, it had actually been contrived as a dictatorship by one man, *"le citoyen B."*, who was to make all the decisions himself; that, on the other hand, the actual looseness of the Alliance made sensible concerted action impossible, so that its units, aroused by cataclysmic visions, were actually exposed to immediate suppression; and that, so far from following the anarchist precept to abstain from playing any official role in the politics of the existing order, the adherents of Bakúnin in Spain in the uprisings of 1873 had not hesitated to accept office in the juntas which, instead of proceeding to abolish the State, were simply setting up provincial governments.

It would have been impossible for Bakúnin and Marx ever to have worked together as equals. The Bakúninists at Bâle had attempted but had failed to get the headquarters of the General Council transferred from London to Geneva. At the next congress, held at The Hague, which did not take place till September 2, 1872, Marx and Engels for the first time made a point of attending the sessions in person, and, since the Italian Bakuninists stayed away, succeeded in dominating the proceedings. They produced the threatening letter which Necháev had written to the Russian who had arranged for Bakúnin to translate *Das Kapital*, and they got Bakúnin and Guillaume expelled.

Yet their opponent was still very strong. The Paris Commune had had the effect of encouraging the program of the Bakúninists, who advocated direct action as against the patient strategy of Marx. Bakúnin had rushed into action at Lyons in the September of 1870, when a republic had been proclaimed there and a Committee of Public Safety set up; in pursuance of his anarchist policy, he had lost no time in issuing a decree in which the State was declared abolished; but, as Marx and Engels pointed out, the mere force of the anarchist will was so far from being able to abolish it, that it had sufficed for the State to assert itself in the shape of two battalions of the National Guard to put the society of the future to rout. Yet the Commune had been startlingly successful. Bakúnin had been enraptured when he had heard about the burning of the Tuileries: "He entered the group room with rapid strides —though he generally walked very slowly—struck the table with his stick and cried: 'Well, my friends, the Tuileries are in flames. I'll stand a punch all around!'" And the revolutionists of the Mediterranean countries were all for rising against priests and princes rather than waiting for the industrial development without which Karl Marx had been insisting that all attempts at revolution were vain.

And Marx now had to fight the French Blanquists as well on somewhat similar grounds. These followers of Louis Blanqui, a socialist who believed in direct action, were clamoring to announce "the militant organization of the revolutionary forces of the proletariat" as one of the immediate aims of the International. The position of Marx and Engels was furthermore weakened in England itself by the fact that the trade union movement, which had succeeded in obtaining the vote and which had been frightened by Marx's address in favor of the Paris Commune, was now turning toward the parliamentary Liberals, and had insisted on having a special council for their own sections of the International distinct from the General Council. Engels, who had moved to London in the autumn of 1870, had proved in some ways not a very great success as a member of this General Council: the British trade union members could not forget that he was a manufacturer—he had in fact in his commerce with the British merchant classes more or less acquired their manners; and they resented the martinet methods which he had carried over from his military training. They were even saying that Marx put him forward only because Engels gave him money. In Germany, the growing socialist movement had been obliged, in order to keep out of prison, to dissociate itself from the International. And Marx himself was now old, ill and tired, and he wanted to finish *Das Kapital*. Marx and Engels sabotaged the International at the moment when they could no longer control it, just as they had done with the Communist League. They had the headquarters transferred to New York.

The American workers had been slow and reluctant about affiliating themselves with the International, though there had been German-American members since 1869 and the membership, principally immigrant, had at one time reached five thousand. The pressure of the panic of '73, when there were a hundred and eighty thousand men out of work in New York

State alone, gave the organization a certain importance. It had a hand in the immense unemployed demonstrations in Chicago and New York, and it gave support to the great anthracite strike of 1873. But it encountered insurmountable obstacles. One of the sections, headed by the feminist Victoria Woodhull, tried to launch a separate American movement, which included among its aims woman's rights and free love and which called for the affiliation of all English-speaking citizens. When London suspended this section, Miss Woodhull, paying no heed to the rebuke, went on to convoke a convention of "all male and female human beings of America," which advocated a universal language and nominated Miss Woodhull for president. And the International very soon split on the question of adapting it to American conditions by making it more inclusive. The secretary of the General Council was an old friend of Marx's named Sorge, who had left Germany after '48. The Marxists stuck to their principles, and the American sections split off and founded new labor parties. The International was finished off in 1874 by a resolution of the General Council, which forbade the American members to join any political party, however reformist in character, that had been organized by the owning classes.

In Europe, the Bakuninists' International also went to pieces during the seventies, due to the impracticabilities of anarchist doctrine. Bakúnin died July 1, 1876, announcing his disillusionment with the masses, who "did not want to become impassioned for their own emancipation," and asserting that "nothing firm and living can be built upon Jesuitical trickery." A young girl student from Russia had come to him as the last of his disciples; and he used to make her tell him over and over again about the countryside at home. The frogs in the garden of his Italian villa reminded him of the frogs in Russia, as he had used to hear them in the fields and ponds around the Bakúnin house; and while he listened, she says, "the hard cunning light would go out of his eyes, and sadness would contract his features and lie like a shadow about his lips." All his trickery and all his eloquence, all his defiance and all his threats, had been powerless to effect the escape of the man who had got out of Siberia, from that family estate of boyhood. The purely emotional character of his rebellion against society is indicated in one of the last things he said. He had left the hospital one evening to call on a friend, who played Beethoven for him on the piano. "Everything will pass," said Bakúnin, "and the world will perish, but the Ninth Symphony will remain."

But the real climax of all this period of working-class organization and agitation was the Paris Commune of 1871.

The Commune was a pivotal event in European political thought. We have seen how the news of the civil war laid Michelet out with a stroke; how two months of a socialist government in Paris so filled Taine with terror that he devoted the rest of his life to trying to discredit the French Revolution; how Anatole France in his twenties shuddered at the sight of the Communards. Inversely, for that later movement which looked for historical progress to the victory of the working class, the Commune broke through into the real stream of history as the first great justification of their theory. And just as the bourgeois historians shied away from it, so these other philosophers of history took heart from it, celebrated it, studied it. "The struggle of the working class against the capitalist class and its State," Marx wrote Kugelmann in April, before the fall of the Commune, "has entered upon a new phase with the struggle in Paris. Whatever the immediate results may be, a new point of departure of world-historic importance has been gained." Three years later, the anarchist Kropotkin, shut up in a St. Petersburg prison, had a solace which Bakúnin had not had: he spent a week rapping out on the wall of his cell for the benefit of a young man next door the story of what had happened in Paris.

Napoleon III, through his own weakness and through the corruption of his racketeering government, had by the latter part of the sixties forfeited the confidence of all those groups save the peasants among which he had formerly kept the balance. The shell of the Second Empire collapsed with his defeat at Sedan; and now the classes quickly came to blows, as Marx had predicted they would. A provisional republican government was set up by the liberal wing of the Chamber, and

Blanqui was given a small post in it as commander of a battalion of the National Guard. Blanqui demanded the arming of the whole adult population of Paris in order to defend the city against the Prussians; but the bourgeois government was now afraid of a working-class insurrection. The fall of Metz and the approach of the Prussians precipitated an attempt at revolution by Blanqui and other socialists, which was suppressed by the Provisional Government. This government signed an armistice with the Germans on January 29, '71, agreeing to the surrender of Alsace-Lorraine and the payment of an enormous indemnity. The National Assembly which met at Bordeaux and proclaimed the Republic in February elected Thiers as its head and was committed by him to a crushing program of raising money to pay off the Germans before proceeding to internal reforms. This program put an end to the moratorium on debts and to the suspension of the requirements to pay rent which had been in operation during the siege, and stopped the pay of the National Guard. When, finally, the government of Thiers attempted to take away from the National Guard the guns that had been cast at their own expense, there was a revolt which resulted on March 26 in the election of the Paris Commune.

The Parisians had had five months of siege, were reduced to the direst privation, and saw France, which had been involved by the Empire in a humiliating and disastrous war, now bound over to the Germans by the Republic. The new government, led by social revolutionists—though Blanqui had just been arrested for his part in the earlier uprising—announced the abolition of the police force and the army and the assumption of their duties by the people, the opening to the people of the public schools, the expropriation of the clergy, and the making elective of all public offices, which were to be salaried at a yearly maximum of 6000 francs. Yet this government was afraid to go too far: they lost time on elections and organization for fear of incurring the reproach of dictatorship; they scrupulously refrained from requisitioning the three billions in the National Bank; and they hesitated to march on Versailles, to which the National Assembly had retreated, for fear of provoking civil war. The Thiers government, with no hesitation, itself laid siege to Paris. During a single week in May, when the Commune was defeated (May 25), between twenty and forty thousand Communards were cut down by the Versailles troops. The Communards themselves shot hostages, burned buildings. It is a proof of the divergence of the tendencies of the socialist and the bourgeois pictures of history—and from now on there will be two distinct historical cultures running side by side without ever really fusing—that people who have been brought up on the conventional version of history and know all about the Robespierrist Terror during the Great French Revolution, should find it an unfamiliar fact that the Terror of the government of Thiers executed, imprisoned or exiled more people—the number has been estimated at a hundred thousand—in that one week of the suppression of the Commune than the revolutionary Terror of Robespierre had done in three years.

The Workers' International, officially, had had nothing to do with the Commune; but some of its members had played important roles. Marx and Engels had watched from England, greedily clipping the papers, with the most intense excitement. Engels had tried to give them the benefit of his studies in military strategy by advising them, without effect, to fortify the north slopes of Montmartre. And two days after the final defeat, Marx had read to the General Council his address on *The Civil War in France,* which had aroused British indignation. "I have the honor to be at this moment," he wrote to his friend Dr. Kugelmann, "the best calumniated and the most menaced man in London. This really does me good after a tedious twenty-years' idyl in my study."

Yet the Commune had not really followed the course that Marx and Engels had previously laid down for the progress of the revolutionary movement. In so far as it had succeeded, it had justified rather the direct force idea of their opponents Blanqui and Bakúnin. And now Marx, who had always insisted that the State of the bourgeoisie would have to be taken over by the proletarian dictatorship and could be abolished only gradually, allowed himself some inconsistency in praising the bold action of the Communards in simply decreeing the old institutions out of existence.

Afterwards, he and Engels used the Commune for all it was worth, "improving its unconscious tendencies," as Engels once admitted, "into more or less conscious plans." The truth was that it had been much too busy during the brief two months of its existence to get far with the reorganization of society, and that it had been, in fact, from the beginning perhaps as much a patriotic as a social revolutionary movement. Yet Engels asserted, also, that the socialist pointing-up of these events was "under the circumstances justifiable, even necessary." He was himself, on the twentieth anniversary of the Commune in 1891, to declare that if the socialist "Philistine" wanted to know what the dictatorship of the proletariat would be like, he should simply look at the Paris Commune. Let us note that a myth-making tendency is already beginning to appear in connection with that socialist view of history which most prides itself on being realistic.

And let us note that this is closely bound up with the myth of the Dialectic. It is in such terms as the following that Marx, in *The Civil War in France* and in his letters to Ludwig Kugelmann, habitually discusses the Commune: "What elasticity, what historical initiative, what a capacity for self-sacrifice in these Parisians! . . . History has no comparable example of such greatness . . . working, thinking, fighting, bleeding Paris, almost forgetful, in its incubation of a new society, of the enemies at its gates—radiant in the enthusiasm of its historical initiative. . . . They know that, in order to work out their own emancipation, and along with it that higher form to which modern society is irresistibly tending by its own economic agencies, they will have to pass through long struggles, through a series of historic processes, transforming circumstances and men. . . . In the full consciousness of their historic mission, and with the heroic resolve to act up to it, the working class can afford to smile at the coarse invective of the gentlemen's gentlemen with the inkhorn and the pen, and at the didactic patronage of well-wishing bourgeois-doctrinaires, pouring forth their ignorant platitudes and sectarian crotchets in the oracular tone of scientific infallibility. . . . Working-man's Paris, with its Commune, will be celebrated forever as the glorious harbinger of a new society. Its martyrs are enshrined in the great heart of the working class. Its exterminators History has already nailed to that eternal pillory from which all the prayers of their priests will not avail to redeem them."

History, then, is a being with a definite point of view in any given period. It has a morality which admits of no appeal and which decrees that the exterminators of the Commune shall be regarded as *wrong* forever. Knowing this—knowing, that is, that we are *right*—we may allow ourselves to exaggerate and simplify. At such a moment the Marxism of Marx himself—and how much more often and more widely in the case of his less scrupulous disciples—departs from the rigorous method proposed by "scientific socialism."

15 Karl Marx: Poet of Commodities and Dictator of the Proletariat

Karl Marx's great book *Das Kapital* is a unique and complex work, which demands a different kind of analysis from that which it usually gets. At the time when Marx was working on the first volume, he wrote Engels (July 31, 1865) that whatever the shortcomings of his writings might be, they had "the merit of making an artistic whole"; and in his next letter to Engels (August 5) he speaks of the book as a " 'work of art,' " and mentions "artistic considerations" in connection with his delay in getting it finished. Certainly there went into the creation of *Das Kapital* as much of art as of science. The book is a welding-together of several quite diverse points of view, of several quite distinct techniques of thought. It contains a treatise on economics, a history of industrial development and an inspired tract for the times; and the morality, which is part of the time suspended in the interests of scientific objectivity, is no more self-consistent than the economics is consistently scientific or the history undistracted by the exaltation of apocalyptic vision. And outside the whole immense structure, dark and strong like the old Trier basilica, built by the Romans with brick walls and granite columns, swim the mists and the septentrional lights of German metaphysics and mysticism, always ready to leak in through the crevices.

But it is after all the poet in Marx who makes of all these things a whole—that same poet who had already shown his strength in the verses he had written as a student but whose equipment had not been appropriate to the art of romantic verse. Marx's subject is now human history; and that bleak inhuman side of his mind which disconcerts us in his earlier writings has been filled in with mathematics and logic. But it is the power of imagination as well as the cogency of argument which makes *Das Kapital* so compelling.

Let us, then, before we go behind *Das Kapital,* take into account the tremendous effect which it produces on us the first time we read it.

It is characteristic of Marx's work in general that there is more of the Hegelian interplay between opposites than of the Hegelian progression from the lower to the higher about his use of the dialectical method. His writings tend to lack formal development; we find it hard to get hold of a beginning or an end. But this is less true of the first volume of *Das Kapital,* as Marx finally got it into shape, than perhaps of any other of his productions. Once we have worked through the abstractions of the opening, the book has the momentum of an epic.

It is a vision which fascinates and appals us, which strikes us with a kind of awe, this evolution of mechanical production and of the magnetic accumulation of capital, rising out of the feudal world, with its more primitive but more human handicrafts; wrecking it and overspreading it; accelerating, reorganizing, reassembling, in ever more ingenious complexity, ever more formidable proportions; breaking out of the old boundaries of nations; sending out the tracks and cranes of its commerce across countries and oceans and continents and bringing the people of distant cultures, at diverse stages of civilization, into its system, as it lays hold on the destinies of races, knocks new shapes out of their bodies and their minds, their personalities and their aspirations, without their really grasping what has happened to them and independently of any individual's will. Yet all this development is not merely technological; it is not actually the result of the operation on humanity of a remorseless non-human force. There is also a human principle at work—"those passions which are," as Marx says, "at once the most violent, the basest and the most abominable of which the human breast is capable: the furies of personal interest." For another element of Marx's genius is a peculiar psychological insight: no one has ever had so deadly a sense of the infinite capacity of human nature for remaining oblivious or indifferent to the pains we inflict on others when we have a chance to get something out of them for ourselves.

In dealing with this theme, Karl Marx became one of the great masters of satire. Marx is certainly the greatest ironist since Swift, and he has a good deal in common with him. Compare the logic of Swift's "modest proposal" for curing the misery of Ireland by inducing the starving people to eat their surplus babies with the argument in defense of crime which Marx urges on the bourgeois philosophers (in the so-called fourth volume of *Das Kapital*): crime, he suggests, is produced by the criminal just as "the philosopher produces ideas, the poet verses, the professor manuals," and practising it is useful to society because it takes care of the superfluous population at the same time that putting it down gives employment to many worthy citizens.

Marx has furthermore in common with Swift that he is able to get a certain poetry out of money. There is in Swift a kind of intellectual appetite for computations and accounts and a feeling almost sensuous for currency. In the *Drapier's Letters,* for example, we seem to see the coins, hear them, finger them. But with Marx the idea of money leads to something more philosophic. We have seen how, in writing of the wood-theft laws, he had personified the trees on the landowner's estate as higher beings to which the peasants had to be sacrificed. Now—improving on Sir Thomas More, who, at an earlier stage of capitalist development, at the time when the great estates were being depopulated and turned into sheep-runs, had said that the sheep were eating the people—Marx presents us with a picture of a world in which the commodities command the human beings.

These commodities have their own laws of movement; they seem to revolve in their orbits like electrons. Thus they keep the machinery moving, and they keep the people tending the machines. And the greatest of the commodities is money, because it represents all the others. Marx shows us the metal counters and the bank-notes, mere conventions for facilitating exchange, taking on the fetishistic character which is to make them appear ends in themselves, possessed of a value of their own, then acquiring a potency of their own, which seems to substitute itself for human potency. Marx had stated the whole theme in a sentence of an English speech of 1856: "All our invention and progress seem to result in endowing material forces with intellectual life, and in stultifying human life into a material force." Mankind is caught helpless in a web of wages and profits and credit. Marx's readiness to conjure up these visions of independent and unpetitionable fetishes, which, though inanimate, usurp the rights of the living, is evidently primarily derived from his own deficiency in personal feeling, which he projected into the outside world. Like other great satirists, he punished in others the faults he felt to be dangerous in himself; and it was precisely this blinded and paralyzed side of Karl Marx's peculiar personality which had made it possible for the active and perceptive side to grasp and to explain and to excoriate, as no one else had been able to do, that negation of personal relations, of the responsibility of man to man, that abstract and half-unconscious cruelty, which had afflicted the life of the age.

Marx, to be sure, loves his abstractions, too; he elaborates them at inordinate length. A good deal of this part of *Das Kapital* is gratuitous and simply for show; and one's interest in it is naturally proportionate to one's capacity for enjoying exercises in pure logic. Marx's method does possess a certain beauty: it enables him, as Mehring has said, to make distinctions infinitely subtle—though, if one looks at it the other way round, he may appear to be almost perversely turning concrete industrial processes into the slippery definitions of metaphysics. (Engels used to complain that it was difficult to recognize the historical processes behind the steps of the dialectical argument.) But the chief value of these abstract chapters which alternate with the chapters of history is—in the first volume, at any rate—an ironic one. It is a great trick of Marx's first to hypnotize us by the shuttling back and forth of his syllogisms, to elevate us to the contemplation of what appear to be metaphysical laws; and then, by dropping a single phrase, to sting us back to the realization that these pure economic principles that lend themselves to such elegant demonstration are derived simply from the laws of human selfishness, and that if they may be assumed to operate with such sureness, it is only because the acquisitive instinct is as unfailing as the force of gravitation. The meaning of the impersonal-looking formulas which Marx produces with so scientific an air is, he reminds us from time to time as if casually, pennies withheld from the worker's pocket, sweat squeezed out of his body, and natural enjoyments denied his soul. In competing with the pundits of economics, Marx has written something in the nature of a parody; and, once we have read *Das Kapital,* the conventional works on economics never seem the same to us again: we can always see through their arguments and figures the realities of the crude human relations which it is their purpose or effect to mask.

For in Marx the exposition of the theory—the dance of commodities, the cross-stitch of logic—is always followed by a documented picture of the capitalist laws at work; and these chapters, with their piling-up of factory reports, their prosaic descriptions of misery and filth, their remorseless enumeration of the abnormal conditions to which the men and women and children of the working class have had to try to adjust themselves, their chronicle of the sordid expedients by which the employers had almost invariably won back, minute by minute and penny by penny, the profits that legislation, itself always inadequate and belated, had tried to shave down a little, and with their specimens of the complacent appeals to morality, religion and reason by which the employers and their economist apologists had had the hypocrisy to justify their practice— these at last become almost intolerable. We feel that we have been taken for the first time through the real structure of our civilization, and that it is the ugliest that has ever existed—a state of things where there is very little to choose between the physical degradation of the workers and the moral degradation of the masters.

From time to time, with telling effect, Marx will light up for a moment the memory of other societies which have been fired by other ideals. The disgrace of the institution of slavery on which the Greek system had been founded had at least, in debasing one set of persons, made possible the development of an aristocracy of marvelous taste and many-sided accomplishment, whereas the masses of the people in the industrial world had been enslaved to no more impressive purpose than "to transform a few vulgar and half-educated upstarts into 'eminent cotton spinners,' 'extensive sausage makers' and 'influential blacking dealers.'" The feudal system of the Middle Ages, before it had been thrown into disorder by the rebellion of the nobles against the king, had at least guaranteed certain rights in return for the discharge of certain duties. Everybody had in some sense been somebody; whereas when the industrial depression occurred and the mill closed its door on the factory worker, neither his employer nor the State was responsible for him. Where the baron had blown in his plunder in such a way as to give his dependents a good time, the great new virtue of the bourgeois was thrift, the saving of money in order to reinvest it. And though Marx has always kept our nose so close to the counting-house and the spindle and the steam hammer and the scutching-mill and the clay-pit and the mine, he always carries with him through the caverns and wastes of the modern industrial world, cold as those abysses of the sea which the mariner of his ballad spurned as godless, the commands of that "eternal God" who equips him with his undeviating standard for judging earthly things.

Something like this is our first impression of *Das Kapital*. It is only later, when we come to think about it coolly and after some further acquaintance with Marx's writings, that its basic inconsistencies become plain.

The most obvious of these is the discrepancy between the scientific point of view of the historian and the moral point of view of the prophet. "What astonished me most in Marx," writes the Russian sociologist, Maxím Kovalévsky, "was his passionate partisanship in political questions, which did not jibe with the calm objective method which he recommended to his disciples and which was supposed to be intended as an instrument for investigating economic principles." And H. M. Hyndman was also struck by "the contrast between [Marx's] manner and utterance when thus deeply stirred to anger [over the policy of the Liberal Party] and his attitude when giving his views on the economic events of the period."

On the one hand, Marx is telling you in *Das Kapital* that a certain "historic" development, indispensable for the progress of the race, could only have been carried out by capitalism; and, on the other hand, he is filling you with fury against the wickedness of the people who have performed it. It is as if Darwin had been a kind of Luther Burbank and had caused the blood of his readers to boil over the inadequacies, in the sight of the ideal, of the species produced by evolution and the wrongs of those animals and plants which had been eliminated in the struggle for life. Marx, the scientific historian, declares that the centralization required for socialism could have been provided in no other way than by the competitive processes of capitalism. In a striking passage in the second volume, he accepts the very horrors of the system as an aspect of its beneficent development: "Looking upon capitalist production in its details . . . we find that it is very economical with materialized labor incorporated in commodities. But it is more than any other mode of production prodigal with human lives, with living labor, wasting not only flesh and blood, but also nerves and brains. Indeed, it is only by dint of the most extravagant waste of individual development that human development is safeguarded and advanced in that epoch of history which immediately precedes the conscious reorganization of society. Since all the economies here mentioned [on the part of the operators of coal mines] arise from the social nature of labor, it is just this social character of labor which causes this waste of the life and health of the laborer." The capitalist forces, then, could not have operated otherwise: even in their destruction of human beings, they are somehow the agents of human salvation; and yet every individual manufacturer must be blasted as either a cold-blooded slave-driver or a canting and rationalizing fraud.

We may allow ourselves at first to be persuaded that Marx has somehow proved "scientifically" the turpitude of the capitalist class, that the triumph of the cause of the worker is somehow guaranteed by "economics." There is the Marxist Theory of Surplus Value.

The worker, according to Marx, has sold his capacity to

labor like any other commodity on the market; and its value has been determined by the minimum amount required to keep him alive and capable of working and of procreating a fresh supply of workers—which is all the employer has an interest in enabling him to do. The worker, then, is hired for this minimum amount, which is due him for, say, six hours of labor, and is then compelled to work by the employer, on penalty of losing his job, for as long as eight or ten hours. The manufacturer thus robs the worker of from two to four hours of work and sells the product of this work at its value. This value of the stolen work is characterized as "surplus value" and said to constitute the manufacturer's profit. On this the manufacturer grows fat and insolent while the worker is kept down as close as possible to the necessaries of bare subsistence.

Now, certainly the manufacturer, left to himself, will tend to work his labor as hard as possible and to pay them the least possible wages. But what does it actually mean to say that labor determines value?—an idea which Marx had found in embryo in Ricardo and Adam Smith. It was easy to point out many things of which the value was obviously *not* determined by labor: old furniture, old masters, radium; and in the case of manufactured products themselves, it by no means held true that their value on the market was proportionate to the amount of work that had gone into them. It was not true that the profits of a manufacturer who employed a great many workers and spent relatively little on plant was larger than the profit of another manufacturer who spent a great deal on plant and employed relatively little labor—though on Marx's theory it seemed that it should be so. The English Fabians, taking their cue from Stanley Jevons, elaborated a counter-theory which made value dependent on demand: the price of any commodity is determined by the degree of its utility to the persons to whom it is available, and this in turn may be said to determine the value of the labor which has gone to make it.

Marx did not attempt to deal with this problem in the only section of *Das Kapital* he published. The solution was put off till a later volume, which he never lived to complete; and it was not until 1894 that Engels was able to bring out the post-humous section (Volume III) of Marx's manuscript which contained it. It now turned out that Marx had frankly recognized that "as a general rule, profit and surplus value are really two different magnitudes." All profits did come out of surplus value; but the effect of the competition of the capitalists—since the pouring of capital into some lucrative line of industry tended to scale down the rate of profit, while its withdrawal from some less profitable line had the effect of bringing it up—was to level out this rate of profit so that everybody made about the same. The total amount of profit would correspond to the total amount of surplus value; but the individual surplus values had, as it were, been pooled by the individual capitalists, and the profits divided up in such a way that each one got a share which was proportionate to the amount of the capital he had invested. As for the merchant, he did not create value in the same way that the worker did; he merely saved money for the manufacturer in distributing the latter's product and he got a cut out of the latter's surplus value. The people who worked for the merchant did not really create value either; they, too, got a cut out of the manufacturer's profit, but they were cheated out of a part of what they had earned in the same way that the factory workers were cheated by the manufacturer. As for the landlord in capitalist society, he collected *his* cut of the surplus value in the shape of the rent which was paid him by the manufacturer and the merchant.

Thus the value that was supposed to be derived from labor appeared as a purely abstract conception which had nothing to do with prices and relative profits, and which indeed exhibited a character almost mystical inasmuch as it was an essence inhering only in farm and factory labor and not possessed by the labor of the merchant or of the manufacturer himself, or even by that of the merchant's clerks. In order to prove that this value of labor had any objective reality, it would have been necessary to show that the total profit realized at a given moment was equal to that part of the combined prices on the market of the total amount of goods produced which was appropriated by the manufacturer after he had paid his workers

—a calculation that Marx never attempted. And it is hard to see how Marx's abstract argument in Volume III—of which John Strachey has recently made so much in his book on *The Nature of Capitalist Crisis*—can be accepted as proving anything at all. If profit is equal to surplus value, says Marx, then as industry becomes continually more mechanized and needs to employ less and less human labor, one would expect the rate of profit to decrease. Now the rate of profit does decrease. But, assuming that the rate of profit does fall, how does this prove that there is any direct relation between the proportion of human labor employed and the manufacturer's rate of profit, which is reckoned on his whole investment? It was quite possible, as we shall see in a moment, to show the mechanism of capitalist crises without invoking the Labor Theory of Value; and certainly the former does not prove the latter. The Labor Theory is thus simply, like the Dialectic, a creation of the metaphysician who never abdicated before the economist in Marx—an effort to show that the moral values which he wished to impress on people were, independently of our ideas about them, somehow involved in the nature of things.

But in the meantime, for more than a quarter of a century, from 1867 to 1894, the idea that all value was created by labor had been steadily marching on. It had been accepted by Marx's followers as one of the fundamental tenets of their faith, and they had been confidently looking forward to the day when the master would resolve all problems and give the irrefutable reply to their enemies. And now when the third volume of *Das Kapital* came out, even economists sympathetic to Marx expressed disillusion and disappointment.

One is almost inclined to conclude that there may have been something in the contention of the Italian economist Loria, who thought that Marx had never really wanted to face the world with the later developments of his theory but had purposely left it for Engels to deal with them after his death. Certainly the moral effect of the overwhelming first volume of *Das Kapital* is likely to be weakened by an acquaintance with its successors. If all value is created by labor only in some metaphysical sense, then there may be more in those utility theories of value which Marxists regard as capitalist frauds than we had formerly been willing to admit. If it is possible for values to be reckoned as Marx reckoned them, in units of an abstract labor power, why was it not possible—what Marx had denied—to reckon them in units of an abstract utility?—especially when the supposed value of labor seems to have nothing to do with fixing prices, whereas the demand of the consumer obviously has.

But the truth is that all such theories are incomplete: real prices are the results of situations much more complex than any of these formulas, and complicated by psychological factors which economists seldom take into account. The economist tends to imagine that value—and value in the sense of actual prices is easily confused with value in a moral or philosophical sense—is something mainly created by the group to which he belongs or whose apologist he aims to be. The stupider type of old-fashioned manufacturer was practically under the impression that he was creating both the product and the labor by supplying the brains and the capital which gave the factory hand his opportunity to work. The Fabian Socialists represented the middle-class British consumer, and they believed that the human being as consumer rather than as farm laborer or factory hand determined the value of commodities by his demand for them. Henry George, who as a poor printer in California had been appalled to see that land of plenty transformed into a merciless monopoly where the rich were crowding the poor off the earth, had been led to conceive all value as primarily derived from the land. Karl Marx, who was not only on the side of the worker but wanted to see him inherit the earth, asserted that all value was created by labor. His effort to support this assertion with a theoretical justification exhibits clearly—it is perhaps the most striking example—the inconsistency in Dialectical Materialism between the tendency to represent everything as relative, every system of economics as an ideology projected by special class interests, and the impulse to establish principles with some more general sort of validity, upon which one's own conduct may be based.

Engels of course was furious with Loria and in a reply to those who had complained of the third volume—it was one of the very last things that he wrote, and he did not live to do a projected second section—advanced one preposterous argument which gave the whole Marxist position away. Falling back on his studies in anthropology, he tries to prove that among primitive peoples the actual prices for which commodities are exchanged are determined by the labor that has gone into them. "The people of that time," he declares, "were certainly clever enough—both the cattle-breeders and their customers—not to give away the labor-time expended by them without an equivalent in barter. On the contrary, the closer people are to the primitive state of commodity production— the Russians and Orientals, for example—the more time do they still waste today, in order to squeeze out, through long tenacious bargaining, the full compensation for their labor-time expended on a product." This is a droll picture of the innocent Engels buying some brass jewelry from a Persian merchant and accepting the protestations of the latter as simply the efforts of an honest fellow to get from the buyer the full value of his work—a picture which appears all the stranger when we remember the youthful Engels' little drawing of the smirking commercial traveler who has just sold the connoisseur some bad wine. And it shows up a central fallacy of Marxism. After all, Marx and Engels had devoted a large part of their lives to demonstrating that human beings will sell things for a good deal more than they have cost them. "Human beings?" Engels would have retorted. "No: only the bourgeoisie." But this lands him in the ridiculous position of assuming that, say, the Caucasian horse-trader or the oriental seller of trinkets is incapable of overcharging his customer. No: the desire to get the highest possible price for something we have to sell seems to have distinguished the human race from a period antedating capitalist society.

We shall return to this point a little later; but in the meantime let us note the crudity of the psychological motivation which underlies the world-view of Marx. It is the shortcoming of economists in general that each one understands as a rule only one or two human motivations: psychology and economics have never yet got together in such a way as really to supplement one another. Marx understood sordid self-interest and its capacity for self-delusion, and he understood the proud human spirit throwing off degradation and oppression. But he tended to regard these as exclusively the products of class specialization rather than as impulses more or less common to humanity which might be expected to show themselves, or to be latent, in people of any class.

Marx would have run up against more complicated questions of the motivation of economic groups if he had gone on with his class anatomy of society. What he shows us in the first volume of *Das Kapital* is always the factory worker immediately confronting the manufacturer, the peasant confronting the landowner; in this section it is always the direct exploiter who is meant when Marx speaks of the capitalist. But in the second and third instalments, which deal with the circulation of capital, Marx must reckon with the tradesmen and the bankers and with what we now call the white-collar class, who work for them; and the picture becomes much more complex. Marx did not, however, get around to discussing the interrelations between these class forces until the very last pages of his manuscript; and it seems significant that of the chapter called *The Classes* he should have written only a page and a half. Modern capitalist society, Marx says here, may be divided into three great classes: "the owners of mere labor-power, the owners of capital, and the landlords, whose respective sources of income are wages, profit and ground-rent." But there are also "middle and transition stages," which "obliterate all definite boundaries." The question is, What constitutes a class? "At first glance, it might seem that the identity of the revenues and of the sources of revenue" of each makes the basis of each of the three great classes. But from this point of view the physicians and the officials would constitute classes, too. "The same would also be true of the infinite dissipation of interests and positions created by the social division of labor among laborers, capitalists and landlords. For example, the landlords are divided into owners of vineyards, farms, forests, mines, fisheries. [Here the manuscript ends.]"

Marx dropped the class analysis of society at the moment when he was approaching its real difficulties.

What Karl Marx, then, had really based his prophecies on—as Reinhold Niebuhr has recently pointed out—was the assumption that, though the employer had always shown himself to be grasping, the socialist worker of the future—having made what Engels describes in *Anti-Dühring* as the "leap from the realm of necessity into the realm of freedom"—would always act for the good of humanity. The dominant class of the capitalist era had never willingly done anything but rob the poor in the interests of the well-being of their own group; but the dominant class of the proletarian dictatorship would never dream of abusing its position.

It ought also to be noted at this point that Marx and Engels had come to believe that there had been an epoch in the prehistoric past when a different standard of morality had prevailed. Since writing the *Communist Manifesto,* they had had occasion to revise their opinion then expressed, that "the history of all human society, past and present, has been the history of class struggles." In the later editions, Engels added a note in which he explained that in 1847 little had been known about the communism of primitive societies. In the meantime, he and Marx had read the books of certain recent anthropologists who had convinced them that a communistic *gens* had been the true primitive form of social organization. Especially had they been impressed by the work of Lewis H. Morgan, the American ethnologist and socialist, who had lived among the Iroquois Indians. As a result, Marx and Engels now looked back—and thereby nourished their faith in the future—to something in the nature of a Golden Age of communist ownership and brotherly relations.

Marx himself had intended to write on this subject, but he had never got to the point of doing so—so that Engels, after Marx's death, published an essay on the German mark (a free rural commune), based on the researches of G. L. von Maurer, and a little book called *The Origin of the Family, Private Property and the State*. Here he attempted to demonstrate from Morgan that the "simple moral grandeur" of the "old gentile society without classes" had been "undermined and brought to its ruin by the most contemptible means: theft, violence, cunning, treason," and that, in consequence, the "new system of classes" had been "inaugurated by the meanest impulses: vulgar covetousness, brutal lust, sordid avarice, selfish robbery of the common wealth."

Now this raises the same sort of question in regard to this communist past that the rule of the proletariat does in regard to the socialist future. How had the members of the human race, who had once been happy and good, managed to become so unhappy and bad? This latter condition, on Engels' own showing, had been brought about by these primitive peoples themselves in the course of their intertribal warfare. The victors had never hesitated a moment in taking advantage of their ascendancy over the vanquished to plunder them and reduce them to slavery. Here again we are brought up against the inadequacy of the Marxist conception of human nature. Certainly there is some plausibility in the assumption that a primitive community of equals is sounder within its limits than modern society—as the Pueblo Indian villages of the American Southwest have survived with their communist economy in the teeth of their more predatory nomad neighbors and of the massacres and bankruptcies of the white man; and that any society of the future which is to be stable must have gravitated to some such equilibrium. But is it really only impulses which may be characterized as "vulgar," "brutal" and "selfish" that have given rise to the class societies?

With this question of the primitive past we need not attempt to deal at length, since Marx gave it but little attention in his writings and since I cannot find that even Engels made very much effort to fit it into the dialectical theory of history. But the question for the future is important. Why should we suppose that man's brutal and selfish impulses will all evaporate with a socialist dictatorship?

The answer is simply that there remained with Marx and Engels, in spite of their priding themselves upon having developed a new socialism that was "scientific" in contrast to the old "utopian" socialism, a certain amount of this very utopianism they had repudiated.

Let us consider why Marx should have assumed that the morality of the revolutionary proletariat would necessarily be more improving for humanity than the morality of the exploit ing bourgeoisie. The moralities which people profess are, ac cording to Marx's theory, inextricably tied up with their clas interests; so that there are a morality of the bourgeoisie and a morality of the proletariat, and the two are antagonistic. The morality of the bourgeoisie has had for its purpose to cultivate those virtues which were necessary to build up its own position and to justify the crimes of which it has been guilty in dis possessing and destroying the workers; the morality of the proletariat consists in the loyalty, the self-sacrifice and the courage which will make it possible for it in turn to dispossess and destroy the bourgeoisie. Yet it is *right* for the proletariat to expropriate the bourgeoisie, and even to imprison them and kill them, in some sense in which it has *not* been right for the bourgeoisie to do the same things to them. Why? Because, the Marxist would answer, the proletariat represents the *antithesis*, which, in the course of the dialectical evolution from the lower to the higher, is coming to carry the *thesis* into the *synthesis*. But in what way is the revolutionary morality dis tinguishably superior to the morality with which it struggles and which it will ultimately supplant?

It is distinguished by its recognition of certain fundamental human rights. Karl Marx in his early writings has had a great deal to say about these rights. Later on, when he is writing *Das Kapital,* he no longer invokes them so explicitly; and Engels asserted in *Anti-Dühring* (of 1877) that "the idea of equality both in its bourgeois and in its proletarian form" was "itself an historical product" and "therefore anything but an eternal truth"; that it owed its popularity merely to what he called "the general diffusion and the continual appropriateness of the ideas of the eighteenth century." Yet for Marx it had been certainly something more; its "appropriateness" had been felt with passion. And the inheritor of the eighteenth-century Enlightenment, with a faith, not unlike Rousseau's, in the fun damental worthiness of man, and even haunted, as appears from his attitude toward the primitive communities described by Morgan, by the phantom of the "noble savage," is always there behind the scientific historian, who indicates coldly that "human development" has been "safeguarded and advanced in that epoch of history which immediately precedes the conscious reorganization of society" at the cost of an immense waste of "flesh and blood." We have seen how Marx had ridiculed Proudhon for introducing into contemporary economics the eighteenth-century abstraction of a universal natural man endowed with a fundamental right to own property. But Marx himself was to be assuming throughout his life that every human being was entitled to what was described by another exponent of the eighteenth-century philosophy as "life, liberty and the pursuit of happiness." When a governing-class Englishman like Palmerston asserted that "the legislature of a country has the right to impose such political disabilities upon any class of the community as it may deem necessary for the safety and the welfare of the whole . . . This belongs to the fundamental principles on which civilized government is founded"; Marx would be prompt to retort: "There you have the most cynical confession ever made, that the mass of the people have no rights at all, but that they may be allowed that amount of immunities the legislature—or in other words, the ruling class—may deem fit to grant them."

And now we have got to the real bottom of Marxism—to the assumption that class society is wrong because it destroys, as the *Communist Manifesto* says, the bonds between man and man and prevents the recognition of those rights which are common to all human beings. If no such human rights exist, what is wrong about exploitation? But there is no ultimate way of *proving* they exist any more than there is of proving that in the sight of God all souls are of equal value. You cannot reason an English Tory into a conviction that the lower classes are not unalterably inferior to the upper; and it would be useless to dispute with a Nazi over the innate inferiority of non-Nordics. Engels was later to provide in *Anti-Dühring* an admirable *historical* account of the development in the modern world of the belief in equal rights—showing how the idea of equality was maintained under the medieval hierarchy by the claims of the various national states; how the industrial middle class, as it progressed out of handicraft to manufacture, required freedom from the restrictions of the guilds in order to sell their labor, and freedom from discriminative trade laws in order to exchange their commodities; and how the working class eventually created by the new economic system, the "shadow" of the bourgeoisie, had taken over from it the ideal of equality and demanded, not merely the abolition of class privileges, as the bourgeoisie had done, but the "abolition of the *classes themselves*." But even with the aid of historical evidence, you cannot necessarily convince people that the progress of human institutions involves a process of progressive democratization: you can only appeal to them by methods which, in the last analysis, are moral and emotional. And this Karl Marx knew magnificently how to do. The great importance of his book is not at all that it establishes an incomparable essence of value inherent in agricultural and factory work, but that it shows in a concrete way how the worker has been misused by the employer and that it makes the reader indignant about this. While Karl Marx is pretending to tell us that all these horrors have advanced human civilization and that all morality is a relative matter, he is really convincing us that a true civilization will be impossible without our putting an end to them and is filling us with fervor for amorality of his own.

It was here that Karl Marx as a Jew had his great value for the thought of his age. The characteristic genius of the Jew has been especially a moral genius. The sacred books of the people of Israel have served as a basis for the religions of three continents; and even in the case of those great men among the Jews who do not occupy themselves with religion proper, it is usually a grasp of moral ideas which has given them their peculiar force. Freud's discovery of emotional compensations is in reality a kind of moral insight: the irrational and the destructive in personality must be distortions of the creative and the natural; and to correct them, the patient and the analyst alike are required to exert a self-discipline which is the only price of mastery and adjustment—a point of view distinctly different from that of the more purely Germanic Jung, who leads his patients away from their troubles into the dreamland of primitive myths and is likely to leave them there. It was probably the Jew in the half-Jewish Proust that saved him from being the Anatole France of an even more deliquescent phase of the French belletristic tradition. Certainly the moral authority of the Jews has figured to a considerable extent among the factors that have caused the Nazis in Germany to persecute them. To a people who are attempting to recapture a barbarian self-confidence and ruthlessness, such moralists are disconcerting: they are always trying to remind one of principles that transcend country and class when one wants to believe in a hierarchy based on race. It is interesting to look back on the role which the Jews have already played in this chronicle: Renan's Semitic studies, the influence on Anatole France of Mme. Caillavet, the Jewish disciples of Saint-Simon; the working-class leader Andreas Gottschalk; the communist Moses Hess; the socialist Ferdinand Lassalle. And so Karl Marx brought into economics a point of view which was of value to his time precisely in proportion as it was alien to it. Nobody but a Jew in that middle nineteenth century could have commanded the moral weapons to crack the fortress of bourgeois self-satisfaction.

Nobody but a Jew could have fought so uncompromisingly and obstinately for the victory of the dispossessed classes. The great Jewish minds of these first generations that had been liberated from the closed Judaic world, still remembered the mediaeval captivity, and they were likely to present themselves as champions of other social groups or doctrines which had not been freed or vindicated yet. So Freud saw the vital importance of those sexual impulses that civilization had outlawed or that puritanism had tried to suppress, and forced psychiatric science to take account of them. So Einstein became preoccupied with the few unemphasized anomalies in the well-operating system of Newton and made them the corner-stone that the builder had rejected on which to build a new system that should shake the authority of the old. So Lassalle took up the cause of feminism at a time when German women were largely at the mercy of their fathers and their husbands; and so Proust transferred from a persecuted race to the artist and the homosexual both that race's tragic fate in society and its inner conviction of moral superiority. So Marx, as has been shown already, had substituted for the plight of the Jew the plight of the proletariat.

But Marx is of the tradition of the Old Testament, not of that of the New. His daughter Eleanor tells us that the version of the life of Jesus which he was in the habit of recounting to his children showed Jesus as primarily a poor carpenter's son who had been executed unjustly by the rich. Marx could rub in the sufferings of the wronged; he could blast the exploiters with hatred. But he could not much love the first any more than he could pity the second. He was not among those working-class leaders who have merged themselves with working-class life. He himself had had no experience of modern industry; it was from Engels and the parliamentary blue-books that he had accumulated his mountains of data. And if he exposes the dark depths of the industrial system, it is less to move us to fellow-feeling with the workers than to destroy the human aspect of their masters. The bourgeoisie, in Karl Marx's writings, are created mainly in caricature; and the proletariat figure mainly as their crimes. There is in Marx an irreducible discrepancy between the good which he proposes for humanity and the ruthlessness and hatred he inculcates as a means of arriving at this—a discrepancy which, in the history of Marxism, has given rise to much moral confusion.

Now where does the animus behind *Das Kapital* come from? It is the bitterest of all Marx's bitter books. It has hardly a trace of the exhilaration which gives his earlier work a kind of fire. "Reading your book again," he wrote Engels April 9, 1863—the book was *The Condition of the English Working Class in 1844*—"has sadly made me feel my age. With what freshness and passion and boldness of vision and freedom from learned and scientific scruples you have handled the subject here! And the illusion that tomorrow or the day after tomorrow the result will spring to life as an historical reality before our eyes gives the whole a warm and spirited humor —with which the later 'gray on gray' makes a damnably unpleasant contrast."

But it is not only age which makes the difference between Engels' book and Marx's. It is impossible to read *Das Kapital* in the light of Marx's life during this period without concluding that the emotional motivation, partly or totally unconscious no doubt, behind Marx's excoriation of the capitalists and his grim parading of the afflictions of the poor is at once his outraged conviction of the indignity and injustice of his own fate and his bad conscience at having inflicted that fate on others. Marx himself is not only the victim, the dispossessed proletariat; he is also the exploiting employer. For has he not exploited Jenny and Engels? Is he himself not responsible, not merely for the being of his beloved daughters, but for the handicaps and hardships they have been born to? In a letter to Siegfried Meyer, written April 30, 1867, when he has finally got *Das Kapital* off to the printer, he speaks of it as "the task to which I have sacrificed my health, my happiness in life and my family."

True—as he goes on to say—it has all been done for the ideal and for mankind: "I laugh at the so-called 'practical' men and their wisdom. If one had the hide of an ox, one could naturally turn one's back on the sufferings of humanity and look after one's own skin; but, as it is, I should have considered myself very unpractical if I had died without completing my book, at least in manuscript form." "To work for humanity," says Lafargue, "was one of his favorite phrases." For that science to which one sacrifices others "should not be," as Marx writes elsewhere, "an egoistic pleasure: those who are in a position to devote themselves to scientific studies should be also the first to put their knowledge at the service of humanity."

Yet if you choose to work for humanity, if you will not write for money, why then you must make other people earn it for you or suffer and let others suffer, because you haven't got it.

If it was true, as I have suggested, that Marx and Engels in relation to one another were like the electrodes of the voltaic cell, it became more and more obvious as time went on that Marx was to play the part of the metal of the positive electrode, which gives out hydrogen and remains unchanged, while Engels was to be the negative electrode, which gradually gets used up. "There's nothing I long for more," Engels wrote Marx, April 27, 1867, just after the last pages of the first volume of *Das Kapital* had finally been got off to the printer, "than to escape from this miserable commerce, which is demoralizing me completely by reason of the time it makes me waste. So long as I remain in it, I can't accomplish anything—especially since I've been one of the bosses, it's got to be a great deal worse on account of the increased responsibility." He is going to give it up, he says; but then his income will be very much reduced, "and what I always have on my mind is what are we going to do about you?" Marx replies on a note of contrition: "I confidently hope and believe that I shall be within a year's time enough of a made man so that I can fundamentally reform my economic situation and stand finally on my own feet again. If it had not been for you, I should never have been able to bring this work to completion, and I assure you that it has always weighed like an incubus on my conscience that it should have been principally on account of me that you have been allowing your splendid abilities to be wasted and rusted in business and have had, besides, to live through all my *petites misères* with me."

But, he adds, he cannot conceal from himself that he has "a year of trial" still ahead of him; and he intimates, without explicitly asking for it, that an immediate advance of money would be helpful. "What—aside from the uncertainty—frightens me most is the prospect of going back to London [he was in Germany arranging the publication of his book], as I must do in six or eight days. The debts there are considerable, and the Manichees [the creditors] are eagerly awaiting my return. That means family worries again, domestic collisions, a hunted life, instead of going freely and freshly to work."

We have seen what the situation at home was. The next year Laura Marx was to succumb to the fate which her parents had been trying to stave off and to take a position as governess. Poor Marx, more in torment than ever, with on the one hand the needs of his family and on the other the exactions of his book, had been suffering from a chronic insomnia. He had been visited by a succession of plagues which were none the less physically agonizing because they were probably partly due to the strain of the domestic situation, as Marx himself suggested, combined, as Engels thought, with his difficulties over his book. For years he was tormented almost incessantly by outbreaks of carbuncles and boils—an ailment of which only those who have had it can appreciate the exasperating character, with its malignant and nagging inflammations always coming out in new places, often inaccessible and sometimes crippling, as if a host of indestructible little devils were hatching under one's skin. And these were diversified with influenza, rheumatism, ophthalmia, toothache and headache. But his most serious complaint was an enlarged liver. He had had trouble with his liver all his life: his father had died of cancer of the liver; and the fear of it had always hung over Karl. During the sixties his trouble became acute; later on, he was to be forced to take a cure. In the meantime, during the years when he is in labor with *Das Kapital,* he passes through a Valley of the Shadow of Death. He will write Engels that his arm is so sore with rheumatism that he cries out without being aware of it every time he moves it in his sleep, that his liver attacks have stupefied his brain, paralyzed all his limbs. We have seen how, unable to read or write, he had given himself up at one period, to "psychological reveries as to what it would be like to be blind or mad." And he extends his afflictions to all about him in a way which betrays a conviction that he is doomed to be a bringer of grief. When Jenny takes a trip to Paris to arrange about a French translation of *Das Kapital,* she finds that the man she has gone to interview has just had a paralytic stroke; and on her way back in the train something goes wrong with the locomotive so that she arrives two hours late; then the omnibus in which she is riding upsets; and when she finally gets back to London, the cab in which she is driving home has a collision with another cab and she is obliged to walk the rest of the way. In the meantime, Lenchen's sister, who had been staying at the Marxes', had suddenly fallen ill and, just before Jenny's arrival, had died. When Marx's mother, upon whose demise he had, as we have seen, been counting, does finally die, he writes strangely to Engels that Fate has been demanding some member of his family: "I myself have one foot in the grave (*unter der Erde*)." And in one of his letters to Engels during his visit to Lassalle in Berlin, he reveals by another fantasy the symbolic significance which he attaches to illness: "*Apropos* Lassalle-Lazarus! Lepsius has proved in his big work on Egypt that the exodus of the Jews from Egypt is nothing more nor less than the story that Manetho tells about the expulsion from Egypt 'of the race of lepers,' led by an Egyptian priest called Moses. Lazarus the leper is thus the prototype of the Jews and Lazarus-Lassalle. Only in the case of our Lazarus, the leprosy has gone to his brain. The disease from which he is suffering was originally secondary syphilis, imperfectly cured. He developed a caries of the bone from it . . . and something has still remained in one of his legs . . . neuralgia or *something of the sort*. To the detriment of his physique, our Lazarus now lives as luxuriously as his antithesis, the rich man, and this I regard as one of the main obstacles to his cure."

And the better times to which Marx looked forward when the first volume of *Das Kapital* was finished, were never really to come. Engels had hoped, as he told him, that his outlook would now become less gloomy. But Marx's poverty and his dependence on others were permanent features of his life; and as their consequences had become more painful, he could only grow more bitter. Hyndman tells us that, unlike certain other aging men, he grew less tolerant instead of more. *Das Kapital* is the reflection of this period. He said that he had written the terrible chapter on the *Working Day* at a time when, as a result of his illness, his head had been too weak for theoretical work; and when he had finally finished his book, he wrote Engels: "I hope that the bourgeoisie as long as they live will have cause to remember my carbuncles." Thus, in attacking the industrial system, he is at the same time declaring his own tribulations, calling the Heavens— that is, History—to witness that he is a just man wronged, and damning the hypocritical scoundrel who compels others to slave and suffer for him, who persists in remaining indifferent to the agony for which he is responsible, who even keeps himself in ignorance of it. The book has behind it the exalted purpose, it is a part of the noble accomplishment, of Karl Marx's devoted life; but the wrong and the hurt of that life have made the whole picture hateful or grievous. The lofty devotion and the wrong are inextricably involved with one another; and the more he asserts the will of his highest impulses, the blacker the situation becomes.

Marx may appear to have kept the two things apart when he has set the bad capitalist on one side and the good communist of the future on the other; but, after all, to arrive at that future, the communist must be cruel and repressive just as the capitalist has been; he, too, must do violence to that common humanity in whose service the prophet is supposed to be preaching. It is a serious misrepresentation of Marx to minimize the sadistic element in his writing. In his address to the Communist League of April, 1850, he had declared to the revolutionary working class that, "far from opposing so-called excesses, the vengeance of the people on hated individuals or attacks by the masses on buildings which arouse hateful memories, we must not only tolerate them, but even take the lead in them." Nor was this, as we have seen from his correspondence, a tendency which he reserved for politics. In the letter to Engels just quoted, for example, there is a passage in which Marx tells his friend that the publisher who had let them down twenty years before by being afraid to bring out *The German Ideology* and who had unloaded "that young fellow Kriege on our necks" had recently fallen out of a window and "if you please (*gefälligst*), broken his own neck."

If we isolate the images in Marx—which are so powerful and vivid in themselves that they can sometimes persuade us to forget his lack of realistic observation and almost produce the illusion of a visible and tangible experience—if we isolate and examine these images, we can see through to the inner obsessions at the heart of the world-vision of Marx.

Here all is cruel discomfort, rape, repression, mutilation and massacre, premature burial, the stalking of corpses, the vampire that lives on another's blood, life in death and death in life: "The Abbé Bonawita Blank . . . operated on magpies and starlings in such a way that, though they were free to fly about as they pleased, they would always come back to him again. He cut off the lower part of their beaks so that they were not able to get their food themselves and so were obliged to eat from his hand. The good little bourgeois who looked on from a distance and saw the birds perched on the shoulders of the good priest and apparently dining with him in a friendly fashion, admired his culture and his science. His biographer says that the birds loved him as their benefactor. And the Poles, enchained, mutilated, branded, refuse to love their Prussian benefactors!" "But capital not only lives upon labor. Like a magnificent and barbarous master, it drags with it into its grave the corpses of its slaves, whole hecatombs of workers, who perish in the crises." "If the silkworm's object in spinning were to prolong its existence as caterpillar, it would be a perfect example of the wage-worker" (both are condemned, thus, to living graves). "This miserable Assembly left the stage, after it had given itself the pleasure, two days before the anniversary of its birthday, May 4, of rejecting the notion of amnesty for the June insurgents. Its power shattered, held in deadly hatred by the people, repulsed, maltreated, contemptuously thrown aside by the bourgeoisie, whose tool it was, forced in the second half of its life to disavow the first, robbed of its republican illusions, with no great creations in the past, with no hope for the future, and with its living body dying bit by bit, it was able to galvanize its own corpse only by continually recalling the June victory and living it over again, substantiating itself by constantly repeated damnation of the damned. Vampire, that lives on the blood of the June insurgents!" "But from 1848 to 1851 there was nothing more than a walking of the ghost of the old revolution—now in the form of Marrast, *'le républicain en gants jaunes,'* dressed up as Bailly; and now in the form of the adventurer who hid his commonplace and unpleasing physiognomy behind the iron death-mask of Napoleon." "Universal suffrage seems to have survived only for a moment, in order that it might before all men's eyes draw up a holograph will, declaring in the name of the people: 'Everything that exists is fit for the scrap-heap.'" "Neither a nation nor a woman can be forgiven for the unguarded hour in which a chance comer has seized the opportunity for an act of rape." "Thetis, the sea-goddess, had foretold to her son Achilles that he would perish in the heyday of his youth. Like Achilles, the constitution has its weak spot; and, like Achilles, it has a foreboding of premature death." "If, subsequently, the constitution was bayoneted out of existence, we must not forget that while in the womb it had been guarded by bayonets directed against the people, and that by bayonets it had been brought into the world." "The champions of the Party of Order were still seated upon the shoulders of armed force, when they realized, one fine morning, that the seat had become prickly, for the shoulders had turned into bayonets." "The bourgeois order, which at the beginning of the century had stationed the state as a sentry before the newly created petty land-holdings and dunged them with laurels, has now turned into a vampire, which sucks out their heart's blood and brain-marrow and casts it into the alchemist's retort of capital." (This last has been pointed out by Max Eastman as an example of Marx's bad taste. The metaphor is certainly mixed; yet the style is not so very much different from the apocalyptic parts of the Bible. It may be noted that Marx himself was always pitiless to the mixed metaphors of his opponents.)

These images have been excerpted almost as they come from the Marx of the most brilliant period: from his writings in the *Neue Rheinische Zeitung* and from *The Class Struggles in France* and *The Eighteenth Brumaire;* and they might be multiplied by countless examples from his more unrelievedly saturnine works. Here is his description of the worker from *Das Kapital.* We have seen, says Marx, "that within the capitalist system all the methods for increasing the social productivity of labor are carried out at the cost of the individual worker: that all the means for developing production are transformed into means of domination over and exploitation of the producer; that they mutilate the worker into a fragment of a human being, degrade him to become a mere appurtenance of the machine, make his work such a torment that its essential meaning is destroyed; cut him off from the intellectual potentialities of the labor process in exact proportion to the extent to which science is incorporated into it as an independent power; that they distort the conditions under which he works, subjecting him, during the labor process, to a despotism which is all the more hateful because of its pettiness; that they transform his whole life into working time, and drag his wife and children beneath the Juggernaut wheels of capital's car."

There is a German expression *"lasten wie ein Alp,"* which

means something like "weigh like an incubus," to which Marx was very much addicted. We find it on the first page of *The Eighteenth Brumaire,* where he says that, "The tradition of all the dead generations weighs like an incubus on the brain of the living." We have seen it in the letter already quoted, in which he tells Engels that the injury to his friend's career for which he feels himself responsible has weighed like an incubus on his conscience; and he had written to the Countess Hatzfeldt after Lassalle's death that this event—in a similar phrase—had weighed upon him "like a hideous and evil dream." In writing about *Das Kapital* to Engels, he says that the task weighs upon him like an incubus; and he complains that the Workers' International "and everything that it involves . . . weighs like an incubus on me, and I'd be glad to be able to shake it off." It is always the same oppression, whether Marx has objectified it and generalized it as the oppression of the living by the dead or felt it personally as his own oppression under the conviction of his own guilt or under the greatest of his own achievements. It is always the same wound, as to which it is never quite clear—as in the case of the Dialectic, which is now a fundamental truth of nature, now an action performed by human agents, as in the case of the development of the capitalist economy, which is now an inevitable and non-moral process, now the blackest of human crimes—whether the gods have inflicted it on man or man has inflicted it on himself. It is always the same burial alive, whether it is the past trying to stifle the present or the future putting away the past. The French constitution of 1848, which, according to Marx in one of the passages just quoted, has been guarded in the womb by bayonets, is brought out of the womb by bayonets only to be bayoneted to death.

"You see," he had once written Engels, "that I'm the object of plagues just like Job, though I'm not so godfearing as he was." No: he is not so godfearing. He sees himself also as "Old Nick," the Goethean spirit that denies. Yet Old Nick is not the right symbol either: this Devil has been twisted and racked. Though he is capable of satanic mockery of the publisher who had sent Kriege on their necks and then fallen and broken his own, the mocker cannot jeer at such a doom without breaking, by a dialectical joke, his own neck as well; and, after all, had not the publisher buried Marx's book alive? It is Prometheus who remains his favorite hero; for Prometheus is a Satan who suffers, a Job who never assents; and, unlike either Job or Satan, he brings liberation to mankind. Prometheus turns up in *Das Kapital* (in Chapter Twenty-three) to represent the proletariat chained to capital. The Light-Bringer was tortured, we remember, by Zeus's eagle's tearing, precisely, his liver, as Karl Marx himself—who is said to have reread Aeschylus every year—was obsessed by the fear that his liver would be eaten like his father's by cancer. And yet, if it is a devouring bird which Father Zeus has sent against the rebel, it is also a devourer, a destroyer, fire, which Prometheus has brought to man. And in the meantime the deliverer is never delivered; the slayer never rises from the grave. The resurrection, although certain, is not yet; for the expropriators are yet to be expropriated.

Such is the trauma of which the anguish and the defiance reverberate through *Das Kapital*. To point it out is not to detract from the authority of Marx's work. On the contrary, in history as in other fields of writing, the importance of a book depends, not merely on the breadth of the view and the amount of information that has gone into it, but on the depths from which it has been drawn. The great crucial books of human thought—outside what are called the exact sciences, and perhaps something of the sort is true even here—always render articulate the results of fundamental new experiences to which human beings have had to adjust themselves. *Das Kapital* is such a book. Marx has found in his personal experience the key to the larger experience of society, and identifies himself with that society. His trauma reflects itself in *Das Kapital* as the trauma of mankind under industrialism; and only so sore and angry a spirit, so ill at ease in the world, could have recognized and seen into the causes of the wholesale mutilation of humanity, the grim collisions, the uncomprehended convulsions, to which that age of great profits was doomed.

And now how far may the diagnosis in *Das Kapital* be taken

today as valid? To what extent have Marx's expectations actually been borne out by events?

Marx believed that the capitalist system involved fundamental contradictions which ensured its eventual destruction. His theory of these contradictions—which he thought of in terms of Hegelian opposites—may be stated with much simplification as follows:

The capitalist system was based on private property and so was inevitably competitive. The aim of every manufacturer was always to undersell the rest, so that there would be a continual stimulus to more efficient methods of production. But the more efficient an industry became—the faster the machines were able to do the work and the fewer people were needed to tend them—the more people would be thrown out of jobs and the more would wages be reduced. That is, the more the commodities produced, the fewer the people who would be able to buy them. In order to get rid of his goods under these continually tightening conditions, the manufacturer would have to undercut his competitors, and that would mean further reduction of wages and still more efficient machinery, and, consequently, again in the long run, fewer people able to buy what he was making. This situation had already produced a jam and a depression about every ten years; and the only way for the manufacturer to get a reprieve from the vicious cycle was to find new foreign markets for his products—an escape which would not in the long run save him.

The more efficiently goods were manufactured, the more money would be needed for the plant; and it would seem to pay the manufacturer to build the plants bigger and bigger. Thus the industries would keep growing and the companies keep merging till each industry would be well on its way to becoming one great unified organization, and the money which kept them going would have been concentrated in a very few hands. But actually the bigger big business grew, the larger the sums of money it dealt in, the smaller its rate of profit became. At last the contradictions involved in this process would jam the whole system so badly—there being no more fresh markets available—that it would become intolerable, impossible, for society to function at all unless the money and the great centralized plants were taken away from the people who claimed to own them and who were incapable of conceiving them as a means to any more beneficent end than that of making themselves rich out of the profits, and were run for the public good. The working class would be able to accomplish this, because it would have increased to enormous proportions and have grown conscious of its interests as a class as incompatible with the interests of its employers; and it would now find itself so hard-pressed by privation that no alternative would be possible for it. All its scruples would be overcome by the realization that this privation coincided with an era when the production of what they needed had become possible with an ease and on a scale which had never been imagined in history.

Now we may reject the Hegelian-Marxist Dialectic as a genuine law of nature, but we cannot deny that Marx has here made effective use of it to exhibit the impossibilities of capitalism and to demonstrate the necessity for socialism. Nothing else had so brought home the paradoxes of destitution imposed by abundance, of great public utilities rendered useless by the property rights of those who controlled them. Nor was it necessary to accept the metaphysics of the Labor Theory of Value and to argue from it *a priori,* as Mr. Strachey does, in order to be convinced by Marx that this process must land capitalism in an *impasse.* The great thing was that Marx had been able, as the bourgeois economists had not, to see the capitalist economy in the perspective of the centuries as something which, like other economies, had had a beginning and must have an end. Mathematician, historian and prophet, he had grasped the laws of its precipitate progress and foreseen the disasters of its slumps as nobody else had done.

Marx was not able to foresee with the same accuracy the social phenomena which would result from these collapses. There were several fallacies involved in the picture he had made of the future.

In the first place, the identification by the Jew of the Jew with the proletariat gives rise to a miscalculation. In Marx's time, both the Jew and the worker had been disfranchised and shut off from society; but there was this difference between them, that the proletarian had been stunted intellectually as well as physically, that the proletarian children, as Engels had said, were not aware that they were unfortunate or unhappy because they had never been anything else; whereas the Jews, though their outlook had been narrow, had been accustomed to intellectual training; through all their migrations and their bondages they had preserved a deep cultivation; they had behind them a noble past and they looked forward to a national resurrection. Once the enclave of old Jewry was broken open, it was quite natural for a man like Marx to take up the instruments of modern thought like one who was coming into his own. Furthermore, he had inherited from his rabbinical forebears a tradition of spiritual authority.

But the proletarian, on his side, had no training and, even when he came to organize trade unions and to oppose the employer effectively, no tradition of the kind of responsibility required of a governing class. He knew little about the history of society, little about the rest of the world; and he had little opportunity to learn. The men who employed him had an interest in keeping him ignorant. By virtue of his very position, he was deprived of the things that would enable him to rise to a higher status. The medieval disabilities of the Jew were in the nature of a mere national accident; the disabilities of the proletarian were disabilities indissoluble from his class. Yet Karl Marx was quite sure that the workers would be able to acquire the science, the self-discipline and the executive skill which had been developed by the governing class, in proportion, precisely, as the gulf itself between them and these possessing classes would come to be more deeply dug, in proportion as their antagonism itself would become more acutely developed. Would there not be communists like Marx to teach them?—and would they not learn as quickly as he had?

With this basic misconception was associated (if the latter was not derived from the former) another analogy also partly false: the analogy between, on the one hand, the advance of the bourgeoisie during the seventeenth and eighteenth centuries and, on the other, the victory of the proletariat which the communists predicted for the future. Now the European bourgeoisie, when it had taken over the governing power, had already been equipped with education and with a good deal of administrative experience; it had much property and a certain amount of authority. But the proletariat of industrial England—which is what Marx is chiefly dealing with in *Das Kapital*—have apparently, through their long stultification in the mines, through their long subordination to machines, through the meager opportunities of their lives in their allotted compartment of the caste frame, become unfitted for class politics and class action. Marx never seems to have taken into account an aspect of the industrial working class in regard to which Antoine Barnave, that early explorer of the economic categories, had made already an ominous observation: "The poor in this age of society are no less enslaved by their poverty; they have lost that natural sagacity, that boldness of imagination, which characterized the men who roamed the woods." The bourgeoisie, before they had won their ascendancy, had already possessed property and culture, their right to which they had only to vindicate; but certainly the English proletariat had to fight hard to get any of either, and when by exception they succeeded in doing so, it brought with it the middle-class point of view. When they had succeeded, through trade union negotiation, in obtaining their better pay or lighter hours, they did not think about world revolution; when they produced an able parliamentary leader, he was bought up or absorbed by the governing class. Least of all was Marx the man to foresee that, following a wholesale killing-off of workers in the next of the big competitive wars, a small allowance of money judiciously administered by the governing classes, always resourceful in avoiding crises, would be enough to prevent their causing a scandal at the same time that it would keep them dependent and make it possible for them to degenerate gradually.

Nor was Marx himself very well fitted to sympathize with or even to imagine what the psychology of the workers would be when they should better their standards of living.

For Marx, the occupations and habits, the ambitions and desires, of modern man, which he himself had never shared, tended to present themselves as purely class manifestations, the low proclivities of an ignoble bourgeoisie. He could not imagine that the proletariat would take to them. When a proletarian gave any indication of wanting what the bourgeois wanted, Marx regarded him as a renegade and pervert, a miserable victim of petty bourgeois ideas. He could not conceive that in his own country and Italy it would become possible for a new kind of state socialism combined with an intensified nationalism to buy the acquiescence of the workers by making it possible for the more ambitious of them to create a new kind of governing class not unlike the old bourgeoisie; nor that even a revolutionary Russia with a dictatorship which had started out on Marxist principles would end up in very much the same way.

Above all, Marx did not know the United States. At the time of the American Civil War, he characterized the United States government, in his articles to *The New York Tribune*, as "the highest form of popular government, till now realized" and solicited the sympathy of the working class "for the only popular government in the world." But he afterwards described the Republic in one of his letters to Engels as "the model country of the democratic imposture"; and, as appears from the last pages of *Das Kapital*, he regarded the United States after the war as a vast field for capitalist exploitation, which was then proceeding "at giant strides" and unhindered. What Karl Marx had no clue for understanding was that the absence in the United States of the feudal class background of Europe would have the effect not only of facilitating the expansion of capitalism but also of making possible a genuine social democratization; that a community would grow up and endure in which the people engaged in different occupations would probably come nearer to speaking the same language and even to sharing the same criteria than anywhere else in the industrialized world. Here in the United States, our social groupings are mainly based on money, and the money is always changing hands so rapidly that the class lines cannot get cut very deep. There is among us as compared to Europe—Mr. Lundberg to the contrary, notwithstanding—relatively little of the kind of class solidarity which is based on group intermarriage and the keeping of businesses in the hands of the same families. And it is also true that the democratic aims which the Republic announced to the new country, put forward though of course they were by a government of property-holders, have still preserved for us enough of their prestige so that it is still usually a serious matter in politics—something which is rarely the case in Europe—to bring charges of undemocratic conduct.

There has been plenty of industrial violence in America, a great deal more than is usual in Europe; but we do not work up to cumulative crises as they do in the more feudal European countries: we have the class quarrel out as we go along. And this is possible because in the United States, even where class interests divide us, we have come closer to social equality: our government does not guarantee a hierarchy to the extent that the European systems do. We are more lawless, but we are more homogeneous; and our homogeneity consists of common tendencies which Marx would have regarded as bourgeois, but which are actually only partly explicable as the results of capitalist competition. The common man, set free from feudal society, seems to do everywhere much the same sort of thing—which is not what Marx had expected him to do because it was not what Marx liked to do himself. The ordinary modern man wants a home with machine-made comforts (where Marx had never cared enough about a home to secure for his wife and his daughters even moderately decent living conditions); he wants amusement parks, movies, sports (Marx claimed that he had once studied horsemanship, but Engels, who had had him on a horse once in Manchester, said that he could never have got beyond the third lesson); he wants an opportunity to travel in his country: cheap excursions such as they have in Nazi Germany, proletarian boat-trips down the Volga, American road-camps and trailers; he wants Boy Scout Clubs and Y.M.C.A.'s, German walking clubs and youth organizations, Komsomol "Physkultur." He wants social services—hospitals, libraries, roads—whether he gets them through taxation by the State or by the State's taking business over or, as has occurred on such a large scale in America, by the philanthropy of private persons. All these things that the peoples of the Soviet Republics as well as the fascist peoples want, the Americans have more or less managed to get during those periods when their capitalist economy was booming; and they have managed to get other things too, which other peoples will learn to want and will get: free movement and a fair amount of free speech.

It looks today as if some such conditions as these were the prerequisites for any socialist revolution which is to perpetuate as well as set up a new form of group domination. Socialism by itself can create neither a political discipline nor a culture. Even where a group of socialists come to the helm, they are powerless by themselves either to instil their ideals or to establish their proposed institutions. Only the organic processes of society can make it possible to arrive at either. And it seems today as if only the man who has already enjoyed a good standard of living and become accustomed to a certain security will really fight for security and comfort. But then, it appears, on the other hand, that from the moment he has acquired these things, he is transformed into something quite other than Karl Marx's idea of a proletarian.

Marx could recognize as worthy of survival only those who had been unjustly degraded and those who rose naturally superior through intellect and moral authority. He had no key for appreciating the realities of a society in which men are really to some degree at liberty to make friends with one another indiscriminately or indiscriminately to bawl one another out—in other words, in which there is any actual approximation to that ideal of a classless society which it was the whole aim of his life to preach. And we must remember—unless we are willing to accept it as a simple act of faith in Scripture, as the people of the year 1000 expected the world to come to an end—that Karl Marx's catastrophic prophecy of the upshot of capitalist development, the big short circuit between the classes, is based primarily on psychological assumptions, which may or may not turn out to have been justified: the assumption that there can be no possible limit to the extent to which the people who live on profits will continue to remain unaware of or indifferent to the privations of the people who provide them. The Armageddon that Karl Marx tended to expect presupposed a situation in which the employer and the employee were unable to make any contact whatever. The former would not only be unable to sit down at the same table with the latter on the occasion of an industrial dispute; he would be inhibited from socking him in the jaw until the class lines had been definitely drawn and the proletarian army fully regimented.

In other words, Marx was incapable of imagining democracy at all. He had been bred in an authoritarian country; and he had had some disappointing experiences with what were supposed to be popular institutions. His expectations of what was possible for democratic parliaments and tribunals had evidently been qualified by his memory of the ineptitudes of the Frankfort Assembly, which had dispersed like a dandelion top when Friedrich Wilhelm had puffed it away, and by his failure to obtain redress against Vogt. Furthermore, he was himself, with his sharp consciousness of superiority, instinctively undemocratic in his actual relations with his fellows: he was embittered by the miscarriage of many projects undertaken with the various groups of his associates and his working-class constituents. Finally—what is doubtless fundamental—it is exceedingly difficult for one whose deepest internal existence is all a wounding and being wounded, a crushing and being crushed, to conceive, however much he may long for, a world ruled by peace and fraternity, external relations between men based on friendliness, confidence and reason. So that Marx was unable either to believe very much in the possibilities of such democratic machinery as existed in the contemporary world or to envisage the real problems which, failing this, would be created by the coming to power of an untrained proletariat in the future. He was sometimes willing to admit in his later years—see his conversations with H. M. Hyndman and his speech at a workers' meeting in Amsterdam, September 8, 1872—that in democratic countries like England, Holland and the United States there was a chance that the Revolution might be accomplished by peaceful means; but in practice the main effect of his teaching (in spite of the revisionist efforts of the German Social Democrats) has been to get people into a state of mind where they expect a gigantic collision of class forces.

Since the events of 1848, with their failures of the French and German parliaments, Marx had added to his body of doctrine a new feature, not explicit in the *Communist Manifesto,* which he asserted to be one of his original contributions to socialist political theory: the dictatorship of the proletariat. It seemed clear to him that it would not be enough for the proletariat to seize political power: it would be obliged to destroy bourgeois institutions, to start socialism with a completely clean slate; and in order to accomplish this, it would be necessary for it to beat down all those forces which would inevitably keep on working to restore the capitalistic state. The government which Marx imagined for the welfare and elevation of mankind—though he sometimes spoke of democratic institutions inside the new dominant class—was an exclusive and relentless class despotism directed by high-minded bigwigs who had been able to rise above the classes, such as Engels and himself.

Yet Marx's thought is not really a closed system, though it has supplied so many sects with dogmas. *Das Kapital*—unless we approach it as Scripture—should open the way to realistic inquiry.

Marx experienced throughout his life the utmost difficulty in finishing his works. He left documents of cardinal importance like the *Theses on Feuerbach* and the *Introduction to the Critique of Political Economy* in a fragmentary or sketchy state; and even the *Communist Manifesto* was extorted from him only under pressure. It took years of the combined insistence of Engels and the anguish of Jenny Marx to get him to bring out the first volume of *Das Kapital*. This difficulty was probably partly neurotic: the never-resting apprehension of the man who, like the hero of his ballad, building his fortress out of a "patchwork of weaknesses," is always afraid lest it may not prove to be strong enough—just as his learning and his elaborate logic are partly for academic show. But his long labors were also the consequence of the scope of his inquiries and interests and of the immensity of his undertaking: interests which were always to remain insatiable, an undertaking which could never be completed. Marx had expected, when he was seeing the first volume through the press in the spring of 1867, to have the second finished the following winter. He speaks then, in writing to Engels, of the "much new material" which has come in on the subject of landed property; and he seems to have decided at some point after this to make Russia his great example of the development of ground-rent in the second part, as he had used England for that of industry in the first. He learned Russian at the end of the sixties, read up Russian literature and history, and had documents sent him from Russia. It was probably an anxiety, however exaggerated, to deal authoritatively with the Russian economy rather than trepidation as to the fate of the Labor Theory of Value, which was the obstacle to his progressing with his work. He accumulated stacks of statistics to the volume of two cubic meters; and at the time when *Das Kapital* in its second volume had rolled back on the Marxist household like an infernal Sisyphean stone that had to be propelled up the mountain again, Engels once remarked to Lafargue that he would like to burn all this material up. One of the last of Marx's unfinished writings was, as we shall presently see, an attempt to formulate some ideas on the revolutionary future of Russia and the possibilities of its presenting an exception to the capitalist laws he had demonstrated.

It is true, as Edward Bernstein says, that, though "where Marx has to do with details or subordinate subjects he mostly notices the important changes which actual evolution had brought about since the time of his first socialist writings, and thus himself states how far their presuppositions have been corrected by the facts," he, nevertheless, "when he comes to general conclusions, adheres in the main to the original propositions based upon the old uncorrected presuppositions [of 1848]." But the point is that he *was* aware of the changes: his mind was always reaching out to know more, straining to understand better. It was colossal to have summed up as Marx had done the copious literature of his predecessors; but since his subject extended into the present and stretched away into the future, he was confronted with what was really the more difficult task of seizing the trend of contemporary events. If he devoted hours and weeks to reconstructing from documents in Old Slavonic the history of the land system in Russia, he also found it necessary to learn Rumanian in order to follow what was happening in the Balkans.

So *Das Kapital* was not only unfinished: it is, in a sense, endless—and this not merely in the sense that, after Marx's death, Engels continued to work on the manuscript over a period of twelve years and that, even after the death of Engels, Karl Kautsky brought out further volumes (Marx's critical summing-up of his predecessors) from 1904 to 1910— not merely that there still half-loom even beyond all this the unwritten or unfinished supplements: the philosophical book on Dialectical Materialism which was to hitch the Revolution up with the Universe, the anthropological work which was to justify the communism of the future from the communism of primitive times, the literary book in which Balzac was to be examined as the anatomist of bourgeois society, the studies in higher mathematics which were to illustrate the laws of the Dialectic by "putting the differential calculus on a new basis." Not only must *Das Kapital*, like Michelet's history, eventually break down as a *Kunstwerk*, because events will not accommodate themselves to its symmetry—since Marx himself became diverted while he was writing it into pursuing new researches into phenomena which were not allowed for by his original plan; but it leads inevitably to further thought and further writing—beginning with Engels' addenda to the later volumes, to the whole growth of Marxist thought since Marx's time—failing which, one may actually say, as one can say of few other books, that the original work would not continue to be valid. And its primary impulse deserts literature altogether when it animates such activities as those of Marx himself in connection with the Workers' International which interrupted the writing of his book and that later participation by Engels in the organizing of the Social Democrats which delayed him in patching up the unfinished work (if it is difficult to give a really consistent and well-organized account of Marxist doctrine, it is precisely because Marx and Engels were continually being impeded and disorganized in the systematization of their ideas by the necessity of taking part in political movements under the pressure of contemporary events). Out of the brooding and laboring thought comes an instrument that is also a weapon in the actual world of men.

16 Karl Marx Dies at His Desk

Yet Karl Marx was far, as we have already seen, from backing cordially that one of his followers who had learned to wield this weapon most effectively. Marx had pursued the Lassallean movement with a peculiar intensity of intolerance. He had resented the glorification of Lassalle which had taken place after his death and the piety with which the German workers sang songs about him and put his picture up in their houses. He credited a story of the Countess Hatzfeldt's that Lassalle had made a deal with Bismarck to support the annexation of Schleswig-Holstein in return for certain concessions to the workers, and he unjustly accused Lassalle's party, for whom Mehring says it was vital to profit by such concessions as Bismarck might make to labor, of playing Bismarck's game. The party, he wrote Engels, needed "cleansing from the lingering stink of Lassalle."

Liebknecht and Bebel had in the meantime succeeded in 1867 in getting themselves elected to the North German Reichstag, and they founded the following year at a trade union congress at Eisenach a new Social Democratic Labor Party. ("A hell of a name!" Engels had written Marx when the term "Social Democrat" had been invented.) At the time of the Franco-Prussian War, the Lassalleans voted for war credits in the July of 1870 when Liebknecht and Bebel refrained from voting at all; but in December, after the victory was won, both parties refused to vote further credits. Liebknecht and Bebel protested against the annexation of Alsace-Lorraine and applauded the Paris Commune, and were indicted for high treason and condemned to two years of prison. Schweitzer, the leader of the Lassalleans, had also been arrested; and after the War the common fight against Bismarck brought the two parties together. Liebknecht arranged a merger which took place at the town of Gotha on May 22, 1874.

A program had already been drafted by a committee of seven Lassalleans and seven Eisenachers, and it had been sent for Marx's approval. He might well have been pleased that German labor should finally have been united, but he took the occasion to make himself unpleasant at the expense of the false doctrine of the Lassalleans. Liebknecht was not seriously concerned about these criticisms. A few minor changes were made in the program, and the merger took place and prospered; and the whole incident might be ignored as one of the instances of Marx's misdirected virulence if he had not been stimulated by the occasion to develop, in the long letter which has come to be known as the *Critique of the Gotha Program,* some general ideas on a very important question to which he had hitherto devoted no attention.

Marx began by raising an outcry—he may perhaps have been nervous on the subject—over an attempt on the part of the framers of the program to ground it on the Marxist Theory of Value. They had asserted that "labor is the source of all wealth." No! Nature was also a source of use-value. You not only had to work: you had to have something to work on and with.

And he went on to another matter, which the charges brought against him by Bakúnin may have induced him to discuss more fully. Bakúnin had promised a society set free from the burdens and the restraints of the State, and had declared that Marx, as a German, wanted to impose authoritarianism and regimentation. It was true that Marx had insisted a good deal, in discussing the future of Germany, on the importance of working for a strong centralized State rather than for a federal republic; and he now tried to make it plain that he was opposed to the State in itself, that he also aimed at ultimate freedom, at the accomplishment of the tasks of humanity through voluntary association.

This led him to try to prefigure more definitely than he had ever done before what would happen in a socialist society inaugurated by a working-class revolution. Hitherto, as in the *Communist Manifesto*, he had said merely that the old society would be "replaced by an association in which the free development of each will lead to the free development of all"; but he had always failed to explain how this condition was to be arrived at after the dictatorship he contemplated had been clamped down. He never did really explain it; but he threw out, in the *Critique of the Gotha Program*, some intimations as to how socialist society was to be constituted in its initial stages. The exalted vision of release which swims beyond the range of his early writings here gives way to a prolongation of something like the world we know. The new order, which has been molded in the womb of the old, will inevitably be born with its likeness. The classes will have been abolished; but inequalities will still exist. There will not yet be any such thing as an equal right to pay and what it purchases. Such phrases as "equal right" and "equitable distribution," which occur in the Gotha program, though they once had a certain significance, are today obsolete rubbish. "No higher system of right can be recognized than is permitted by the configuration of the economic level and the phase of cultural development determined by this configuration." (*"Das Recht kann nie höher sein als die ökonomische Gestaltung und dadurch bedingte Kulturentwicklung der Gesellschaft."*) Since there will still persist differences in ability, physical and intellectual, produced by the society of the past, so that there will be differences in the extent or intensity of the work that different men will be able to perform, and since value is created by labor, the workers of the socialist society will have unequal, not equal, rights. (The whole question of whether the work of a stronger or more intelligent man *does* necessarily exceed in "extent or intensity"—from the point of view of effort expended—the work of a weaker or duller is always ignored by Marx; as is also the question of the incentive provided by higher pay for more or more exacting work, which has contributed in the Soviet Union to creating a new class inequality.)

It will be only "in a higher phase of communist society, after the enslaving subordination of individuals subjected to the division of labor shall have been done away with, and thereby also the antithesis between physical and intellectual work, after labor has ceased to be merely a means to live but has become itself the prime necessity of life, after the forces of production have also increased with the all-around development of the individual and all the springs of coöperative wealth are more abundantly flowing," that "the narrow horizon of bourgeois rights" can finally "be quite overpassed and society inscribe on its banners: 'From each according to his ability, to each according to his needs!'"

It will be seen that, though Marx had pointed out the naïveté of the utopias of his socialist predecessors, the prospect of the future he invoked, with its more abundant flowings of the springs of coöperative wealth, was still itself rather utopian. He had simply thrust the happy consummation a little farther off into the future.

It was the last important act of Marx's public career. The closing ten years of his life did bring him certain consolations: Engels was living in London; he was able to take trips for his health. But all these years he is helplessly sinking, forced to relinquish his work at sixty—succumbing to that mortal wound which he had brought with him into the world. He had banished the International when he had felt it slipping out of his hands; now he was losing his grip on *Das Kapital,* the first volume of which had failed to bring him the public recognition he had expected. He had had the humiliation of seeing a review of his book, which Engels had written for the *Fortnightly Review* and which the historian Beesly had promised to publish, sent back by John Morley on the ground that it was too dry for the *Fortnightly's* readers; and was to see his friend and disciple Hyndman bring out a book called *England For All,* based partly on Marx's ideas, in which, for fear of antagonizing *his* readers, he respectfully acknowledged his debt "to the work of a great thinker and original writer" without mentioning Marx's name.

Jenny Longuet, who was living in France with her husband, had a baby in the spring of 1881, and her parents went over to see her that summer. But Jenny Marx came back ill. She had developed an incurable cancer, and her nerves had pretty badly given way. She had had herself on occasion to write begging letters to Engels, and she had eventually become rather jealous of him and bitter about their obligations to him. When Marx had gone back to Trier at the time of his mother's death, he had written to the wife he had met there: "I have been making a daily pilgrimage to the old Westphalen house (in the Rosnerstrasse), which has interested me more than all the Roman ruins, because it reminds me of happy youth and used to shelter my sweetheart. And every day people ask me right and left about the quondam 'most beautiful girl' in Trier, the 'Queen of the ball.' It's damned agreeable for a man to find that his wife lives on as an 'enchanted princess' in the imagination of a whole town." He had indeed made her drink the poisoned cup, which the lover had proffered his beloved in that ominous poem of his youth; and he, like the lover of the poem, was growing cold from the poison, too.

By December Jenny was dying; and Marx himself was in bed with pleurisy. "I shall never forget the morning," their daughter Eleanor writes, "when he felt strong enough to go into Mother's room. It was as if they were young again—she a loving girl and he a loving young man, embarking on life together, and not an old man shattered by illness and a dying old lady taking leave of one another forever." Liebknecht says that she followed with the eagerness of a child the first elections held in Germany after the enactment of the Anti-Socialist Law, and was delighted when the results showed a gain for the outlawed Social-Democrats; and Marx wrote Sorge that it was a source of gratification that she should have been cheered up just before she died by the appearance, with a certain amount of publicity, of an article on him by Belfort Bax. The last thing she said that was understood was, "Karl, my strength is broken." He was too ill to attend her funeral. When Engels arrived, he said: "The Moor is dead, too."

He was right: Marx went the next year to Algiers, to Monte

Carlo, to Enghien, to the Lake of Geneva, but the pleurisy went with him all the way. Back in England, he took refuge in the Isle of Wight to escape from the London fogs, but there he caught cold again. The death of Jenny Longuet, about whose health he had worried so when he had had no money to send her to the seaside, followed her mother's in January, 1883. Marx by March had an abscess of the lung. When Engels came to call on him on the afternoon of the 14th, he found the household in tears: they told him that his friend had had a hemorrhage. Lenchen went up and found her master in his study, half asleep, as she thought. He had gotten up from his bed, and gone to his study and sat down at his work-table. Engels went in, and felt his pulse and listened for his breath, and found they had both stopped.

Marx's collaborator outlived him twelve years. Lizzy Burns had died in '78, and Engels had married her to please her on her deathbed. When the Marx ladies had come to call on him, he had had to send Lizzy out marketing, giving her money for a drink at a pub and a ride home through the park in a hansom. He hoped and searched to the end of his days to prove that Lizzy and her sister were the descendants of Robert Burns. After Lizzy's death, a young niece of hers named Mary Ellen, who had been brought up in Engels' household, made an attempt to keep house for him. But she got into trouble with the son of a well-to-do business contractor, and Engels compelled him to marry her, to the indignation of the young man's family. He had been surprised to find out that this young fellow was neither a revolutionist nor a man of any intellectual ability. He tried to help the young couple get started, but Mary Ellen's husband failed in business, and Engels had to take them in. "The family is very numerous," he wrote Regina Bernstein. "Two dogs, three cats, a canary, a rabbit, two guinea-pigs, fourteen hens and a rooster." When the baby also arrived, Engels used to like to play with him. He advanced a great deal of money to Mary Ellen's husband, but the young man was never able to make a go of it. After the deaths of both the Marxes, Lenchen came to take care of Engels.

He seems to have enjoyed these last years. In the streets of that London of which the atomized population had so shocked him when he had come there in his twenties, he still walked erect and slender, almost with the energy of youth. He was living, as Marx had done, in one of those monotonous rows of houses—with so much soot, as Liebknecht says, on the back gardens that it was impossible to tell the gravel from the grass —where the fronts were so much alike that his near-sighted friend had not infrequently attempted to unlock the wrong door when he had been coming back home after dark. But in London he had more interesting companionship and the leisure to pursue his studies and pleasures. Eleanor Marx, who had been staying with him in Manchester at the time he finally quitted the office, tells how he shouted, "For the last time!" when he drew on his top-boots in the morning, and how, at the end of the day, "when we stood waiting for him in the doorway, we saw him coming across the little field . . . flourishing his stick in the air and singing and laughing all over his face." In London, he gave convivial Sunday evenings, to which he invited men of all social classes who had either distinguished themselves intellectually or done some service to the socialist cause. He did not insist on their professing the correct doctrine and even entertained Prussian conservatives. His cellar was always full of good Bordeaux, great quantities of which he had sent to Marx. The conversation was unrestrained, and the host, when things had reached a certain point, used to start up old students' songs. He was so delighted with *The Vicar of Bray*—from which he said it was also possible to learn a good deal of English history—that he translated it into German. A fortnight before Christmas he would have the ladies of his acquaintance come in and chop great heaps of apples, nuts, raisins, almonds and orange peel, which were put into an enormous tub. "Later in the evening," says Bernstein, "the male friends of the house would arrive, and each of them was required to lay hold of a ladle that stood upright in the tub, and stir the paste three times round—a by no means easy task, which required a great deal of muscular strength. But its importance was mainly symbolical, and those whose strength was inadequate were mercifully exempted. The concluding touch was given by Engels himself, who descended into the wine-cellar and brought up champagne, in which," sitting around the great kitchen, "we drank to a merry Christmas and to many other things as well." At Christmas he sent everyone a pudding out of the enormous tub, and gave an enormous dinner at his house, at which the pudding came in flaming.

When the goading of Marx was removed, the natural bon-homie of Engels tended to reassert itself. He stuck loyally to Marx's old feuds: he would not have anything to do with H. M. Hyndman or with anyone whom he thought to have injured Marx; and he continued to fight the Lassalleans and to hold it against Wilhelm Liebknecht that he had disregarded Marx's criticisms of the Gotha program. But his advice to the various groups, which he gave only when people asked him for it, was full of good sense and moderation. He adopted, as Mehring has remarked, very much the same realistic policy which Lassalle had pursued in Germany in supporting the agi-tation for the franchise: Let the working class formulate their own demands; there will be time for doctrine later. He wrote to Sorge that he need be in no hurry to publish Marx's criticism of Henry George, who ran for mayor in New York on the ticket of a United Labor Party in 1886: George would compro-mise himself in the long run, and in the meantime "the masses must be set in motion along the road that corresponds to each country and to the prevailing circumstances, which is usually a roundabout road. Everything else is of secondary importance if only they are really aroused."

With the whole field now to himself, falling heir to the Marxist glory, he became more modest than ever. He insisted in reply to praise that if perhaps he had been a little under-rated at the time when Marx was alive, he was now being overrated. In the summer of '93, he appeared for the first time in person at a congress of the Second International, which had been founded by the Social Democrats in 1889. The repeal of the Anti-Socialist Law had made it possible for him to go back to Germany, and the socialists had begged him to come. When he saw the towers of Cologne cathedral from the train that took him through the Rhineland, tears came into his eyes, and he said: "What a lovely land, if only one could live in it!"

When he appeared at the congress in Zürich, he was amazed at the ovation given him and passed it all back to Marx. At the house of the Russian socialist Axelrod, he was delighted to meet and to kiss a group of pretty little Russian comrades, who, he said, had wonderful eyes; "but my real darling," he wrote his brother, "is a delicious little factory girl from Vienna, with the sort of alluring face and charming manners that are really very rare." "The people were all very nice," he afterwards wrote to Sorge, "but it isn't for me—I'm glad it's over." The next time he would write them beforehand, so that he shouldn't "have to parade before the public." He would leave all that to the parliamentarians and the spell-binders: "that sort of thing belongs to their role, but it hardly fits in with my kind of work."

He had counted on elaborating the *Peasant War* into a really considerable book, which should present his whole theory of German history; but the confused and illegible manuscripts, the brain-racking subtleties of *Das Kapital* consumed all the rest of his life. He only succeeded in bringing out the third volume—in which the Labor Theory of Value is discussed—in October, 1894, the year before he died; and he had to bequeath the remaining material to Kautsky.

It is ironic and characteristic that Engels should in the end have been left by Marx holding the bag, as we say, for the two most questionable features of Marxism: the Dialectic and the Labor Theory of Value—those two dogmas on our acceptance of which the whole philosophy as a system depends. Engels had written at Marx's request a polemic against the Berlin philosopher Dühring, who, in default of any systematic exposition by Marx and Engels of their own fundamental ideas, was getting a hold on the younger German socialists. Engels tried to defend the Dialectic and he did not make a very convincing job of it, though his book had the approval of Marx. Later, after Marx's death, he had to answer the questions of young socialists who were having difficulties with Marxist theory. Marx himself had with telling effect and with acrid satisfaction to himself brought into play the materialistic aspect of Marxo-Hegelian Dialectical Materialism to blight the shimmering mirages of the utopians and to make the blood of the bourgeois run cold. Conscientiously, almost morbidly, reluctant to put himself on record about anything which he had not completely excogitated, Marx had never far pursued the inquiries which would have led him down to dialectical first principles. It is significant that in the preface to *Das Kapital* he should, instead of expounding himself the materialistic view of history, be content to quote with approval a rather inadequate attempt to state it, but a version which made it seem extremely grim, volunteered by a Russian admirer. Engels with his readier fluency and his relative superficiality now tried to explain everything plausibly; and as he did so the old German idealism which he had drunk in with his first Rhine wine began to flow back into the Dialectic. We have already discussed the varying emphasis which Marx and Engels gave to their doctrines at different moments of history and different periods of their own careers; but it ought to be added here that the widely diverging interpretations which have been put upon Dialectical Materialism have also been partly due to certain fundamental divergences between the temperaments of the two different men.

And now Engels had on his hands the Labor Theory of Value, against which a great outcry went up. He died (August 5, 1895) earnestly trying to defend it, leaving the last of his polemics unfinished. He was suffering from cancer of the oesophagus and was no longer able to speak, but could write. He carried on conversations with his friends by chalking his remarks on a slate, and they could see from them that he was bearing his pain "with stoicism and even with humor."

He left legacies to both the Marx daughters and to the niece of Mary and Lizzy Burns (who nevertheless made trouble about the will in an effort to get more than he had left her), and twenty thousand marks to the Party. He wrote Bebel to "take care above everything that . . . it doesn't fall into the hands of the Prussians. And when you feel sure on that score, then drink a bottle of good wine on it. Do this in memory of me." He left directions for the disposal of his body, which were carried out by his friends. They had him cremated, and on a windy autumn day threw his ashes out to sea off Beachy Head.

In the memoir of Wilhelm Liebknecht there is a nightmarish and haunting story told at a length which implies that it had for him some special meaning. He had taken out the two little Marx girls, then respectively seven and eight, to see the Duke of Wellington's funeral in London. Their mother had warned him as they were leaving not to let them get mixed up with the crowd; but he had no money for a window or a place in a stand and was obliged to find a perch on a staircase in the neighborhood of Temple Bar. The roar of the crowd rolled towards them, and then the long procession went past, with its great catafalque and its gold-laced horsemen. But now, just as they were about to leave, the crowd, which was following the procession, came driving into the street behind them. At first he had tried to stand his ground, but they were like a canoe caught in an ice-jam. Forced along, he clasped the little girls close to him and tried to keep clear of the main current. They just seemed to be almost free, when another surge of people debouched on them and pushed them out into the Strand. There the crowd had made a rush and were packed solid. He clenched his teeth and tried to lift the children so that they would be up above the crush on his shoulders, but he found they were squeezed against him too tightly. He seized their arms; they were dragged away. He felt a force that was shoving between him and them; he grasped a wrist of each with each of his hands, but the force was wedging them apart; he knew that unless he let go, he would dislocate or break their arms. He let go. Against Temple Bar Gate, unable to get through the three passages, the mass was piling up like a solid surf driven against the pillars of a bridge; people were screaming, being trampled down. He shouldered and elbowed like a madman, trying to get pushed through the passage, but again and again he missed: the stream that entered hurled him aside. Then he was caught in the flood with a shock, squeezed horribly, sucked through the passage, and spat forth on the other side. There the people had more freedom to spread out. He ran among them looking for the children. Just as he was beginning to feel sick with fear, he heard two voices calling "Library!", the name they had given him on account of his learning (because even the children of communists must not address comrades as "Mister"). They had got through much easier than he, and never knew they had been in danger. He said nothing to their people at home. Several women had been killed there that day.

Had he foreseen in that moment—we have noted already that the image of a whirlpool had occurred to him in remembering the down-drift of exile from which he felt that Jenny Marx had saved him—had he foreseen that his own child was to be caught in the fury of that blind and brutal tide which the father had found the strength to oppose—Karl Liebknecht, clubbed and riddled, trampled under, when he had tried to stand against it, too? Certainly those children of the great nonconformist and their sister not yet born were to suffer no other fate than that Wilhelm Liebknecht had feared for them the day of the Duke of Wellington's funeral.

Jenny Longuet died, as we have seen, before her father; and one of her little boys died six days later than he. Eleanor, so much younger than her sisters—the family called her "Tussy" —was twenty-eight at the time of her father's death. She was much the brightest of the children and his favorite. She had been born just before Edgar's death and had as a child been so much like a boy that it was as if she were trying to fill the gap which had been left by Marx's loss of his son. As she grew up, she became for her father a secretary, companion and nurse. She understood the working-class movement, and conducted her father's correspondence, and had in her hands all the threads of the International. When she was sixteen, the French socialist Lissagaray, who afterwards wrote a history of the Commune, fell in love with her and wanted to marry her. Her father in this case decided, for reasons which may have been unconsciously selfish, that the young man had an unreliable character, and poor Tussy, though she wanted to accept him and though her mother approved of the match, was obliged to remain at home. It seems to be to this affair that she refers in a letter to Olive Schreiner, when she writes: "If you had ever been in our home, if you had ever seen my Father and Mother, known what *he* was to me, you would understand better both my yearning for love, given and received, and my intense need of sympathy. Of my Father I was so sure! For long miserable years there was a shadow between us . . . yet our love was always the same, and despite everything, our faith and trust in each other. My Mother and I loved each other passionately, but she did not know me as Father did. One of the bitterest of many bitter sorrows in my life is that my Mother died, thinking, despite all our love, that I had been hard and cruel, and never guessing that to save her and Father sorrow I had sacrificed the best, freshest years of my life. But Father, though he did not *know* till just before the end, felt he must trust me—our natures were so exactly alike!"

She was the daughter who most resembled Marx. She had black hair and bright black eyes, as well as his broad forehead and short and broad body. She had vivacity, a quick smile, high color and a remarkably musical voice. She loved to recite and act, and her father had let her take dramatic lessons and thought her "very good in the passionate scenes." But she later mostly devoted these abilities to public speaking for the socialist cause. She played, with the encouragement of Engels, an active and important part in organizing the unskilled workers of the East End of London into the Gasworkers' and General Laborers' Union, at whose meetings she used to be greeted by cries of "Good old stoker!" She taught Will Thorne, the labor leader, to read and write; and she took part in the great London dockers' strike of 1889, which her work had helped to prepare. She also edited her father's writings after his death, made the first English translation of *Madame Bovary*, translated Ibsen for Havelock Ellis and edited *A Warning to Fair Women*, an anonymous Elizabethan play, for Ellis' Mermaid Series. But her edition of *Fair Women* never appeared. The series was taken over by a new publisher who thought it prudent to dissociate it from the author of *Studies in the Psychology of Sex* and even removed his name from the title pages.

Eleanor Marx was a part of that world of advanced intellectuals of the eighties upon whom the conventional British looked with a chilling horror. Beatrice Potter, then interested in organized charity and not yet Mrs. Sidney Webb, met her just after her parents had died, in the spring of 1883, at a time when she was editing a free-thinkers' magazine. The editor had been imprisoned for blasphemy, and Eleanor was "very wrath." "It was useless to argue with her," Miss Potter noted in her diary. "She refused to recognize the beauty of the Christian religion. . . . Thought that Christ, if he had existed, was a weak-headed individual, with a good deal of sweetness of character, but quite lacking in heroism. 'Did he not in the last moment pray that the cup might pass from him?' " She declared that it was the aim of the socialists to make the people "disregard the mythical next world and live for this world, and insist on having what will make it pleasant to them." "In person she is comely, dressed in a slovenly picturesque way, with curly black hair flying about in all directions. Fine eyes full of life and sympathy, otherwise ugly features and expression, and complexion showing the signs of an unhealthy excited life, kept up with stimulants and tempered by narcotics. Lives alone, is much connected with Bradlaugh set."

A year after her father's death, she had entered into a serious alliance with a member of this set, a man who had a legal wife living. She had had a job in a better-class boarding-school; but when she announced the situation to her superiors, they regretted to have to let her go. "I need work much," she wrote Havelock Ellis, "and find it very difficult to get. 'Respectable' people won't employ me."

Her friends had done their best to discourage her interest in Dr. Edward Aveling. He was a brilliant young teacher of science of mixed French and Irish origins, who, with Bradlaugh and Annie Besant, had been one of the leaders of the Secularist movement. After his association with Eleanor Marx, he enlisted in the socialist movement and worked hard for it by fits and starts as an agitator, lecturer and writer. But there was something very odd about Aveling. He was an inveterate and shameless dead-beat—if it is possible to use so brutal a phrase for the man who suggested Louis Dubedat, the slippery but talented artist of Bernard Shaw's *Doctor's Dilemma*. Though startlingly and repulsively ugly, his eloquence and his charm were so great that H. M. Hyndman says that he "needed but half an hour's start of the handsomest man in London" to fascinate an attractive woman—a power which he used very unscrupulously. But what was more serious for his standing with his associates, he was extremely undependable about money: he not only skipped out of hotels without paying the bills, but he borrowed money from his friends right and left, and even when he knew they had little, without ever paying it back, and he did not hesitate to use for his own purposes the funds which had been given for the cause. He was emotional and artistic, had "temperament." At one time he had tried being an actor, had gone off with a stock company to the provinces. He wrote several one-act plays, in which he and Eleanor acted. He had also luxurious tastes and liked to have everything for himself of the best.

The English used to say that "nobody could be as bad as Aveling looked." But the Executive Council of Hyndman's Social-Democratic Federation did not want to take him in. They deferred, however, to Eleanor Marx and to the French and German friends of Marx, who wrote them letters in behalf of Aveling. Engels, who was devoted to Tussy, continued to receive Aveling at his evenings even when other guests told him that if Aveling came, they must stay away. Edward Bernstein found that the Fabians, with an evasiveness which he regarded as typically English and rather offensive, would say when he mentioned the Avelings: "Oh, the Avelings are very clever people. . . . Oh, everybody must admit that they have been of great service to the movement." "I am beginning," Olive Schreiner wrote Ellis, "to have such a horror of Dr. A. To say I dislike him doesn't express it at all. I have a fear and horror of him when I am near. Every time I see him this shrinking grows stronger. . . . I love her, but *he* makes me so unhappy."

Aveling was unfaithful to Eleanor. He finally disappeared and then later turned up very ill. Knowing he was in love with another woman, she saw him through an operation—in 1898—and nursed him until he was well. "I realize more and more," she wrote Lenchen Demuth's son at this time, "that wrong behavior is simply a moral sickness. . . . There are people who lack a certain moral sense just as others are deaf or shortsighted or are in other ways afflicted. And I begin to realize the fact that one is as little justified in blaming them for the one sort of disorder as the other. We must strive to cure them, and if no cure is possible, we must do our best." It was as if her loyalty to Aveling were an attempt to repeat the pattern of her loyalty to her father, himself at once brilliantly gifted and always in trouble about money—as if she had substituted "moral sense" for "money sense." When Aveling was nearly well, Eleanor suddenly took poison. She had received a letter that morning which Aveling took care to destroy but which is believed to have broken the news that during the time when he had been away, he had—his first wife in the meantime having died—legally married a young actress. He tried also to tear up the note which she had left for him, but the coroner's officer saved it. It said: "How sad life has been all these years."

Aveling inherited what was left of the money that Engels had left to Eleanor and went to live with his new wife. A few months later he died—in an easy chair in the sunshine, quietly reading a book.

Paul and Laura Lafargue lost all their children, and this is said to have been one of the causes that led to a sort of demoralization which seems to have overtaken them. Lafargue dropped his medical practice and made a very meager living by running a photographer's studio. He had the reputation of being a miser and the French socialists called him *le petit épicier*. He had taken part in the Paris Commune, but, though he was once elected to the Chamber, he never played the role in the movement that his abilities seemed to warrant. Engels had left Laura £7000. Laura divided it up into ten parts and decided that when they came to the end of them, they might as well kill themselves. In 1912, when they were nearly seventy, they both took injections of morphine and were found dead in their beds.

Such pain and such effort it cost to build a stronghold for the mind and the will outside the makeshifts of human society.

Jenny Longuet had five children, and three sons and a daughter survived: they were the only descendants of Marx. One of them, Jean Longuet, became, after the murder of Jaurès, the leader of the Left wing of the French Socialists and opposed the continuance of the World War after the Austrian proposals of peace. His son, Robert-Jean Longuet, Karl Marx's great-grandson, is, as I write, getting out a magazine in Morocco in defense of the interests of the natives against the military regime of the French, who have allowed them to sink into misery since the slump of 1931 has impelled the home government to protect the home market at the expense of the products of Morocco.

III:

1 Lenin: The Brothers Ulyánov

It had been difficult for Marx and Engels to see Russia as anything other than a bugbear. As Germans, they lived in dread of the Tsar. In the days of 1848 and the *Neue Rheinische Zeitung*, they had regarded a war against Russia as the only means by which Germany could be united and the revolution brought to pass. On the eve of the Crimean War, they declared that there had been in Europe since 1789 "in reality only two powers: Russia and Absolutism, on the one hand, and the Revolution and Democracy on the other." And as Germans, they had at the same time always cultivated a contempt for the Slavs. When Engels was studying Russian in 1852, he wrote Marx that he thought it was important that "one of us at least should know . . . the languages, the history, the literature and the details of the social institutions of those nations with which, precisely, we shall immediately be coming into conflict. The truth is that Bakúnin has got to be somebody only because nobody has known Russian. And the old Pan-Slavist *dodge* of turning the ancient Slavic commune into Communism and representing the Russian peasants as born Communists, will be amply taken care of." Engels scoffed at the belief of Herzen that Russia, with her roots in these primitive communes, was destined to bring socialism to Europe.

It was not until the accession of Alexander II, which brought a revolt of the peasantry and a constitutional agitation by the nobility, that Marx and Engels began seriously to consider the possibility of revolution in Russia. But they still remained very distrustful of the flighty ideology of Russians: "Herr Bakunin,"

Marx wrote Engels in 1868, after a congress of the International, "is so condescending as to desire to take the whole workers' movement under Russian leadership. . . . The association, as *old Becker* writes, is to supply the 'Idealism' that is lacking in our association. *L'idéalisme Russe!*"

It was, then, with considerable surprise that Marx learned in the fall of 1868 that a translation of *Das Kapital* into Russian was actually being printed in St. Petersburg. He had hoped much of an English translation, and yet, during Marx's lifetime, the book was never to reach the English; but now it was coming out in Russian, the very next year after it had been published, before it had been translated into any other language. "It is an irony of fate," he wrote Kugelmann, "that the Russians, whom I have fought for twenty-five years, and not only in German, but in French and English, have always been my 'patrons' "; and he growlingly put it down to the fact that the Russians "always run after the most extreme ideas that the West has to offer": it was pure intellectual "gourmandise."

He did, however, in response to this interest, turn his serious attention to Russia. It was at this time that he learned the language and that he resolved, as we have seen, to make Russia the main subject of the second part of *Das Kapital*. But Marx never seems to have succeeded in deciding what he thought about Russia.

A very curious and interesting document is his answer to a young Russian Marxist, Vera Zasúlich, who wrote him on behalf of her comrades in February, 1881, to ask him whether he had meant in *Das Kapital* to imply that agrarian Russia would be obliged to pass through all the stages of capitalist industrial exploitation before it could hope for a revolution. Marx's effort to reply to this question was perhaps the last vital flicker of his mind; and his several draughts of an attempt to deal with it show the difficulty the problem gave him. He was not now quite so certain as Engels had been in 1852 that the Russian peasant commune was entirely without possibilities as an eventual basis for socialism. Marx replied that what he had said in *Das Kapital* was merely that *Western* European countries would have to evolve through the capitalist exploitation and that he had spoken only of "*private* property, based on individual labor," turning into capitalist private property—so that the primitive *communal* economy of an *Eastern* European country would not necessarily be meant. In his drafts, in which he had at first been attempting to treat the subject *au fond,* he reviews several considerations which seem favorable to the contrary assumption: the Russians *had* established, as it were, overnight the whole modern banking system which had taken centuries to develop in the West; "the physical configuration of the Russian land" invited mechanical farming "organized on a vast scale and coöperatively run," and the agricultural science and mechanical tools produced by the industrial West would be at the disposal of Russia; after all, the mediaeval communes which he had seen around Trier in his youth had survived all the vicissitudes of the Middle Ages and endured to their own day. On the other hand, the so-called emancipation of the serfs had delivered the peasants up to the taxes and the money-lenders, so that they would rapidly be dispossessed or driven off the land altogether as the decurion farmers had been in the last days of the Roman Empire, unless a revolution came to their rescue.

But the letter he sent at last was brief and cautious: he said simply that he had become convinced that the peasant commune was "the *point d'appui* for social regeneration in Russia," but that if it were to "function as such, the deleterious influences that assail it from all sides would have to be got rid of first, and then the normal conditions of a spontaneous development ensured."

As for Engels, he had already in 1874, in controversy with the Russian Tkachóv, expressed the opinion that the peasant communes in Russia could develop in a revolutionary direction only if they were not destroyed before a proletarian revolution in Western Europe had made possible for them a general collectivization. In the foreword by him and Marx to the second translation of the *Communist Manifesto*, published in 1882, they said that the western revolution itself, which was to facilitate this development, might in the first instance be set off by the signal of an uprising against the Tsar.

Among these young Russians who were already reading

Marx in the eighties and early nineties were the two older sons of the director of schools of the province of Simbírsk on the Volga, Ilyá Nikoláevich Ulyánov.

Ilyá Nikoláevich himself was a man of high character and ability. The rank of Councillor of State, to which he had attained by virtue of his office, gave him an hereditary title of nobility; but he had come out of the petty bourgeoisie of Astrakhan and had short fingers, high cheek-bones, a flat nose. His father had died prematurely and had left the family nothing, and Ilyá Nikoláevich's brother had had to turn to and support the rest. Forced to give up his own hopes of education, he set himself, by stiff work and stern saving, to make it possible for his seven-year-old brother to finish school at the Astrakhan *gimnáziya* and to go on to the University of Kazán, where he qualified himself to teach Physics and Mathematics.

This industry and austerity and devotion of Ilyá Nikoláevich's older brother set the key for the whole subsequent development of the Ulyánovs, and give them a character quite distinct from anything the ordinary foreigner will be likely to associate with Russia. In understanding this remarkable family, with their orderly and disciplined life, their habits of self-denial and their passion for education, we shall do better to remember New Englanders of the plain-living and high-thinking period. Ilyá Nikoláevich consolidated the Ulyánov qualities with those of a woman of German stock. María Alexándrovna Blank was the sister-in-law of a fellow-professor and the daughter of Volga-German parents, who belonged to the Lutheran Church and had brought her up in the German tradition. María Alexándrovna's father was a physician, who had bought an estate and given up his medical practice, and the family as a whole were more cultivated, as they were considerably better off, than the Ulyánovs. But María Alexándrovna, too, had suffered somewhat from family reverses, which had made it impossible for her father to give her tutors as he had done for his other children. They had had to fall back on a German aunt, who had instructed her in languages and music. The family had been a large one, and they had been trained to be diligent and thrifty. The father, besides, had Spartan ideas and had not allowed María Alexándrovna and her sisters, even when they were grown-up young ladies, to drink either coffee or tea. They had had two dresses apiece, both of calico, with short sleeves and open necks, which they had had to wear summer and winter.

Ilyá Nikoláevich and María Alexándrovna were married in the summer of 1863, when he was thirty-two and she twenty-eight. In 1869, he was given the post of inspector of primary schools in the province of Simbírsk, and came to live in the capital of the province, the city of Simbírsk (now renamed Ulyánovsk); later he was made director and became—through his work alone: he had no bureaucratic ambitions—a figure of some eminence in his field. The recent emancipation of the serfs and the judicial and educational reforms of the early years of Alexander II had opened for serious professional men of the type of Ilyá Nikoláevich an opportunity to work among the people. Ulyánov had grown up in the heartbreaking years of the oppression of Nicholas I, when it had been as much as the students at the universities could do to gather in secret and sing the songs of the Decembrist poet, Ryléyev. Ilyá Nikoláevich used sometimes to sing them to his children when they were walking in the woods and the fields at a safe distance outside the town. He had the career of a loyal official, and he remained, as did María Alexándrovna, a practicing Christian, whose faith was real; but he was known in Simbírsk as "the Liberal," and his sense of responsibility to the people had given him an absorbing purpose which was not always quite well-regarded. As a *gimnáziya* teacher, he had never taken money for working with the poorer students to get them through their examinations; and now he applied himself eagerly to the task of building up a school system in Simbírsk. Through roads thick with mud in spring and autumn, rutted and icy in winter, he traveled all over the province. Sometimes he would be gone for weeks. Wrestling with officials, training teachers, sleeping in peasants' huts, he acquired a special ability to deal easily with people of all kinds. In the course of seventeen years he succeeded in getting the better of the laziness and ignorance whose vacuity matched the vast flat spaces of Russia to the extent of building four hundred and fifty schools and doubling the school attendance.

And in the meantime the Ulyánov children were growing up in the house in Simbírsk. The town, on a steep and towering cliff, rises straight from the river-bank and looks away to a great view of the Volga, which lies broad between its level plains. You can see, for an immense distance which is nothing in the immensity of the river's length, where it is flowing from and whither it is flowing away in its slow and placid progress through Russia. The little city, five hundred and sixty miles from Moscow and nine hundred and thirty-five from St. Petersburg, which today looks rather shabby with its dull brick and white-washed buildings and its old houses in fancy fretwork of wood-lace, with its precipitous cobbled streets, was the seat of the Simbírsk government and a haven of provincial officials. The slopes are bristled with orchards that give little green Volga apples and whose blossoms for a few weeks in the spring are said to make of Simbírsk one of the loveliest towns in Russia; later, they give place rather dismally to the dust and dried-up verdure of summer and to the sticky and slippery mud.

The hierarchy of Russian society was in the Ulyánovs' time plainly visible in the stratification of the town. On the summit, which was called the "Crown," were the residences of the upper classes, with their gardens in which lilacs bloomed. Among these there were two distinct groups: the nobility and the government officials; the former prided themselves on their pedigrees and looked down on the not truly noble officials, who were themselves graded in fourteen ranks. There was a certain tradition of culture in Simbírsk. Karamzín, one of the pioneering scholars who at the end of the eighteenth century had founded modern Russian language and literature, the author of a history of Russia which glorifies the early tsars and derives from Walter Scott, had resided for some time in Simbírsk; and Goncharóv, the creator of Oblómov, the great pathetic-comic type in fiction of the demoralized Russian gentleman, had been the son of a Simbírsk merchant and had at one time served the governor as secretary. The Kerénskys as well as the Ulyánovs were a part of academic Simbírsk. Down the hill from the aristocratic "Crown" were the markets, the bigger business houses, and the streets where the merchants lived; and at the bottom, beside the docks, were the lees of the population, evidently much as they are today, slopping about among the pigs and the dogs, the stands selling sausages and kvas.

The Ulyánovs had at first taken a lodging on the edge of the aristocratic "Crown." They did not fit in very well in Simbírsk. With Ilyá Nikoláevich's plebeian origins and María Alexándrovna's Lutheranism, they were not acceptable to the circles of the nobility; they were too serious for the circles of officials, who were disgruntled over the recent reforms; and they had nothing in common with the merchants. María Alexándrovna occupied herself with her family and with the exercise of a stringent economy, which only just allowed them to make ends meet. She had a baby, whom they christened Vladímir, the spring after they came to Simbírsk: April 22, 1870—her third child and second son; and afterwards had two sons and two daughters, of whom one of the sons died. In 1878, when Vladímir was eight years old, they were able to move into a bigger house.

This house is still in existence, and has been turned into a memorial museum, in which the Ulyánov sisters have recreated the original interior. From outside, the low yellow frame-house on the broad provincial street without curbs that is hollowed out like the bed of a river, seems to verge on the oriental; but, going inside, the American visitor finds himself in the presence of something so perfectly comprehensible and familiar that he can hardly believe he has traveled so far from Concord and Boston, that he is back in tsarist Russia. And it is surprising to find in Soviet Russia an interior so clean and so definite, so devoid of the ornateness and messiness characteristic of more pretentious places. The furniture is mostly mahogany, and almost exactly the sort of thing that you would find in your grandmother's house. In the living-room, low-ceilinged and simple, there is a long old-fashioned grand piano, on whose music-rack rests the score of Bellini's *I Puritani*, with dried ferns pressed between the pages. Between two windows, a level-topped mahogany mirror and slim-legged mahogany table show clear against the pale patterned wallpaper—most of these rooms are in light yellow or light gray;

and the leaves of potted rubber-plants and palms show sharp against the white of the window-frames, with their white curtains looped up along the tops but not dropping down at the sides—windows through which one can see the small green leaves of the trees cut out on the white sky outside. Brass candlesticks; oil-lamps in brackets, with shining tin reflectors behind them; Russian stoves made of smooth white tiles; a red pillow embroidered in black by one of the Ulyánov daughters. In the dining-room, the big family table is covered with a cloth of coarse white lace. This was evidently also a place where people read, studied their lessons and played chess. There are chessmen, a map on the wall, a little sewing-machine. Elsewhere there are book-cases and book-shelves: Zola, Daudet and Victor Hugo, Heine, Schiller and Goethe, as well as the Russian classics; and many maps and globes: Russia and Asia, the two hemispheres, the world.

The house seems somewhat larger than it is, because a large family have filled it. Upstairs, the little boy and the two little girls slept all together in one room in three little white iron cots. You see their hoops, paper dolls and wooden horses; and, from a later age, drawings and school diplomas; a bound magazine of 1883, in which *The Adventures of Tom Sawyer* was appearing; blue and lavender butterfly nets. The older sister had slept in a room that opened out of this one; and the nurse, who had come to them when Vladímir was born, slept in a little room just below.

On the same floor with the other children, but cut off from their sisters' quarters in a separate part of the house, only accessible by a stairway of its own, the two older boys had their rooms. Sasha was four years older than Volódya (these were the nicknames of Alexander and Vladímir); and Volódya used to imitate Sasha at the same time that he tried to compete with him. It got to be one of the jokes of the household that he would always reply, "Like Sasha," when any such question was put to him as whether he wanted his cereal with milk or butter. If Sasha took a hill on skates, Volódya had to take it, too. You can see it all in the two small rooms that open into one another: Volódya's with its school Xenophons and Ovids; Sasha's, a little larger, with Darwin and Huxley, Spencer and

Mill, and the test-tubes and glass pipes, with which he performed his chemical experiments. Their towels hang on nails on the wall. When any of their cousins came to visit and attempted to invade these quarters, they would say: "Oblige us by your absence."

The small low windows of Sasha's and Anna's rooms look out on a little balcony, where morning-glory vines, trained on strings, screen it in with their purple-pink flowers. Beyond is the apple orchard, which had been one of the most delightful features of the new house on the Úlitsa Moskóvskaya. The crowing of a neighbor's rooster is the only sound that breaks the silence of the provincial afternoon.

Alexander was all inside himself. As a child, he rarely cried; and as a youth, was reserved and reflective. He was good-looking and tall; but his gaze was rather melancholy and slow. In school he was a model student, always stood first in his class and graduated a year or two ahead of the boys of his own age. When he lost his religious faith, he said nothing about it to the family. They only found out one evening when Ilyá Nikoláevich asked him whether he was going to vespers and he answered "No," in a way that kept his father from pursuing the matter. He liked the novels of Dostoévsky, which appealed to his subjective nature; but he had decided to study science.

Vladímir, on the other hand, liked Turgénev, whose novels he read over and over, lying on the cot in his room. He was noisy, energetic, rather aggressive. He had red hair, and the high cheekbones and slanting eyes of the Tatars of Astrakhan. He had been clumsy as a child: it had taken him a long time to learn to walk—probably, as his sister suggests, because his head was too big; and he had usually broken his toys as soon as he began to play with them. Unlike Sasha, who was scrupulously truthful, he was capable of a certain slyness. On one occasion, he had lied to an aunt about breaking a decanter in her house, and then burst into tears three months later just as his mother was putting him to bed, and confessed to her what he had done. He had a great sarcastic turn and was always teasing his younger sisters and brothers. There was a song about a gray wolf and a helpless kid that they sang at the piano with their mother, and whenever they came to the part where there was nothing but the horns and the halter left, little Mítya would always cry; but whereas the other members of the family would try to induce him not to take it so seriously, Volódya would lay the pathos on heavier in order to make Mítya break down.

Vladímir turned out to be as good at school, though not so well-behaved, as Sasha. He was quick, and he had a capacity for attention that enabled him to grasp the lessons so promptly and so tenaciously in class that he rarely had to study them at home. But he ridiculed the French master so openly that the man finally gave him a bad mark, and his father had to call him down. He ceased to believe in religion when he was somewhere around fifteen, and threw away the little cross he wore. Unlike Sasha, he had no turn for the sciences: he was much better at History and Classics. He attained such mastery of Latin that he was able to coach his older sister Anna and a none-too-bright friend and get them through the eight-year course in two or three years.

When Alexander was twenty years old and Vladímir was sixteen, Ilyá Nikoláevich suddenly and unexpectedly died. He had always more or less overworked. As the motor that kept the school system going, he had been obliged to cope with all the problems of all the schoolmasters of the province, who were continually coming to him for help; and he had made a practice of taking their classes when they were ill. But now when he had used himself up in twenty-five years of service, he was to see all his work being destroyed by the reaction against popular education which followed the assassination of Alexander II in 1881, and to find himself professionally humiliated and seriously embarrassed for money. He was retired four years earlier than was customary; and, though he was recalled by a subsequent official, he spent his later years under the oppression of the Statute of 1884, which effected the dismissal of liberal professors and the exclusion of unreliable students, administered by a Minister of Education who forbade the education of "the children of cooks." Ilyá Nikoláevich had a stroke, and died in January, 1886.

The first effect on Vladímir of Ilyá Nikoláevich's death was to release the natural arrogance which his father had held in check. He even became rather offhand with his mother. On one occasion, when she asked him to do something at a moment when he was playing chess with Sasha, he answered curtly and went on playing. Sasha told him he must do what she wanted or he would not finish the game. One evening, writes their brother Dmítri, the younger children were playing in the yard. Through the screened and open window, they could see Sasha and Volódya inside, sitting absolutely motionless and silent, bent over the lighted chessboard. A little girl came up to the window and shouted: "They're sitting in there like convicts that have just been sentenced to hard labor!" The two brothers suddenly turned and looked out, while the little girl ran away.

The relation between Sasha and Volódya was a good deal less intimate now. Sasha was studying at the university in St. Petersburg. "How do you think our Vladímir's coming on?" Anna, their older sister, asked Alexander once at this time. "There's no question he's very able," said Sasha, "but he and I don't understand one another."

Alexander was studying Zoölogy, and he presently wrote home to his mother that he had just been awarded a gold medal for a paper on annelid worms. When he and Anna had gone up to St. Petersburg, their father had given them each an allowance of forty rubles a month. Alexander had told his father that thirty was enough for him, and when he continued to send him forty, he saved ten rubles every month—saying nothing, so as not to embarrass Anna—and at the end of the eight months of the college year gave his father back eighty rubles.

One day in the March of the year after Ilyá Nikoláevich's death, a woman schoolteacher whom the Ulyánovs knew came round to the *gimnáziya* where Vladímir was and showed him a letter she had just received from a relative of theirs in St. Petersburg. Alexander had been arrested with a number of other students for taking part in a plot to kill the Tsar. The youngest of the boys was twenty and the oldest twenty-six. A letter full of terroristic talk, which one of them had written to a friend, had given one of the names away to the police, and they had nabbed a group of six on the Névsky Prospékt, carrying a bogus medical dictionary, which contained dynamite and bullets treated with strychnine. Alexander was arrested later. It turned out that, due to his knowledge of Chemistry, he had been assigned the task of making the bomb, and had been alternating between the university laboratory and a private one, where he had been working with explosives. He had pawned the gold medal that he had won at school in Simbírsk in order to get nitric acid from Vilna.

Anna had happened to be calling on him at the moment the police arrived, so she had been arrested, too. Close to her brother though she was, she had known nothing of his political activities. It was only afterwards that she attached significance to his having said on two occasions lately, in connection with some action of which he had heard: "I wonder whether I'd have the courage to do that. I don't think so."

Vladímir now had the task of breaking the news to his mother. But María Alexándrovna gave him no chance for tact: she took the letter as soon as he began and immediately got ready to go. There was no railroad as yet through Simbírsk, so that she had to make part of the journey on horseback, and Vladímir tried to get someone to go with her. But when people heard what had happened, their attitude toward the Ulyánovs became more careful, and he found that there was not one of their friends in Simbírsk who was willing to be seen with his mother.

It was not till the end of the month that she was allowed to visit Alexander. They talked across the interval between two rows of bars in the visitors' room of the Peter-Paul Fortress. She spent another month in St. Petersburg, calling on her children in jail and appealing to public officials. They allowed her to be present at the hearing. Alexander had been neither the originator nor the organizer of the plot; but he tried to take all the responsibility in order to get his companions off. He affirmed his political position with an eloquence that terribly touched his mother. Since they had seen him last in Simbírsk, he had completed his adolescence, and he had now the voice and assurance of a man. María Alexándrovna found that the scene was too much for her, and got up and left the court. She continued to petition the authorities, in the hope of getting him off with life imprisonment; and, in the furtive Russian manner, they allowed her to go on applying, though they already knew her son had been sentenced. One day in early May, when she had seen him the night before, she learned from a paper she had bought in the street that Sasha had just been hanged.

A few days afterwards Anna was liberated, but banished to the estate of her grandfather Blank. María Alexándrovna went back home to Simbírsk. She had made it a duty to keep up and to go on as if nothing had happened, so that the lives of the younger children should not be demoralized or darkened. The neighbors admired her fortitude, but they ceased to cultivate her acquaintance. Even an old schoolmaster, a friend of the family, who had used to play chess with her husband, no longer came to the house.

It had been during these weeks that Volódya had had to prepare for his final examinations. He passed them with grades so high that the masters had to give him the gold medal, though they knew what had happened to Sasha's.

He was seventeen now, and he had to be the man of the family. Anna says that he was "hardened" by the affair of Alexander. He had already a reputation with his masters for what Kerénsky, the director, called "excessive reserve" and "unsociability": he was described as having "a distant manner even with people he knows and even with the most superior of his schoolmates." It may be a myth, as Trotsky believes, that when he had heard of Alexander's execution, he had said: "We shall never get there by that road!"; but we have the word of Anna that his brother's death set him thinking seriously about the problems of revolution. To the schoolteacher who had brought him the news, he had said: "That means, then, that Sasha couldn't have acted in any other way."

The eighties had proved a crushing period for everything the Ulyánovs lived for. The new tsar, Alexander III, coming to the throne at the beginning of the decade, after the murder of Alexander II, had resolved not to dally with those policies of reform which had ended for his predecessor so disastrously. His first act had been to throw out a project for setting up consultative commissions which had been intended by Alexander II as a concession to the educated classes; and he had embarked on a career of reaction of the frankest and most thoroughgoing kind. He strengthened the Orthodox Church; and he weakened the local councils and put the peasant communes under autocratic control. He did his best to dam the flood of Western influence, and made his German, Polish and Finnish subjects speak Russian. On the margin of the document which young Alexander Ulyánov had drawn up as a program for his group, the Tsar had written opposite a statement to the effect that the political regime now made it impossible to elevate the people: "This is reassuring." All that eager acquisition of ideas, that ardor to make of Russia a modern country, which the Russian intelligentsia represented, was colliding with a relapse into feudalism of a kind that they had never imagined.

Now Volódya was to find his own progress blocked. Kerénsky had done his best to give him a clean bill of health. He had affirmed in a recommendation that the boy had been given by his parents a training "based on religion and rational discipline," and that he had shown no signs of insubordination. He gave his assurance that young Ulyánov's mother would be with him at the university. The chief of police in St. Petersburg had advised María Alexándrovna to send her son as far away as possible to some quiet place of learning in the provinces.

It was arranged that he should go to Kazán, a hundred and fifty miles up the Volga. And María Alexándrovna, with the three younger children, went to live with him there. Vladímir started in at law school; but he found that he could not get away from repercussions of what had happened to his brother. The student plot had had the effect of aggravating even further the pressure on academic institutions: more liberal professors were fired, more dubious students excluded. By December a current of student revolts which had been generated in Moscow struck the University of Kazán. The students called a meeting, summoned the university inspector, and demanded the restoration of certain rights of which they had recently been deprived. That night the police came to the Ulyánov apartment and took Vladímir away. He had participated in the demonstration, but had not played any important role. It was simply that the brother of the assassin Alexander was now being watched by the police. He was excluded from the University and expelled from the city of Kazán.

He joined Anna at his grandfather's place, and the rest of the family followed. The next spring he applied for permission to reënter the University; but the director of the Department of Education turned his petition down. "Wouldn't this be the brother of the other Ulyánov?" the official had written on the margin. "Didn't he come from Simbírsk, too?" A request to finish his studies abroad was also refused that autumn. But María Alexándrovna still had sufficient pull to get the authorities to let him live in Kazán.

They took a little two-floor apartment on the hill just outside the town; and there in the old Eastern city, with its population that still partly spoke Tatar, Vladímir first read Karl Marx.

It was a time when the principal political ideas that Russians had depended on in the past had pretty completely run into the sands. The liberal nobility, deprived by a world crisis of the market for their grain, had had to fall back on the help of the Tsar and could no longer afford to be liberal. The eighties had been the period when the landowner Leo Tolstoy had attempted to divest himself of his property and to concoct a new kind of Christian life distinguished by lack of possessions, nonresistance, sexual abstinence and manual labor. The great political movement of the seventies had been the party of the People's Will, which had hoped to find the Russian peasantry, with their tradition of rebellion and violence, receptive to the socialism of Bakúnin. But the subversive possibilities of the peasantry had gone down with the rise in the price of wheat which had made the more enterprising of them well-to-do; and the socialism that Bakúnin had brewed in the West made no contact with the peasant commune. The Tsar had done serious damage to the strength of the People's Will by exiling and imprisoning its members; and the party had resorted to the terrorism that had culminated in the assassination of Alexander II. For the young people of Alexander Ulyánov's generation there had seemed to be no other possible course than to kill the new and worse tsar, too. "We have no classes that are strongly united so that they are able to restrain the government . . . ," young Ulyánov had said in court. "Our intelligentsia is so unorganized and so physically weak that they are at the present time in no position to engage in an open fight. . . . This weak intelligentsia, not possessed by the interests of the masses, . . . can defend its right to think only by the methods of terrorism."

But actually the affair in which Sasha figured was the last gesture of the terrorist movement. The group that had succeeded in doing away with Alexander II had realized to an amazing degree the half-insane dream of Necháev: a compact, devoted and disciplined band ready to die in order to strike; but its leaders had thus to destroy themselves in carrying out their aims, and the intellectuals of a younger generation lacked their leadership and were chilled by their fate. The fate of young Ulyánov and his associates chilled them still further. He had said that they were passing through a period when nothing but terrorism was practical, and now that did not seem to be practical. He had read Marx, as appeared from the program he had drafted, but he had believed that it would be impossible for a Marxist to carry on an agitation among the Russian working class until the political regime had been got rid of. Now, faced with the blank of his brother's grave, Vladímir read Marx himself, and he found in it what did seem to him a practical way.

In the meantime, since the days of the People's Will, the industrial development of Russia, though still far behind that of the Western countries, had been going ahead at a pace which made it seem as unlikely as Karl Marx had thought it, that the Russians would be able to make a short cut straight from the peasant commune to the socialism of a mechanized society. In the twenty years between 1877 and 1897, the production of textiles doubled and the production of metals trebled; in the ten years between 1887 and 1897, the three hundred thousand textile workers doubled and the hundred thousand metal workers increased to a hundred and fifty thousand. The eighties had been a period of desperate strikes which had been repressed with the utmost brutality, but which had had the result of procuring some rudimentary industrial legislation: factory inspection, the abolition of child labor, certain restrictions on the work of adolescents and women, and the regular payment in cash of wages which had hitherto been dribbled out—sometimes only twice a year—by employers as capricious with their hands as the landlords had been with their servants. In that dim house of the Russian spirit, the Marxist view seemed to Vladímir realistic: it was the only theory in sight that could make sense of the Russian situation and relate it to the rest of the world. And Vladímir's peculiar temperament had fitted him to be its spokesman. His trenchant intellect, his combative nature, his penchant for harsh and caustic criticism, his deep feeling combined with detachment, all made him sympathetic to Marx.

Vladímir studied the first volume of *Das Kapital* in a little extra kitchen that he had fitted up as a study. His sister Anna describes how, "sitting on the kitchen stove, which was strewn with the back numbers of newspapers, and making violent gesticulations, he would tell me with burning enthusiasm about the principles of Marxist theory and the new horizons it was opening to him, when I would come downstairs for a chat." Vladímir had a kind of exuberance quite foreign to Marx himself. "There emanated from him," Anna goes on, "a cheerful faith that communicated itself to the people with whom he was talking. Even then he already had the gift of persuading people, of carrying them with him. Even then, when he was studying anything and discovering new lines of thought, he could not help telling his friends about it and making recruits for his side." Others came to hear him talk about Marx, students at the University; but they did not come often to the Ulyánovs', where they could not afford to be seen. The principal Marxist in Kazán at that time was a student named Fedoséyev, a man of about Vladímir's age, whom young Ulyánov, however, never met—a fact which is explained by Trotsky on the ground that even a resolute Marxist would shun the society of the brother of an assassin. Neither was he able to read the publications of the Marxist group called

"Liberation of Labor," which had been founded in Switzerland in 1883 by a small circle of Russian exiles. But he was already in touch with something that could be felt as a new force in Russia.

And he had now, with his career at the University cut off, nothing to do but study Marx—and to play chess with his younger brother. Vladímir—this brother has recorded—got to be good at chess and insisted on a rigorous game, but did not care about winning. He would make Mítya accept a handicap, but would not let him go back and change his moves. That winter (1888-89) a young man to whom Anna was engaged organized for Vladímir a match by correspondence with a lawyer in Samára, who was an expert. Vladímir started to smoke at this time; but his mother disapproved, and when arguments based on considerations of health had failed to have any effect on him, she reproached him with needless expense. They were living at that time on her pension, and he stopped and never smoked again.

His mother was also fearful lest his political associations should get him into trouble in Kazán; and she made him come with her into the country, where she had had Anna's fiancé buy her a small estate in the government of Samára, below Simbírsk on the Volga. She had got him out of Kazán just in time. A few weeks after they had left—in the May of '89—the Marxist group of which Fedoséyev was leader as well as the group to which Vladímir had belonged were arrested and given heavy sentences.

But Vladímir as a landlord was not a success. "My mother," he afterwards told his wife, "wanted me to go in for farming. But I saw that it wasn't working out: my relations with the peasants became abnormal." He evidently considered abnormal any relationship that took on the character of the relation between master and underling. (It is worth noting that the next proprietor of the land was murdered by these peasants during the period of the 1905 revolution.) Certainly he knew how to talk to the country people with a view to achieving his own ends: that is, to making them tell him how they were living and what they were thinking. It was as if he had taken over from his father the gift of meeting all sorts of people and dealing with them on their own terms. He used to have long conversations with Anna's brother-in-law, a *kulak* who had done well for himself by buying up land and selling it to the peasants; and Valdímir would laugh delightedly over the sly deals that the man had put over; the farmer thought him a wonderful fellow. These brief years at Alakáevka gave him his only first-hand contact with the peasants, but he studied them with the single-minded attention which he was coming now to train more and more steadily on the social development of Russia. He also collected and scrutinized agricultural statistics on the locality, and satisfied himself that the peasantry, so far from constituting the homogeneous element that the Populists had counted upon, had been exemplifying the Marxist principles by differentiating themselves, since the abolition of serfdom, into something like a bourgeoisie on the one hand and something like a proletariat on the other.

In the fall of 1889, he appealed to the Minister of Education to let him take the final examinations as an outside student at the University; he explained that he had to support the family and that, without a university degree, it was impossible for him to follow any profession. The Minister made a memorandum to ask the police about him, noting "He's a bad fellow"; and later refused the request. In the meantime, the Ulyánovs went swimming, sometimes twice a day, in a little pond on the place: Vladímir's younger brother tells how beautifully Vladímir used to float, with his arms behind his head. They were floating with the slow provincial life. The little sister liked "the wind from the steppe and the silence all around." Here as elsewhere now they did not see very much of their neighbors; and when anyone did come to call, Vladímir usually climbed out the window. He had a work-table outside, which he had fastened to the ground in the shade of the linden trees, and he went there every morning; he had also rigged up a horizontal bar. In the evenings they all sat with the samovar in a summerhouse on the terrace, reading or playing chess around a lamp. Dmítri remembers seeing Vladímir boning out Ricardo with a dictionary. Anna wrote a little poem about one of their evenings in autumn, in which she described the moths and mosquitoes swarming in on them out of the darkness and dancing around the light, as if, feeling its warmth, they were deceived and thought summer was coming again.

The next May, María Alexándrovna went up to St. Petersburg to appeal to the Minister of Education herself. She wrote him that it had become for her "an actual torture to look at my son and see how the best years of his life are passing away without his being able to make use of them." She succeeded in eliciting permission for Vladímir to take his final examinations at the law school of one of the universities. Vladímir made a trip to St. Petersburg to find out what he had to do, and took advantage of the opportunity to get hold of Engels' *Anti-Dühring*, in which he found an exposition of the whole Marxist point of view. He got up the four-year course in something less than a year and a half. We may form some conception of his habits of study from his advice to Albert Rhys Williams at a meeting of the Constituent Assembly in the winter of 1918, when Mr. Williams was studying Russian. "You must go at it systematically," he said, leaning over the box with sparkling eyes and driving his words home with gestures. "I'll tell you my method of going at it." This method, says Mr. Williams, turned out to be nothing less than: "First, to learn all the verbs, learn all the adverbs and adjectives, learn all the grammar and rules of syntax; then to keep practicing everywhere and upon everybody." When he took the examinations, he came out first among a hundred and twenty-four.

But at this moment another tragedy occurred. His sister Olga was also a student in St. Petersburg and just at the time he was taking his examinations, she came down with typhoid fever. She was the most brilliant of the girls of the family and the one who was closest to Vladímir. In the country they had read together and talked about serious subjects. She had wanted to study medicine, but the medical school was closed to women, and she was working in Mathematics and Physics. She had overworked when she was already ill—in the tradition of the Ulyánov family—tutoring her classmates for nothing to help them get through their examinations. Vladímir took her to a hospital, which turned out to be a bad one—and anyone who has had experience of Russian hospitals knows how very bad it must have been. María Alexándrovna came up to St.

Petersburg again in time to see Olga die on the anniversary of Sasha's execution.

There was nothing for Vladímir to do but go back to Samára with his mother. Her influence on her children was deep and lasting. When they were little, she had never raised her voice with them and had hardly ever punished them; nor had her love for them ever been demonstrative. Vladímir, who had been eager to escape, imposed upon himself the duty of spending two years more in the provinces in order to be with his mother. It took him still five months more to get the certificate of political loyalty that he needed to practice law. He had made friends with the Samára attorney with whom he had played the chess match by mail, and he now became his assistant. He acted for the defendants in a few petty criminal cases, and in every instance lost. His only success was in prosecuting a suit brought by himself against a local merchant who was racketeering a crossing of the Volga and who had held Vladímir up one day and compelled him to cross on the man's little steam-launch instead of in the fishing-boat that Vladímir had hired. The man had long been a nuisance to the neighborhood, but no one had ever had the pertinacity to see a prosecution through. Vladímir bucked the efforts of the authorities not to let the case come into court, and got a judgment against the merchant.

In 1891-92, the famine and the cholera epidemic that followed it brought the intellectuals into the field. Tolstoy at sixty-three set an example by turning in with all his family and working his head off for two years: he and his sons established hundreds of soup-kitchens, and he tried to get the people on their feet again by distributing seed and horses. Vladímir Ulyánov, however, according to one of his friends, was one of the only two political exiles in Samára who refused to do anything about the soup-kitchens, and he would not belong to the relief committee. Our only knowledge of his position at this time is derived from the indictment of a Populist opponent, who declares that Vladímir welcomed the famine as a factor in breaking down the peasantry and creating an industrial proletariat. Trotsky says that it would have been quite improper for a Marxist to serve in any official capacity, that the business of a revolutionary was to bring pressure on the tsarist government by continuing to threaten it as an antagonist.

Certainly the Marxist point of view at this period was stiffening for Vladímir Ulyánov into a ruthless and rigid conviction. Abroad, under the stimulus of the dockers' strike in England and the recovery after the disaster of the Commune of the working-class movement in France, Marxism was getting its second wind with the founding of the Second International. The Russian Marxist, G. V. Plekhánov, the leader of the Liberation of Labor group, had appeared at the first congress of the Second International in 1889 and made a speech that had carried weight in Russia. "The Russian revolutionary movement," he had said, "will be victorious as a revolutionary movement of workers. There is and can be no other alternative." In the elections of 1890 in Germany, the Social Democratic Party, which had been outlawed in 1878 by Bismarck's anti-Socialist law but which had continued to send its men to the Reichstag, got a vote of a million five hundred thousand, with the result that the law was repealed as useless. Workers in the St. Petersburg factories were tearing up volumes of Marx and Lassalle that they had succeeded in getting hold of and passing them around in chapters. By 1893, a manuscript essay by Fedoséyev was being circulated surreptitiously in Samára. It was an original application of Marxist principles to the peculiar situation in Russia. Fedoséyev had become convinced from a study of the condition of the peasantry under Alexander II, that the liberal instincts which the liberals had indulged themselves in imputing to the Tsar had had nothing to do with the freeing of the serfs. This reform had been put through by the big landlords, especially the Baltic barons, who had found that it would be easier and more profitable to rationalize their farming and use hired labor. Backed thus by larger forces behind him, Vladímir developed the self-confidence of his dynamic and intellectual genius. He became more and more contemptuous of the Populists and in his polemics he pressed them closer and closer. His sister says that they came to regard him as "an exceedingly presumptuous and rude young man."

One must imagine for this harshness of Vladímir a background of the inertia, the corruption and the frivolity of Russian provincial life. "What a pity!" one of their neighbors in the country, a bibliophile, had exclaimed, when he had heard of Sasha's arrest. "He borrowed a book of mine, and now I'll never get it back!"

One night during the last winter he spent in Samára, Vladímir read a story of Chékhov's which had just appeared in a magazine, a story called *Ward No. 6*. Ward No. 6 was the psychiatric wing of a hospital in a little Russian town, two hundred versts from the railroad. Surrounded by burdock and nettles, the place presented, as Chékhov says, that peculiarly depressing and accursed appearance that prison and hospital buildings have in Russia. The entrance hall had a horrible smell from the mountains of old hospital clothes and mattresses that were heaped up rotting there; and on one of these piles lounged a guard, an old soldier who beat and robbed the patients. The ceiling of the ward was smoked up like the inside of a peasant's hut, so that one could imagine how stifling it must be in winter. In this room was confined a young man, who suffered from delusions of persecution. When he was not quailing in abject terror at the idea that the police were after him, he would babble about human meanness, about the forces that were trampling down the truth, about the wonderful life that in the fulness of time would come to pass upon the earth, about the bars on the window that reminded him of the stupidity and cruelty of the strong. The head doctor was an educated man, who had always had the hospital on his conscience: he well knew how out of date it was, how badly run and how rotten with graft, but he had never had the force of character to modernize it or clean it up. He would sit at home every night reading and mechanically pouring himself vodka at intervals of half an hour, and, brooding muzzily at last over his book, would try to see all that was wrong with the hospital as insignificant from the point of view of the great sum of human suffering and the inevitability of death, as unimportant in prospect of the depopulated globe which would one day be revolving in space after the sun should have lost its heat.

One day he visited Ward No. 6 and got into a long conversation with the victim of persecution mania. He had attempted to calm down the young man, who had denounced him immediately as the jailer who was keeping them in that terrible place, and whose first idea had been to kill him, by explaining that a truly philosophical mind did not depend on things outside itself, that it could be as happy in a hospital as anywhere, that the Greek Stoics had learned to despise suffering. The young patient had replied with vehemence that to learn to hold suffering lightly was to learn to despise human life, that he himself had always suffered and always expected to suffer, whereas the doctor's life had always been comfortable, and that it was easy enough for him to despise suffering because he had never known what it was. The young patient had been the son of a well-to-do official, but the family had gone to pieces: his brother had died of galloping consumption; his father had been convicted of forgery; he had been obliged to give up the university and to come back to the slow little town. The sight of a group of manacled prisoners had set off his delusions of persecution. The doctor got into the habit of visiting this patient often. One day he was overheard by an assistant who had recently been sent him, an ignorant and vulgar young man, who coveted the doctor's post. The doctor was telling the patient that all disagreements between them were as nothing compared to the solidarity implied by the supremely important fact that they were the only two people in the town who were capable of thinking and talking about really serious subjects.

The rest of the story follows the processes by which the doctor himself is gradually railroaded into Ward No. 6. There were in the story, of course, certain features that were calculated to affect Vladímir Ulyánov in connection with his own recent experience: a disreputable Russian hospital, a man whose education had been aborted, an official laid off for bad reasons after twenty years of service. But Chékhov had made of the story, one of his masterpieces, a fable of the whole situation of the frustrated intellectuals of the Russia of the eighties and nineties. When the blow finally falls and the reader sees that the head doctor is to be lured into the ward, it comes with a terrible force. The doctor has been perfectly passive, he has been unable to resist his fate; but, once trapped, he makes a scene, demands to be let out of the hospital. The old soldier beats him up, and then, lying in pain on his bed, the doctor feels at last that he is sharing in the suffering of these others, which his apathy and timidity have permitted. The young patient had reached his conscience; at the bottom of the doctor's acquiescence had been an impulse toward expiation. But he and the young rebel both are helpless prisoners now, disqualified as insane by their fellows. The doctor has a stroke of apoplexy and dies in Ward 6.

When Vladímir finished reading this story, he was seized with such a horror that he could not bear to stay in his room. He went out to find someone to talk to; but it was late: they had all gone to bed. "I absolutely had the feeling," he told his sister next day, "that I was shut up in Ward 6 myself!"

2 Lenin: The Great Headmaster

This flaccid provincial life conditioned, by a law of antagonism, a purpose of irresistible intensity.

From the moment of Vladímir's departure from Samára in the fall of 1893, when he was twenty-three years old, his story strikes out on new lines and must be dealt with in a different way. For Vladímir Ulyánov, the leader of the Social Democratic movement in Russia, the prohibitions and repressions of the Tsar, the ineptitudes and apathy of his subjects, present themselves as merely a set of obstacles which have to be watchfully circumvented, a series of temporary delays which may be utilized at the same time that they are endured, by a will that never doubts for a moment its superiority and its ultimate success.

In Vladímir a variety of elements had fused to produce this result. He evidently owed to his German blood that solidity and efficiency and diligence that were so untypical of the Russian intelligentsia. The moral consistency of Vladímir seems to belong to a different system from that uncontrollable fluctuation between emotional and moral extremes—good for drama but bad for real action—which makes even so great a Russian as Tolstoy seem a little ridiculous to the West. Vladímir knew no truancies into skepticism, no drops into self-indulgence or indifference. He had more in common—in his soberer and more scrupulous way—with another kind of Russian that was being bred by the tsarist regime. The effect of the Tsar's obduracy and cruelty was to make the courageous fierce, and the effect of the general fear and futility was to cause them to concentrate their forces in an effort to make themselves felt as individuals or in small devoted groups, at the expense of their own annihilation. Necháev had lived such a role in a fantasy which did not engage with reality, had paid the real and terrible penalty in the Peter-Paul Fortress; the Terrorists had lived it in earnest. Vladímir had talked in Samára with exiles of the earlier movement, and he had learned how it was necessary to live if you would pit yourself against the Tsar. To such a man so situated in Russia, there came finally the word of Marx to add to his moral conviction the certainty that he was carrying out one of the essential tasks of human history.

Vladímir, released, becomes Lenin. The son of the Councillor of State divests himself of his social identity, assumes the anti-social character of a conspirator; and, in graduating into the world-view of Marxism, he even partly loses his identity as a Russian and is occupied with lines of force that make of national boundaries conventions and extend through the whole human world.

He did not, despite his natural aloofness, have the right instincts for a conspirator at first. He was too confident and too enthusiastic. His sister Anna had used to have to restrain him from writing letters that might compromise their recipients; and even after his return from Siberia, when it was vital for him to avoid the police, he got himself arrested again by attempting to enter St. Petersburg by way of Tsárskoe-Seló, which was particularly closely guarded because the Tsar spent his summers there—a naïve ruse which the Okhrána made a joke of. But he applied himself to the technique of conspiracy with the same close but objective attention that he had brought to the study of law; and, set free on the occasion of this second arrest after only ten days in prison and with his list of political connections still safe in invisible ink, he immediately made the rounds of his collaborators, instructing them in the use of cipher.

Nor had he the oxlike constitution of a Bakúnin. Already in his twenties he was suffering from tuberculosis of the stomach; at the time when he went abroad in 1895 to establish relations with Plekhánov, he took a cure in a Swiss sanitarium.

And the strain of overworking at illegal work told on him, during these years, severely. He was already nervous and ill when he was arrested for the first time; Siberia built him up; but the suspense of the last days, when he was worrying for fear his sentence might capriciously be prolonged, made him thin again. He lost almost all his hair in his twenties. And in later years the anxious tension created by party crises sometimes reduced him to complete collapse. Yet he trained himself to economize his energies and to adjust himself to the vicissitudes of his life. During his three months in prison, in a cell five by ten with a ceiling six feet high, he rubbed the floor every morning with wax for exercise as well as neatness and executed fifty floor-bends every evening before going to bed. In Siberia he skated and hunted; and he was in the habit of leaving the company and bracing himself with long vigorous walks when the exiles would be sitting up till all hours, gossiping, disputing and speculating, over their cigarettes and their tea.

More successfully than Marx he kept clear of the personal entanglements and squabbles that are the disease of the exile's life. Considerate, as Marx was not, of the convenience and health of his associates, he made a point, as Marx was unable to do, of never becoming involved in or even of criticizing their private affairs. It was characteristic of him that, after the Revolution, he should have averted a severe chastisement which his colleagues had contemplated visiting upon the polyandrous Kollontaí when she suddenly went off to the Crimea with a handsome young naval officer—turning it off with the suggestion that they should be sentenced to spend five years together. If he was threatened with becoming embroiled, he simply broke off relations with people. Thus when there was danger of the exiled Social Democrats' quarreling personally with the older exiles from the People's Will Party, Lenin insisted that they must drop them altogether. "There's nothing worse than these exiles' scandals," he wrote. "They pull us back terribly. These old men have gotten bad nerves. Just think of all they've been through, the penal sentences they've served. But we can't allow ourselves to be distracted by scan-

dals of this kind. All *our* work still lies ahead of us—we mustn't
waste ourselves on such affairs."

It was harder to keep steady in the presence of the real
tragedies of demoralization. A disaster that shocked Vladímir
profoundly occurred during his Siberian exile. The pioneer
Marxist Fedoséyev, who had also been sent to Siberia and
with whom Vladímir had been corresponding, committed suicide as the result of a slander which had been started against
him by another exile. Fedoséyev had been accused of spending
for his own uses a general exiles' fund; and, already broken
down by prison, he had been driven to the indignant gesture
of renouncing the resources that were due him from his writing
and from the funds of the party, and trying to live on the eight
rubles a month which were the allowance made by the government to exiles. He broke down, found he could not work, came
to the conclusion that he was useless, and shot himself. Yet he
had left a message for Lenin that he was not dying, "from
disillusion," but that he had still his "faith in life, unshakable
and complete." Another comrade, an intimate friend of
Fedoséyev's, shot himself when he heard the news. Another,
a working-class man, went mad, with delusions of persecution.
Another died of tuberculosis, which he had contracted in
solitary confinement. Julius Cedarbaum, a young Jew from
Odessa, whose conspiratorial name was Mártov, had been sent
to the Arctic circle by the anti-Semitic Alexander (Lenin and
Mártov were both exiled to the Yeniseí river, two thousand
miles from Moscow, but Lenin had a more comfortable climate,
nine hundred miles further south), and there he, like
Fedoséyev, had been pursued by the calumnies of a comrade,
had had a breakdown, had ceased to work. "God save us
from 'exiles' colonies'!" Vladímir wrote to his mother, in telling
her of Mártov's misfortunes. When other exiles were busy pull-
ing wires to get themselves transferred to places where they
would be able to see one another, Vladímir insisted on remaining in the town to which he had been assigned, where there
were only two other exiles, both workers.

He did, however, have one comrade join him: Nadézhda
Konstantínovna Krúpskaya. The radical young people de-

spised legal marriage, but Vladímir and Nadézhda Konstantínovna went through the ceremony when she arrived, as it was
only on condition that they should do so that the authorities
had allowed her to go.

Her parents had belonged to the gentry, but they were both
orphans and had married on nothing. Her mother had gone
to work as a governess as soon as she got out of school. Her
father had been an army officer. He had been sent as a very
young man to put down the Polish insurrection of 1863,
and he had at that time conceived a sympathy for the
Poles which had prompted him later to serve in Poland as
military governor of a district. There he had found the Russians tormenting the Jews by making them submit to having
their hair cut in the public square, and the Poles by forbidding
them to fence in their cemeteries and then driving pigs in to
dig them up. Krúpsky stopped all this; he built a hospital,
became popular with the inhabitants. Soon he was arraigned
for disloyalty on a whole catalogue of charges, which included dancing the mazurka, talking Polish and neglecting to
go to church. He was dismissed from the service, without the
right to reënlist. The case dragged through the courts ten
years, during which Krúpsky found work as an insurance agent
and factory inspector. They were always moving from town to
town, and Nadézhda saw a good deal of life. Her father was
finally vindicated by the Senate, just before he died. Nadézhda
was then fourteen. She and her mother now had nothing to
live on but a small government pension.

Whether her father had himself been a revolutionary,
Nadézhda never knew, but revolutionaries had used to come
to their house. Once when they had gone to visit a family in
the country whose children her mother had taught, the peasants, taking them for landlords, had held them up as they were
leaving, beaten the coachman and threatened to kill them.
Her father had not been indignant, and the little girl had
heard him say to her mother that the landlords had earned
the peasants' hatred. When Nadézhda Konstantínovna was
ten, she became devoted to a young woman schoolteacher,
who talked to the children seriously and belonged to the
People's Will Party. She vowed that when she grew up, she

would be a teacher in a village school. That spring Alexander
II was assassinated by the People's Will. Nadézhda's teacher
had already been arrested, and spent two years in a cell without windows.

As soon as Nadézhda was old enough, she went to work, like
her mother, as a governess, and at the same time took courses
at a night school, so that she was able to graduate from a
small woman's college in St. Petersburg. She read Tolstoy and
began to do all her own housework and to eliminate such
features of her life as she had come to regard as luxuries.
During the early years of the nineties, she taught Geography
in workers' Sunday schools, and she presently discovered that
one of her classes was a Marxist reading circle. She read Marx,
became a Marxist. The photographs of her in her girlhood,
in the high necks and bulging sleeves of the period, show a
rebellious girl-boy, with hair brushed straight back, contemptuous narrowed eyes, a wilful nose and a full-lipped but sullen
mouth.

She met Lenin at the beginning of 1894 (she was a year
older than he), when he had not been long in St. Petersburg
and was still spending his time, as he said, walking the streets
looking for Marxists. She worked with him on the League of
Struggle for the Emancipation of the Working Class, which he
organized the following year. Avoiding the intelligentsia except as active Social Democratic agitators, he was trying to
deal directly with the workers. He questioned them with his
penetrating attention, saw behind them into their dwellings
and shops that lay beyond the immense public buildings, the
fizzing restaurants and gold-and-white opera-houses of the
spacious imperial avenues: brick barracks, low and dirty
wooden buildings, trailing out along unpaved and ill-lighted
streets. Krúpskaya helped him to reach them. At first she got
him information from her pupils; then she dressed like a working-class woman and visited the factory barracks. Lenin wrote
leaflets on factory fines and industrial legislation, and Krúpskaya and the other women of the Union of Struggle group
distributed them at the factory gates when the workers were
leaving the plant or followed them home and stuck them
under their doors. The group carried on the agitation after

Lenin had been arrested, and they played an important role in a general textile strike in the summer of 1896. Krúpskaya was arrested and exiled. She had handled communications with Lenin in prison; and had attempted, at his request, a little to soften his solitary confinement by standing at a point on the pavement where he thought he could catch a glimpse of her on his way to exercise, but, though she was there several days in succession, he was never able to see her. When she finally joined him in Siberia, she brought her mother, with whom she had always lived and who had helped them evade the police. Lenin rented adjacent apartments, one for himself, one for them.

Through all this—even watched by the police, locked up in solitary confinement, transported two thousand miles away —he continued to direct his lieutenants and to lay his plans of campaign. In prison, he had communicated with comrades outside through messages written in milk out of inkstands molded from bread that he could swallow when the guard came round. He had thus composed a May Day manifesto which was smuggled out and circulated among the workers, and which had helped to set off the big strike. And through all these sidetrackings, hardships and distractions, he steadfastly carried forward his solid Marxist book on the development of capitalism in Russia. He managed to get blue-books and statistics in prison; he devoted part of his three-days leave between the time of his getting out of prison and the time of his leaving for Siberia, to working in the Moscow library; he took advantage of the opportunity presented by a stop-over of a month on his way to his destination to work in the library of a local merchant, to which he walked two miles every day; and as soon as he had arrived in the place of his exile, he had begun writing his family insistently to send him the books he needed. Sometimes it took him a year and a half to get them. "It's no trifle," he says in one of his letters, "to contend with 'enormous distances'!" But figuring on the dates of departure of the mails, calculating the delay from the spring torrents, testing out the speed of the express trains, Lenin succeeded in engineering a correspondence that kept him in touch with the West.

From these letters we get the impression that he is now controlling his family as he does his political associates. His mother, his sisters, his brother and even his brother-in-law are all working to further his projects, and they have all more or less been brought into the current of his revolutionary activity. It is strange, reading their letters and memoirs, not remarkably different in tone from those of such a British family as that of A. E. and Laurence Housman, to see these cultivated people of the nineties turning rapidly into a group of outlaws who exercise the most admirable qualities in outwitting and subverting society. Even María Alexándrovna was obliged to abet the escapes of her children. Vladímir had been arrested for the first time through the discovery of a double-bottomed suitcase in which he had brought illegal literature back from his trip to Western Europe. The police, who had found this out at the frontier, had allowed him to go on with the suitcase in order to follow his movements; and Vladímir, who had told his inquisitors that the suitcase had been left with his family, asked Nádya through a letter in cipher to have Anna get hold of one like it that it would be possible to produce in court. Anna tells how this problem obsessed her: how she secretly acquired a suitcase, how she tried to make it look less new, how she despairingly came to realize that it was entirely unlike her brother's, how she got so that she would turn away when she passed shop-windows with suitcases in them. María and Dmítri were arrested while Vladímir was in Siberia, and Anna and María and Dmítri were all arrested in Kíev in 1904.

If these letters of Lenin to his family, occupied mainly with directions about the posts and arrangements for the publication of his writings, are of a dulness which must have been felt by their recipients as it is by the ordinary reader, this is not due to indifference on Vladímir's part. The paradox of his attitude toward humanity in general is first apparent here. Intent on an ulterior purpose to which the ordinary personal relationships must always in the long run give place, he yet enters into the lives of others with a peculiarly sensitive sympathy. Unconcerned about and uninterested in himself save as an instrument for accomplishing that purpose, he readily identifies himself with others. In Siberia and throughout his life, he follows the activities and the misfortunes of his family, lecturing, encouraging, prescribing, in his role of elder brother. "Dear Mítya!"—even in 1910 he was still writing his younger brother in this vein—"It's a very long time since I received your letter, and to my shame I'm very late in answering. How is your recovery coming on? I hope that the doctors are wise and aren't starting in with their work until you're completely well. I've often been obliged to think about the danger of accidents here when I've been crossing the center of Paris on a bicycle, where the traffic jam is hellish. But to get yourself thrown off the way you did, right in the country in winter! It must have been a wild kind of horse—and your way of riding him, too!—Find a moment to scribble me a few words about your health: are you absolutely all right again? Anyúta writes me that they hope to cure your leg completely, but not the shoulder. Will you be able to ride a bicycle afterwards? And your shoulder? It is hard for me to believe that they can't cure a broken clavicle. You must give serious attention to your treatment and go through with it to the end." And Vladímir, knowing that chess will help console Mítya in his crippled state, begins corresponding with him about problems: "I've felt like playing again," he says. In later years, he seems to have transferred to Maxim Gorky something of this half-protective attitude toward Mítya. He likes to spend holidays with him at Capri, laughing and drinking wine a little; and he cherishes at the same time that he chides him. When he came to see Gorky in London, knowing the delicate health of his friend, he made a point of examining the bedding to see whether it were well-aired.

Nadézhda Konstantínovna, taken away from her party work, succumbs a little more to Siberia. "With the monotony of the life," she writes, "one ends somehow by losing the idea of time. Volódya and I have got to a point where we find that it costs us some effort to remember whether V. V. came to see us three days or ten days ago." Late in the autumn, before the snow, when the rivers were just beginning to freeze, they would take long walks on the banks of the streams and would be able to see every pebble, every little fish, quite distinctly through the ice, "just like some enchanted kingdom." When

he rivers were solid to the bottom and the mercury froze in
he thermometers, they would warm themselves by skating a
ew versts. Elizavéta Vasílevna, Nadézhda Konstantínovna's
mother, had rather a bad fall on the ice. The wild swans would
bring the end of the long winter. When they would stand at
the edge of a forest and hear the woodcocks clucking and the
burbling of the spring brooks, and Vladímir would go into the
wood while Nádya held back the dog, which was trembling
with excitement for the hunt, she would feel herself overwhelmed by the tumult of awakening nature. Vladímir was
not much good at hunting, though he liked to plunge through
the swamps and pit himself against all kinds of obstacles. "On
one occasion," says Krúpskaya in her memoirs, "we organized
a fox-hunt, with little flags. Vladímir Ilyích was very much
interested in the whole enterprise. 'Very skilfully thought out,'
he said. We posted the hunters in such a way that the fox
ran straight at Vladímir Ilyích. He seized his gun, but the fox,
after standing and looking at him a moment, darted away into
the wood. We were puzzled: 'Why on earth didn't you shoot?'
we asked. 'Well, he was so beautiful, you know,' said Vladímir
Ilyích."

In the meantime, they translated together the Webbs' book
on English Trade Unionism, in order to make a little money;
and Vladímir finished his *Capitalism in Russia* and started in
on a study of philosophy for the purpose of getting ammuni-
tion to annihilate Edward Bernstein, who was trying to correct
Marxism by Kant. He taught the storekeeper how to keep his
accounts, and he explained to him that he, the storekeeper,
was a parasite of the capitalist system. He sent for children's
books for the six children of the poor Polish hatmaker who
was one of his companions in exile and who was having a
hard time making hats appropriate to the Siberian climate. He
gave the peasants free legal advice, unraveling their unintelligible stories and backing their claims with such success that
it presently got to be enough merely to say that one had been
to Vladímir Ilyích. He drew up and sent to Plekhánov a program for the Social Democratic Party.

When his three years' exile was up in the February of 1900,
he took Nadézhda Konstantínovna to Ufá, where she had

still to serve a year under surveillance, and went on to see hi
family in Moscow. Mítya came to meet him at the train and
says that as soon as he had asked about everybody, he began
"cruelly to criticize Bernstein," whose book on socialism had
reached him in Siberia and whom he stigmatized as a danger
ous perverter of Marx, with whom "a decisive and relentles
struggle had now become imperative." The moment he arrived
home, he asked about telegrams and letters and whethe
Mártov had not arrived. He was so much disconcerted at no
receiving any news of his ally that he insisted on composing
a telegram and making Mítya go out to send it—thereby, say
Anna, disappointing them, as they had hoped to have him al
to themselves during at least the first few moments of his home
coming.

For a few years at first in the nineties Marxism had flourished in Russia, because the authorities had not understood
it. But now the police were on the trail of the Social Democrats: there were new arrests in the South in the spring of
1900; and Lenin opposed as too risky a plan to hold a Social
Democratic congress. He decided that the only move possible
was to bring out a paper abroad. He stayed in Russia only
so long as was necessary to raise money and to arrange with
his collaborators; then he established himself in Munich,
where Krúpskaya eventually joined him. The first number of
Iskra (*The Spark*), set up by Social Democratic printers,
came out December 21, 1900; and in 1902 he published at
Stuttgart a pamphlet called *What Is to Be Done?*, in which
he outlined a program for the creation of a revolutionary
party.

All the writing of Lenin is functional; it is all aimed at accomplishing an immediate purpose.

Karl Marx had still been heavily loaded with the old
paraphernalia of culture: *Das Kapital,* with its wealth of il-
lustration, its footnotes and sidelights and learned jests, its
quotations from many literatures, ancient and modern, in their
original many tongues, has still something in common with
such a treatise as the *Anatomy of Melancholy;* if its father was
the moral genius of Judaism, its mother was the Renaissance.

But Lenin is not only not a scholar in the old-fashioned sense in which Marx was; he is not really a writer at all. Even his longest and most ambitious work, *The Development of Capitalism in Russia*, which is intended as a sort of supplement to Marx, has no literary, no purely intellectual, side as *Das Kapital* has: Lenin simply assembles the statistics and indicates the processes they represent. That the book is altogether lacking in the irony and indignation of Marx is unquestionably due partly to the fact that—as Lenin explains later in the similar case of *Imperialism: the Last Stage of Capitalism*—he was obliged to get it by the censor. But his other writings show to what degree he is indifferent to literary form. He is simply a man who wants to convince. His expression has an aspect of austerity: he detested all kinds of rhetoric and used to castigate the jargon of the Left. "He is perhaps," says D. S. Mírsky, "the only revolutionary writer who never said more than he meant." He is impersonal, plain and hard-hitting; and he has a gift for striking off his meaning in epithets and slogans that stick. The Russians say that his early addiction to Latin influenced his literary style, and certainly he took advantage of the special opportunities for terseness presented by the highly inflected Russian language. But the repetitiousness of his polemical writing and his monotonous addiction to a vein of rather flat-footed Marxist invective show a clumsiness which is never present in even the rancorous hair-splitting of Marx. It is simply that these are the best methods which Lenin is able to think of to gain his objective, to drive home his point. "His correspondence with his close colleagues," says Trotsky, was carried on "in a telegraphic language . . . Complicated explanations were replaced by a double or triple underlining of separate words, extra exclamation points, etc." What renders his writings impressive is simply the staunchness, the sincerity, the force, that make themselves felt behind them.

To appreciate fully the distinction of Lenin's intellectual equipment, one would probably have to have heard him speak. Gorky tells us that Lenin's speeches always made upon him the impression of "the cold glitter of steel shavings," from which "there rose, with amazing simplicity, the perfectly fashioned figure of truth."

But this truth is always the truth of some particular situation with which Lenin wants his hearers to grapple.

It is not that his powers were narrowly specialized: his natural range was probably wide; he had a schoolmaster's high esteem for and even genuine appreciation of other departments of thought. But he had deliberately narrowed his interest. Like almost all educated Russians, he loved music and literature. Gorky tells how he once came to see him and found *War and Peace* on the table: "'Yes, Tolstoy [Lenin said]; I wanted to read the scene of the hunt, then remembered that I had to write to a comrade. Absolutely no time for reading. Only last night I managed to read your book on Tolstoy.' Smiling and screwing up his eyes, he stretched himself deliciously in his armchair and, lowering his voice, added quickly, 'What a colossus, eh? What a marvelously developed brain! Here's an artist for you, sir. And do you know something still more amazing? You couldn't find a real muzhík in literature till this count appeared on the scene.'" On another occasion, he and Gorky were listening to Beethoven's *Appassionata*: "'I know nothing [Lenin said] that is greater than the *Appassionata*; I'd like to listen to it every day. It is marvelous superhuman music. I always think with pride—perhaps it is naïve of me—what marvelous things human beings can do!' Then screwing up his eyes and smiling, he added rather sadly: 'But I can't listen to music too often. It affects your nerves, makes you want to say stupid nice things and stroke the heads of people who could create such beauty while living in this vile hell. And now you mustn't stroke anyone's head—you might get your hand bitten off. You have to hit them on the head, without any mercy, although our ideal is not to use force against anyone. Hm, hm, our duty is infernally hard.'" And when he studied the natural sciences, it was to prove that the new theories of matter, for which he had the utmost respect, did not conflict with the materialism of Marxism.

Lenin, in a sense, is without intellectual curiosity, because he cannot allow himself to indulge in gratuitous intellectual activity. Even in the field of Marxism, he was at no time very deeply interested in the fundamentals of Marxist thought. His only extensive work on the philosophical principles of Marxism, *Materialism and Empirio-Criticism,* is one hundred per cent a polemic, directed against what he regarded as dangerous idealist tendencies on the part of the Russian Marxists, who had been coming under the influence of Ernst Mach.

It is enough for him to feel that he has refuted a philosophical theory for him to have been able to produce a text from Marx or Engels that has the appearance of controverting it. That something has been "confirmed by Marx and Engels hundreds of times" is all the assurance he needs; and "the desire to find a 'new' viewpoint in philosophy betrays the same poverty of spirit as the desire to create a 'new' theory of value or a 'new' theory of rent." He has evidently not always understood the actual positions of his opponents or imagined the possible implications of the scientific discoveries they were based on—it was the period, 1908, when the atom was tending to resolve itself into a system of stresses in space. For Lenin, our sense-perceptions represent external realities; we verify them—as Marx had indicated in the *Theses on Feuerbach*—by entering into action; our knowledge of the world is relative, but it is always approaching an absolute; and this process is guaranteed by the progress of the Dialectic. The Dialectic is the "*only* conception that offers the key to the understanding of the 'self-movement' of everything in existence; it alone offers the key to the understanding of 'leaps,' to the 'transformation into the opposite,' to the destruction of the old and the appearance of the new." "The destructibility of the atom, its inexhaustibility, the mutability of all the forms of matter and the variability of its motion, have been the stronghold of Dialectic Materialism"; and in the social sciences the Dialectic is exemplified by the processes of the class struggle. The only alternative conception is "dead, poor and dry"; the Dialectic is vital. If we hold these ideas as dogmas and act upon them, the triumph of socialism will be "inevitable." His conception of Marxism may be indicated by his comparison of "Marxist philosophy" to "a solid block of steel, from which you cannot eliminate even one basic assumption without abandoning objective truth, without falling into the arms of the bourgeois-reactionary falsehood."

Nor has he even as an historical critic the same interest a Marx and Engels. Even *The Development of Capitalism i Russia* differs from Marx in its limited scope and through th emphasis of its special local bearing as a polemic against th Russian Populists. And even in this political field, the concen tration of Lenin is more limiting. There is a letter of Engel to Marx, to which I have already referred, in which he speaks after the defeat of '48, of the conditions of an actual revolu tion as having a demoralizing effect on such critical thinker as Marx and himself, and tells his friend that, when the mo ment comes, they must try to avoid, "at least for a time becoming involved in that whirlpool." To Lenin this point o view would have been utterly inconceivable; he could no have imagined that it would be possible to lose anythin worth having by becoming involved in action. Even in a simi lar situation—the reaction that followed the defeat of the revo lution of 1905—he did not withdraw, as Marx and Engels had been glad enough to do, in order to look at things more closel and to elaborate their ideas more completely. The roots o Lenin's activity were instinctive, unquestioning, irresistible his explicit convictions are derived from whatever will serv his purpose in Marx. His whole object is still to build a party and his critical activity is confined to what he regards as in dispensable for whipping his party into shape.

It would be tedious to trace in detail the stages by whicl Lenin steered his followers through the rocks and shoals o revolutionary politics. As we follow his windings in those in terminable polemics that make dreary enough reading today we may be tempted to imagine with certain of his opponent that he is the victim of a theological obsession with doctrine or to be struck, as Boris Souvarine is, by the apparent incon sistencies of his course. But to approach Lenin thus throug his writings, even in these utterances to his party, is not t understand him at all. If his controversial writings are usuall dull to read, it is because the issues involved are not reall being fought out by Lenin in terms of ideas at all. These issue are not—though Lenin thinks they are—really questions o Marxist theory. They are invariably questions of practica policy; and his real aim is not to justify theoretically the policy that he feels is the right one, but simply to make people pursue it. The theoretical side of Lenin is, in a sense, not serious; it is the instinct for dealing with the reality of the definite political situation which attains in him the point of genius. He sees and he adopts his tactic with no regard for the theoretical positions of others or of his own theoretical position in the past; then he supports it with Marxist texts. If he is mistaken, he declares his error, and adopts a new tactic, with new texts. Yet in all this ready shifting of tactics, he had always in his mind a single purpose related to theory in a larger sense: the making in Russia of a revolution which should be not merely Russian but Marxist.

He had thus a double problem: to implement Marxism itself and to guide the Russian movement along the Marxist rails.

In connection with the first of these, he had really to reload the weapons that had been hung up by Marx and Engels after the campaign of 1848, to bring back into Marxism the "dynamic principle" of Marx's college dissertation, the will to change the world of the *Theses on Feuerbach*, the human force that made Marxism "not a dogma," as Lenin was fond of quoting from Engels, but indefeasibly "a guide to action." And Lenin's character was totally free from that personal ambition and vanity which had betrayed Ferdinand Lassalle when he had tried to take Marxism into action.

In Western Europe the doctrine of Marx had been falling into what the Marxists called "reformism" and "opportunism." When Lenin, in 1895, had gone to see Paul Lafargue in Paris, Marx's son-in-law had told him it was impossible that the Russians should understand Marx, since nobody understood him any longer in Western Europe. The very parliamentary successes of the Social Democratic Party in Germany had had the effect of cooling the ardor of the revolutionary purpose of German Marxists and of impelling them to question the Marxist credo. Edward Bernstein began in 1898 to advocate a revision of Marxist theory. The Social Democrats, he pointed out, were no longer a revolutionary party in the sense that, say, the Communist League had been: they were simply reformers who went to the Reichstag in the hope of putting through certain measures. Bernstein proposed that they should frankly take stock of the assumptions implied by their altered point of view. It seemed evident to Bernstein that the Marxist expectation of the eventual elimination of the middle class had already been disappointed: the impoverished and multiplied working class was not finally to be left confronting a small group of capitalists, who had grown more powerful as their number had dwindled; the working class was better off, the middle class was multiplying, the capitalists were multiplying, also; the contradictions between the interests of these classes were becoming less, not more, acute, and the periodical crises of the system less serious instead of more so. The increasing control of industry by the monopolistic trusts would probably avert the final catastrophe, and it would be possible in the meantime for socialists to effect the transformation of society along lines not dissimilar to those by which Bismarck and Wilhelm II, under pressure of the earlier socialist agitation, had been granting reforms from above.

Moreover, the moral aspects of Marxism were in need of new clarification. The scientific point of view it insisted on provided no moral motivation. The truth was that it disguised a doctrine of the natural rights of man, which it was important to bring out into the open. What was needed was a standard of morality, such as one found in Kant, that was independent of the interests of class. Such a standard would have the effect of establishing a human solidarity with those who had been regarded by Marxism as the irreconcilable antagonists of one's class, so that one would seek to avoid class violence and to benefit society as a whole. As the growth of moral consciousness was gradual, so the development of socialism must be gradual: "evolution" was to take the place of "revolution." Thus the procedure of the Social Democrats in the Reichstag of the Kaiser was justified.

Now for Lenin, with the Tsar for antagonist, there could be no question whatever of a gradual evolution toward socialism; a moral code which should include both him and Nicholas was to him inconceivable. Disregarding the perfect justice of much of the negative side of Bernstein's criticism, he reacted against the whole Bernstein exploit with an aggressive bull-headed fury. These doctrines were calculated to demoralize the convictions of Russian revolutionists, and hence they threatened his vital interests; so he denounced as the most damnable of heresies any attempt on the part of the revisionists to bury Marx the fighter.

In Russia he had to contend with a whole series of special heresies, often connected with the revisionist movement. There were, in the first place, as we have already indicated, the Populists, who persisted in believing in the revolutionary potentialities of a peasantry that they still regarded as homogeneous. Lenin analyzed the differentiations that had appeared since the Emancipation and demonstrated that the various strata could not be depended on to act in unison. And when the Populists opposed capitalist advances because they destroyed the old life of the countryside, Lenin insisted on their progressive aspect. Later, he had to fight the school of Marxist "Economists," who represented a kind of Trade Unionism: they advocated giving up politics and working exclusively in the economic field; trusting in the certainty that the working class would come eventually to socialism by themselves, they renounced the responsibilities of Marxist leadership at the same time as the obligations of the struggle against the Tsar. These Marxists were suffering from a form of the disease to which Marxism seems inevitably prone in periods of political reaction: the delusion that the processes of history will automatically do the Marxist's work without his direct intervention. The shift had occurred, as it were, overnight as the result of that campaign against the Marxists which had resulted in Lenin's arrest; and he was confronted, after his year in prison, with a group of "legal" Marxists, who were content to remain Liberals in politics. Lenin himself was incapable of this voluntary suspension of the Marxist will and, even after the defeat of 1905, he did not for a moment abrogate the mission to make Marxist history. In this period the Russian intellectuals, frustrated in the field of politics, began to droop into various forms of mysticism. *Materialism and Empirio-Criticism*, published in 1908, was an effort to combat these tendencies as they were manifesting themselves in the

cases of certain of the Russian Marxists. Lenin was fearful les
any doubt on the part of the Social Democrats that thei
sense-perceptions represented realities might divert them
from the path of Marxist action; and though, as we have said
he failed to take account of what Physics was really up to
he did his duty as the watch-dog of Marxism—and this aspec
of his book has some validity even in our own day, when the
findings of filmy experiments provide pretexts for theologica
systems; he fulfilled the only function in which he was in
terested in warning his followers that the new idealism made
possible for modern thought by the insubstantial characte:
which matter seemed to be assuming, might let God bac]
into the world again and sap the morale of those who be
lieved that mankind, without help from above, must create
its own future.

But the prime urgency behind both these problems is tc
make people follow his lead.

Lenin's capacity for dominating others does not derive, a:
Marx's did, from the authority of a great doctor or prophet
who may be content with a few disciples. He had to have
loyal adherents, with whom he could actually work and whc
were trained to accept his direction; and there appeared i:
his relation to his group something of the attitude of the olde:
brother, carried over from his relation to his family, and a
good deal of the inspired schoolmaster. "What a professor we
have lost in Vladímir Ilyích!" said Maxím Kovalévsky wher
he heard Lenin lecture in Paris; and his opponents at the
1907 Congress shouted, "Don't play the teacher with us: we're
not schoolboys!" Sukhánov, who saw Lenin with his followers
in Petrograd in 1917 and was able to observe them with de
tachment, constantly refers to them as "the teacher" and "the
pupils."

First with his associates, then with the masses, Lenin was
always laboring, explaining, making sure they had learnec
their lessons, supervising all that they did, so delighted wher
they gave the right answers that it made people feel bette:
to go along with him, scolding them and dropping them from
the class if they persisted in giving the wrong ones. Even in

dealing with philosophical questions, he treats his opponents like pupils who are obtuse about grasping the point: "If Plekhánov is an idealist who has deviated from Engels, then why aren't you a materialist, since you are supposed to be one of Engels' followers? This, Comrade Bazárov, is merely a miserable mystification! . . . Another warning, Comrade Dauge: the road from Marx to 'Dietzgenism' and 'Machism' *is a road into the mire*—and not merely for individuals, not merely for Iván and Sídor and Paul, but for the whole direction of the movement." The slower students and those who were badly prepared he worked over with the same earnest patience that his father and he himself had displayed in the *gimnáziya* at Simbírsk, leading them from one step to another, pounding in every precept till they had got it well fixed in their minds; and even with the brightest students he never ceases to be exacting and vigilant. Unlike Marx, he was incapable of envy, never embroiled himself personally with people, never harbored personal grudges; and, on the other hand, though he was susceptible, as we shall see, to very strong personal attachments which survived political differences (as was not the case with Marx), he could no more allow these feelings to influence his political action than the headmaster can allow himself to be influenced in the matter of grades or discipline by his affection for a favorite pupil. So we see him in the last vivid glimpse we have of him in the historical film patched together from old newsreels, *From the Tsar to Lenin,* a short sturdy man with a big bald boxlike brow, leaning forward as if on the edge of his chair, arguing, insisting, smiling, screwing up his eyes in the shrewd Russian way, gesturing to drive his points home: a rapid-fire of lips, eyes and hands in which the whole of a man's energy is concentrated. Here there is none of the self-dramatization of the orator, none of the public geniality of the politician: it is the sure dignity of the respected headmaster who deals directly and frankly with his charges yet who stands on a higher ground and always preserves a certain distance between him and them, a distance the most insolent rebel will be powerless to get across.

Thus, though Lenin had none of Marx's nervous pride, none

of his impulse to pontificate and humiliate, he was in his political procedure almost as undemocratic. He was fond of his associates, he appreciated their qualities, but it never occurred to him to doubt for a moment that he could tell them what they ought to do; and he could never relinquish the final responsibility for what was said or done by the group any more than the headmaster with even the ablest faculty, the most promising crop of boys, can submit to a vote of the school. Sukhánov says that, skilful though Lenin was at preparing and presenting his ideas, he avoided the direct give-and-take of debate.

This, of course, was not merely a matter of Lenin's peculiar personality or of his conditioning by his early life. If he gravitated into the role of dictator, it was because the social physics of Russia made it inevitable that he should do so. In his drive toward personal domination there was nothing either of the egoism of genius or of the craving for honor of the statesman. Lenin was one of the most selfless of great men. He did not care about seeing his name in print, he did not want people to pay him homage; he did not care about how he looked, he had no pose of not caring about it. He regarded his political opponents not as competitors who had to be crushed, but as colleagues he had regrettably lost or collaborators he had failed to recruit. Unlike certain of the other great revolutionists, Marx or Bakúnin, for example, he is imaginable as a statesman of the West, developing in a different tradition.

But in Russia the difference in culture between the people and the educated classes was so extreme that a leader of the people had inescapably to direct them from above. Tolstoy had spent the latter part of his life alternating between his actual role of a great landowner with a troublesome conscience and the intensive impersonation of a muzhik, whose humility always became a fraud. Lenin knew how to talk to the people, he could readily put himself in their shoes, he believed that they had the stuff to contribute members to his trained corps of professional revolutionists. But with his hard sense of social realities, he is quite clear about the intellectual inequalities between the intelligentsia and the masses. He quotes in *What Is to Be Done?* as "profoundly true and important" a statement by Karl Kautsky to the effect that the proletariat, left to itself, can never arrive at socialism; socialism must be brought them from above: "the vehicles of science are not the proletariat, but the *bourgeois* intelligentsia." And "our very first and most pressing duty," he writes in the same book, "is to help turn out worker-revolutionists on the same level *in regard to party activity* as intellectual revolutionists (we italicize the words 'in regard to party activity,' because in other connections the attainment of such a level by the workers, although that, too, is needful, is neither so easy nor so pressing). Our attention then must chiefly be directed to raising the workers to the level of revolutionists, not at all necessarily to degrading ourselves to the level of the 'labor masses,' as the Economists want to do, or to the level of the 'medium workers,' as *Svoboda* wants to do." These masses are mostly illiterate, and when they exchange their submission for insurrection, they fall as readily into a filial attitude toward the man who takes the helm in their rebellion as toward the man who had kept them in bondage.

On the other hand, the Russian intellectuals with whom Lenin had to collaborate had been demoralized by the same paternalism: hunted, thwarted, with no experience of power, they were irresolute, irresponsible, unready. At a time when the Social Democrats were bitterly complaining against the domination of Lenin, an old friend of Lenin's, Krzhizhanóvsky, lost patience and demanded of Fyodr Dan how it was possible, as they said, for one man to ruin an entire party while everybody looked on helpless. "Because," said Dan, "there is nobody who is occupied with the Revolution twenty-four hours a day, who has no thoughts except the thought of the Revolution, and who even when he goes to sleep, dreams only of the Revolution. See what you can do with a man like that!" In *What Is to Be Done?*, Lenin characterizes Russia as "a politically enslaved state, in which nine hundred and ninety-nine of the inhabitants have been corrupted to the marrow of their bones by political subservience and by a complete incomprehension of party honor and party ties."

Lenin's rigor was thus intensified by the slackness of the

material he worked in, his habit of command developed in relation to the unsureness of his colleagues. And the schoolmaster turned into something that was new to Russia and to the world: the professional trained revolutionist, who marshaled his troops with the science of a general, backed his procedure with the learning of a scholar, and kept up the standards and discipline of his calling with the stringency of a Medical Association. He tells in *What Is to Be Done?* how he and his friends had suffered, in the days of the League for the Emancipation of Labor, "to the point of actual torture, from the consciousness that we were proving ourselves primitive handicraftsmen at such an historic moment, when, paraphrasing a well-known saying, it would have been possible for us to say: Give us an organization of revolutionists, and we shall turn Russia upside down! And since then whenever I have remembered the burning sense of shame I experienced, my bitterness is increased against those pseudo-Social Democrats who through their teachings 'disgrace the revolutionist's calling,' who do not understand that our task is not to effect the degradation of the revolutionist to the level of primitive handicraftsmen [of revolutionary politics, he means], but to *elevate* the primitive craftsmen to the level of revolutionists."

That task he was now to undertake; and *What Is to Be Done?*, a document of cardinal political importance, gives a description of the formidable machinery with which he proposes to supplant the "primitive handicraftsman."

The general organization of those working for revolution is to be dominated by a small band of persons, by the smallest number of persons possible, who have devoted their lives to this aim. It is easy for the political police to demoralize however large a movement which is loose and uncentralized; but it will be difficult for them to fight a movement directed by a permanent and secret staff who have themselves been trained, as the police have been, objectively to judge situations and to keep out of the hands of the authorities. This will set the mass membership free to circulate illegal literature and engage in other forms of agitation—since the police, unable to catch the leaders, will have to give up trying to curb this activity—as well as guarantee them against the dangers of being diverted by demagogues, while the "dozen experienced revolutionists will concentrate all the secret side of the work in their hands—prepare leaflets, work out approximate plans, and appoint bodies of leaders for each town district, for each factory district, and for each educational institution." "I know," he adds in a parenthesis, "that exception will be taken to my 'undemocratic' views, but I shall reply later on at length to this altogether senseless objection." The central committee will thus hold in its hands all the threads of the subsidiary bodies, but it will remain always apart from them and above them, set off from them by a sharp demarcation. This, so far from restricting the scope of the movement, will make it possible to include the greatest variety of revolutionary organizations—and not only working-class organizations: trade unions, workers' circles for self-education and the reading of illegal literature; but also socialist and even simply democratic circles in all the other layers of society. And beyond these will be the fringe of sympathizers who are to be found in all walks of life: "office employees and officials, not only in factories, but in the postal service, on the railroads, in the Customs, among the nobility, among the clergy, even in the police service and at the Court," who will help them when they can. The party would not be in a hurry to admit such sympathizers as these to the heart of the organization; "on the contrary, we should husband them very carefully and should train people especially for such functions, bearing in mind that many students could be of much greater service to the party as 'abettors'—as officials—than as 'short-term' revolutionists."

Such a system, Lenin says, does not imply that the "dozen" will " 'do the thinking' and that the rank and file will not take an active part in the movement. On the contrary, the crowd will advance from its ranks increasing numbers of professional revolutionists." As for the talk about the "broad principles of democracy," you cannot, under a despotism like Russia's, have democracy in a revolutionary party any more than anywhere else. For democracy, you need first full publicity, and, second, election to all functions. The German Socialists can

396

afford to have democracy, because even their party congresses are public; but how can there be anything democratic about a group which has to work in secret and which requires from its revolutionary following even a good deal more secrecy than it gets? How on earth can you have democratic elections where it is not possible for the rank and file really to know much about the outstanding workers, where even their identity is not known to most? It is only the vaporing exiles "playing at generals" in Western Europe who go on about "anti-democratic tendencies." "Think it over a little and you will realize that 'broad democracy' in party organization, amidst the darkness of the autocracy and the domination of the gendarmes, is nothing more than a *useless and harmful toy*." What their movement will have if it is successful is something greater than democracy: "complete comradely mutual confidence" in the tradition of revolutionary history. "They have not to think about the toy forms of democracy . . . , but they have a lively sense of their *responsibility*, because they know from experience that an organization of real revolutionists will stop at nothing to rid itself of an undesirable member."

Thus the configuration of Russian society has brought the Marxist Lenin to a plan of organization not unlike that of Necháev and Bakúnin. He complains that "the very idea of a militant centralized organization" which declares a determined war on tsarism should be associated, in an attempt to disparage it, with the terrorist movement of the seventies. This is "absurd both historically and logically, because no revolutionary tendency, if it seriously thinks of fighting, can dispense with such an organization."

In the realization of this program, Lenin was able to carry with him only the toughest and most determined. There was an issue involved in the splits and regroupings of intra-party politics which is not reducible to formulation in terms of ideas or even of tactics. It has been said truly that the difference between Bolsheviks and Mensheviks was at bottom a temperamental one.

This crucial division took place at the Second Congress of

the Social Democrats in the summer of 1903. The congress began in Brussels in a flour mill, infested within by rats and surrounded by Russian and Belgian detectives; and continued, after two of the delegates had been arrested by the police and deported, in the dirt and the August heat of the Tottenham Court Road in London.

The atmosphere was terribly strained: political conflicts were wrecking personal relations. Lenin himself was so keyed up that he could hardly sleep or eat. It is difficult for us, with our parliamentary habits, to understand an assembly like this, in which the chairman, Plekhánov, the father of the movement, was unable to refrain from interrupting those of the speakers with whom he did not agree, with such gibes as—the government Remount Department having been mentioned in connection with the question of the equal status of languages—"Horses don't talk, only asses do." One of the younger delegates begged Krúpskaya to get Vladímir Ilyích to take the chair before Plekhánov had made everything worse. To gauge Lenin's superiority among his associates, we must note that Krúpskaya thinks it worth mentioning that "no matter how fiercely Vladímir Ilyích spoke in the discussion, he was utterly impartial as a chairman, and never indulged in the slightest injustice toward an opponent." He did, however, once lose his temper—something that happened rarely—and left the meeting, slamming the door. When the congress was over, he collapsed.

But he won. "Of such stuff are Robespierres made," said Plekhánov to one of the minority. His chief opponent was his old ally, Mártov. Mártov, on the testimony of his antagonists themselves, was an exceptionally gifted man. Gorky calls him "amazingly attractive." His intelligence was penetrating and subtle; and he had, says Krúpskaya, "shown a keen sense for grasping Ilyích's ideas and developing them in a talented manner." He was, in fact, Lenin's favorite pupil; and his revolutionary instincts were real; but they were subject to Hamlet-like let-downs. Trotsky speaks of Mártov's "thin shoulders" and his "drooping and never quite clean *pince-nez*," and Henri Guilbeaux records that he exhibited "*une totale et invraisemblable négligence de son extérieur*." Describing him on a later occasion, Gorky says that he was "deeply affected by the tragic drama of the dissension and split. He trembled all over, swayed backward and forward, spasmodically unfastening the collar of his starched shirt and waving his hands about."

The split came about ostensibly over a mere clause in the program for the party which Plekhánov and Lenin had prepared. Mártov wanted to admit to the party all the liberals who might think themselves in sympathy with it; Lenin insisted on restricting it to persons who would work actively and submit to discipline. He knew that discontent in Russia was mounting up to a crisis—which came in 1905. The peasants, crushed with debts and starving, and no longer since the Emancipation able to rely on the landlords to keep them alive, had been raiding and burning the manor houses and demanding a distribution of the land. The protests of the industrial workers had finally got to a point where it was possible for the first time for socialists to speak at workers' meetings without the police's daring to interfere. At the moment when the congress was being held, a gigantic general strike was taking place in the South of Russia. The insurrectionary movement had been going ahead so fast that the Marxists had hardly been able to keep up with it; and Lenin was driven by the urgency of getting a grasp on it before it got hopelessly away from them and plunged on a blind course. "The root of the mistakes made by those who are supporting Mártov's formula," Lenin said in a speech at the congress, "lies in the fact that they not only ignore one of the main evils of our party life, but actually sanctify it. That evil lies in the fact that in an atmosphere of almost universal political discontent, in conditions which require complete secrecy in our work, in conditions where most of our activity is concentrated in narrow underground circles and even meetings of individuals, it is to the last degree difficult, almost impossible, for us to distinguish talkers from workers. And there is hardly another country in which the mixing of these two categories is so common, causes such a plague of confusion and harm as in Russia. We suffer from this evil cruelly, not only among the intelligentsia, but also in the ranks of the working class, and Comrade Mártov's formula legitimatizes it."

He carried a majority for his program. His adherents came to be known thereafter as "*Bolsheviki*," or members of the majority, and his adversaries as "*Mensheviki*," or members of the minority; and these labels, by their associations with the Russian words for *greater* and *less*, came in time to carry, for the public, connotations of strength and weakness, plenty and scarcity, maximum and minimum demands. From this moment, the terms "hards" and "softs" were much in vogue in the party itself.

The split lopped off Mártov from *Iskra;* the editors were now Lenin and Plekhánov. But soon Lenin lost this ally, also. Plekhánov, the first exponent of Russian Marxism, thirteen years older than Lenin, was a member of a noble family, who had at twenty rejected a career in the army to take part in the Populist movement. He had led a great Populist demonstration in the seventies, but had left the Populists when they had taken to terrorism. He had mastered the analytical instruments of Marxism and learned to exploit its stinging wit at the same time that he had carried to chilling lengths the Marxist intellectual superciliousness. Gorky says that Plekhánov resembled a Protestant pastor, buttoned up tight in his frock-coat and "confident that his ideas were incontrovertible, every word and every pause of great value." When workers came to see him from Russia, he would receive them with folded arms and lecture them so magisterially that they found they were unable to talk to him about the things that were on their minds. He had been away from Russia so long that he was unable to form any correct conception of the working-class movement when it came. Krúpskaya says that she once showed him the correspondence about the movement for which Lenin waited so eagerly and which excited his gift of divination, and then realized at once that such news was only demoralizing to the older man—"he seemed to lose the ground beneath his feet, a look of mistrust came over his face"—and she never tried to do so again.

He and Lenin had already had something in the nature of a struggle for power over the original direction of *Iskra,* though Plekhánov had finally capitulated; and it was not long after the Bolshevik-Menshevik split before Plekhánov was unable to resist the pull exerted on him by his old associates. He proposed bringing back the old Menshevik members to the editorial board of *Iskra;* and Lenin, still hoping for unity, acquiesced but resigned. The Mensheviks now made war on him; Plekhánov attacked *What Is to Be Done?* in *Iskra;* Lenin was characterized as an "autocrat," who aimed at a "bureaucratic centralization" and had been "transforming party members into cogwheels and screws," and he was accused of having projected an "organizational utopia of a theocratic character." As a result of all this protest, some Mensheviks were admitted to the Central Committee. The victory of the majority was destroyed. In Russia the local committees, accepting Lenin's principles of party discipline, had supported the Bolsheviks; but the Russian Central Committee, afraid to lose such famous leaders as Mártov and Plekhánov, finally demoted him from his position as director of its foreign business and imposed on him a prohibition to print anything without its consent, thus putting him in a situation where it would have been impossible for him either to state his case or to communicate with Russia.

He resigned from the Central Committee. He was now isolated, with only twenty-two followers. In the Socialist International, Karl Kautsky gave his verdict against him; and even Rosa Luxemburg, who had been close to him in his opposition to the reformists, sided with the Mensheviks, too.

The break with his friends had been difficult. There is in Lenin's polemics of this period no real venom and no personal rancor. Implacable as he was as a fighter, he was essentially a good-natured man. His revilings are the routine of Marxist controversy: there is no malice in them, merely disappointment that his opponents cannot see what is necessary to meet the Tsar on his own ground. In spite of his menacing assertion that real revolutionists would "stop at nothing to get rid of an undesirable member," he tended to trust people perhaps excessively, and was to believe in the reliability of the spy Malinóvsky at a time when Krúpskaya herself suspected him, until Malinóvsky himself one day walked into a Bolshevik meeting, threw down his Party credentials and fled. "His personal affections for people," says Krúpskaya, "made these political ruptures incredibly painful. I remember how miserable Vladímir Ilyích felt at the time of the Second Congress when it became clear that a break with Axelrod, Zasúlich and Mártov was inevitable. He and I sat up a whole night shivering. Had he not been so passionate in his attachments, he would have lived longer." He and Mártov had been arrested together, had worked on *Iskra* together. "Afterwards, Vladímir Ilyích vehemently fought the Mensheviks, but every time that Mártov, even in the slightest degree, showed signs of taking the correct line, his old attitude toward him revived." "I am sorry, deeply sorry," he said to Gorky after the Revolution, "that Mártov is not with us. What a splendid comrade he was, what an absolutely sincere man!" Mártov remained in Russia, but when he began coming out against trial without jury and capital punishment for the opponents of the Bolsheviks, he was requested by the police to leave. On his deathbed, Lenin asked about him. "He said with sadness," reports Krúpskaya: " 'They say Mártov is dying, too.' There was in his voice a note of tenderness."

But now in the moment when he has stripped away so much and won only political outlawry, he has a kind of austere exultation: "The battle to kill the organizations was inevitably terribly fierce. The fresh wind of open struggle soon became a high gale. This gale swept away without exception every remnant—and a fine thing it did!—of circle interests, sentiments and traditions, and produced official bodies that were for the first time really organs of the Party." And in the defense of his position which he publishes now, *One Step Forward, Two Steps Back*, he bases his role in the struggle on the action of the Dialectic. It would seem, he says (or so I interpret this very curious passage) as if the minority of Lenin's group before the Second Congress had turned into the majority of the Bolsheviks, and that the majority had then turned into the minority; that the negation had been negated. "In a word, not only do oats grow according to Hegel [the sprouting of a grain of oats had been one of the dialectical illustrations in Hegel's *Logic* and Engels' *Anti-Dühring*], but the Russian Social Democrats wage war among themselves according to Hegel." And yet the dialectical process can never be retrograde, as it would be if this were really it. The true *antithesis* is the revolutionary, not the opportunistic wing of the party. "It would be criminal cowardice to doubt for a moment the inevitable and complete triumph of the principles of revolutionary Social Democracy, proletarian organization and party discipline."

When Lenin had published his statement and resigned from the Central Committee, he and Krúpskaya took their rucksacks —it was the summer of 1904, and they were living now in Geneva—and spent a month in the mountains. A new woman comrade, whose party name was Zvérka, "Wild Creature," and who had just escaped from political exile and was "full of a joy and energy with which she infected those about her," started off with them but was soon discouraged: "You like to go where there's not even a cat to be seen, and I can't get along without people!" "Indeed," Krúpskaya says, "we always chose the wildest paths and got away into the heart of the mountains, far from human beings." They had loaded themselves with books, but never read them. At night they fell right into bed. They had almost no money, and their diet was mostly cheese and eggs; but at one inn they found a Social Democrat worker who advised them to eat not with the tourists but with the coachmen and the chauffeurs. This they did and found that everything was cheaper. They looked at the "mountain tops, covered with eternal snow, the blue lakes and the tumultuous waterfalls"; and "Vladímir Ilyích's nerves became quite normal again."

3 Trotsky: The Young Eagle

There had been present at the London Congress another brilliant young Jew who came, like Mártov, from the province of Khersón on the Black Sea—the delegate who had suggested to Krúpskaya that Lenin ought to take the chair.

Almost ten years younger than Lenin, Lev Davýdovich Bronstein had been born—November 8, 1879—in the little country village of Yánovka in the neighborhood of Elizávet-grád. The village was the estate of a colonel who had had it as a present from the Tsar but had not made a go of farming on the immense uninhabited steppe. The tsarist government, in its effort to populate this area, had also been giving it away to the Jews; and the Bronsteins had come down to Khersón from a Jewish town in Poltáva, to get away from the cramped and hunted Jewish life. Young Lev Davýdovich's father had exhibited a kind of enterprise not usually characteristic of these Jews, who mostly became simply small tradesmen and stuck together in their little rural colonies: he bought or leased some six hundred and fifty acres of Colonel Yanóvsky's estate, went to live in the house, made of mud and thatched with straw, which the Colonel had had built for himself, and raised grain, cattle, pigs and horses. He persisted where the Colonel had faded out, and by relentless labor and saving, made himself what was called a *kulak*, that is, a rich peasant. He had a ten-horsepower steam-engine that ran a thresher and the only grist-mill in the countryside. The peasants would bring their grain from miles away and wait for weeks to get it ground, paying the master ten per cent. He stopped selling to the local merchants when he found that he could get more for his grain by working through a commission merchant in Nikoláev and waiting for the market to rise.

Lev Davýdovich thus grew up in a household which, though only just emerged from poverty and not yet relaxed from its strain, occupied a pretty sound position. He was conscious of social classes—the peasants and servants—beneath him, who sometimes taunted him with eating better food than they; but did not suffer any constraint imposed by the consciousness of classes above him. The aristocrats of that uninviting region had been parvenus, who had flourished for a time, acquired billiard-rooms and French, and then been wiped out by the wheat slump that had occurred in the early eighties. By the time the young Bronstein was observing such things, there was little left of the third generation. In the case of one of the wealthiest of these families, which had given its name to a whole county, the elder Bronstein leased from the heirs the mortgaged remnant of their once vast estate and took in the younger son as apprentice in the machine-shop on his farm. When the mother and father of this family came to call on the Bronsteins, they would talk about their former splendors and hide tobacco and lumps of sugar up their sleeves.

Nor were they much injured by the campaign against the Jews which went elsewhere to such terrible lengths. Though it was a part of the anti-foreign-influence policy of Alexander III to make life difficult for the Jews by new restrictions, so that it was impossible, after his accession, for Bronstein the father to buy more land, and though the son lost a year at school, due to the fact that the quota of Jewish boys was limited to ten per cent—nevertheless, the former went on increasing his property by subterfuge and the latter always led his grade. As they prospered, they dropped the synagogue and the observance of the Jewish Sabbath—the father had always said openly that he did not believe in God; and the son, though he was made to study Hebrew, had never spoken Yiddish. Odessa, when he went there to school, was a seaport where the nations were so mixed that racial discords did not become disruptive, and where the Orthodox animus against Jews presented itself to him on the same level as the animus against Roman Catholics. "This national inequality," he says in his autobiography, "was probably one of the underlying causes of my dissatisfaction with the existing order, but it was lost among all the other phases of social injustice. It never played a leading part—not even a recognized one—in the list of my grievances."

Lev Davýdovich's sense of injustice seems first to have become self-conscious in connection with the peasants on his father's farm. During the years when he was going to school in Odessa, he lived with a nephew of his mother's, an intelligent and cultivated man, who had taught him the Russian grammar and how to wash and hold a glass, and whose liberal tendencies, though moderate enough, had kept him out of the University; and when Lev Davýdovich in his teens would go back to Yánovka in the summer "in a freshly laundered duck suit, with a leather belt that had a brass button, and a white cap with a glittering yellow badge," and would show his incompetence at harvesting the wheat, he was disquieted at being made aware that his father's hired men and women were sullenly sneering at him. There was a sharp-tongued mower from the village, with a skin as black as his boots, who would sometimes make digs about the meanness of his masters in young Lev Davýdovich's presence, and the boy would be torn between anger and a desire to shut the man up, on the one hand, and admiration for his "smartness and daring" and a desire to have him on his own side. One day when this man had said to him, "Go home and eat cakes with your mother," he had found when he got to the house a barefooted country woman, who had walked in seven versts to collect a ruble they owed her. She was sitting on the ground in front of the house, because she hadn't the courage, as he thought, to sit down on the stone doorstep; and she would have to wait there until evening, because there was no one to give her the ruble. He knew that the peasants who worked for them got only porridge and soup to eat and were never given any meat unless they made a silent demonstration by congregating in the courtyard of the farmhouse and lying down on their faces. One day when Lev Davýdovich came back from a game of croquet, he found his father having a scene with a peasant.

The man's cow had got into their field, and old Bronstein had locked her up, telling the owner he would not let him have her till the damage to the crops had been paid. The peasant was protesting and pleading, and Lev Davýdovich felt as he listened that there was hatred in the man's heart against his father. He went to his bedroom and burst into tears and did not answer when they called him to dinner. Then his father told his mother to go in to him, and let him know that the peasant had his cow back and that he had not made him pay for the crops.

In his second year of school in Odessa, Lev Davýdovich was suspended (with the right to come back, however) for leading a demonstration against an unpopular French teacher, who, as the students thought, through nationalistic prejudice, had been bullying one of the German boys and giving him worse marks than he deserved. Lev Davýdovich's mother was so indignant that she refused to acknowledge his presence when he came back into the house after the news had been broken by someone else; but his father surprised him a few days later by saying suddenly, "Show me how you whistled at your head master. Like this? With two fingers in your mouth?" He illustrated and burst out laughing. The boy did his best to explain that they had only howled in unison with their mouths closed; but the old man would have it that he had whistled.

His progress in that world of the intellect in which he was beginning to shine, so different from the dust and the sweat of the farm, estranged him more and more from his parents. Old Bronstein was proud of his scholastic achievements, but was himself altogether illiterate, only learned to spell out the alphabet later on in order to read the titles of his son's books, and now denounced as an abhorrent affectation the glasses that the doctor in Odessa had told Lev he had to wear. The cousin with whom he had been boarding was a publisher, later the head of the biggest publishing house in South Russia, and had infected him with a passion for letters. With a friend he had started a magazine when he was in the second grade at school, and he later did extra tutoring in order to get money to go to the theater. "In my eyes," he writes, "authors, journalists and artists always stood for a world that was more attractive than any other world, a world open only to the elect."

And—what was a great deal more serious from his parents' point of view—he fell into revolutionary company. The school he had been attending in Odessa did not give the highest grade, and he had gone to finish to a town called Nikoláev in order to be nearer his family. There for the first time—he was now sixteen—he made the acquaintance of Populists and Marxists in the circle of a self-educated Czech gardener, whose little one-room house was a center for radical students and former exiles, and who circulated illegal literature. Old Bronstein looked his son up and read him the riot act one day when he had come in to see his commission merchant; he threatened to cut him off. The boy had shown an aptitude for mathematics, and his father was exceedingly anxious for him to study engineering, so that he could help run the sugar-mills and breweries which the old man now contemplated building. Lev Davýdovich refused: he set to work to support himself as a tutor and arranged a communal scheme of living with his friends of the radical garden.

Up to the time of his coming to Nikoláev, young Bronstein had called himself a conservative and spoken contemptuously of "socialist utopias." Odessa, "perhaps the most police-ridden city in police-ridden Russia," had been politically extremely backward, and he had not really yet been exposed to the revolutionary movement. Now, though he says that he went left with a rapidity that even scared away some of his new friends, he sided with the Populists against the Marxists. Marxism, he says, repelled him "partly because it seemed a completed system." The principal Marxist in the provincial town was a young woman named Alexándra Lvóvna Sokolóvskaya, six years older than Lev Davýdovich. Her childhood had been spent in poverty and she had been aroused while still a little girl by the trial of Vera Zasúlich, who had tried to shoot General Trépov. Later she had studied midwifery at Odessa and had there made the acquaintance of students who had attended the University of Geneva and had worked in the Emancipation of Labor group with Plekhánov and Lenin and Vera Zasúlich herself, now converted from Populist terrorism to Marxism. Alexándra Lvóvna has been described as "gentle-eyed" and "iron-minded": she had a great many male admirers in the Nikoláev circle. Young Bronstein had already acquired a formidable reputation as a debater, and the Populist sympathizers announced to her that he would be able to demolish her arguments. He seems to have had very strongly from the beginning the sense of his own importance. At this time he was opposing Marxism—it was a part of the Populist case—as a threat to individuality; and there was enacted a whole youthful comedy between Alexándra Lvóvna and him, in which political issues were confused with the war between the sexes. Whenever they met, there would be a skirmish. "So you think you're still a Marxist, do you?"—thus Alexándra Lvóvna, as reported by Max Eastman, describes these sarcastic encounters. "I can't imagine how a young girl so full of life can stand that narrow dry impractical stuff!" "I can't imagine," she would reply, "how a person who thinks he is so logical can be satisfied with a headful of vague idealistic emotions." When a paper which had formerly been Populist took on a new Marxist board and became the first legal Marxist sheet in Russia, he got up and posted a petition to the Nikoláev public library to stop its subscription to it. But when he and one of Alexándra Lvóvna's younger brothers came to try to write a play together, it turned out that the Populist hero was rather a feeble character, and that his love was finally rejected by an attractive young Marxist girl "with a merciless speech about the failure of Populism." The whole affair came to a climax in a boorish adolescent joke which Lev Davýdovich perpetrated when he came back after an absence in Odessa. He had the gardner tell Alexándra Lvóvna that he had finally seen the light and invited her to a New Year's party. That evening he treated her with friendliness, but when they sat down to supper at midnight, he rose and proposed the toast: "A curse upon all Marxists, and upon those who want to bring dryness and hardness into all the relations of life." Alexándrovna Lvóvna got up and left the room, saying, "There are some things too important to joke about." Lev Davýdovich presently collapsed like Paul on the road to Damascus, though, in embracing Alexándra Lvóvna, he did not admit that he had changed his position.

He says that he had been furious all the time because he had not been able to grasp the theory on which the Marxists based their point of view. Their literature seems to have consisted of a copy of the *Communist Manifesto,* transcribed by hand and badly garbled, and young Bronstein's intellectual ambitions, spurred by his need to impose his personality, had far outrun his actual competence. But he had already been compelled by events to see the importance of factory agitation. The industrial development of Russia was shifting from the north to the Ukraine. In Nikoláev there were now two big plants, employing eight thousand people. The great St. Petersburg textile strike, led by Lenin and the League of Struggle, occurred in 1896. The next spring Lev Davýdovich, now eighteen, and one of Alexándra Lvóvna's younger brothers set out to organize the local workers. They got into contact with an electrician, who, like many of the Russian workers of that period who had mastered a mechanical skill, belonged to the more intelligent level of the ordinary population; and, calling their organization the South Russian Workers' Union, began circulating illegal pamphlets, which they brought in through Odessa from abroad, and leaflets, which Lev Davýdovich printed out by hand for the hectograph at the rate of two hours to a page.

Their agitation lasted a year before the police came down on them in January, 1898. The six intellectuals in the movement had agreed in this event not to hide, so that the authorities could not undermine the morale of the union members by telling them that they had been deserted by their leaders. Two hundred people were arrested, and the police tried to flog them into compliance: one man jumped out the second story of the prison and another went insane. Lev Davýdovich spent three months in solitary confinement in a miserable provincial prison, with no clean clothes, no soap, no books or writing materials, no opportunity for exercise and no neighbors, but a continual plague of lice. The window was sealed for winter, so that it was impossible to get any ventilation: he could imagine how bad it must smell from the face the warden made when he visited him. He would compel himself to do a thousand, a hundred and eleven, steps on the diagonal from one corner to the other, while he made up to the tunes of familiar songs new revolutionary stanzas, which were later actually sung, became popular and lasted through the great revolution. Then he was moved to a modern jail in Odessa, where he was able to get clothing and food from his family and to communicate with the other prisoners. His sister brought him the Bible in four languages, and he worked over French, German and Italian. In the meantime, the papers of the agitators had fallen into the hands of the police: the gardener's old housekeeper who had been told to hide them had simply buried them under the snow, but when the snow had melted, the package was found by a workman cutting the grass and turned over to the owner of the estate. At the end of two years of prison, Lev Davýdovich was sentenced to four years' exile, spent six months more in various prisons, and then was shipped with Alexándra Lvóvna, who had been arrested, too, and whom Lev had married in prison, to the Léna River in Siberia, where they lived in a series of little towns some distance above the Arctic Circle and more than a thousand miles farther east than the Yeniseí, to which Lenin and Mártov had been exiled.

Life out there—nearer Alaska than Moscow—says Trotsky, was "dark and repressed, utterly remote from the world." In summer they were eaten by mosquitoes, which sometimes stung the cattle to death, and the houses were infested with cockroaches, which they would have to brush off the pages of their books as they read. They had a ten-months-old girl by that time, and it was so cold that when they were obliged to travel they would put a funnel of fur over her head and fearfully take it off at every stop to see whether she were still alive. They lived with a couple who drank, as was common in that desolate region, and had knock-down-and-drag-out fights, in which an incalculably aged relative would be likely to become involved, so that Lev Davýdovich would have to go to the rescue.

Lev Davýdovich wrote literary criticism and sketches of life and character, which were published in a Siberian paper.

His pieces went over so well that he was offered sixty rubles a month to become a regular contributor, but before he had a chance to begin, an order came out from the St. Petersburg censor that further articles by this writer were forbidden.

In Siberia he finally applied himself to getting to the bottom of Marxist economics. At the time of his imprisonment in Odessa, he had still been resisting Marxism; but in his enforcedly intensive perusal of the conservative religious and historical magazines which had constituted the prison library and had been at first the only reading matter he could get, had been led to try to explain for himself a definite historical problem: the growth of Freemasonry in Europe from the beginning of the seventeenth century. He had not then accepted historical materialism, and he regarded the phenomena of history as the products of a variety of factors; but when it was possible for him to get books from outside, he had got hold of some translated essays by the Italian Hegelian-Marxist Labriola, which led him to ask how these factors had arisen. He had been dogged by Labriola's refrain, "ideas do not drop from the sky," and he had begun to see the progress of Freemasonry as an attempt on the part of the old artisan class during the period of the dissolution of the mediaeval guilds to maintain a system of ethics whose extinction was being threatened by the break-up of their social institutions. In the transfer prison in Moscow he had heard for the first time of Lenin and read his *Development of Capitalism in Russia*. In Siberia he studied *Das Kapital*, and he left exile a convinced Marxist, who could argue the Marxist case.

The doctrine of the Social Democrats had been threading its way through the East along the line of the Trans-Siberian railway, and Lev Davýdovich had been writing them proclamations. The spirit of revolution was spreading in Russia again. When they had read of the excommunication of Tolstoy for such heresies as denial of the Immaculate Conception, they had been at first astounded, then reassured: "we felt absolutely certain that we should get the better of that lunatic asylum." A new terrorist movement had commenced and two heads of government departments had been assassinated; but the Social Democratic exiles declared themselves against it.

Lev Davýdovich had received in 1902, concealed in the binding of books, a few copies of *Iskra*, which were reaching him a year and a half after they had been printed. Then *What Is to Be Done?* arrived. Young Bronstein had already written and circulated among the communities of exiles an essay on the importance of organizing a centralized Social Democratic party; and now he saw that the comrades in the West were going full speed ahead. He was eager to be there, to be with them.

The quickening of the pulse of rebellion was leading to a train of escapes. Almost everywhere in Siberia there were peasants who had been influenced by Populist exiles, and the same conditions—the vast spaces, the broad rivers and pathless forests—that were supposed to prevent escaping made it difficult for the police to pursue. The various colonies of exiles took turns.

The Bronsteins had now two little daughters, but Alexándra told Lev he ought to go, even suggested it first herself. When Lev was living in Western Europe, they found it impossible to keep in touch with one another; and then later, she was exiled again. "Life separated us," he says.

He got away in the August of 1902 under the hay of a peasant's cart while Alexándra Lvóvna nursed the dummy of a sick man in his bed. When he had reached the Siberian railroad, friends handed him a suitcase full of clothes and a faked passport, which he filled in at random with the name of the head warden in the Odessa jail, who happened to be called Trotsky.

He stopped off at Samára, which was the Russian headquarters of the organization founded by *Iskra*, and enrolled himself in the group. The comrades at Samára were amazed by him and called him "the Young Eagle." Lenin's old ally Krzhizhanóvsky gave him "Peró" (Pen) as a conspiratorial name and was in doubt as to whether to have him go abroad to write or to keep him at home as an organizer, but finally decided to send him to *Iskra*. He got across the frontier with less trouble from the police at the railroad station than from a student who was supposed to smuggle him out but who involved him in an argument on the way and became so indignant over the attacks that *Iskra* had recently been making on the terrorists that he threatened to drop the escape there and then.

Arrived in Vienna with no money, he went straight to the offices of the newspaper published by Victor Adler, the head of the Austrian Social Democracy, and there found his progress impeded by a prodigious Social Democratic bureaucrat, the editor-in-chief of the paper. This person was wearing two pairs of glasses, and when the young man asked to see Comrade Adler, he looked at him coldly and inquired whether he meant "the Herr Doktor." "Yes," said Lev Davýdovich. "Do you know what day this is?" the other then demanded sternly. The young eagle didn't know, as he had lost track in the carts, barns and houses among which he had been hiding and dodging. "Today is Sunday," the editor announced and tried to pass him and go on down the stairs. Trotsky insisted that his business was important. "Even if your business were ten times as important—even if you had brought the news—do you hear me?—that your tsar had been assassinated, that a revolution had broken out in your country—do you hear? Even this would not give you the right to disturb the Herr Doktor's Sunday rest!" Trotsky realized at that moment, he says, that the man was talking nonsense, and he continued to bar his way till he had extorted Victor Adler's address. It turned out to be perfectly true that the Social Democratic leader was tired: he had been busy with an election campaign. "I'm a Russian," Trotsky explained, introducing himself at Adler's house. "I've been able to gather that," said Adler. He reassured the young man by declaring that if a revolution in Russia did occur, he need not hesitate to ring his bell even late at night.

In Samára, Lev Davýdovich had been given a sum of money which was supposed to get him to Zürich, but he had allowed himself to be held up by the people who had sheltered him and helped him on his journey and had been careless in other ways, so that he had boarded the train for Vienna without a kopek left. And so, though Adler had sent him off with twenty-five kronen, he got to Zürich in the middle of the night with no money for transportation or lodging. (This inability to refrain from squandering money is worth noting because it is one of the traits of a certain princely aspect of Trotsky's character—a tendency which he has since learned to check by handing his funds over to other people to manage.) He took a cab straight to Axelrod's house, got Axelrod out of bed and made him pay the fare.

Axelrod despatched him to London. He arrived there in the early dawn—it was October now—and went immediately to Lenin's lodgings in the Tottenham Court Road, where he and Krúpskaya were masquerading as a German couple named Richter, and loudly knocked three times on the door, as he had been instructed to do. Krúpskaya came down and let him in. "Peró has arrived!" she announced. Lenin was still in bed and received him with cordiality but surprise. Krúpskaya paid off the cabman, then went to make them coffee. When she came back, she "found Vladímir Ilyích still sitting on the bed in animated conversation with Trotsky on some rather abstract theme." But he had already had a chance to tell Lenin all that he knew about the movement in Southern Russia, where he had been sent on a brief trip by Krzhizhanóvsky. The connections in general were bad; the secret *Iskra* address in Khárkov was wrong; the editors of the *Southern Worker* were opposed to amalgamation with *Iskra* because—or so they said—they differed from it on certain matters, such as the former's sharp polemics against the Liberals, though Trotsky could see that what was really behind it was simply the provincial desire to preserve their regional independence—still he believed that it would be possible to work with them; and the crossing of the Austrian frontier was in the hands of a *gimnáziya* student who was hostile to the followers of *Iskra*. Lenin was very much pleased with the young man: he liked the way that he had grasped and could formulate the situation at the *Southern Worker*.

Lenin took him for a walk around London. Trotsky tells of an impression he received on this occasion in a passage so remarkable that it must be given direct in his own words: "From a bridge, Lenin pointed out Westminster and some other famous buildings. I don't remember the exact words he used, but what he conveyed was: 'This is their famous Westminster,' and 'their' referred, of course, not to the English but to the ruling classes. This implication, which was not in the least emphasized but, coming as it did from the very innermost depths of the man and expressed more by the tone of his voice than by anything else, was always present, whether Lenin was speaking of the treasures of culture, of new achievements, of the wealth of books in the British Museum, of the information in the larger European newspapers or, years later, of German artillery or French aviation. They know this or they have that, they have made this or achieved that—but what enemies they are! To his eyes, the invisible shadow of the ruling classes always overlay the whole of human culture —a shadow that was as real to him as daylight."

For Lenin had succeeded completely, as Marx had not been able to do, in putting himself outside the owning classes. Quite clear and quite frank, as we have seen, about his equipment as a bourgeois intellectual and his function as a director of the working class, he had now, by his actual mode of life, identified himself with the dispossessed. It has been said, and it is not unlikely, that he and Krúpskaya refrained from having children because they knew that, with their meager resources, their constant shifting from place to place, the danger with which they always had to reckon of landing in exile or jail, a family could only have hampered them in following their prime line of duty. And Lenin cared so little for luxuries that it was not difficult, as time went on and he became more and more dependent on a salary from the party that was sometimes hardly enough to live on, for him to dispense with ordinary comforts. He had been in his early years so indifferent to what he wore that his mother and his sister Anna had made periodical trips to St. Petersburg to outfit him with new clothes. When Krúpskaya had arrived in Munich, she had found him living in a small furnished room and drinking tea out of a tin mug, which he washed every time he used it and hung up on a nail by the tap. In attempting after Lenin's death to destroy what she regarded as the legend that their life had been "full of privations," Krúpskaya only succeeds in showing the unconscious austerity of their standards. They were never, she says, in such straits as certain others of the émigré comrades, who sometimes "had no means of earning a living for as long as ten years, received no money from Russia, and literally suffered from hunger." But in her more detailed *Memories of Lenin,* she tells how they lived in Munich, first with a working-class family of six, who crowded into a small room and kitchen while they themselves had a single room; and then in a small house in the suburbs, with furniture which they bought themselves and which they sold, when they left, for twelve marks. When they had been forced to move *Iskra* to London by the imminence of the tsarist police, they had at first inhabited a dreary bed-sitting-room, and later, when Krúpskaya's mother arrived, the two rooms in which Trotsky found them. They did all their work themselves and had also to cook for the comrades who were always around the apartment and often spent the night on the floor: their rooms were the headquarters of *Iskra.* Lenin possessed no stock of books like Marx, but did most of his reading in libraries.

And so, in denying that Lenin was "ascetic," she only throws into relief the relentless concentration with which he pursued his purpose. Vladímir Ilyích, she insists, was interested in all phases of life and liked to amuse himself; but these amusements turn out to have consisted of frequenting those theaters in Paris where he could hear a singer—the son of a Communard —who wrote revolutionary songs; in London, of making excursions to Primrose Hill because it was near the grave of Marx, and of bus-rides in the more respectable thoroughfares, supplemented by walks in the working-class districts; Lenin would mutter, in English, Disraeli's phrase, "Two nations!" Ordinary museums bored him; but he could hardly tear himself away from the Museum of the Revolution of 1848 in Paris, where "he examined every little item, every single drawing." Nor had Krúpskaya any other recreations. When Elizavéta Vasílevna arrived, she took over the care of the household so that Nádya would be set free for political work. She was secretary of the *Iskra* board and stood, says Trotsky, "at the very center of all the organizational work. She received comrades when they arrived, instructed them when they left, established connections, supplied secret addresses, wrote letters, and coded and decoded correspondence. In her room there was always a smell of burned paper from the secret letters she heated over the fire to read. She often complained, in her gentle insistent way, that people did not write enough, or that they got the code all mixed up, or wrote in chemical ink in such a way that one line covered another, and so forth." Bobróvskaya, the Bolshevik party worker, says that, though Krúpskaya sometimes smiled, she never heard her laugh aloud, and that when she saw her in Finland in 1907, she seemed to be wearing the same gray blouse that she had had in Geneva in 1903.

Whoever has known the Russian revolutionaries of these pre-War generations at their best has been impressed by the effectiveness of the tsarist regime as a training school for intellect and character in those who were engaged in opposing it. Forced to pledge for their convictions their careers and their lives, brought by the movement into contact with all classes of people, driven to settle in foreign countries whose languages they readily mastered and whose customs they curiously studied with a quick and realistic observation, compelled by long sojourns in prison to accommodate themselves to the criminal outlaw and therefore to understand him, while the months or the years of confinement in the solitude of the Peter-Paul Fortress or the gloom of the Arctic Circle have imposed upon them the leisure to read and to write—these men and women combine an unusual range of culture with an unusual range of social experience and, stripped of so many of the trimmings with which human beings have swathed themselves, have, in surviving, kept the sense of those things that are vital to the honor of human life. And even among such men and women, Lenin had grown in moral power in proportion as he had divested himself of everything that might give him an interest in common with those who profited by the social system. It is true perhaps, as Lenin is reported to have said, that Trotsky had in him something of Lassalle. He was sounder and more sober than Lassalle, and he had developed a revolutionist's self-discipline which cut him off from such temptations as Lassalle's; but certainly he admired Lassalle at this time, as the references in his writings show, and like Lassalle he loved to shine. Lunachársky, who first met Trotsky in 1905, describes him as arrogant and handsome, dressed with an elegance a little offensive for a Marxist revolutionist in exile, and with none of Lenin's human charm. Where Lenin, says Lunachár-sky, never "glanced in the mirror of history, never even thought what posterity would say of him—simply did his work," Trotsky "looked often at himself."

Nor could he specialize himself so narrowly as Lenin. He always liked to read French novels, and in Paris he met a young comrade who even induced him to visit the Louvre. This was Natálya Ivánovna Sedóva, who had begun her revolutionary career by persuading her whole class at boarding-school to go in for reading radical literature and refuse to attend prayers, who at the time of Trotsky's advent from Russia was the head of the welcoming committee for Social Democrats arriving in Paris, and who has lived with him ever since and is the mother of his two sons. She took him around Paris. At first, he says, he fought against art, but later came to understand it and even wrote about it a little; and he has followed the tradition of Lassalle and Engels rather than that of Marx and Lenin: the tradition of the socialist as man of the world and all-around personality.

Yet an unquestioning, almost an involuntary, recognition of Lenin's superiority comes out in such comments on Lenin as that which I have quoted above. Marxist though Trotsky is and uncompromising fighter though he is, when he writes about Lenin it is always as one who is approaching something noteworthy and rare, of a breed almost above the human; and he has found in presenting Lenin an art of traits carefully picked and quietly placed, a portraiture affectionate and deli-cate, made sober by the deepest respect, quite outside the vein of Marxist vehemence and recalling in an unmistakable way the picture of Socrates by Plato.

It was not time yet for Trotsky to follow Lenin's lead. In the early part of 1903 Lenin proposed taking him on *Iskra* in a letter to his colleagues in which he described the young writer as "a man of rare abilities, he has conviction and energy, and he will go much farther." He deprecated the floridity of Trotsky's style, but predicted that he would outgrow it. Plekhánov, evidently antagonized by the appearance of another brilliant writer and afraid that Lenin and Trotsky would combine against him, refused to have Trotsky on the board and treated him with the studied coldness of which Trotsky says he was a master. But when the split of the Second Congress came, Trotsky sided with the members of the minority. He says that, as a man of twenty-five, his respect for the older leaders was still so great that he could not understand Lenin's ruthlessly cutting them off, and shared the general indignation at his behavior. Thereafter, he was engaged for some years in criticizing the dictatorial tendencies of Lenin and advocating, as an independent Social Democrat, a member of neither faction, a reconciliation between Bolsheviks and Mensheviks.

The crisis for which Lenin was trying to prepare came before he had forged his engine and found him more or less helpless at a time when the younger man, through his very position of freedom, was able to take over the leadership.

The massacre of January 22, 1905, roused the Russian exiles from their studies, polemics and debates. The fiasco of the war with Japan had wrecked the morale of the army and the navy, and disgusted the people with the tsardom. A demonstration led by an Orthodox priest and carrying religious banners had petitioned the Tsar for political amnesty, the separation of Church and State, the eight-hour day, the transference of land to the people, and the calling of a Constituent Assembly based on universal suffrage. The petition was drawn up in a language reminiscent of the days of Borís Godunóv: "If thou refusest to hear our supplication, we shall die here in this square before thy palace." The Tsar had lived up to his role in this scene by having them shot down on the spot, men, women and children indifferently; and the revolutionary movement, from that moment, leaving Holy Russia behind, launched upon a series of the most colossal and comprehensive industrial strikes that the world had yet known. The conspiracy of the Decembrists had been a revolution of the nobility; the terrorist movement had been middle-class; now for the first time a revolutionary movement arose among the people themselves, with the industrial workers at its head. "Only then," Lenin wrote about it afterwards, "did the old serf-bred, bearish, patriarchal, pious and submissive Russia cast out the old Adam; only then did the Russian people succeed in getting a really democratic, a really revolutionary education."

He himself was largely forced to look on. Father Gapón, who had led the demonstration and who was now learning to ride and shoot, came to see Lenin in Geneva, and Lenin, extremely excited, tried to help him to get guns to the Petersburg workers; but the ship ran aground and the cargo was lost. Lenin resorted to the Geneva library and read up military strategy and everything he could find on city insurrections. In April he attended the Third Congress of the Social Democratic Party, which had to be held in London, and found that the delegates from Russia were opposed to the leadership from abroad, where the exiles had lost touch with what was happening. In June, when the news reached him of the mutiny on the *Potyómkin*, the general strike in Odessa and the running-up of the red flag by the first ship of the Black Sea squadron, he sent a Bolshevik party worker to Odessa, with instructions to seize the city, to spread the revolt in the fleet, and to send a torpedo-boat for him. But by the time the man had arrived the rebellion had already been put down. At last, on the twentieth of November, Lenin succeeded in returning to Russia; but it was by this time too late in the day for him to play any very effective part. There were Bolsheviks in the Petersburg Soviet, though only in its later days, and a young Bolshevik engineer named Krásin, who bought and distributed arms, was one of the key men of the movement; but it turned out at that time to be a misfortune of the personal dictatorship of Lenin that his followers, without their leader, were not able to act with any boldness and that a Trotsky had been unable to be his collaborator.

Trotsky himself had gotten back in February; he had been one of the first exiles to arrive; and he made his way by a series of ruses up from Kíev, where he resumed the writing of leaflets and had them printed by Krásin in an underground press, to St. Petersburg, where he emerged, at the age of twenty-six, as the most important public figure in the capital, between whose flinchless will and the vapid Tsar the power seemed to hang for a moment. Sedóva was caught in a cavalry raid on a May Day meeting that had been held in the woods, and Trotsky retired to Finland during the summer. But when the immense October strike got under way, he returned and, together with the Mensheviks, organized—the first meeting took place the night of October 13—a Soviet (Council) of Workers' Delegates, in which both factions of the Social Democrats and the inheritors of the Populist tradition were to join in giving the unions a centralized direction. The Bolshevik leaders, however, afraid of merging their faction, would not act in the absence of Lenin, and did not take part till he arrived in November. Trotsky became chairman on December 9, when his predecessor was arrested, and he drafted all the documents of the Soviet as well as wrote articles for three revolutionary papers—one of which, undertaken with the Mensheviks, achieved an enormous circulation and quite eclipsed the Bolshevik sheet. He had developed, through much lecturing in exile, into an extraordinary public speaker —it was the opinion of Lunachársky that he even surpassed Jaurès—a master of both delivery and argument, who, whatever the imperfections of his relationships with people as individuals, had the genius for compelling them in the mass. He could handle the grim Marxist logic with a freer and more sweeping hand so as to make it an instrument for persuasion and wield the knife of the Marxist irony for purposes of public exhibition, when he would flay the officials alive and, turning their skins inside out, display the ignominious carcasses concealed by their assurances and promises; he could dip down and raise a laugh from the peasant at the core of every Russian proletarian by hitting off something with a proverb or fable from that Ukrainian countryside of his youth; he could point epigrams with a swiftness and a cleanness that woke the wonder of the cleverest intellectuals; and he could throw wide the horizons of the mind to a vision of that dignity and liberty that every man among them there should enjoy. Between the vision and the horrible carcasses that stood in the way of their attaining it, the audience would be lashed to fury.

He had to meet fury with fury. The government was intimidated into issuing on the thirtieth of October a manifesto that promised a constitution; but the liberal pretensions of the Minister of the Interior were contradicted by the Chief of Police, who had invested the city with troops and commanded them not to spare their cartridges. Not a soldier of the guard was removed, and provocatory attacks began. Trotsky was not to be spared the anti-Semitic rabies which he had escaped on the farm in his youth, always one of the last resorts of a government that can no longer conceal from its people its inability to allow them to live. The police, by dint of bands and vodka, were able to mobilize certain elements of that miserable population, the small shopkeeper, the pickpocket, the barfly, the hungry muzhik adrift in the town, against others as wretched as themselves, in pogroms of which Trotsky was afterwards to put on record a searing description. In these massacres, which took place in a hundred cities, there were known to have been four thousand people killed and ten thousand mutilated.

But the protest of the people against the government seemed for a time to be irresistible. Soviets were being organized in the principal industrial cities, and in some places republics were declared. A railroad strike which had started in Moscow on October 24, involving also the telegraph and telephone lines, had spread in a week to every railroad in the country and paralyzed the whole life of Russia. The peasants burned two thousand estates and sent delegates to a congress in Moscow, which organized a Peasant Union. When an attempt was made at Sebastopol to forbid the sailors to go to political meetings, one of them coolly shot two of his officers, who had given orders not to let the men leave the barracks. Most of the Black Sea fleet and many of the soldiers at Sebastopol revolted, showing that Lenin had been right in his opinion of the possibilities of the *Potyómkin* incident. These revolts combined the protest against specific conditions with the demand for a Constituent Assembly. And in Poland, in Finland, in Latvia, in Georgia, the subject peoples of the Russian Empire were burning Russian school-books and throwing out Russian landlords and officials. Altogether, during the year 1905, there were some two million eight hundred thousand people involved in demonstrations against the tsarist government. The movement spread to other countries, as it had done in 1848, and great strikes took place in Austria, in Germany, in Bulgaria, in Italy and in France.

The Soviet proclaimed the freedom of the press, the censorship having gone by the board, and directed a strike for the eight-hour day and a strike against the execution of the sailors of Kronstadt, who had mutinied, and against the declaration of martial law in Poland. The Soviet helped to organize new unions, distributed relief to the jobless, and found itself—Trotsky bade the Anarchists note well—taking over all sorts of functions that had got out of the control of the government. By the end of November it represented one hundred and forty-seven factories, thirty-four ateliers and sixteen trade unions—some two hundred thousand persons. People were coming to it from all over Russia for redress of grievances that ranged from the oppression of whole provinces to the complaints of old war veterans who had nothing to live on and old Cossacks who had been dismissed from lifelong posts. Finally, the Soviet issued a Financial Manifesto, in which it instructed the people to cease to pay taxes and insist on getting gold or full-weight silver in payments from state institutions, and warned the capitalists of foreign countries that the revolutionary government, if successful, would not recognize the debts of the Tsar.

The Soviet lasted fifty days. The Minister of the Interior gave orders to shoot the peasants and burn their houses. The ships that had rebelled at Sebastopol were bombarded from the fortress, from the city and from the ships that were still amenable to discipline, and those of the crews who were not drowned or torn to bits were slaughtered when they reached the shore. The St. Petersburg Soviet was arrested two days after it had issued its Financial Manifesto. A general strike which was called three days later than the arrest of the Soviet collapsed after a terrible civil war, as bitter as the Paris Commune, around the working-class quarter of Moscow, in which a band of about eight thousand workers, probably only about two thousand of them armed, carried on a war of sniping against the dragoons of the Tsar and stood up to them for nine days, at the end of which time they were crushed by the Semyónovsky Guard, sent down from St. Petersburg for the purpose. The troops had been turning their artillery not merely on the barricades but also on the people's houses. In front of the ruins of one of these houses was set a piece of human flesh on a plate, with a placard that said, "Give your bit for the victims." The soldiers of the Guard, who had been ordered to "Be merciless, make no arrests," burnt up a good part of the workers' quarter and killed something like a thousand people, including women, young children and babies; they dragged the wounded out of the ambulances and finished them off in the streets. Between the day of Father Gapón's plea to the Tsar and the calling of the First Duma on April 27 of the following year, the authorities had slaughtered fourteen thousand, executed a thousand more, wounded twenty thousand, and arrested seventy thousand.

At his trial, Trotsky unleashed a fine speech in the manner of Ferdinand Lassalle that turned defense into accusation. "The prosecution invites you, Gentlemen of the Bench," he said in his peroration, "to declare that the Soviet of Workers' Delegates armed the workers for a direct struggle against the actually existing 'form of government.' If you ask me to answer that question categorically, my reply will be: Yes!—Yes, I accept this indictment, but I accept it on a certain condition. And I do not know whether the public prosecutor will be willing to admit this condition or whether the Court will be willing to agree to it. I ask, what precisely does the indictment mean when it speaks of a certain 'form of government'? Does it mean that we have in Russia a genuine form of government? The government for a long time now has been retrenching itself against the nation; it has retreated into the camp of its police and military forces, and of the Black Hundreds. What we have at this moment in Russia is not a national power: it is an automatic machine used to slaughter the population. I do not know how to define otherwise the governmental machine that is tormenting the living body of our country. And if you tell me that the pogroms, the murders, the burnings, the rapes—if you tell me that all that has happened at Tver, at Rostóv, at Kursk, at Sedlitz—if you tell me that the events that have occurred at Kishinyóv, Odessa, Belostók, represent the form of government of the Russian

Empire—then I shall be willing to recognize, in agreement with the public prosecutor, that we took up arms in October and November for the purpose of struggling directly against the form of government that exists in this Empire of Russia." There is an interesting photograph of Trotsky in his cell in the House of Detention. Short of stature, but with big shoulders and with a shock of black hair, with down-slashing nose and mustache, and eyes, blue and piercing, truly eagle-like, staring out through the ribboned *pince-nez* or perhaps staring into his own fierce spirit, with one leg crossed over the other and his hands clasped on his knee, he sits in his prison not abashed, not indignant, hardly even defiant, but like the head of a great state who has sat still at a time of crisis to give the photographer a moment.

He was sent back to the Arctic Circle, this time for an indefinite sentence; but he succeeded in escaping again before he had even reached his destination. He pretended to be sick at one of the stops, and no precautions were taken to guard him, because anyone would have been sure to be caught trying to get back along the river by which they had come and any other way seemed out of the question. Between the river Ob and the Uráls, there was not a single Russian settlement— nothing but snow and a few huts of natives, who spoke languages of their own; and it was February, the season of blizzards. But Trotsky persuaded a peasant to drive him into the wilderness in a deer-sleigh, and, following a deer track, impossible for horses, they traveled four hundred and thirty miles in a week. He got through the Uráls on horseback, pretending to be an official; then took a train, wired Sedóva to meet him, and got away with her safely to Finland, where Lenin and Mártov were.

In the years immediately following, Trotsky described and analyzed the revolution in a remarkable book called *1905*. The Marxist writing of history by revolutionaries who have actually taken part in it had been inaugurated by Engels in his study of 1848; but Trotsky here has gone beyond Engels. His role has been more important, the subject itself is larger, and he has brought to both role and book a more dramatic sense of life. *1905* is a brilliant forerunner of his history of the great revolution. The Marxist does not yet really dominate events, but he has been able at least, on the one hand, to exert some actual influence on them and, on the other, to set them down in the chronicle fresh from the scene of action. History acted and history written still proceed along separate lines, but they are tending to come together.

Trotsky's Marxist diagnosis of the failure of 1905 was that the Tsar, when it came to the showdown, had been in a position to control the fighting forces, and that this had been due to the predominance in the army and the navy both of the element recruited from the peasantry. These peasants, held together and provided for in the services so that they had not the stimulus of the starving ex-serfs to assert themselves against their superiors, were bound to succumb to their natural passivity and let the technically-trained elements down. He thought, however, that the peculiar situation in Russia had forced the proletariat forward to do the work and claim the position that had been assigned to the bourgeoisie in France at the end of the eighteenth century. The proletariat had produced the Soviet; and the Social Democratic Party, which alone had the clue to what was happening, had inevitably taken the helm.

To decide what the revolution had been heading for and what to steer for when the tide turned again, was the great problem of the Russian Social Democrats, who knew that no western precedent could direct them. The Mensheviks looked forward to a bourgeois democracy, in which capitalism would not be abolished but the government would be run by liberals, with the socialists as an opposition. Lenin believed in a period of dictatorship by a combination of the proletariat and peasantry, which would not, however, be a social revolution but merely a means of setting up a democracy of the western model. Trotsky worked out in Finland a theory of "permanent revolution," which was almost identical with that held later by Lenin, and dominant after the Bolsheviks seized power in 1917. Engels had written in his *Principles of Communism* of 1847 that it would be impossible for a socialist revolution to maintain itself in a single country: the other advanced capitalist countries would have to follow suit. Now Trotsky

insisted that not only would a proletarian revolution in Russia
be unable to remain purely democratic—since it would be necessary to resort to socialism in order to satisfy the workers
at all, in face of the inevitable resistance of the capitalist;
but even that, in view of the primitive economy of Russia,
it would be impossible to have socialism there at all without
socialist revolutions in other countries. Such was the line of
historical development to which Trotsky adjusted his en-
deavors, and he has stuck to it ever since.

His further adventures up to the time of his return to
Russia in 1917 need not concern us here. A figure independent of faction, he completed his international education by
sojourns in Vienna, in Berlin, in Zürich, in Belgrade, in Paris
and in Madrid. He was hunted from country to country after
the beginning of war in 1914: a Russian colonel in the troops
sent to France was assassinated by his soldiers, and Trotsky,
who had been publishing a paper in Paris, was expelled from
France on suspicion. He eventually came to the United States
and had been in New York ten weeks when the new Russian
revolution occurred. He arrived this time rather late because
the British held him a month in Halifax. The Provisional
Government in Russia encouraged the authorities to keep him
there; but the Soviet insisted on his release.

He had, he says, been disillusioned with the Mensheviks
when he worked with them in 1905: though the masses had
pressed them forward, "I observed with astonishment and a
sense of estrangement how every event caught even Mártov,
the most intelligent of them, unawares and threw him into
confusion." In 1917 the two ablest of the Marxists, Trotsky
and Lenin, were brought finally to work together.

4 Trotsky Identifies History with Himself

It will be seen that the Marxist movement had arrived by the beginning of the century at a point where it could provide a base and frame for an ambitious and gifted young man. Trotsky is not, like Marx, a great original thinker; he is not a great original statesman, like Lenin; he was perhaps not even inevitably a great rebel: the revolution was, as it were, the world in which he found himself living. He is one of those men of the first rank who flourish inside a school, neither creating, nor breaking out of, its system.

The young student who had impressed his fellows by the eloquence and force of his reasoning at a time when he did not yet know what he was talking about, because he had at any cost to play a role, found his place in the army of Marxism—in the drama of progress, on the stage of the earth, conceived in a certain way. This is not, of course, to imply that there has been anything insincere or specious about the relation of Trotsky to this role. On the contrary, he has staked upon it not only such things as comfort and peace of mind, but his own life and the lives of his followers and family, and that enjoyment of political power itself which is the only worldly satisfaction that Marxism allows to its true priesthood; and he has learned in the Marxist academy a perfection of revolutionary form and standards of revolutionary honor that seem almost intended to rival that of the Tsar's dueling officers.

There is a passage in which Trotsky tells of the effect on

him of reading the Marx-Engels correspondence which is worth quoting as a description of the tradition that Marx and Engels had founded. Trotsky had been trying to work with the Austrian Social Democrats, who had been both stultified by the Germanic academicism—the workers sometimes addressed them as *"Genosse Herr Doktor,"* and demoralized by the Viennese skepticism: Victor Adler had once shocked Trotsky by declaring that, as for him, he preferred political predictions based on the Apocalypse to those based on Dialectical Materialism.

"In this atmosphere," says Trotsky, "the correspondence between Marx and Engels was one of the books that I needed most, and the one that stood closest to me. It supplied me with the principal and most unfailing test for my own ideas as well as for my entire personal attitude toward the rest of the world. The Viennese leaders of the Social Democracy used the same formulas that I did, but one had only to turn any of them five degrees around on their own axes to discover that we gave quite different meanings to the same concepts. Our agreement was a temporary one, superficial and unreal. The correspondence between Marx and Engels was for me not a theoretical, but a psychological revelation. *Toutes proportions gardées,* I found proof on every page that I was bound to these two by a direct psychological affinity. Their attitude to men and ideas was mine. I guessed what they did not express, shared their sympathies, was indignant and hated as they did. Marx and Engels were revolutionaries through and through. But they had not the slightest trace of sectarianism or asceticism. Both of them, and especially Engels, could at any time say of themselves that nothing human was strange to them. But their revolutionary outlook lifted them always above the hazards of fate and the works of men. Pettiness was incompatible not only with their personalities, but with their presences. Vulgarity could not stick even to the soles of their boots. Their appreciations, sympathies, jests—even when most commonplace—are always touched by the rarefied air of spiritual nobility. They may pass deadly criticism on a man, but they will never deal in tittle-tattle.* They can be ruthless, but not treacherous. For outward glamor, titles or rank they have nothing but a cool contempt. What philistines and vulgarians considered aristocratic in them was really only their revolutionary superiority. Its most important characteristic is a complete and ingrained independence of official public opinion at all times and under all conditions."

But even here we can see that it is the attitude itself, rather than what is to be accomplished through the attitude, that appeals to the imagination of Trotsky: he sees himself as the aristocrat of revolution. Lunachársky tells of Trotsky's exclaiming of the Social Revolutionary leader Chernóv, who had accepted a place in the coalition government before the October revolution: "What contemptible ambitiousness!—to abandon his historic position for a portfolio." But the position of honor is only removed to the end of a longer perspective. "Trotsky," Lunachársky adds, "treasures his historic role, and would undoubtedly be willing to make any personal sacrifice, not by any means excluding that of his life, in order to remain in the memory of mankind with the halo of a genuine revolutionary leader." Bruce Lockhart wrote in his diary in February, 1918, after his first interview with Trotsky: "He strikes me as a man who would willingly die fighting for Russia provided there was a big enough audience to see him do it." And there is somehow the impression created that the cause of human progress stands or falls with Trotsky: Truth's quarrel is Trotsky's quarrel. He tells in his autobiography of his judgment on the boys at his school when he went back after having been suspended over the demonstration against the French teacher. He divided them into three distinct groups: those who had "betrayed" him, those who had "defended" him, and those who had "remained neutral." The first

* This was written before Trotsky had been able to read the complete text of the correspondence, published by the Marx-Engels Institute in Moscow. It did not begin coming out till 1929, the year that *My Life* was finished. But of course the very expurgation to which Bebel and Bernstein subjected the letters is evidence of the ideal of self-discipline that the Marxists had come to set themselves.

group he "cut completely"; the second group he cultivated. "Such, one might say," he goes on, "was the first political test I underwent. These were the groups that resulted from that episode: the tale-bearers and the envious at one pole, the frank courageous boys at the other, and the neutral vacillating mass in the middle. These three groups never quite disappeared even during the years that followed. I met them again and again in my life, in the most varied circumstances." So even the reader of Trotsky inevitably finds himself involved in something in the nature of an issue of personal allegiance to the author. Trotsky is not content, as Lenin was, to present the course of events, which he or another in this or that case may have interpreted more or less correctly: he must justify himself in connection with them.

We who of recent years have seen the State that Trotsky helped to build in a phase combining the butcheries of the Robespierre Terror with the corruption and reaction of the Directory, and Trotsky himself figuring dramatically in the role of Gracchus Babeuf, may be tempted to endow him with qualities which actually he does not possess and with principles which he has expressly repudiated. We have seen the successor of Lenin undertake a fabulous rewriting of the whole history of the Revolution in order to cancel out Trotsky's part; pursue Trotsky from country to country, persecuting even his children and hounding them to their deaths; and at last, in faked trials and confessions more degrading to the human spirit than the frank fiendishness of Iván the Terrible, try to pin upon Trotsky the blame of all the mutinies, mistakes and disasters that have harassed his administration— till he has made the world conscious of Trotsky as the accuser of Stalin's own bad conscience, as if the Soviet careerists of the thirties were unable to deny the socialist ideal without trying to annihilate the moral authority of this one homeless and hunted man. It is not Trotsky alone who has created his role: his enemies have given it a reality that no mere self-dramatization could have compassed. And as the fires of the Revolution have died down in the Soviet Union at a time when the systems of thought of the West were already in an advanced state of decadence, he has shone forth like a veritable pharos, rotating a long shaft of light on the seas and the reefs all around.

But we must try to see the man inside the role and to examine his real tendencies and doctrines.

The boy who came back to the farm from Odessa with his book learning and his new glasses, his new habits of cleanliness and his new city clothes, found himself cut off from his kindred, a creature of another order, who felt that he was superior to them; and the relationship established here seems to have persisted all Trotsky's life in connection with human beings in general. He tells us in *My Life* with that candor that sets him off sharply from the ordinary public figure, that his first emotions of "social protest" consisted of "indignation over injustice" rather than of "sympathy for the downtrodden," and "even when my revolutionary ideas were already taking shape, I would catch myself in an attitude of mistrust of action by the masses, taking a bookish, abstract and therefore skeptical view of the revolution. I had to combat all this within myself, by my thinking, my reading, but mainly by means of experience, until the elements of psychic inertia had been conquered within me." Lunachársky has said, and his impression is amply confirmed by other persons who have known Trotsky, that "a tremendous imperiousness and a kind of inability or unwillingness to be at all caressing or attentive to people, an absence of that charm which always surrounded Lenin, condemned Trotsky to a certain loneliness." It is characteristic of Trotsky that—in an article on a book by Céline—he should argue, as no other of the great Marxists would have done, in favor of the revolutionary movement on the ground that it "leads humanity from out the dark night of the circumscribed I."

Possessing neither Lenin's gift for establishing personal relations of confidence nor the cunning political sense which has made it possible for Stalin to build up his machine and manipulate public opinion, Trotsky has ended by finding himself today in essentially the same position that he occupied between the split of 1903 and the revolution of 1905, and then again after 1905 up to the time of his return to Russia

PART III: TROTSKY AND HISTORY 433

in 1917: that of an independent Marxist with a few devoted
followers but no real popular constituency behind him. It is
when he has been brought by a moment of crisis to a position
of unquestioned authority and is free to act for himself that
he becomes powerful as a political force, for he has the genius
of making people do things. As Commissar for War in 1918
and 19, he managed, traveling in his armored train, to speed
so fast from front to front, to appeal to the soldiers with such
passion, to telegraph so promptly for supplies, to write and
despatch so many resonant press stories, to put pressure so
effectively on the military experts who had been trained
under the old regime to lend their skill to the Revolution, and
to catch and shoot so many disaffected officers, that the sixteen Soviet armies, feeling behind them this demon of will,
held their fronts against the Kolcháks and Deníkins and saved
the Revolution; and when Yudénich was advancing on
Petrograd and Lenin was in favor of abandoning it, when the
regimental commander had given his men the order to fall
back and his troops were running away and had already
reached division headquarters, Trotsky mounted the first
horse he could find and, chasing one soldier after another
with his orderly behind him brandishing a pistol and shouting,
"Courage, boys: Comrade Trotsky is leading you!", compelled
the whole regiment to turn and recover the positions it had
left; the commander now appeared at the most dangerous
points and was wounded in both legs; the men attacked the
tanks with bayonets. And in politics itself it is evidently true,
as Bruce Lockhart said years ago, that Trotsky is never so
formidable as when he has been driven into a tight place.
Certainly his stature never appeared so imposing as at the
time when, denied asylum by all the nations of Europe, he
was forced to defend himself against the murderous persecution of Moscow.

And so the drive of the ideal behind all this is less the
desire for human happiness than the enthusiasm for human
culture, for that "first truly human culture," as he says in
Literature and Revolution, which socialism is eventually to
make possible, that blazes out from the shut-in man to illuminate this twilight of society. And so it is the *theory* of

Marxism, the diagram of social development, rather than the immediate vicissitudes of the lives of his fellow creatures, that is present to Trotsky's mind. The Marxist must act, of course; but he cannot consent to do so unless he can understand the situation and explain his own intervention in terms of Marxist theory. "The feeling," he writes, "of the supremacy of general over particular, of law over fact, of theory over personal experience, took root in my mind at an early age and gained increasing strength as the years advanced. . . . [This feeling] became an integral part of my literary and political work. The dull empiricism, the unashamed cringing worship of the fact which is so often only imaginary, and falsely interpreted at that, were odious to me. Beyond the facts, I looked for laws. . . . In every sphere, barring none, I felt that I could move and act only when I held in my hand the thread of the general."

At its worst, this results in the substitution of a kind of logical demonstration—recalling his mathematical aptitude—for the appreciation of men in their milieux, as is likely to be the case particularly with certain of his political predictions, written remote from the seat of operations. At its best—when he is examining events that have already taken place, so that the foundation of reality is given—it produces historical studies of extraordinary subtlety and solidity. Trotsky differs from the typical Marxist pedant, with his spinning of abstract "theses," in that the dominance in his mind of Marxist theory still leaves the play of his intelligence pretty free: one finds in his writings not only the Marxist analysis of mass behavior but a realistic observation—in regard to personality particularly—in the tradition of the great Russian writers; and not only a sense of development and form which gives dignity to the least of his articles but also a vein of apt imagery which lends beauty to even his polemics and makes some passages in his books unforgettable. 1905, *The History of the Russian Revolution, My Life,* the biography of Lenin, and *Literature and Revolution* are probably a part of our permanent literature.

"The social-revolutionary radicalism," he goes on in the passage already quoted, "which has become the permanent pivot for my whole inner life grew out of this intellectual enmity toward the striving for petty ends, toward out-and-out pragmatism, and toward all that is ideologically without form and theoretically ungeneralized." Yes, but a permanent pivot in the center of one's inner life is also a stake beyond which one cannot range. Trotsky has told us how in the course of his formative years he several times lengthened his tether: he had "resisted" first revolution, then Alexándra Lvóvna and Marxism, then art. And up to 1917 he had also resisted Lenin. Yet for letting out the rope to the stake, one does not the less remain confined to the circle. In the most serious undertakings of mankind, we are forced to distrust the mentality which resists having its pattern upset: there is always the danger that it might fail to take account of the emergence of important new factors. It has been the burden of all Trotsky's later writings and the chief basis of his self-justification that from the beginning of the Revolution he has been orientated toward Lenin (he admits, of course, his conflicts with Lenin, but the fact that he should attempt to minimize them shows his need for a fixed "pivot" of authority); and since Lenin's death, toward the memory of Lenin. And Trotsky's Marxism is as dogmatic as Lenin's. He is as far from the exploratory spirit that distinguished Marx and Engels; and, being essentially a writer and a doctrinaire rather than like Lenin an inspired worker in the immediate materials of humanity, the implications of this dogmatic Marxism are all the more clearly exposed in his work.

Let us see what these implications are. First of all: there has been, so far as I know, no other first-rate Marxist for whom the Marxist conception of History, derived from the Hegelian Idea, plays so frankly teleological a role as it does in the work of Trotsky. Here are some references from his book on the 1905 revolution, written soon after the events it describes. "If the prince was not succeeding in peacefully regenerating the country, he was accomplishing with remarkable effectiveness the task of a more general order for which history had placed him at the head of the government: the destruction of the political illusions and the prejudices of the middle class." "History used the fantastic plan of Gapón for the purpose of arriving at its ends, and it only remained for the priest to

sanction with the priestly authority its [history's] revolutionary conclusions." "When one rereads the correspondence of
our marvelous classics [Marx, Engels and Lassalle], who from
the height of their observatories—the youngest in Berlin, and
his two ranking seniors in the very center of world capitalism,
London—observed the political horizon with never-relaxing attention, taking note of every incident, every phenomenon, that
might indicate the Revolution's approach; when one rereads
these letters, in which the revolutionary lava is boiling up,
when one breathes this atmosphere of an expectancy impatient but never weary, one is moved to hate that cruel dialectic of history which, in order to attain momentary ends,
attaches to Marxism *raisonneurs* totally devoid of talent in
either their theories or their psychology, who oppose their
'reason' to [what they regard] as the revolutionary madness."
History, then, with its dialectical Trinity, had chosen Prince
Svyatopólk-Mirsky to disillusion the middle class, had pro-
pounded revolutionary conclusions which it had compelled
Father Gapón to bless, and will cruelly discredit and destroy
certain Pharisees and Sadducees of Marxism before it summons the boiling lava of the Judgment. These statements make
no sense whatever unless one substitutes for the words
history and the *dialectic of history* the words *Providence*
and *God*. And this Providential power of history is present in all the writing of Trotsky. John Jay Chapman said
of Browning that God did duty in his work as noun, verb,
adjective, adverb, interjection and preposition; and the same
is true of History with Trotsky. Of late, in his solitude and
exile, this History, an austere spirit, has seemed actually to
stand behind his chair as he writes, encouraging, admonish-
ing, approving, giving him the courage to confound his ac-
cusers, who have never seen History's face.

What it may mean in moments of action to feel History
towering at one's elbow with her avenging sword in her hand
is shown in the remarkable scene at the first congress of the
Soviet dictatorship after the success of the October insurrection of 1917, when Trotsky, with the contempt and indignation
of a prophet, read Mártov and his followers out of meeting.
"You are pitiful isolated individuals," he cried at this height

of the Bolshevik triumph. "You are bankrupt; your role is played out. Go where you belong from now on—into the rubbish-can of history!" These words are worth pondering for the light they throw on the course of Marxist politics and thought. Observe that the merging of yourself with the onrush of the current of history is to save you from the ignoble fate of being a "pitiful isolated individual"; and that the failure so to merge yourself will relegate you to the rubbish-can of history, where you can presumably be of no more use. Today, though we may agree with the Bolsheviks that Mártov was no man of action, his croakings over the course they had adopted seem to us full of far-sighted intelligence. He pointed out that proclaiming a socialist regime in conditions different from those contemplated by Marx would not realize the results that Marx expected; that Marx and Engels had usually described the dictatorship of the proletariat as having the form, for the new dominant class, of a democratic republic, with universal suffrage and the popular recall of officials; that the slogan "All power to the Soviets" had never really meant what it said and that it had soon been exchanged by Lenin for "All power to the Bolshevik Party." There sometimes turn out to be valuable objects cast away in the rubbish-can of history—things that have to be retrieved later on. From the point of view of the Stalinist Soviet Union, that is where Trotsky himself is today; and he might well discard his earlier assumption that an isolated individual must needs be "pitiful" for the conviction of Dr. Stockman in Ibsen's *Enemy of the People* that "the strongest man is he who stands most alone."

Then the confusions of the Marxist morality become more and more obvious in Trotsky as its conceptions are brought into question, no longer merely by the mild Kantianism of Bernstein, but by the harsh and inescapable critique of the development of events in that State which the Marxist morality founded. I quote from the first volume of his biography of Lenin, published in French in 1936, in which these matters are not yet being specifically debated. Trotsky writes of Lenin's mother, for example, that, "An inexhaustible spring of moral force would make it possible, after every fresh blow of fate, for her to reëstablish her interior equilibrium and to sustain those who needed her support. Moral genius, not supplemented with other gifts, does not make itself conspicuous at a distance: it can only be seen at close range. But if there were not in the world such generous feminine natures, life would not be worth living." And when he tells the story of the lie that the boy Vladímir confessed to, he remarks, "Thus we see that the categorical imperative of morality was by no means so foreign to Vladímir as has subsequently been asserted by Lenin's innumerable enemies." Yet later on he says of Anna's statement that her brother Alexander was incapable of lying and that this was vividly brought out at his trial: "One is tempted to add, What a pity! Such a mentality, in a merciless social struggle, leaves you defenceless in politics. However the austere moralists may reason, professional liars that they are, lying is the reflection of social contradictions, but also sometimes a weapon for fighting them. It is impossible by a mere individual moral effort to escape from the web of the social lie." Finally, he explains, apropos of the charge of "amoralism" brought against Lenin by one of his early opponents: "Now, it appears that this amoralism consisted in accepting any means as admissible so long as it led to the end. Yes: Ulyánov was not an admirer of that morality of the Popes or of Kant, which is supposed to be appointed to regulate our lives from the height of the starry heavens. The purposes he was pursuing were so great and super-personal that he openly subordinated moral standards to them."

Two years later, after the Moscow trials of March, 1938, he wrote a long article called *Their Morals and Ours* (*New International,* June, 1938) against persons who had been asserting that the systematic falsehoods of the Kremlin and its remorseless extermination of the old Bolsheviks had grown quite logically out of the Jesuitical policy pursued by the Bolsheviks themselves. This article must be regarded as the *locus classicus* of Trotsky's ideas on this subject. What do we find in it? We find first of all that the Jesuits have been maligned. The notion that they ever believed that the end could justify *any* means is a malicious invention of their opponents: what they did hold was that a given means may be neither bad nor good in itself, but may become either through the purpose it serves. Thus it is a criminal act to shoot a man "with the aim of violation or murder," but an act of virtue to shoot a mad dog which is about to attack a child. "The Jesuits represented a militant organization, strictly centralized, aggressive, and dangerous not only to their enemies, but to their allies as well." They were superior to the other Catholic priests of their day because they were "more consistent, bolder and more perspicacious." It was only in so far as they became less Jesuits, less "warriors of the Church," that is, in so far as they were perverted into "bureaucrats," that their order degenerated.

Thus such means as lying and killing are morally indifferent in themselves. Both are necessary in time of war, and it depends on which side we want to win whether we approve them or reprobate them. Trotsky illustrates this phenomenon strikingly, and evidently without being aware of it, in the very essay under discussion, by bitterly complaining of the "hypocrisy" and the "official cult of mendacity" of the Kremlin and denouncing one of his calumniators of the GPU as a "bourgeois without honor or conscience." When the Bolsheviks calumniated the Mensheviks, then, the reader is moved to inquire, this did not imply anything derogatory to their conscience or their honor? One finds the answer in another passage: "The question does not even lie in which of the warring camps caused or itself suffered the greatest number of victims. History has different yardsticks for the cruelty of the Northerners and the cruelty of the Southerners in the [American] Civil War. A slave-owner who through cunning and violence shackles a slave in chains, and a slave who through cunning and violence breaks the chains—let not the contemptible eunuchs tell us that they are equals before a court of morality!" There is, then, a court of morality above the warring classes, and this court is presided over by, precisely again, the Goddess History. For anyone but a Marxist it would appear as if history in the ordinary sense of the description or study of past events might well approach without moral animus the casualties of both North and South in the American Civil War. Should the historian, even in assuming that one side in a given conflict represents a progressive force and the other a retrograde one, have "different yardsticks" for the heroism or cruelty of the one and of the other? In using the word *cruelty* itself, Trotsky implies a moral judgment which is independent of partisan feelings and belongs to the common language. (It is, however, worth noting that the Russian word for *cruelly*, used in a generalized sense, as in the passage quoted from Lenin on page 398, is likely to be translated into English as "severely." *Severely* has no moral connotations, whereas *cruelly* has; but the element of cruelty in life had been, as it still is, in Russia so much a matter of course that it almost loses its moral implications. Where the conflict becomes so acute, it is difficult for either side to admit common concepts of morality. What is true here is also true of the other "means" with which Trotsky is dealing. A foreigner who has been lied to by Russian officials over a long enough period of time will end by losing his native candor.)

It would be possible to work out a point of view which would take care of these contradictions, which would explain in what proportion our notions of good and evil are universal and in what proportion they are determined by class, much more adequately than Trotsky has done here; I have tried to suggest how it might be put at the end of my chapter on the Dialectic. But it could perhaps never really be developed by anyone who, as Trotsky is, was trying to fight the class struggle himself. The shell of party polemics, that convention which is in itself an abrogation of peacetime relations and an obstacle to serious discussion, interposes itself here between Trotsky and the real problems at issue. There is a good deal of the mere argument *ad hominem*—or rather, argument to social class—of the kind exploited first by Marx and Engels in the *Communist Manifesto*. In reply to the objection that communism "repudiates, instead of refashioning them, religion and morality," the "eternal truths . . . that are common to all social systems," the founders of Marxism retort that since these social systems are all built on exploitation, they may well arrive at similar values; and in answer to such complaints as that communism destroys marriage and the family, throw back into the teeth of their opponents the disintegration of family relations produced by industrial work. In this way the question of whether, and if so, to what degree, certain qualities and types of behavior may be agreed to be desirable in themselves by human beings of different classes—this question never gets discussed at all; and Trotsky meets it here even less squarely than the *Communist Manifesto*: Who are these creatures who dare to probe our morality? They are the "petty pickpockets of history," etc. The very title *Their Morals and Ours* attempts to divert attention by putting the debate on a polemical plane.

But again he invokes Lenin: "The 'amoralism' of Lenin," he says, "that is, his rejection of super-class morals, did not hinder him from remaining faithful to one and the same ideal throughout his whole life; from devoting his whole being to the cause of the oppressed; from displaying the highest conscientiousness in the sphere of ideas and the highest fearlessness in the sphere of action, from maintaining an attitude untainted by the least superiority to the 'ordinary' worker, to a defenseless woman, to a child. Does it not seem that 'amoralism' in the given case is only a pseudonym for higher human morality?" It is true, of course, that Lenin followed a moral logic of his own; but he lived it, and we can see how he was torn in feeling, if not perplexed in decision, by its difficulty. Even less than Trotsky did Lenin examine it or try to formulate it; yet today the best that Trotsky can do is to point into the past toward Lenin—that is, to show that there was once a great Bolshevik who was a humane and dedicated person.

It cannot be said that Trotsky has shown himself particularly humane. It seems to have been principally the planning side of socialism, the opportunity for increasing efficiency, and the ruthless side of Marxism, that attracted him when he was actually in power. The whole Bolshevik dictatorship, of course, was fundamentally undemocratic. With a people quite untrained in political democracy, it was inevitable that a revolutionary government should itself have to resort to despotism. And it is true that during the years of civil war the brutal methods of war-time imposed themselves as a matter of life or death for the Revolution itself. It is true that the first impulses of the Bolsheviks to be generous with their political enemies brought extremely disillusioning results: when they had released the monarchist general Krásnov, after his raid on Petrograd, in return for his word of honor that he would cease to fight the Bolshevik regime, he immediately returned to the attack. But through this crisis, which called forth Trotsky's best, he did not respond in any very sensitive way to the feelings and needs of the people. Read the pamphlet, *The Defense of Terrorism*, published in 1920, in reply to a pamphlet by Kautsky that attacked the Bolshevik regime, in which he defends both the Bolshevik shooting of military and political enemies and his own project for a compulsory labor army. True it was written "in the car of a military train and amid the flames of civil war" and Trotsky begs us to bear this in mind; but what we feel in it is the terrific force of a will to domination and regimentation with no evidence of any sympathy for the hardships of the dominated and regimented.

For when he had whipped the Red Army into shape at the cost of many drumhead executions and definitely routed the Whites, he proceeded, against Lenin's advice, to turn his admirable military machine into a conscript army of labor. But the soldiers, who had stuck it out against the enemies of the Revolution, began to vanish when they were put on public works. So, also, the Commissar of War was opposed to allowing trade unions, insisting that since trade unions were by definition class weapons against the employees and since they were living in a workers' republic, they had no longer any need for such instruments. Lenin pointed out to him that the Bolshevik regime was not yet really wholly a workers' republic, but rather—since the workers were to a considerable extent directed by officials not of working-class origin—a "workers' republic with bureaucratic distortions."

The inauguration of the New Economic Policy (at the beginning of 1921), which allowed a certain amount of private exchange and let up on the requisitions from the peasants, relieved the whole situation by restoring the old motive of personal gain in place of the ideal of communist discipline. It is to the credit of Trotsky's sagacity that he had advocated the adoption of such measures in February, 1920, at a time when they were rejected by Lenin. But there had in the meantime taken place an incident which, instead of being eventually forgotten, has come to take on a more sinister significance in view of subsequent developments in Russia. In February, 1921, the sailors of the Kronstadt fortress, who had played an heroic part in the 1917 revolution, rebelled in behalf of the peasants, and troops were sent against them by the Bolsheviks and the mutiny was ruthlessly extinguished. Trotsky has recently defended his action on the ground that the personnel at Kronstadt were no longer the heroes of October and that the mutiny meant counter-revolution. But, after all, it was thought proper immediately afterwards to accede to the mutineers' demands by the establishment of the N.E.P., and in the meantime—as we learn from other sources—the men's families had been taken as hostages, and the sailors themselves, with such women as were with them, including the prostitutes of the barracks, had been massacred with every circumstance of ferocity by that child of the Tsar's Okhrána and father of Stalin's GPU, the Cheká. One remembers Trotsky's satisfaction at the time of the 1905 revolution when the action of the St. Petersburg Soviet in connection with a similar mutiny on the part of the Kronstadt sailors prevented their execution by the Tsar; and one realizes that Trotsky's enthusiasm for freedom is less a positive than a negative affair, that it is expressed mainly in indignation against other people who will not let his side be free. Even in *Literature and Revolution* (of 1924), where Trotsky is dealing with a field that is more or less his own, and despite the range of his appreciation and his opposition to the more vulgar kind of attempt to break literature to the yoke of party doctrine, he is trying to bring the other Soviet writers inside his Marxist intellectual circle or chiding them when they stray.

Lenin was moved to rebuke Trotsky during the period of which I have spoken and which was the occasion of their only serious falling-out, for his addiction to "intellectualistic formulas that fail to take into account the practical side of the question"; and his "testament," Lenin's notes to the Central Committee written down not long before his death, in indicating Trotsky as "the ablest man" on the Central Committee, he criticizes his "too far-reaching confidence and a disposition to be far too much attracted by the purely administrative side of affairs." And it is as a hero of the faith in Reason that Trotsky must figure for us. He tells us in his autobiography how he used to be driven mad at school by hearing boys who were studying science talk about " 'unlucky' Monday or about meeting a priest crossing the road," and how he would "get all excited and use harsh words" (as he was to do in the above case, with Kautsky) when he could not convince the people at Yanóvka that the measure of the area of a trapezoidal field which he got quickly by applying Euclid was more accurate than the different one which they arrived at after "many weary hours" of measuring it bit by bit. But Marx, after all, is not Euclid; you may be able to calculate to some extent in moments of revolution what Trotsky is so fond of describing as the parallelogram of social forces; but to mold the living growth of a society you must be aware of what people want. Trotsky has illustrated by his whole career in a very instructive way what is valid and what is blind in this rationalistic aspect of Marxism.

5 Lenin Identifies Himself with History

It had been one of the features of Bernstein's "revisionism" that he sought to discredit the doctrine of Marx and Engels laid down in the *Communist Manifesto* that "the proletariat has no fatherland"—a situation which they themselves, as we have seen, were very far from consistently assuming—by pointing out that the German worker was now a citizen represented in the Reichstag and owed his country certain obligations that must come before his duty to his class. Engels himself in the early nineties, when the prospect was beginning to loom of a general European war, had been in favor of having the German Social Democrats approve the voting of war-credits by the Reichstag, in case of an attack by Russia, and the international congresses of this period were disturbed by a conflict between him and a Dutch ex-clergyman named Nieuwenhuis, the head of the small Dutch party, who was able to enlist a minority for the policy of calling upon the workers of all countries, in the event of a European war, to refuse to serve in the army and to declare a general strike. But Engels, with characteristic optimism, thought that the great social revolution would arrive before the great war; and he began to have doubts when he realized—he had never been able to accept the ascendancy of Prussia—that the government's idea of strengthening the army involved enlarging the officers' corps. In 1893, he published a series of articles, in which he advocated the gradual liquidation of the German standing army and the substitution of a popular army based on universal service.

In August, 1914, the Social Democratic members of the Reichstag voted for war-credits to a man. Only two years before, the Second International had drafted a resolution opposing the participation of the working class in any kind of war, since a war could only mean for them "shooting one another for the sake of the capitalists' profits, for the sake of the ambitions of dynasties, for the accomplishment of the aims of secret diplomatic treaties," and declaring that it would become the duty of socialists to take advantage of such a crisis for rousing the people against the capitalist order.

The effect on Lenin was terrific. At first he refused to believe it. When he read the news in the *Vorwärts,* the organ of the German party, he thought it was a forgery by the government. Then he learned that Plekhánov in Paris had been urging the Russian exiles there to enlist in the French army. He kept saying, "Can Plekhánov have turned traitor, too?" and tried to explain it to himself by the fact that he had once been in the army. And at last he had to reckon with the fact that Karl Kautsky, the intellectual heir to the tradition of Marx and Engels, a man whom Lenin had respected, had succumbed to the patriotic cause to the tune of a patter of sophistries that were a scandal to the Marxist movement. The leaders of the Second International were jumping for places in the war governments.

Krúpskaya says that that incident of his boyhood at the time of his brother's arrest—the refusal to a man of their liberal friends to go along with his mother on her journey, had made a permanent impression on Lenin and imbued him with a lifelong bitterness over the cowardice of liberals in a pinch. This bitterness had returned in his anger and scorn at the Constitutional Democrats of 1905, who, as deputies in the series of Dumas that the Tsar had been dismissing like footmen, had turned from liberal to roundly reactionary; and now it was as if the disillusion of those days in Simbírsk were repeated. And as that earliest crisis of his life, in isolating him among his associates and loading him with a new responsibility, had brought him to maturity at seventeen, so the desertion of 1914 forced upon him again the position of head of an outlawed group and inaugurated a new phase in his life. "The experi-

ence of the war," he is writing in June, 1915, in his pamphlet
on *The Collapse of the Second International*, "like the experience of every crisis in history, of every great disaster and every
sudden turn in human life, stuns and shatters some, *but*
[italics Lenin's] it enlightens and hardens others."

He grew thin, so that his features stood out; his old buoy-
ancy and confidence gave way to something like settled gloom.
That "virile good nature" of which Trotsky speaks turned into
something grimmer, which remained with him up to the end
and which made some find his amusement uncomfortable: he
had a way of bursting out laughing when he heard of anything
particularly atrocious that had happened. The mere strong
language of Russian party debating, which has always a
slightly burlesque flavor for the foreigner, turns into the most
deadly earnest. When Plekhánov comes to lecture in Lau-
sanne, preaching the defense of the fatherland, Lenin goes
to confront him, speaks calmly but with a face pale with passion, and will not shake hands with him or call him comrade.
He damns Kautsky with invective more blasting—calling him
hypocrite, prostitute, coward—than any that he has ever allowed himself to an old companion-in-arms. He made short
work—as it was his habit to do—of those precedents from Marx
and Engels which his opponents were quite correct in invoking. No, the situation then had been different: when Marx
and Engels had supported a war, it had been always because
it represented the interest of the bourgeois revolution, which
had not yet fully triumphed over feudalism; whereas the bourgeoisie today was in its decadence, and the socialist revolution
was due. And he wrote, in the spring of 1916, a little work
called *Imperalism: The Last Stage of Capitalism*, in which he
brings Marx up to date by describing the growth of monopoly
and the domination of finance-capital; the development of
the export of capital abroad in place of the earlier export
of commodities; the division of the exploitable world between
England, Germany, France and the United States—these four
powers now owning between them nearly eighty per cent of
the world's finance-capital, and the first three controlling more
than eighty per cent of the total colonial area; the increasingly
parasitic relationship of the mother countries to the colonies;

and the inevitability, when all this had been accomplished—the Marxist economic contradictions having become continually more acute—of the nations' having finally come to clinches in a gigantic death-struggle for profits. The big profits had been used in the meantime as bait for an upper layer of workers, and the socialists had turned imperialist, too.

In the September of 1915 and the April of the following year, the socialists who opposed the war managed to get together for two conferences held in Switzerland. They were obscure enough, Lenin and his allies, hunted, scattered and few, behind the roaring holocaust of patriotism. Lenin was back where he had been in 1904: in a flatly defeated minority. And from his solitude he derived a new dignity.

He and Krúpskaya had been in Cracow in the August of 1914, and they had seen from their window the casualties being brought back from the battle of Krasnik. They had watched the wives and families of the dead and dying running along after the stretchers, afraid to recognize those they were looking for. You will find in the writings of Lenin little expression of humanitarian feeling. One of the strangest and most characteristic incidents in the whole of his extraordinary career occurred at the time of his funeral, when Krúpskaya began a brief speech as follows: "Comrades, in the course of these days when I have been standing by Vladímir Ilyích's coffin, I have been in my mind over the whole of his life, and this is what I want to say to you. He loved with a deep love all the workers, all the oppressed. He himself never said this—nor did I; I should probably never have spoken about it at any less solemn moment." He himself had never spoken of this, and yet it is only now that we take account of the fact. His language has been all indignation, insistence that action be taken; he has assumed that the cruelties of the tsardom, the diseases of the industrial system, the slaughters of the great war, did not need any eloquence of appeal to persuade people that they must not continue. He is the most male of all these reformers because he never weeps: his attitude begins with impatience. "I have never," declares Gorky, "met in Russia, the country where the inevitability of suffering is preached as the general road to salvation, nor have I ever known of any man anywhere, who hated, despised and loathed all unhappiness, grief, and suffering so deeply and strongly as Lenin did. . . . He was particularly great, in my opinion, precisely because . . . of his burning faith that suffering was not an essential and unavoidable part of life, but an abomination that people ought to and could sweep away."

It was this that now made him harsh, and that later, under the stress of the civil war, led him to accept the rigors of the new machine that had to govern Russia. Trotsky tells of Lenin's misgivings in the first days of the Revolution over a military order that looters should be executed on the spot, the first infliction of the death penalty by the Bolsheviks; but afterwards, when some emissary from the West asked questions about political executions, Lenin retorted: "Who wants to know?—the statesmen who have just sent sixteen million men to their deaths?" He said to Gorky one day in the country, when they had been talking to some Soviet children: "These children will have happier lives than we had. A good deal that we have had to go through they will never know. There will not be so much cruelty in their lives."

He lost himself now in events, seems to have been conscious of himself solely as the agent of an historical force. Those who knew him have noted with surprise his complete lack of self-importance. Angélica Balabánova says that she cannot remember when she first met him in exile, that "externally he seemed the most colorless of all the revolutionary leaders." Nor did the shift from the Zürich library to the dictatorship of the Kremlin release a love of power for its own sake or an impulse to play the great man. Bruce Lockhart, when he saw Lenin after the October Revolution, thought "at the first glance" that he "looked more like a provincial grocer than a leader of men. Yet in those steely eyes there was something that arrested my attention, something in that quizzing, half-contemptuous, half-smiling look which spoke of boundless self-confidence and conscious superiority." And Clara Zetkin tells a story of his receiving a delegation of German Communists: accustomed to the Marxists of the Reichstag, with their frock-coats and their official inflation, these Germans had expected something else; and Lenin kept his appointment so punctually, entered the room so unobtrusively and talked to them so naturally and simply, that it never occurred to them they were meeting Lenin. The Berlin doctor who was called in at his last illness has left an account which indicates the habitual asceticism implied by Lenin's identification of himself with his purpose: "I saw him first in his bedroom," says Dr. Klemperer, "a large plain apartment which contained only an old iron servant's bed, a plain desk, many wooden chairs and a table covered with books. There were no decorations or pictures on the wall, no rugs. . . . When I saw him again in June of the same year, 1922, he was established in the magnificent country estate of the former Mayor of Moscow, where he hoped to find rest and relaxation. But he did not live in the fine house itself; instead, he lay in a poor room of a small house near-by, which had been used by servants. I was forced to argue with him that his health would suffer in this room before he would permit himself to be taken to the larger house."

The only feature of Lenin's appearance that people do seem to have found striking was his small hazel eyes, which are described as sharp, quick and glittering. These eyes now looked out on Europe through the lens that Marx and Engels had polished, and brought sharply into focus through it the real conflict behind the fumes of the battle. The writer will make no attempt to re-create the psychological atmosphere of this period of the War, which most of his readers will be able to remember. The nationalism of our time, at once debased and inflamed, has since, in particular countries, run to manifestations more fantastic; but it has never raged so universally or so completely to the extinction of reason. Lenin concentrated on Europe an attention, objective and yet taut with expectation, that studied to locate the controls of a mechanism which most could not see. He could look into the big businesses, the banks, the parliaments, the foreign offices, the colonial populations, the factories, the fighting forces, and see the latent antagonisms of classes, the opposition, eventually to prove fatal, between the processes of combination, on the one hand, the monopolies and the international trusts, and, on the other, the processes of disruption themselves, the differentiations of both class and nationality. An American who saw Lenin in the Kremlin tells of the eagerness with which he would pick up a fresh newspaper and read it "as if he were burning a hole in it." "His words always gave one the impression," says Gorky, "of the physical pressure of an irresistible truth"; he seemed to speak "not of his own will, but by the will of history."

He does not live in theory like Trotsky: he sees always a real situation, and he seizes a situation wherever he is able to take hold, without caring whether his story hangs together. Nor is history quite the anthropomorphized spirit, at once Recording and Guardian Angel, that it has become for Trotsky. We find Lenin identifying history with his will, as when he writes to the Central Committee on the eve of the October Revolution: "History will not forgive delay by revolutionists who could at once be victorious." We even hear of—what seems to happen with every Marxist, when events get beyond his control—his tending to put off on history, as though it were a force outside himself, developments for which he does not want to feel responsible: "History is a cruel stepmother, and when it retaliates, it stops at nothing," he said to Gorky— gloomily, notes Gorky, and closing his eyes, after a sidelong glance—when the latter had told him a story of a princess who had just tried to drown herself in the Neva. But in general what is in Lenin's head is actual places and people, contingencies immediately to be reckoned with.

He had given so little thought to the ultimate goals of social- ism and the development of society under dictatorship that when, feeling the revolution imminent—in February, 1916— he tries to formulate some notions on the subject, he can only look it up in Marx and Engels and repeat the meager indica- tions of the *Critique of the Gotha Program*, in respect to in- equality of wages and the withering-away of the State. There is nothing in *State and Revolution* except the qualified utopi- anism of his masters. He himself is still sufficiently utopian to imagine that the bureaucratic duties, the "bookkeeping and control," that will be "necessary for the smooth and correct functioning of the first phase of Communist society" have al- ready been "simplified by capitalism to the utmost, till they have become the extraordinarily simple operations of watching, recording and issuing receipts, within the reach of anybody who can read and write and knows the first four arithmetical rules," and that these functions may be easily discharged by the "majority of the citizens," who will "keep such accounts and maintain such control over the capitalists, now converted into employees, and over the intellectual gentry who still retain capitalist habits." It is characteristic of Lenin that he should have waited till the very last moment before turning his attention to these matters, and that he should not have had time to finish the book in which he attempted to discuss them. *State and Revolution* was written in the interval when he was in hiding in Finland in the summer of 1917, between the time of his first advent in Russia and the time of his return in the fall, and was interrupted by the events of October. "It is pleasanter and more profitable," he wrote when he brought it out after the seizure of power, "to live through the experience of a revolution than to write about it."

Yet Lenin's failure to elaborate a social philosophy or to give much thought to prefiguring the future, implies no lack of imagination. It is simply that the imagination for history has been transferred to practical politics, and hence is mainly preoccupied with the present. Lenin's conception of this present has unquestionably proved itself one of the great imaginative influences of our age—a world-view which gives life a meaning and in which every man is assigned a place. After all, even Stalin, the Georgian bandit-politician, who started on the road to power with a few Marxist texts in his head, thought for a time he was a character in Lenin.

Isolated among the Socialists of Western Europe, Lenin had, nevertheless, an assurance of support in Russia.

A revival of the revolutionary movement had begun in 1912. In the February of that year a critical incident had taken place in the Lena goldfields. These fields, from which huge profits were made, lay far above the Arctic Circle, in the region of Trotsky's first exile, where there were six months of night in winter and a plague of mosquitoes in summer. The workers had been reduced to a slavery of the most impoverished and degraded kind. The men worked unlimited hours, and their

wives were made to wait on and to sleep with the officers of
the company. A wage cut of from twenty to twenty-five per
cent and the finding of the genitals of a horse in the food
finally drove them to strike. St. Petersburg, at the instance of
the owners, sent out an infantry company, commanded by one
of the officers who had shot down Father Gapón's petitioners.
He arrested the strike committee, and the next morning shot
down an unarmed demonstration, who had come to demand
their release. Two hundred and seventy people were killed,
and two hundred and fifty wounded. The Minister of the Interior, when interrogated in the Duma about the massacre,
declared simply that "so it was and so it would continue to
be."

In April there was a protest strike of more than three hundred thousand; on May Day, a strike of half a million. The
resolutions drawn up by the strikers usually ended now with
the slogan, "Long Live Socialism!" The policy conceived by
Stolýpin of building up a stratum of rich peasants as a buffer
between the peasantry and the landlords had resulted in cutting deeper the difference between the well-to-do peasants
and the others, and reducing the latter to a new destitution.
They would sell their land and go to work in the factories and
bring the factory wages down. That year seven Mensheviks
and six Bolsheviks were elected to the Fourth Duma. The
Bolsheviks brought out a paper called *Právda* (*Truth*) in
April, and its circulation outdistanced the Menshevik paper.
The trade union movement grew up again despite the determined persecution of the government, and by 1913 and 1914
there was a strike wave on a scale even bigger than that of
1905. In the spring and early summer of 1914, the grievances
of the Bakú oil-workers and the women factory workers of St.
Petersburg, who had been poisoned by certain ingredients of
the rubber and chemical products, aggravated by the shooting of workers in the Putílov munitions plant, led to a movement which brought the proletariat again to the barricades.
The Bolsheviks calculated now that they had the backing of
two-thirds of the industrial workers.

Both the Bolsheviks and the Mensheviks in the Duma, not
susceptible to the patriotism of a tsar's war, had opposed the

war appropriations and walked out of the session in protest. They had been tried for treason and sentenced, on the evidence mainly of the writings that Lenin was sending in from abroad, to lifelong exile at hard labor in Siberia. The majority of the Mensheviks had, however, in the period of discouragement after 1905, advocated the "liquidation" of the illegal party organization, on the ground that it only made the repression worse, a policy which Lenin believed would mean giving up the class struggle altogether; and at a congress in the January of 1912, the Bolsheviks finally cut loose from the Mensheviks and became no longer merely a Social Democratic faction, but an independent party. At the general socialist anti-war conference at Zimmerwald in September, 1915, the Bolsheviks formed an international committee which was the nucleus of the Third International. Lenin could thus, even from Cracow and Zürich, feel the growth, as it were under his hand, of that disciplined organization that he had projected in 1902.

Of the people who were to realize this project, Max Eastman, who was in Russia in the early twenties, has put on record an eloquent description: "A wonderful generation of men and women was born to fulfill this revolution in Russia. You may be traveling in any remote part of that country, and you will see some quiet, strong, exquisite face in your omnibus or your railroad car—a middle-aged man with white, philosophic forehead and soft brown beard, or an elderly woman with sharply arching eyebrows and a stern motherliness about her mouth, or perhaps a middle-aged man, or a younger woman who is still sensuously beautiful, but carries herself as though she had walked up to a cannon—you will inquire, and you will find out that they are the 'old party workers.' Reared in the tradition of the Terrorist movement, a stern and sublime heritage of martyr-faith, taught in infancy to love mankind, and to think without sentimentality, and to be masters of themselves, and to admit death into their company, they learned in youth a new thing—to think practically; and they were tempered in the fires of jail and exile. They became almost a noble order, a selected stock of men and women who could be relied upon to be heroic, like a Knight of the

Round Table or the Samurai, but with the patents of their nobility in the future, not the past."

And—what is so remarkable—this army all now looked to Lenin in exile. Nikolaí Sukhánov, not a Bolshevik himself, who attended the reception given Lenin on the latter's return to Russia, was much struck by the extent to which "the whole Bolshevik effort was kept inside the iron frame of the spiritual center abroad, without which the party workers felt themselves completely helpless, in whose presence they were proud to stand, and to which the best of them regarded themselves as devoted and dedicated servants, like Knights of the Holy Grail."

6 Lenin at the Finland Station

On January 22, 1917, Lenin said to an audience of young people in a lecture on the 1905 Revolution: "We of the older generation may not live to see the decisive battles of this coming revolution." On the 15th of February, he wrote his sister María, asking about certain sums of money which had been sent him without explanation from Russia. "Nádya," he told her, "is teasing me, says I'm beginning to draw my pension. Ha! ha! that's a good joke because living is infernally expensive, and my capacity for work is desperately low on account of my bad nerves."

They had been living on a small legacy which had been inherited by Krúpskaya's mother. A broker in Vienna had taken half of it for transferring it to them in wartime, and there had not been very much more than the equivalent of a thousand dollars left. Their funds were so low in 1917 that Lenin tried to get his brother-in-law in Russia to arrange for the publication of a "pedagogical encyclopaedia," which he proposed to have Krúpskaya write.

They had lodged at first in Zürich at a boarding-house where "Ilyích liked the simplicity of the service, the fact that the coffee was served in a cup with a broken handle, that we ate in the kitchen, that the conversation was simple." But it turned out to be an underworld hangout. There was a prostitute who "spoke quite openly of her profession," and a man who, though he "did not talk much," revealed "by the casual phrases he uttered that he was of an almost criminal type." They were interested in these people, but Krúpskaya insisted they should move, for fear they should get into trouble. So they transferred to a shoemaker's family, where they occupied a single room in an old and gloomy house that went back almost to the sixteenth century. They could have got a better room for the money: there was a sausage factory opposite their windows, and the stench was so overwhelming that they opened them only late at night and spent most of their time in the library. But Vladímir Ilyích would never consent to leave after he had heard his landlady declare that "the soldiers ought to turn their weapons against their governments." They often had only oatmeal for lunch, and when it got scorched, Lenin would say to the landlady: "We live in grand style, you see. We have roasts every day."

The years, as Vladímir had written his sister, had told pretty severely on their nerves. It had been hard, after 1905, to settle down to exile again, and that had been twelve years ago. Their comrades had been cracking up even worse than after the arrests of the nineties. One of them went to pieces in Lenin's house and had delusions about seeing his sister, who had been hanged. Another had caught tuberculosis during a sentence in a penal regiment; they sent him to Davos, but he died. Another, a survivor of the Moscow insurrection, came to see them one day and "began talking excitedly and incoherently about chariots filled with sheaves of corn and beautiful girls standing in the chariots." Vladímir stayed with him while Nádya got a psychiatrist, who said the man was going crazy from starvation. Later, he tied stones to his feet and neck and drowned himself in the Seine. Another, a factory worker in Russia, who, due to his political activities, found it difficult to keep a job and was unable to support his wife and children, broke down and became an *agent provocateur*. He took to drink, and one evening drove his family out of the house, stuffed up the chimney, lit the stove, and in the morning was found dead. Now they were plagued by a new kind of spies: not the old race of obvious dicks who used to stand on the street-corners and wait for them and whom they could easily dodge, but plausible and exalted young men, who talked themselves into posts in the party.

They had gone to see the Lafargues in Paris, and Krúpskaya, a little excited at meeting the daughter of Marx, had babbled something rather inarticulately about the part that women were playing in the revolutionary movement; the conversation had lagged. Lenin had talked to Lafargue about the book, *Materialism and Empirio-Criticism,* that he was writing against the Marxist mystics, and Lafargue agreed about the hollowness of religion. Laura had glanced at her husband and said: "He will soon prove the sincerity of his convictions." Lenin had been deeply moved when he had heard of their double suicide. "If one cannot work for the Party any longer," he had said to Krúpskaya at the time, "one must be able to look truth in the face and die the way the Lafargues did."

Elizavéta Vasílevna, his mother-in-law, used to say to people: "He'll kill both Nadyúsha and himself with that life." She herself died in 1915. She had wanted that last year to go to Russia, but there was no one to look after her there, and just before her death she said to Nádya, "I'll wait till I can go with you two." She had worked hard for the comrades as they came and went, had sewed "armor" into skirts and waistcoats in which illegal literature was to be carried and composed endless bogus letters that were to have messages written between the lines. Vladímir used to buy her presents in order to make her life a little more cheerful; once when she had failed to lay in cigarettes for a holiday, had ransacked the town to find her some. She had always regarded herself as a believer, and would not talk to them about sacred subjects; but had said suddenly, just before her death: "I used to be religious when I was young, but as I lived on and learned about life, I saw that it was all nonsense." And she asked to be cremated after her death. She died after an outing on a warm day of March, when she and Nádya had sat out for half an hour on a bench in the Berne forest.

Krúpskaya herself became ill after her mother's death. It was a recrudescence of an ailment that had first appeared in 1913. Something had gone wrong with her heart then; her hands had begun to tremble. The doctor had said that she had a weak heart and that her nerves were giving way. The cobbler's wife, who did their shopping—they were in Cracow now —was indignant: "Who said you were nervous—big ladies are nervous and throw the dishes around!" But she found that she couldn't work, and Vladímir took her to the mountains. It turned out that she had exophthalmic goiter. It had been always a slightly sore point with Nádya that people thought she looked like a fish. She complains in one of her early letters that Vladímir's sister Anna had said she had the look of a herring, and her conspiratorial names had been "Lamprey" and "Fish"; I once heard her described as "an old codfish" by a lady who had visited her in the Kremlin. Now the goiter, by swelling her neck and causing her eyes to protrude, intensified this effect. Vladímir had her operated on in Berne: the operation turned out to be difficult; they were working over her three hours without giving her an anesthetic—to the usual effect on Lenin that was produced by the presence of suffering. Lenin's letters through all this period show the strain of Nádya's illness.

One day in the middle of March when they had just finished eating dinner and Nádya had done the dishes and Ilyích was about to go to the library, a Polish comrade came bursting in, crying: "Haven't you heard the news? There's been a revolution in Russia!"

This time the defeats of the World War were carrying the tide across the barriers that had curbed it in 1905. The coal mines and factories of Poland had been lost with the Russian defeats; and half the production of the country was being expended on the fighting forces. On January 22, the anniversary of Father Gapón's demonstration, there had been a strike of a hundred and fifty thousand in Petrograd; and on March 8 a new general strike had begun: the workers poured into the streets. Now the army, full of peasant conscripts, could no longer be mobilized against them. Even the Cossacks, even the Semyónovsky Regiment, which had put down the Moscow insurrection, came over to the side of the rebels. The people were disgusted with the war, and they had completely lost confidence in the Tsar; the royal family, under the dominion of Raspútin, were secretly trying to make peace with the Germans; the big landlords and the bourgeoisie, who had an interest in continuing the war, were also eager to get rid of the autocracy. The Tsar himself had gone to General Headquarters in order to get away from the trouble; and when he attempted to return to Petrograd, the railroad workers held up his train. The whole machinery of the monarchy had stopped: the Tsar was forced to send his abdication by telegram, and a few days later was put under arrest. He had tried to dissolve the Fourth Duma, as he had done with its predecessors, but this time they refused to disband, and formed a Provisional Committee, which appointed a Provisional Government. A Workers' Soviet, with an Executive Committee that included both Mensheviks and Bolsheviks, sprang to life from its paralyzation of 1905, like one of the victims of Koshchéy, the deathless enchanter of the Russian folk-tale, who was finally slain by the breaking of an egg; and the Committee decided to bring in the army and make it a Soviet of Workers' and Soldiers' Deputies.

Lenin had to depend on foreign newspapers; but through their blurred and biased despatches he managed to grasp the fundamental factors. In the few articles he wrote for *Právda*, which was now being published again, before he was able to return to Russia, he laid down the general assumptions on which he was afterwards to act. The power hung between the two bodies, Provisional Government and Petrograd Soviet—which represented two groupings of interests, irreconcilable with one another. The Soviet was the spokesman of the people, who wanted peace, bread, liberty, land. The Provisional Government, whatever it might say, was recruited from a bourgeoisie whose tendencies toward liberalism were limited to the desire to get rid of the Románovs: the Minister of War and Marine was Guchkóv, a big Moscow industrialist and real-estate owner; the Minister of Foreign Affairs was Milyukóv, a former professor of History and the founder of the Kadet Party—the principal leader of the Russian bourgeoisie; and the Minister of Justice was a young lawyer only a shade further to the left than the Kadets. This last was the son of old Kerénsky, the director of the *gimnáziya* at Simbírsk, who had given Vladímir Ulyánov a good character after the execution of his brother and had guaranteed that his mother would keep him out of trouble. Kerénsky the younger had grown up

to be a highly successful orator of the emotional and ornamental kind, badly spoiled by the ladies of Petrograd and
cherishing an almost mystical conviction that he had been
chosen for some illustrious role.

This government, Lenin said, could never give the people
what they wanted. It could not give them peace, because it
depended on the subsidy of France and England and was
committed to carrying on their war: it had never yet said a
word about repudiating the imperialistic policy of annexing
Armenia, Galicia and Turkey and capturing Constantinople.
It could not give them bread, because the only way to give
them bread would be by violating the sanctities of both capital and landlordship, and the bourgeoisie by definition were
bound to protect the principle of property. It would not give
them freedom, because it was the government of those landlords and capitalists who had always shown themselves afraid
of the people. The only potential allies of the Soviet were,
first, the small peasants and the other impoverished groups in
Russia, and second, the proletariat of the other warring
nations.

The revolution was only as yet in its first and transitory
phase, and it would still have to wrest the power away from
the bourgeoisie. The workers, the peasants and the soldiers
must organize all over Russia under the leadership of the
Petrograd Soviet. They must do away with the old police and
establish a "people's militia"; and this militia must take upon
itself to distribute such food as there was, seeing to it "that
every child should have a bottle of good milk and that no adult
of a rich family should dare to take extra milk till the children
had all been supplied," and "that the palaces and luxurious
homes left by the Tsar and the aristocracy should not stand
idle but should provide shelter for the homeless and destitute."
The Soviet, once it was dominant, must declare itself not responsible for treaties concluded by the monarchy or by any
bourgeois government, and it must publish all secret treaties;
it must propose an immediate armistice to all the nations; it
must insist on the liberation of all colonies and dependent
peoples; it must propose to the workers of all countries that
they overthrow their bourgeois governments and transfer

power to workers' Soviets; it must declare that the billion-dollar debts contracted by the bourgeois governments for the purpose of carrying on the war should be paid by the capitalists themselves: for the workers and peasants to pay interest on these debts "would mean paying tribute to the capitalists over a period of many, many years for having generously permitted the workers to kill one another over the division of spoils by the capitalists."—And now we must answer the objections of Kautsky, who, writing on the Russian situation, warns us that "two things are absolutely necessary to the proletariat: democracy and socialism." But precisely what does this mean? Milyukóv would say he wanted democracy; Kerénsky would say he wanted socialism—

But here the fifth letter breaks off. Lenin is on his way to Russia and will not now be obliged to finish it.—The first days he had lain awake nights trying to work out ways to get back. The French and British would not give him a passport for the same reason that the British were to take Trotsky off his ship at Halifax—though Plekhánov and other nationalist socialists were to be sent home in a British ironclad with a guard of torpedo-boats. The truth was that Milyukóv himself had telegraphed the Russian consuls not to repatriate the internationalist socialists. Lenin thought seriously about going in an airplane, but in the morning he knew he couldn't manage it. Then he decided he would have to get a false passport—if possible, a Swedish one, because a Swede would be least suspect. Unfortunately he knew no Swedish, and he wondered whether he could get enough up to pass himself off at the frontier; then concluded he ought not to take chances, ought not to try to speak at all; and wrote to a comrade in Sweden asking him to find two Swedish deaf mutes who looked like Zinóvyev and him. "You'll fall asleep," Krúpskaya told him, "and see Mensheviks in your dreams, and you'll start swearing and shouting, 'Scoundrels, scoundrels!' and give the whole plot away."

On March 19 there was a meeting of exiles to discuss getting back to Russia. Mártov had worked up a plan for persuading the German government to let them return through Germany in exchange for German and Austrian prisoners. Lenin leaped at the idea, which hadn't occurred to him; but nobody else wanted to risk it. Mártov himself got cold feet, and it was Lenin who put the scheme through. Appeals to the Swiss government came to nothing, and telegrams to Russia got no answers: the patriots of the Provisional Government did not want the internationalists back, and the socialists themselves were in doubt. "What torture it is for us all," Lenin wrote to the comrade in Stockholm, "to be sitting here at such a time!" He was sitting himself in his low-ceilinged room writing his *Letters from Afar*. At last Lenin wired the comrade in Sweden to send somebody to Chkheídze, the Menshevik who was President of the Petrograd Soviet, to appeal to him on the ground that it was his duty to get the stranded Mensheviks back. Other pressure was brought to bear, and permission was finally wired in the form, "Ulyánov must come immediately." It was arranged with the German ambassador in Switzerland that a party was to be sent through Germany: the Germans were hoping that Lenin would further disorganize the Russian government. It was agreed that while they were passing through Germany, nobody should leave the train or communicate with anyone outside, and that nobody should be allowed to enter without the permission of the Swiss socialist who accompanied them. The German government insisted that Lenin should receive a representative of the trade unions. Lenin told them that if any boarded the train, he would refuse to have anything to do with him.

When Lenin got the news that they could go, he insisted on their taking the next train, which left in a couple of hours. Krúpskaya didn't think she could get packed, settle her accounts with the landlady and take the books back to the library in time, and suggested that she might follow later. But Vladímir insisted she must come with him. They left a lot of their things in a box in the event that they might have to return. Their landlord, who has written an account of their tenancy, had never paid any special attention to them. When Frau Lenin had first come about the room, his wife had not wanted to take her: "You could see that she was the Russian type," and "she wore a dress that was a little bit short"; but when Lenin appeared himself, he made a better impression.

They could see that he had strength in his chest: "My God," their son used to say, "he's got a neck like a bull!" For the rest, they were punctual about paying, and Herr Lenin got along well with his wife. "I think the two of them never quarreled. With Frau Lenin it was easy to get along. She was allowed to cook in our kitchen with my wife. We had agreed to let her do that. The two women always got along well together, which is something to wonder at, if one considers that the kitchen was a narrow intestine of a room, and that they had to squeeze by each other to pass. Frau Lenin would have made a good Hausfrau, but she always had her mind on other work." When Frau Lenin mentioned to Frau Kammerer that she wanted to get to Russia, Frau Kammerer expressed concern about her going into "that insecure country at such an uncertain time." "You see, Frau Kammerer," Frau Lenin said, "that's where I have work to do. Here I have nothing to do." Her husband said to Herr Kammerer just before he left: "So, Herr Kammerer, now there's going to be peace."

In the train that left the morning of April 8 there were thirty Russian exiles, including not a single Menshevik. They were accompanied by the Swiss socialist Platten, who made himself responsible for the trip, and the Polish socialist Radek. Some of the best of the comrades had been horrified by the indiscretion of Lenin in resorting to the aid of the Germans and making the trip through an enemy country. They came to the station and besieged the travelers, begging them not to go. Lenin got into the train without replying a word. In the carriage he found a comrade, who had been suspected of being a stool-pigeon. "The man had made a little too sure of his seat. Suddenly we saw Lenin seize him by the collar and in an incomparably matter-of-fact manner pitch him out on to the platform."

The Germans overpowered them with meals of a size to which they were far from accustomed, in order to demonstrate to the Russians the abundance of food in Germany. Lenin and Krúpskaya, who had never up to now been in any of the belligerent countries during this later period of the War, were surprised, as they passed through Germany, at the absence of adult men: at the stations, in the fields and the city streets, there were only a few women and children, and boys and girls in their teens. Lenin believed they would be arrested as soon as they arrived in Russia, and he discussed with his comrades a speech of defense which he was preparing on the way. But on the whole he kept much to himself. At Stuttgart, the trade union man got on with a cavalry captain and sat down in a special compartment. He sent his compliments to the Russians through Platten, in the name of the liberation of peoples, and requested an interview. Platten answered that they did not want to talk to him and could not return his greeting. The only person who spoke to the Germans was the four-year-old son of one of the Russians, who stuck his head into the compartment and said in French: "What does the conductor do?"

On the way to Stockholm, Lenin declared that the Central Committee of the Party must positively have an office in Sweden. When they got in, they were met and feted by the Swedish socialist deputies. There was a red flag hung up in the waiting-room and a gigantic Swedish repast. Radek took Lenin to a shop and bought him a new pair of shoes, insisting that he was now a public man and must give some thought to the decency of his appearance; but Lenin drew the line at a new overcoat or extra underwear, declaring that he was not going to Russia to open a tailor's shop.

They crossed from Sweden to Finland in little Finnish sleighs. Platten and Radek were stopped at the Russian frontier. Lenin sent a telegram to his sisters, announcing that he was arriving Monday night at eleven. In Russianized Finland, Krúpskaya says, "everything was already familiar and dear to us: the wretched third-class cars, the Russian soldiers. It was terribly good." Here the soldiers were back in the streets again. The station platforms were crowded with soldiers. An elderly man picked the little boy up and fed him some Easter cheese. A comrade leaned out the window and shouted, "Long live the world revolution"; but the soldiers looked around at him puzzled. Lenin got hold of some copies of *Právda*, which Kámenev and Stalin were editing, and discovered that they were talking mildly of bringing pressure on the Provisional

Government to make it open negotiations for peace, and loyally proclaiming that so long as the German army obeyed the Emperor, so long must the Russian soldier "firmly stand at his post, and answer bullet with bullet and shell with shell."

He was just expressing himself on the subject when the train whistle blew and some soldiers came in. A lieutenant with a pale face walked back and forth past Lenin and Krúpskaya, and when they had gone to sit in a car that was almost empty, he came and sat down beside them. It turned out that he, too, believed in a war for defense. Lenin told him that they should stop the war altogether, and he, too, grew very pale. Other soldiers came into the car and they crowded around Lenin, some standing up on the benches. They were jammed so tight you could hardly move. "And as the minutes passed," says Krúpskaya, "they became more attentive, and their faces became more tense." He cross-examined them about their lives and about the general state of mind in the army: "How? what? why? what proportion?" reports a non-commissioned officer who was there.—Who were their commanders?—Mostly officers with revolutionary views.—Didn't they have a junior staff? didn't these take any part in the command? . . . Why was there so little promotion?—They didn't have the knowledge of operations, so they stuck to their old staff.—It would be better to promote the non-commissioned officers. The rank and file can trust its own people more than it can the white-handed ones.—He suggested that they ask the conductor to let them into a car with more space so that they could hold something in the nature of a meeting, and he talked to them about his "theses" all night.

Early in the morning, at Beloóstrov, a delegation of Bolsheviks got in, Kámenev and Stalin among them. The moment Lenin laid eyes on Kámenev, whom he had not seen in several years, he burst out: "What's this you're writing in *Právda*? We've just seen some numbers, and we gave it to you good and proper!" Lenin's younger sister María was also there, and a delegation of women workers. The women wanted Krúpskaya to say something, but she found that words had left her. There was a demand for Lenin to speak, and the train-crew, who knew nothing about their passenger except that he was somebody special, picked him up and carried him into the buffet and stood him on a table. A crowd slowly gathered around; then the conductor came up and told the trainmen that it was time to start on. Lenin cut short his speech. The train pulled out of the station. Lenin asked the comrades whether they thought that the group would be arrested as soon as they arrived in Petrograd. The Bolsheviks only smiled.

Two hundred years before, Giambattista Vico, at his books in a far corner of Europe the whole width of the continent away, in asserting that "the social world" was "certainly the work of man," had refrained from going further and declaring, as Grotius had done, that the social institutions of men could be explained in terms of man alone. Grotius, though one of Vico's masters, had been a Protestant and a heretic, and his great book had been put on the *Index*, so that Vico was afraid even to edit it. In the Catholic city of Naples, in the shadow of the Inquisition, Vico had to keep God in his system.

At the end of the eighteenth century, Babeuf, who not only believed that human society had been made by man but who wanted to remake that society, had said in explaining his failure: "We have but to reflect for a moment on the multitude of passions in the ascendancy in this period of corruption we have come to, to convince ourselves that the chances against the possibility of realizing such a project are in the proportion of more than a hundred to one."

Lenin in 1917, with a remnant of Vico's God still disguised in the Dialectic, but with no fear of Roman Pope or Protestant Synod, not so sure of the controls of society as the engineer was of the engine that was taking him to Petrograd, yet in a position to calculate the chances with closer accuracy than a hundred to one, stood on the eve of the moment when for the first time in the human exploit the key of a philosophy of history was to fit an historical lock.

If the door that Lenin was to open did not give quite on the prospect he hoped, we must remember that of all the great Marxists he was least in love with prophetic visions, most readily readjusted his prospects. "Theoretical classification doesn't matter now," he had just written in *Letters from Afar*, apropos of whether the immediate measures he contemplated for feeding the Russian people should be regarded as constituting a "dictatorship of the proletariat" or a "revolutionary-democratic dictatorship of the proletariat and the poorest peasantry." . . . "It would be indeed a grave error if we tried now to fit the complex, urgent, rapidly-unfolding practical tasks of the revolution into the Procrustean bed of a narrowly conceived 'theory,' instead of regarding theory first of all and above all as a *guide to action.*"

We have watched the attempts of Michelet to relive the recorded events of the past as a coherent artistic creation, and we have seen how the material of history always broke out of the pattern of art. Lenin is now to attempt to impose on the events of the present a pattern of actual direction which will determine the history of the future. We must not wonder if later events are not always amenable to this pattern. The point is that western man at this moment can be seen to have made some definite progress in mastering the greeds and the fears, the bewilderments, in which he has lived.

The terminal where the trains get in from Finland is today a little shabby stucco station, rubber-gray and tarnished pink, with a long trainshed held up by slim columns that branch where they meet the roof. On one side the trains come in; on the other are the doors to the waiting-rooms, the buffet and the baggage-room. It is a building of a size and design which in any more modern country of Europe would be considered appropriate to a provincial town rather than to the splendors of a capital; but, with its benches rubbed dull with waiting, its ticketed cakes and rolls in glass cases, it is the typical small station of Europe, the same with that sameness of all the useful institutions that have spread everywhere with middle-class enterprise. Today the peasant women with bundles and baskets and big handkerchiefs around their heads sit quietly on the benches.

But at the time of which I am writing there was a rest-room reserved for the Tsar, and there the comrades who met him took Lenin, when the train got in very late the night of April 16. On the platform he had been confronted by men come back

from prison or exile, who greeted him with tears on their
cheeks.

There is an account of Lenin's reception by N. Sukhánov, a
non-party socialist, who was present. He came walking into the
Tsar's room at a speed that was almost running. His coat was
unbuttoned; his face looked chilled; he was carrying a great
bouquet of roses, with which he had just been presented.
When he ran into the Menshevik, Chkheídze, the President of
the Petrograd Soviet, he suddenly stopped in his tracks, as if
he had come up against an unexpected obstacle. Chkheídze,
without dropping the morose expression which he had been
wearing while waiting for Lenin, addressed him in the sen-
tentious accents of the conventional welcoming speech. "Comrade Lenin," he said, "in the name of the Petrograd Soviet and
of the whole revolution, we welcome you to Russia . . . *but*
we consider that at the present time the principal task of the
revolutionary democracy is to defend our revolution against
every kind of attack, both from within and from without. . . . We hope that you will join us in striving toward this
goal." Lenin stood there, says Sukhánov, "looking as if all this
that was happening only a few feet away did not concern him
in the least; he glanced from one side to the other; looked the
surrounding public over, and even examined the ceiling of the
'Tsar's Room,' while rearranging his bouquet (which harmo-
nized rather badly with his whole figure)." At last, turning
away from the committee and not replying directly to the
speech, he addressed the crowd beyond them: "Dear comrades, soldiers, sailors and workers, I am happy to greet in you
the victorious Russian revolution, to greet you as the advance
guard of the international proletarian army. . . . The war of
imperialist brigandage is the beginning of civil war in Europe.
. . . The hour is not far when, at the summons of our Comrade Karl Liebknecht, the people will turn their weapons
against their capitalist exploiters. . . . In Germany, everything is already in ferment! Not today, but tomorrow, any day,
may see the general collapse of European capitalism. The
Russian revolution you have accomplished has dealt it the
first blow and has opened a new epoch. . . . Long live
the International Social Revolution!"

He left the room. On the platform outside, an officer came up and saluted. Lenin, surprised, returned the salute. The officer gave a command: a detachment of sailors with bayonets stood at attention. The place was being spotted by searchlights and bands were playing the *Marseillaise*. A great roar of a cheer went up from a crowd that was pressing all around. "What's this?" Lenin said, stepping back. They told him it was a welcome to Petrograd by the revolutionary workers and sailors: they had been roaring one word—"Lenin." The sailors presented arms, and their commander reported to Lenin for duty. It was whispered that they wanted him to speak. He walked a few paces and took off his bowler hat. "Comrade sailors," he said, "I greet you without knowing yet whether or not you have been believing in all the promises of the Provisional Government. But I am convinced that when they talk to you sweetly, when they promise you a lot, they are deceiving you and the whole Russian people. The people needs peace; the people needs bread; the people needs land. And they give you war, hunger, no bread—leave the landlords still on the land. . . . We must fight for the social revolution, fight to the end, till the complete victory of the proletariat. Long live the world social revolution!"

"How extraordinary it was!" says Sukhánov. "To us, who had been ceaselessly busy, who had been completely sunk in the ordinary vulgar work of the revolution, the current needs, the immediately urgent things that are inconspicuous 'in history,' " a sudden dazzling light seemed to flash. "Lenin's voice, issuing straight from the railway carriage, was a 'voice from the outside.' Upon us, in the midst of the revolution, broke—the truth, by no means dissonant, by no means violating its context, but a *new* and brusque, a somewhat stunning note." They were pulled up by the realization "that Lenin was undeniably right, not only in announcing to us that the world socialist revolution had begun, not only in pointing out the indissoluble connection between the world war and the collapse of the imperialist system, but in emphasizing and bringing to the fore the 'world revolution' itself, insisting that we must hold our course by it and evaluate in its light all the events of contemporary history." All this, they could now see, was unquestionable; but did he really understand, they wondered, how these ideas could be made practical use of in the politics of their own revolution? Did he really know the situation in Russia? Never mind for the present. The whole thing was very extraordinary!

The crowd carried Lenin on their shoulders to one of the armored cars that had been drawn up outside. The Provisional Government, who had done their best to bar the streets against the gathering throngs, had forbidden bringing out these cars, which could become formidable factors in a mass demonstration; but this had had no effect on the Bolsheviks. He had to make another speech, standing above the crowd on top of the car. The square in front of the station was jammed: there they were, the textile workers, the metal workers, the peasant soldiers and sailors. There was no electric light in the square, but the searchlights showed red banners with gold lettering.

The armored car started on, leading a procession from the station. The other cars dimmed their lights to bring out the brightness of Lenin's. In this light he could see the workers' guard stretching all along both sides of the road. "Those," says Krúpskaya, "who have not lived through the revolution cannot imagine its grand solemn beauty." The sailors had been the Kronstadt garrison; the searchlights were from the Peter-Paul Fortress. They were going to the Kshesínskaya Palace, the house of the prima ballerina who had been the Tsar's mistress, which the Bolsheviks, in a gesture deliberately symbolic and much to the indignation of its inmate, had taken over for Party headquarters.

Inside it was all big mirrors, crystal candelabra, frescoed ceilings, satin upholstery, wide staircases and broad white cupboards. A good many of the bronze statues and marble cupids had been broken by the invaders; but the furniture of the ballerina had been carefully put away and replaced by plain chairs, tables and benches, set about, rather sparsely, where they were needed. Only a few Chinese vases, left stranded among the newspapers and manifestoes, were still getting in people's way. They wanted to give Lenin tea and to treat him to speeches of welcome, but he made them talk about tactics. The palace was surrounded by a crowd who were shouting for him to speak. He went out on a balcony to meet them. It was as if all the stifled rebellion on which the great flat and heavy city had pressed with its pompous façades since the time of those artisans whom Peter the Great had sent to perish in building it in the swamp, had boiled up in a single night. And Lenin, who had talked only at party meetings, before audiences of Marxist students, who had hardly appeared in public in 1905, now spoke to them with a voice of authority that was to pick up all their undirected energy, to command their uncertain confidence, and to swell suddenly to a world-wide resonance.

Yet at first, as they heard him that night—says Sukhánov, who was standing outside—there were signs that they were shocked and frightened. As Lenin's hoarse accents crackled out over them, with his phrases about the "robber-capitalists . . . the destruction of the peoples of Europe for the profits of a gang of exploiters . . . what the defense of the fatherland means is the defense of the capitalists against everybody else" —as these phrases broke over them like shells, the soldiers of the guard of honor itself muttered: "What's that? What's he saying? If he'd come down here, we'd show him!" They had, however, Sukhánov says, made no attempt to "show him" when he was talking to them face to face, and Sukhánov never heard of their doing so later.

He went in again, but had to return and make a second speech. When he came back, a meeting was called. In the great ballroom, the long speeches of welcome began to gush afresh. Trotsky says that Lenin endured their flood "like an impatient pedestrian in a doorway, waiting for the rain to stop." From time to time he glanced at his watch. When he spoke, he talked for two hours and filled his audience with turmoil and terror.

"On the journey here with my comrades," he said, "I was expecting that they would take us straight from the station to Peter and Paul. We are far from that, it seems. But let us not give up the hope that we shall still not escape that experience." He swept aside agrarian reform and other legal measures proposed by the Soviet, and declared that the peasants themselves should organize and seize the land without the aid of governmental intervention. In the cities, the armed workers must take over the direction of the factories. He threw overboard the Soviet majority, and hauled the Bolsheviks themselves over the coals. The proletarian revolution was imminent: they must give no countenance to the Provisional Government. "We don't need any parliamentary republic. We don't need any bourgeois democracy. We don't need any government except the Soviet of Workers', Soldiers', and Peasants' Deputies!"

The speech, says Sukhánov, for all its "staggering content and its lucid and brilliant eloquence," conspicuously lacked "one thing: an analysis of the 'objective premises,' of the social-economic foundations for socialism in Russia." But he goes on to say that he "came out on the street feeling as if I had been flogged over the head with a flail. Only one thing was clear: there was no way for me, a non-party man, to go along with Lenin. In delight I drank in the air, freshening now with spring. The morning had all but dawned, the day was already there." A young Bolshevik naval officer who took part in the meeting writes: "The words of Ilyích laid down a Rubicon between the tactics of yesterday and today."

But most of the leaders were stunned. There was no discussion of the speech that night; but indignation was to break out the next day when Lenin discharged another broadside at a general meeting of the Social Democrats. "Lenin," declared one of the Bolsheviks, "has just now presented his candidacy for one throne in Europe which has been vacant thirty years: I mean, the throne of Bakúnin. Lenin in new words is telling the same old story: it is the old discarded notions of primitive anarchism all over again. Lenin the Social Democrat, Lenin the Marxist, Lenin the leader of our militant Social Democracy—this Lenin is no more!" And the Left-Wing Bogdánov, who sat just under the platform, furiously scolded the audience: "You ought to be ashamed to applaud this nonsense—you cover yourselves with shame! And you call yourselves Marxists!"

The purpose of Lenin's speech had been to prevent a proposed amalgamation of Bolsheviks and Mensheviks; but at that moment it looked as if he was to have the effect of driving the Bolsheviks in the other direction. To many of the

Bolsheviks themselves, it seemed, as it had done to his opponents after the rupture of 1903, that Lenin had simply succeeded in getting himself out on a limb.

The night of their arrival, Krúpskaya records, after the reception in the Kshesínskaya Palace, she and Lenin "went home to our people, to Anna Ilyínishna and Mark Timoféyevich." María Ilyínishna was living with her brother-in-law and sister. Vladímir Ilyích and Nádya were given a separate room; and there they found that Anna's foster son had hung up over their beds the last words of the *Communist Manifesto*: "Workers of the World, Unite!"

Krúpskaya says she hardly spoke to Ilyích. "Everything was understood without words."

Summary as of 1940*

Marxism is in relative eclipse. An era in its history has ended. It may be worth while at this moment to look back and try to see what has happened.

Let us begin by asking ourselves what we mean, whether we really mean anything definite and fixed, when we casually use the word "Marxism."

The Marxism of Karl Marx himself was, in its original form, a mixture of old-fashioned Judaism, eighteenth-century Rousseauism and early nineteenth-century utopianism. Marx assumed that capitalist society had corrupted the human race by compelling it to abandon spiritual values for the satisfactions of owning things: he believed that the day would arrive when the spirit would come back into its own, when humanity would destroy its false idols and the sheep be set off from the goats: this could only be accomplished by communism—i.e. the common ownership of the means of production which would make possible a society without classes.

Friedrich Engels, the son of a Rhineland manufacturer, who had worked in the Manchester branch of the family textile business and been horrified by the misery of the working class, turned Marx's attention to political economy and supplied him with data on the industrial system. They had both come to the conclusion that the economic factor was of fundamental importance in the development of human society; and, taking

* From THE SHORES OF LIGHT, Copyright, 1952, by Edmund Wilson, Farrar, Straus & Young, Inc., Publishers.

over from the philosophy of Hegel his principle of revolutionary change, they evolved a picture of history in which the machinery of progress was represented as a process of continual class conflict. Every important change in the methods providing the necessaries of life gave rise to new social-economic classes, which had to struggle with the obsolete classes in order to get control of the machine. The bourgeoisie had contended with and disposed of the feudal system, which was obstructing the freedom of the merchant to trade and the freedom of the worker to hire himself that were necessary for the successful functioning of the early competitive phases of capitalism; and the industrial proletariat would, in turn, do the same thing to the capitalist system, when this, in its later phases, should prove obstructive to the logical development of large-scale industry and financial monopoly into the single centralized system which could only be run by the state.

Marx and Engels, therefore, did what they could to promote the success of labor organizations which aimed at the enfranchisement of the working class or at procuring better pay or conditions: the English Chartist movement and the Communist League of the forties, the Workers' International of the sixties and seventies; and they tried to convince the members of these movements that they, the representatives of the working class, were enacting leading roles in the Marxist drama of history.

This drama, as imagined by Marx on the eve of the revolution of 1848, was to move swiftly to a catastrophic climax which would be followed by something in the nature of a millennium. Engels was envisaging the future in terms of the French Revolution plus the Apocalypse. But when, later, parliamentary machinery was set up in that feudal Germany which had made the background for the thought of both men, the German socialists who had been trained on Marx but who were now able to get themselves elected to the Reichstag began to decide that there was nothing inevitable about the social-economic impasse and the class-war Armageddon which Marx had been predicting. Since the pressure of the working class had been effective in securing certain reforms, there was perhaps, after all, no reason to believe that the socialist aims might not be accomplished by orderly and gradual legislation. And Marx himself in his later years began to concede that in democratic countries such as England, the United States and Holland, the socialist revolution might be effected through peaceful parliamentary methods—though he thought this would be likely to stimulate a revolt of the outvoted reactionaries.

Karl Marx sometimes praised the achievements of the democratic countries, as when he backed the cause of the North during the American Civil War; but more often—it represents the bent of his own somber and savage personality—he talks in terms of Armageddon, and Armageddon is what he leads us to expect. He even applauded the Commune, when the workers and soldiers of Paris rose against the bourgeois government and held the city two months—though the procedure of the Commune was a good deal more drastic than that which he had contemplated. He had never believed in the possibility of simply abolishing bourgeois institutions and setting up socialist ones in their place, which was what the Communards had attempted, but had expected that the proletarian dictatorship would begin by taking over the machinery of the existing bourgeois state.

It ought, also, to be noted here that one can find in the whole immense work of Marx and Engels a considerable variety of attitudes toward the main problems with which they were concerned. In the first place, there are two personalities involved, and their emphasis is somewhat different. Engels left to himself, as he was after Marx's death, was more tolerant and flexible politically, and insisted somewhat less on the materialistic side of what they called their Dialectical Materialism; and Karl Marx had within his own nature tendencies so strongly divergent that his formidable machinery of logic never succeeded in making them consistent: he was at the same time a moralist and prophet, who wanted to blast a generation of vipers, and a scientific student of history, who aimed at an objective analysis of economic processes. Add to this that the points of view of Marx and Engels, both, varied in relation to the apparent imminence or the apparent improbability of a revolutionary working-class movement in which they could take an active part; and that the young fighters of '48, who saw the industrial worker on one side of the barricades and the capitalist exploiter on the other, never quite came to terms with the elderly observers of the years of their exile in England, who were forced now to take account of the unexpected situations to which the capitalist system gave rise in its later and more complicated phases.

The writings of Marx and Engels thus lend themselves to being exploited, very much as the Scriptures have been, to furnish texts for a variety of doctrines; and there have even been different Marxist canons prepared by the different creeds. The German Social Democrats did not hesitate to tamper with the texts themselves; and the Russians of the Marx-Engels Institute, in publishing these texts as they were written, were at pains to provide a commentary which supplied the "correct" interpretation.

II   Marxism first reached Russia as early as 1868, when a translation of *Das Kapital* was published there, and it began to take hold in the eighties, after the Terrorist movement had culminated in the assassination of Alexander II. But as the Germans had made Marxism respectable, academic and parliamentarian, so in Russia, of necessity an outlawed movement, it became, in its most effective form, narrow, concentrated, grim and cruel. In Russia, the first problem of the radical was to get rid of a feudal autocracy which would not even hear of a constitution and which excluded the bourgeois liberals from its institutions of learning.

Valdímir Ulyánov, who called himself Lenin, belonged to a section of the professional classes which had been hard hit in the eighties. His father, the director of schools for the province of Simbírsk on the Volga, had made his own career, an energetic and honorable one, which had earned him a patent of nobility, during the period of the educational reforms inspired by Alexander II, and had been prematurely retired from his post and forced to see his work undone when the reaction of Alexander III, came to punish the murder of his predecessor. Lenin's elder brother, a student at the University of St. Petersburg, became involved in a plot to carry on the work of the

Terrorists by assassinating Alexander III, but was caught by the police and hanged. The older Ulyánov had just died of a stroke, perhaps partly as a result of chagrin, and Vladimir was now head of the family. He profoundly admired his mother, who found herself everywhere ostracized as a result of her son's execution; and the succession of family misfortunes caused the iron to enter his soul. During his first eager years of young manhood, he was to find his own progress brutally blocked. As the result of a student demonstration in which he had played no important part, he was dismissed from the University of Kázán on suspicion as the brother of the Terrorist; and he was forbidden to study a profession either at home or abroad. In this period of frustration, he read Marx.

The harshness of the Tsarist autocracy inevitably called forth harshness on the part of the groups who were fighting it; and Russian Marxism took on some of the characteristics of the Terrorist movement of the seventies. The band of trained and dedicated revolutionists projected by Lenin in *What Is to Be Done?*, his pamphlet of 1902, and afterwards realized by him in the Bolshevik and Communist parties is a conception not to be found in Marx, who had never got much further as an organizer than drafting programs and presiding at meetings for the Communist League and the Workers' International. Lenin, confronted with the ignorance of the illiterate Russian masses, had frankly to propose that they should be directed by a nucleus of revolutionary intellectuals; and, confronted with the ineffectual loquacity of the common run of Russian intelligentsia, he had to insist that these upper-class leaders of the proletarian movement should not be merely talkers or even thinkers, but persons who would work actively for the Party and who would be ready to take real responsibility. The springs of Lenin's own activity were profound, irresistible, instinctive. His prime motivations were probably the overpowering hatred of suffering of which Gorky so emphatically speaks, combined with a passion for combat that took a curiously impersonal form and made him regard himself as a naked historical force pitted against other such forces. He had disciplined himself in such a way that the emotion always fed the conviction, and the conviction always led to action. This process was brought to a climax when the Tsarist regime involved Russia in the long devastation and slaughter of what Lenin insisted on characterizing as the Imperialist War.

The fact that the Provisional Government of Kerénsky desired to continue the war and that it did not seem at all disposed to distribute land or food to the starving Russian masses would thus in itself have been almost enough to make Lenin resolve to overthrow it, even without the mesmeric driving force provided by the Marxist conception of history. People like the Menshevik Mártov quite correctly pointed out that Lenin was throwing overboard the procedure expressly prescribed by Marx and formerly accepted by Lenin himself, in not waiting till a bourgeois "democratic" state had made the transition from the Tsarist autocracy to the socialist state of the workers. When Marx had been questioned by young Russians as to whether it would be possible for Russia, with its ancient peasant communes, to pass straight to a socialist economy without traversing all the stages of large-scale capitalist exploitation, he had, despite his earlier approval of the Commune, expressed himself as very doubtful.

But Lenin, for all his endless polemics, was little worried by Marxist theory: he was preoccupied not with ideas, but with actual current events, watching intently for the break, any break, that might make possible the destruction of the Tsardom. When the moment did come during the war, he saw the flimsiness and the impracticability of the bourgeois Provisional Government, and he supplanted it with a new kind of government based on the councils (*soviets*) of workers, peasants and soldiers which, as soon as the grip of the Tsar was relaxed, had been gravitating in 1917, as they had done in 1905, to unofficial positions of authority. But though Lenin disregarded the letter of Marx, he was true to the Armageddon spirit; and it had always been his habit to act first and look up later, when he had the leisure—what, as I have said, is not usually difficult—supporting texts in Marx and Engels.

Lenin's ultimate aims were of course humanitarian, democratic and anti-bureaucratic; but the logic of the whole situation was too strong for Lenin's aims. His trained band of revolutionists, the Party, turned into a tyrannical machine which perpetuated, as heads of a government, the intolerance, the deviousness, the secrecy, the ruthlessness with political dissidents, which they had had to learn as hunted outlaws. Instead of getting a classless society out of the old illiterate feudal Russia, they encouraged the rise and the domination of a new controlling and privileged class, who were soon exploiting the workers almost as callously as the Tsarist industrialists had done, and subjecting them to an espionage that was probably worse than anything under the Tsar. What Lenin had actually effected was a kind of bourgeois revolution; the situation had, in a sense, worked out according to Marx; but it was not at all what Lenin had intended. Lenin himself died, after only six years of power, in great perplexity and anguish of mind, outmaneuvered by one of his lieutenants who knew how to distribute patronage and had no scruples about deceiving the public.

At first, under the dictatorship of Stalin, a serious attempt was made to bring the economy of Soviet Russia up to the level of the capitalist nations, so that socialism might become a reality; but when, due to the mechanical ineptitude and the administrative inefficiency of the Russians, this seemed to be definitely failing, Stalin quickly buried the Leninist ideals, executed or otherwise suppressed all the people who were still disposed to defend them, and consolidated the position of those groups of officials who were doing their best to give Russia the strong bourgeoisie she had lacked and who have ended, it may be, by dominating the dictator Stalin himself.

In the meantime, the short circuit in the capitalist system which Karl Marx had so confidently predicted had actually taken place in Germany, but with results very different from those he had expected. Instead of the processes of capitalism giving rise automatically to a crisis in which a dispossessed proletariat was left facing a small group of capitalists, with nothing to do but to expropriate the expropriators, a new kind of middle class, as in Russia, came out of the petty bourgeoisie and did not find the slightest difficulty in enlisting ambitious members of the working class. This group succeeded in setting up a new kind of state socialism, in which the government planned and directed in the interests of the new governing class, without actually taking over the industrial plant, but eliminating the big capitalists, if necessary, and seeing to it that the working class were well enough off so that they did not become seriously recalcitrant.

III Karl Marx had arrived at his vision of the working class expelling the capitalists by way of two false analogies. One of these was a probably unconscious tendency to argue from the position of the Jew to the position of the proletarian. The German Jews in Karl Marx's time were just escaping from the restrictions of the ghetto, which meant also the system of the Judaic world; and in this case the former victims of a social and economic discrimination, with their ancient religious discipline and their intellectual training, were quite easily able to take over the techniques and the responsibilities of the outside modern world. The proletariat, however, unlike the Jews, had no tradition of authority; they were, by their very position, kept ignorant and physically bred down. The country—industrial England—in which Marx prophesied that the widening gulf between the owning and the working classes would first bring about a communist revolution, had turned out to be the country where the progressive degradation of the underprivileged classes had simply had the effect of stunting them and slowly extinguishing their spirit. The other false analogy of Marx was his argument from the behavior of the bourgeoisie in the seventeenth and eighteenth centuries to the behavior to be expected of the working class, in their turn, in relation to the bourgeoisie. The European middle classes who finally dispossessed the feudal landlords were, after all, educated people, accustomed to administering property and experienced in public affairs. The proletariat, the true ground-down industrial workers on whom Marx was basing his hopes, were almost entirely devoid of any such experience or education; and what we now know invariably happens when the poor and illiterate people of a modern industrial society first master advanced techniques and improve their standard of living, is that they tend to exhibit ambitions and tastes which Karl Marx would have regarded as bourgeois. We have seen it in the United States, where we have produced what is really the earliest example of that new kind of bourgeoisie that they have been getting in Germany and Russia. But ours is a more highly developed, that is, a more democratic, version; and when I say that it is more democratic, I am using the words not in any loose sense, but in the definite sense that, with us, individual responsibility, the ability to make decisions, is a good deal more evenly distributed than it is in these other countries.

Is there nothing left of Marxism, then? Are there no basic Marxist ideas that may still be accepted as true?

I have above, at the risk of banality, discussed it in terms of its historical origins, because it seems to me that the shifting generalities to which the liberal mind is addicted still need to be constantly corrected by the facts of socialist history. But there is, of course, common to the Marxism of Marx and of Engels, of Lenin and of Trotsky, a technique which we can still use with profit; the technique of analyzing political phenomena in social-economic terms. There was this much in the claims of Marx and Engels that they had been able to make socialism "scientific": they were the first to attempt in an intensive way to study economic motives objectively. This does not, of course, mean, however, that we should try to find the key to the events of our time in the conclusions which these men of another time drew from the events of theirs. The Marxist method can get valid results only if applied afresh by men realistic enough to see, and bold enough to think, for themselves.

As for the aims and ideals of Marxism, there is one feature of them that is now rightly suspect. The taking-over by the state of the means of production and the dictatorship in the interests of the proletariat can by themselves never guarantee the happiness of anybody but the dictators themselves. Marx and Engels, coming out of authoritarian Germany, tended to imagine socialism in authoritarian terms; and Lenin and Trotsky after them, forced as they were to make a beginning among a people who had known nothing but autocracy, also emphasized this side of socialism and founded a dictatorship which perpetuated itself as an autocracy.

When all this is said, however, something more important remains that is common to all the great Marxists: the desire to get rid of class privilege based on birth and on difference of income; the will to establish a society in which the superior development of some is not paid for by the exploitation, that is, by the deliberate degradation of others—a society which will be homogeneous and coöperative as our commercial society is not, and directed, to the best of their ability, by the conscious creative minds of its members. But this again is a goal to be worked for in the light of one's own imagination and with the help of one's own common sense. The formulas of the various Marxist creeds, including the one that is common to them all, the dogma of the Dialectic, no more deserve the status of holy writ than the formulas of other creeds. To accomplish such a task will require of us an unsleeping adaptive exercise of reason and instinct combined.

Index

"Absolute Idea" of Hegel, 121, 125–26, 130, 143–44, 180, 190, 233
Abstract Man, 155–56, 185
Adler, Victor, 413, 429
Aeschylus, 116, 317
Alduses (printers), 13
Alexander II, 270, 275, 278–79, 349, 351, 356, 360, 362, 368, 377, 478
Alexander III, 359–61, 372, 375, 404, 478–79
America. *See* United States
American Encyclopedia, The, writing of Marx for, 217, 254
Amiel, Henri-Frédéric, 45
Anarchism, 280, 331
Anatomy of Melancholy, 382
Andrews, Stephen Pearl, 103
Annenkov, P. V., 166–68
Anti-Dühring, by Engels, 182, 185, 215, 302, 304, 305, 338, 366, 401
Anti-Semitism. *See* Jews
Antithesis. *See* Thesis
Apocalypse, the, 41
Apollonius Rhodius, 187
Apology of Socrates, 73
Appassionata, of Beethoven, 384
Arnold, George, 110
Arnold, Matthew, 28
Augustus, 187
Austria, 429
Aveling, Dr. Edward, 343–45; marries Eleanor Marx, 343

Aveling, Mrs. Edward (Eleanor Marx), 219, 242–43, 257, 308, 334, 336, 340–45; suicide, 345
Axelrod, P. B., 338, 401, 414

Babeuf, François-Noel (Gracchus), 32, 69–78, 80, 82, 87, 105, 145, 165, 275, 431, 467; communism of, 74; execution, 77
Babouvism. *See* Babeuf, F. N.
Bacon, Francis, 1, 5
Bailly, Jean-Sylvain, 314
Bakúnin, Mikhaíl Alexándrovich, 260–87, 347, 361, 373, 392, 396, 473; achievement of power, 273; appearance of, 268; birth of, 265; conversion to revolutionary politics, 267; death of, 283; desire to destroy, 267–68; escape, from Siberia, 271; family, 266–67; impotence of, 266; imprisonment, 269–70; internationalism of, 272–73; marriage of, 266; oratory, 274; personality of, 268; political inconsistencies, 280; relations with Marx, 267, 272, 273, 274, 279–80, 331; relations with Necháev, 275–78; role in revolutions, 268–71
Balabánova, Angélica, 449
Bâle, Congress of *1869,* 264, 265, 273, 274

494

502

ANCHOR BOOKS

FICTION

ANCHOR BOOKS

ANCHOR BOOKS

HISTORY

THE END OF THE JEWISH PEOPLE?—Georges Friedmann; Eric Mosbacher, trans., A626

ENGLAND: Prehistory to the Present—Arvel B. Erickson and Martin J. Havran, AO2

ENVY AND OTHER WORKS—Yuro Olesha; Andrew R. MacAndrew, trans., A571

ESSAYS ON OLD TESTAMENT HISTORY AND RELIGION—Albrecht Alt; R. A. Wilson, trans., A544

EUROPEAN DIPLOMATIC HISTORY 1789–1815: France Against Europe—Steven T. Ross, A645

THE FACE OF THE ANCIENT ORIENT—Sabatino Moscati, A289

FIVE STAGES OF GREEK RELIGIONS—Gilbert Murray, A51

FOUR STAGES OF RENAISSANCE STYLE—Wylie Sypher, A44

FROM FERTILITY CULT TO WORSHIP: A Reassessment for the Modern Church of the Worship of Ancient Israel—Walter Harrelson, A713

FROM HEGEL TO NIETZSCHE—Karl Lowith; David E. Green, trans., A553

FROM THE STONE AGE TO CHRISTIANITY: Monotheism and the Historical Process—William Foxwell Albright, A100

THE GATEWAY TO HISTORY—Allan Nevins, revised edition, A314

GOOD-BYE TO ALL THAT—Robert Graves, revised second edition, A123

GUESTS OF THE SHEIK: The Ethnography of an Iraqi Village—Elizabeth Warnock Fernea, A693

HALF-WAY TO THE MOON: New Writing from Russia—Patricia Blake and Max Hayward, A483

A HERO OF OUR TIME—Mihail Lermontov; Vladimir Nabokov and Dmitri Nabokov, trans., A133

HISTORY AND SOCIAL THEORY—Gordon Leff, A781

HISTORY BEGINS AT SUMER—Samuel Noah Kramer, A175

A HISTORY OF EAST AND CENTRAL AFRICA: To the Late Nineteenth Century—Basil Davidson, A677

HISTORY OF ENGLAND: In Three Volumes—G. M. Trevelyan, A22a, b, and c

A HISTORY OF EUROPE: Two Volumes—Henri Pirenne, A156a, b

A HISTORY OF ROME from its origins to 529 A.D. as Told by the Roman Historians—Moses Hadas, ed., A78

A HISTORY OF WEST AFRICA—Basil Davidson, with F. K. Buah and the advice of J. F. Ade Ajayi, A550

HITLER'S SOCIAL REVOLUTION—David Schoenbaum, A590

HOW THE GREEKS BUILT CITIES—R. E. Wycherley, A674

THE IMPERIAL IDEA AND ITS ENEMIES—A. P. Thornton, A627

IMPERIALISM AND SOCIAL REFORM: English Social-Imperial Thought 1895–1914—Bernard Semmel, A618

ISLAM—Fazlur Rahman, A641

ITALY FROM THE RISORGIMENTO TO FASCISM—A. William Salomone, ed., A737